# CHILDREN
# OF JOB

SUNY Series in Modern Jewish Literature and Culture
Sarah Blacher Cohen, Editor

# CHILDREN OF JOB

## American Second-Generation Witnesses to the Holocaust

ALAN L. BERGER

State University
of New York
Press

Portions of chapters 3 and 4 appeared in earlier versions as "Ashes and Hope: Second Generation Literature of the Holocaust," in *The Holocaust: Reflections in Art and Literature*, Edited by Randolph L. Braham, Boulder, Social Science Monographs, 1990; "Bearing Witness: Second Generation Literature of the Holocaust," in *Modern Judaism*, February, 1990; "Job's Children: Post-Holocaust Jewish Identity in Second Generation Literature," in *Jewish Identity in America*, Edited by David M. Gordis and Yoav Ben-Horin, New York, KTAV, 1991; and "The Holocaust, Second-Generation Witness, and the Voluntary Covenant in American Judaism," in *Religion and American Culture: A Journal of Interpretation*, Winter, 1995.

Published by
State University of New York Press, Albany

© 1997  State University of New York

Production by Susan Geraghty
Marketing by Fran Keneston

Printed in the United States of America

For information, address State University of New York
Press, State University Plaza, Albany, N.Y., 12246

Library of Congress Cataloging-in-Publication Data

Berger, Alan L.,
     Children of Job : American second-generation witnesses to the
Holocaust / Alan L. Berger.
         p.    cm. — (SUNY series in modern Jewish literature and
culture)
     Includes bibliographical references and index.
     ISBN 0-7914-3357-9 (hardcover : acid-free paper). — ISBN
0-7914-3358-7 (pbk. : acid-free paper)
     1. Holocaust, Jewish (1939–1945), in literature.  2. American
literature—Jewish authors—History and criticism.  3. Holocaust
(Jewish theology)  4. Children of Holocaust survivors—United
States—Intellectual life.  I. Title.  II. Series.
PS153.J4B468  1997
810.9′358—dc20                                                    96-26918
                                                                          CIP

10  9  8  7  6  5  4  3  2  1

# CONTENTS

*Foreword by Elie Wiesel*                                            *vii*

*Acknowledgments*                                                     *ix*

Chapter 1   Introduction                                               1

    The Second-Generation Witness: Inheriting the
      Holocaust                                                   1
    Particularism and Universalism                               4
    Children of Survivors and Children of Job                    5
    Theological Sequelae                                         8
    Universal Questions                                         8
    The Search for *Tikkun*                                      10

Chapter 2   From Pathology to Theology: The Emergence of
the Second-Generation Witness                                          13

    The American Second Generation: A Brief History              16
    A New Generation of Jewish Writers and Filmmakers            19
    Post-Auschwitz Covenant Theology                            21
    Elie Wiesel and the Additional Covenant                      23
    Irving Greenberg and the Voluntary Covenant                  25
    Emil L. Fackenheim and the Search for a Post-Aushwitz
      *Tikkun Olam*                                            28
    Richard L. Rubenstein: "God after the Death of God"          31

Chapter 3   Second-Generation Novels and Short Stories:
Jewish Particularism                                                   35

    *Damaged Goods*                                              37
    *Summer Long-a-Coming*                                       48
    *Maus*                                                       59
    *Short Stories: A Biographical Note*                         71
    *Stories of an Imaginary Childhood* and *While The*
      *Messiah Tarries*                                        72

*Dancing at the Club Holocaust* and *Forms of Captivity*
    *and Escape*                                                                    75
*Elijah Visible*                                                                       79
Conclusion                                                                             84

Chapter 4    Second-Generation Novels and Short Stories:
Jewish Universalism                                                                    87

*The Flood*                                                                            88
*White Lies*                                                                           95
*Dancing on Tisha B'Av* and *Winter Eyes*                                             110
Conclusion                                                                            126

Chapter 5    Second-Generation Documentaries and
Docudramas: Jewish Particularism                                                      129

*Kaddish*                                                                             131
*A Generation Apart*                                                                  136
*Breaking the Silence*                                                                140
*Half-Sister, Everything's For You,* and *In Memory*                                  146
*Angst*                                                                               150
The Docudramas: *The Dr. John Haney Sessions*
    and *Open Secrets*                                              152
Conclusion                                                                            157

Chapter 6    Second-Generation Documentaries and
Docudramas: Jewish Universalism                                                       159

*As If It Were Yesterday*                                                             162
*Weapons Of The Spirit*                                                               168
*So Many Miracles*                                                                    173
*Voices From The Attic*                                                               177
Conclusion                                                                            181

Chapter 7    Whither The Future?                                                      183

Working through the Holocaust                                                          184
Riders towards the Dawn                                                                187
Children of Job and Covenantal Judaism                                                187

*Notes*                                                                               191

*Index*                                                                               215

# FOREWORD
## BY ELIE WIESEL

This book is important for all of those interested in the destiny of the survivors of the Holocaust and the history of their children.

For reasons that the reader will understand, it is hard for me to speak about it. First, the subject is too close to me. Then, the author has deemed it appropriate to refer often to my work. Normally, in the name of an objectivity so dear to university scholars and researchers, I should therefore refrain from making comments.

I will not do so. I will say what I think of my young friend and colleague Alan Berger and of what he writes on the "children of Job." I will be quick to add that there are in this book deeply moving pages of truth, of new psychological insights, and of profound comments which will leave no one indifferent. He has read much, reflected much on the question which haunts our generation oscillating between necessary hope and absolute despair.

Of whose "children of Job" is it about? There used to be many. Those before the misfortune and those after it. The first ones were taken to a premature and sudden death. The second ones were born after their parents' "reconciliation" with life and perhaps also with God. It is with the latter ones that Professor Berger's work deals. Job's seven sons and three daughters, following the catastrophe which deprived them of everything, had to somehow compensate for their loss.

The children of the survivors could easily identify with them. How are they able to live with the painful and traumatizing memory of their orphaned parents? Should they feel guilty for not being able to spare them their past sufferings, which dominate the very act of remembering them in the present? Where do they draw the courage and the strength to look them in the face while trying to make them smile? How do they manage to make them speak without discomfort but with prudence, or respect their delicate silence without wounding them by appearing uninterested? If one could define as unique the tragedy of the survivors, one can equally designate as without precedent the drama of their heirs.

A drama that is psychological, social, philosophical, and even religious. The author examines it with rigor and compassion. Just like the survivor himself, his sons or daughters must overcome various difficulties and obstacles in order to normalize their behavior. Their parents' past challenges them even in their ambitions and their dreams, their relationships with their friends at school or at work. Is it a privilege or a burden for them to feel compelled to justify the faith their father or their mother placed in a future which they incarnate?

Scrupulous and honest to the end, Berger studies, how should one say, the soul of these "children" now become adults. How does one reveal the wounds that are invisible but are theirs? How does one reconcile the power of memory with that of imagination? And faith in God or revolt against His justice—how does one measure it? Quite like the survivors, certain "children" have become more pious, others less so. Everything they undertake, everything they build has a secret tie to the unnamable experience of their parents. "The children of Job" will never detach themselves from the tragedy that gave birth to them.

In exploring their universe, which is at once darkened and illuminated by memory, as evoked in novels, memoirs, films, and essays, Alan Berger accompanies them with a respect and tact which do him honor. He advances with them, step by step. Along the way, he has stopped being a neutral observer to become a friend moved by his discoveries. A friend that moves his readers by his capacity for understanding. (Translated from French by Mary Ann Gosser Esquilin)

# ACKNOWLEDGMENTS

I wish to acknowledge the support of many people with whom I spoke or corresponded over the course of time in completing this work. In alphabetical order they are: Harry James Cargas, Gloria Cronin, Yaffa Eliach, Morris Faierstein, Ellen Fine, Eva Fogelman, Thomas Friedmann, William Helmreich, Serge Liberman, Edward T. Linenthal, Asher Milbauer, Alan Rosen, Nahum Sarna, H. Daniel Smith, Morton Weinfeld, Charles Winquist, and Arnold Zable. Further, I am grateful to the second-generation witnesses who agreed to be interviewed for this study. My seminar students at the College of William and Mary, and Syracuse University patiently listened and responded to ideas and concepts concerning texts and films that were entirely new to them. I also want to thank Lawrence Baron and Lester Friedman for their generosity in commenting on two of the book's chapters. The work of Emil Fackenheim and Irving "Yitz" Greenberg provided helpful theological markers in determining the framework of second-generation post-Auschwitz Jewish identity.

My indebtedness to the work and vision of Elie Wiesel goes beyond words. His life, teaching, and writing serve as inspiration for women and men everywhere who seek to remember the Holocaust, transmit its legacy, and make the world more humane.

Technical help and support was provided by Ms. Mary Beth Hinton, Mr. Brian McLaughlin, and Ms. Denise Stevens of Syracuse University's Bird Library. Further assistance was rendered by Ms. Deborah Eskan of Florida Atlantic University. I also thank Susan Nowak, Ph.D. for preparing the index, and the Florida Atlantic University Foundation for their support of that project. Ms. Susan Geraghty, the production editor, was a patient and wise guide. All were a joy to work with.

Naomi Benau Berger, herself a second-generation witness, read and improved the work. For this and so much else I thank her.

This book is dedicated to our sons: Ariel, Michael, and Daniel—the third generation.

# CHAPTER 1

# *Introduction*

> The second generation is the most meaningful aspect of our work.
> Their role in a way is even more difficult than ours. They are
> responsible for a world they didn't create. They who did not go
> through the experience must transmit it.
>
> —Elie Wiesel[1]

In Elie Wiesel's haunting novel *The Forgotten*, Ephraim, a sightless survivor of the *Shoah*, seeks to impart a portion of his memory to Malkiel
("God is my King"), a second-generation member. "The blind man,"
writes Wiesel, "leaned toward Malkiel as if to inspect him; their heads
touched. The old man's breath entered Malkiel's nostrils."[2] Wiesel's dramatic depiction focuses attention on several important developments concerning the relationship between the *Shoah* and Jewish identity fifty years
after the event. For example, the Holocaust is a continuing source of
contemporary Jewish identity for daughters and sons of survivors, of
whom there are approximately 150,000 living in the United States alone.[3]
Like the second children of Job, these second-generation witnesses attest
to an event that they never lived through but that ineluctably shapes their
lives. Further, like the transmission of earlier transformative events in
Jewish history such as the story of the Exodus, and the destructions of the
Temple, the telling of the Holocaust story must be passed *l'dor va'dor*,
from generation to generation.

## THE SECOND-GENERATION WITNESS:
## INHERITING THE HOLOCAUST

Second-generation witnesses, the offspring of Jewish Holocaust survivors,
have a personal relationship to the *Shoah*. They inherit the Holocaust as
an irreducible part of their Jewish self-identity. But what are these new
types of Holocaust witnesses to do with an event not personally experienced? Geoffrey H. Hartman perceptively comments that with the passing
from the scene of the eyewitnesses and the fading of even the most faithful memories, "the question of what sustains Jewish identity is raised
with a new urgency."[4] "In this transitional phase," writes Hartman, "the
children of the victims play a particular role as transmitters of a difficult

defining legacy."[5] Cheryl Pearl Sucher, herself a daughter of survivors, employs a biological metaphor in musing on the relationship between first- and second-generation memory of the *Shoah*. She writes, "though a child of survivors, I am parent to the interpretation of their survival."[6] While the second generation is in a "special situation," Hartman notes that it is more than a "temporary dilemma:" "the burden on their emotions, on their capacity to identify, is something we all share to a degree."[7] Consequently, how the second-generation witnesses shape and ritualize Holocaust memory has great bearing on how the event will be commemorated in the future.

The focus of second-generation witness testimony is less on the Holocaust itself than on its continuing aftermath. The beatings, torture, humiliation, gassings, and burnings happened to their parents' generation. It is the survivors who remember living with death and routinized evil as constant companions. With the messengers who brought fateful tidings to Job, they can say, "I alone am left to tell you" (Job 1:15, 17, 19). The situation of the second generation, for its part, is articulated by Ariel—the protagonist in Wiesel's *The Fifth Son*—who sensitively notes, "I suffer from an Event I have not even experienced." Collectively, second-generation writers are, in the words of Ellen Fine, "confronted with a difficult task: to imagine an event they have not lived through, and to reconstitute and integrate it into their writing—to create a story out of History."[8] Affirming who *they* are, second-generation witnesses shed light on contemporary Jewish identity.

But these witnesses are "guardians of an absent meaning." Writing of the second generation in France, Nadine Fresco notes that "these latter day Jews are like people who have had a *hand amputated that they never had. It is a phantom pain, in which amnesia takes the place of memory.*"[9] Alain Finkielkraut, a leading intellectual, speaks for his contemporaries in the French second generation in calling his parents "survivors of an invisible tragedy," whose "crushing presences are also evasive presences, part of an impenetrable world."[10] For Finkielkraut, the second generation forms a new social type in Jewish history, the "imaginary Jew" who lives after the *Shoah* but attempts to identify with the murdered Jewish culture of Europe.[11] Thus, the artistic works of this generation bear witness to the *presence of an absence*. This absence is seen in a variety of ways and consists both of traumatic and positive dimensions. On the one hand, there exist photos of murdered relatives; survivors' flawed parenting skills owing to their Holocaust experience; a life lived under the sign of what Robert J. Lifton terms the "death imprint," defined as "imagery [that] can include many forms of cruel memory . . . the smoke or smell of the gas chambers, the brutal killing of a single individual, or simply separation from a family member never seen again;"[12] and ascribing to the children near magical powers to undo the murderous destruction wrought by the *Shoah*. On the other hand, many survivor families display a fierce loyalty to each other. This loyalty and commitment includes members of the extended family who happened to have survived. Children of survivors feel responsible for "parenting their parents," as Sucher notes, and share a compulsive need to learn about the Holocaust. Further, second-generation witnesses provide a voice for their survivor parents.

Moreover, second-generation witnesses have their own distinctive Holocaust images and ways of bearing witness that reflect their *own* memories. First and foremost, they attest to their parents' continuing survival. Listening to survivor tales provides this generation with the means to both connect with their parents and, therefore, better understand their own identity. Lighting *yahrzeit* (memorial) candles is another second-generation way of remembering. Dina Wardi, an Israeli psychotherapist, argues that children of survivors are themselves frequently viewed as memorial candles.[13] Geographically, pilgrimages to parents' European birthplaces and to locations of death camps as well as to Israel serve as physical markers of second-generation Holocaust remembrance. Part of their Holocaust inheritance includes a desire to tell their children about the event. Indeed, Robert M. Prince identifies this desire as "one of the few discrete traits held in common among children of survivors."[14] Children of survivors also understand themselves and their connection to the Jewish tradition in terms of their parents' Holocaust experience. As Prince notes, "imagery of the Holocaust, mediated by parental experience, serves as an unconscious organizer for the identity of children of survivors and provides basic metaphors for unconscious fantasy."[15] Yet, if second-generation witnesses are very close to their parents, they also differ in a profound way. In Hartman's telling phrase, second-generation witnesses shift the focus to the "sequelae of a catastrophic memory."

Yet there can be no doubt about the impact of the Holocaust on the Jewish identity of the second-generation witness. The texts, both novels and films this book analyzes confirm this observation. Clearly the most graphic illustration of the connection between the *Shoah* and the second generation is seen in the work of Art Spiegelman's *Maus* volumes. For example, in *Maus II*, Spiegelman draws himself seated at his artist board. Through the open window, the reader sees a German soldier standing in a concentration camp guard tower and pointing his rifle at Spiegelman's head.[16] The violence of the European past is very much a part of the American present, and attests to the continuing impact of the Holocaust on subsequent generations. But the second generation's legacy is both constantly present and continually elusive. Further, as Aaron Hass notes, "children of survivors acquired both detrimental and life-enhancing qualities from their parents."[17]

## PARTICULARISM AND UNIVERSALISM

My study suggests that the works of second-generation witnesses take one of two distinct Jewish paths: particularism or universalism. The dialectical tension between universalism and particularism is, in fact, itself a characteristic feature of biblical and rabbinic thought.[18] For example, particularist expressions are seen clearly in the notions of covenant and chosenness, and the portrayal of the Israelites as a "kingdom of priests and a holy nation" (Ex. 19:6). Universalist thinking, for its part, stems from the belief that God is a universal deity; Abraham addresses God as "the Judge of all the earth" (Gen. 18:25). Further, liturgical expressions of universalism are common in the High Holiday services. Universalism is prominent as well in the second part of the *Aleinu* prayer, which calls for the perfection (*tikkun*) of the world under the reign of the Almighty (*"Latakain olam b'malkut Shaddai"*). This tension is also expressed in the post-Auschwitz creative work of the second-generation witnesses. Those who travel the particularist path put God on trial (*din Torah*), abandon the Sinai Covenant while seeking to find an adequate alternative, deal with theodicy within a specifically Jewish context, and raise the issue of Jewish-Christian relations. The particularists seek a *tikkun atzmi* (mending or repair) of the self. Writers whose works are particularist in nature include Thomas Friedmann (*Damaged Goods*), Barbara Finkelstein (*Summer Long-a-Coming*), Art Spiegelman (*Maus*), Melvin J. Bukiet (*Stories of an Imaginary Childhood* and *While the Messiah Tarries*), J. J. Steinfeld (*Dancing at the Club Holocaust*), and Thane Rosenbaum (*Elijah Visible*). Examples of filmmakers whom I term particularist are Stephen Brand (*Kaddish*), Eva Fogelman (*Breaking the Silence*), Abraham Ravitt (*Half-Sister, Everything's For You,* and *In Memory*), Jack and Danny Fischer (*A Generation Apart*), and Owen J. Shapiro (*Alinsky's Children*).

Those who travel the second path, that of Jewish universalism, seek to articulate universal lessons emerging from the Holocaust. The universalists do not abandon Jewish specificity, but strive for *tikkun olam*, the moral improvement or repair of the world, and struggle against all forms of prejudice and racism, ranging from antisemitism to homophobia. This *tikkun* consists of a mission to build a moral society. Writers who walk this path include Julie Salamon (*White Lies*), Lev Raphael (*Dancing on Tisha B'Av* and *Winter Eyes*), and Carol Ascher (*The Flood*). Of the filmmakers in this group, I include Pierre Sauvage (*Weapons of the Spirit*), Myriam Abramowicz and Esther Hoffenberg (*As If It Were Yesterday*), Saul Rubinek (*So Many Miracles*), and Debbie Goodstein (*Voices from the Attic*).

Despite their differing emphases, both groups share several features: their identity is shaped by the Holocaust; the members of each group desire to bear witness; and the daughters and sons of survivors in both groups are frequently "replacement" children, their half-siblings having been murdered by Nazis during the *Shoah*. Wiesel's *The Oath* and *The Fifth Son* portray both the psychosocial and theological sequelae of being raised in a family where one is the second "only" son. So, too, do Thomas Friedmann's *Damaged Goods* and Spiegelman's *Maus*. Julie Salamon's *White Lies* speaks of the second, post-Auschwitz daughters of survivors. Wiesel movingly writes of this phenomenon and its impact. He reports that a student, the son of survivors, described his anguish at being the "only" child of parents who had each lost their first children in the camps. His parents met after liberation. "Each time they look at me," the youth tells Wiesel, "it is not me they see."[19] Consequently, these replacement children remember much in the manner portrayed in the Book of Job. In fact, Job's tale is paradigmatic for those wishing to confront the mystery of humanity and God while seeking to understand the meaning of innocent suffering.

## CHILDREN OF SURVIVORS AND CHILDREN OF JOB

Throughout history, the experience of the enigmatic Job of Uz has riveted humanity's attention. Philosophers and poets, mystics and theologians have looked to this tale in search of insight into the relationship between God and humanity, attempting to plumb the mystery of innocent suffering. The Job of antiquity suffered, and even rebelled, but he was granted a mystical experience of the deity and a divine "confession" that the universe lacked perfection. The Book of Job "answers" the question of theodicy by affirming divine majesty and human penance; Job "despises" himself and repents in "dust and ashes." The text's epilogue even reports that Job is granted a second set of ten children, to "replace" those who were killed—although, and this is the point, a lost child is never "replaced." Further, his wealth and happiness were also restored.

But in light of Auschwitz, Job's theodicy raises far more questions than it answers. The "Jobs of the gas chambers," to use Martin Buber's phrase, did not repent in dust and ashes, they *became* dust and ashes. Further, those who survived did not—and do not—live unscathed by their experience. Many survivors married and had children while living in so-called Displaced Persons camps immediately after the Holocaust. Indeed, the birth rate in the DP camps was the highest of any Jewish community in the world. Some have compared this act of renewal to the covenant at Sinai.[20] Yet, Wiesel notes the need for a sequel to the Book of Job. This sequel should begin where the biblical tale ends. Its focus is a question: What happened to Job's second children? "How," Wiesel wonders, "could they live in a house filled with tragedy? How could Job and his wife live with their memories?" He contends that the real tragedy in the Book of Job is the tragedy of Job's children, the children of the survivors.[21]

*The Testament of Job,* an obscure pseudepigraphic text edited between the first century B.C.E. and the end of the second century C.E., reinterprets the biblical tale of Job.[22] In doing so, it places second-generation artistic works—which are chronologically new—in the context of antiquity. For example, the *Testament* portrays a dying Job, around whose bed stand his second set of ten children, those born after the deaths of their half-brothers and -sisters. Job tells these "replacements" his tale of innocence and tragedy, stressing his steadfastness in the face of misfortune. Job's legacy consists of traditional advice: remember God, help the poor, assist those in need, and marry within the faith.

The *Testament* has neither the poetic beauty nor theological sophistication of its biblical antecedent. Nevertheless, the pseudepigraphic text makes three important points concerning the second generation. For example, Job's children take the place—and inherit the burden—of those killed earlier. Further, the survivor of catastrophe shares the tale of his suffering: "Tell your children of it and let your children tell their children another generation" (Joel 1:3). While not all survivors spoke of their experiences—indeed, for approximately twenty years after the end of the *Shoah* there was a "conspiracy of silence" among certain survivors[23]—recent years have witnessed an ever stronger sense of urgency to bear witness. Finally, the Job of the *Testament* urges his children to maintain their Jewish identity after the disaster.

Further, the names given to the biblical Job's second set of daughters are highly suggestive of a special sense of mission. Jemimah, Keziah, and Karen-happuch are names which have been interpreted in a manner suggesting the societal significance of at least the universalist group of second-generation witnesses.[24] Jemimah, for instance, comes from the word for day (*yom*), and implies brightness. Like the sun's light, Jemimah will brighten things. Keziah is a fragrance whose essence will float over the world. Karen-happuch, a horn of eyeshadow, will shine like a gemstone (*happuch*). Each of these names contains a dimension of outreach to the world. The second generation will have a societal impact by translating the survivors' suffering into a salvific message. As noted earlier, while not all second-generation witnesses are universalists, each does bear witness to the significance of the *Shoah* for contemporary identity and shares the desire to prevent future catastrophe.

Post-Auschwitz Jewish thought seizes on the figure of Job in discussing the relationship of the Holocaust to contemporary Jewish identity. The late theologian Eliezer Berkovits distinguishes between survivors, whom he terms *k'doshim* (holy ones) and nonwitnesses. He writes that "we are not Job and we dare not speak or resound as if we were. We are only Job's brother."[25] In contrast, the historian Deborah Lipstadt movingly writes that students of the Holocaust are not even Job's brother. At best, they are his "nieces and nephews."[26] Both thinkers, despite their different familial metaphors, correctly warn against substituting the imagination of nonwitnesses for the experience of the survivors. The distinguished philosopher Emil Fackenheim, for his part, recognizing the epoch making nature of the *Shoah*, views all subsequent post-Auschwitz generations as, in a manner of speaking, "replacement children."[27] But, as noted, no lost child can be replaced. Consequently, Fackenheim employs a familial metaphor which is neither brother, nor sister, nor nephew. Rather, it is the classical notion of *kl'al Yisrael*, the community of Israel. He writes: "For a new 'generation,' and Jewish generations to come ever after, are not 'the Job of the gas chambers': they are Job's children."[28] Moreover, Fackenheim writes that all subsequent post-Holocaust generations have the task of interrogating both the Jewish Bible and all of Jewish history in light of Auschwitz.

While not referring specifically to the children of Job, the late cultural and literary critic Terrence Des Pres writes perceptively about the impact of the loss of innocence on those who live in the "aftermath":

> Like it or not, we are involved beyond ourselves. To be in the world but not of it, to recover innocence after Auschwitz, plainly, will not work. The self's sense of itself is different now, and what has made the difference, both as cause and continuing condition is simply knowing that the Holocaust occurred. We are in no way guilty but we do not feel blameless. We live decently but not without shame. We are entirely innocent but innocence, the blessedness of simple daily being, no longer seems possible.[29]

With Hartman, Des Pres indicates the universal impact of the *Shoah*.

There is now a generation of children of survivors, most of whom are themselves parents, who—like the children in the *Testament of Job*—have received their parents' testimony and accepted the mission of transmitting it to their own children, the third generation, and to the world at large. Formal acceptance of this legacy occurred at the closing of the World Gathering of Holocaust Survivors which met in Jerusalem in 1981. Nearly two decades later, it is now time to assemble and discuss various second-generation witness texts. The contemporary children of Job have written novels and made films that underscore the meaning of inheriting the Holocaust for post-Auschwitz Jewish identity. Their works bear the indelible imprint of the *Shoah*'s cultural, psychic, and theological legacy. For example, in terms of particularism, how credible is it to assert the idea of a post-*Shoah* covenant? If so, what is the nature of the divine-human relationship? If not, what are the reasons for remaining a Jew? How does one argue with God after Auschwitz? Echoing Jeremiah and Job, second-generation witnesses raise anew the millennial question of innocent suffering.

## THEOLOGICAL SEQUELAE

The works examined in this study exemplify several types of theological sequelae. Their covenantal affirmations display aspects of Wiesel's Additional Covenant, Irving Greenberg's Voluntary Covenant, and Richard Rubenstein's notion of covenant as a way of binding together diverse peoples. Further, the creative works of second-generation witnesses seek to achieve at least a partial *tikkun* of what Emil Fackenheim describes as the total rupture of Jewish, Christian, and Western philosophical thought caused by the Holocaust (these theological positions are discussed below in chapter 2). These paradigms, in turn, are concerned with an applied post-Holocaust theology, one that acknowledges a wounded deity and, consequently, ascribes greater responsibility to the human partner for maintaining the covenant. Further, their Holocaust legacy leads second generation witnesses to search for ways to attest their Jewish commitment that reflect their own experience of shaping Holocaust memory. Those second-generation witnesses who travel the universal covenantal path strive to achieve *tikkun olam*. While this concept has undergone various changes in meaning, those in the second-generation come closest to embracing the understanding of the term given in Eliezer Ben-Yehuda's dictionary, which defines this term as meaning "something for the good of the world."[30]

This "something" is explained by Menachem Z. Rosensaft, an attorney and founding chairperson of the International Network of Children of Jewish Holocaust Survivors. He speaks of the second generation not in terms of privileges or rights, but in terms of mission. Owing to this generation's unique relationship to the Holocaust because of its members relationship to their parents, children of survivors, he attests, have a "particular sensitivity" to the war and the Holocaust. Consequently, this generation has a "specific duty" to share its awareness: "to ensure that others, Jews and gentiles alike, understand why remembrance of these events is important."[31]

## UNIVERSAL QUESTIONS

The phenomenon of the second-generation witness leads inexorably to questions possessing a universal resonance. For example, what does the tragedy of European Jewry have to do with American Jews in particular and American culture at large? Moreover, is there a relationship between second-generation witnesses of the *Shoah* and those of other catastrophic events such as the case of the Armenian genocide and children of Hiroshima and Nagasaki? In this context, Lipstadt notes that some children of survivors have served as "consultants to those working with children whose parents have suffered massive psychic trauma, such as children of Southeast Asian 'boat people,' or children of Japanese Americans who were interned during World War II."[32] Moreover, members of the second generation have volunteered in great numbers to interview survivors as part of Steven Spielberg's "Survivors of the *Shoah* visual history project." What of the relationship between children of survivors and other ethnic or identity groups so popular in America, such as the feminist movement, Afro-Americans, gays and lesbians, and Vietnam veterans? Eva Fogelman contends that groups for survivors and second-generation witnesses are part of America's "renewed interest in ethnic identity, personal roots, and communal systems of support."[33] What types of comparisons can be made between difficult parent-child relationships of survivors and those of children of nonwitnesses, or children of immigrants?

Further, second-generation witnesses live in a postmodern era, a time when questions of memory and ethnic identity appear paramount. Their writings and films are clearly autobiographical and thus mark a distinct break from biblical and rabbinic paradigms that emphasize communal archetypes and collective response to tragedies that befall the House of Israel. Indeed, the works of second-generation witnesses suggest affinities between postmodern and post-Holocaust worldviews. For example, the second generation is concerned with the crisis of representation of memory as well as issues of cultural identity. Nevertheless, this generation employs traditional images—albeit in attenuated form—as theological and psychic markers in their search for a post-*Shoah* Jewish sense of themselves.[34]

Eugene Borowitz, writing in *Renewing the Covenant: A Theology for the Postmodern Jew*, emphasizes the relationship between what he terms the "common self's concentration on immediacy" and the covenant. The covenant, he writes, "renders the Jewish self radically historical."[35] Thus, while the second-generation witness exhibits certain characteristics of postmodernism as an American, this witness also reveals his/her Jewish legacy. The writings and films of this generation comprise a secular midrash on post-Auschwitz Jewish identity. Telling their stories affirms who they are as well as serving to shed light on the nature of contemporary Judaism in America and the outlines of a post-Auschwitz covenant.

In the next chapter I discuss the ways in which Holocaust memory is being shaped by second-generation writings and films. After briefly discussing the history of the second-generation witness in America, I turn to concerns raised by the appearance of this generation's artistic works. First, this study serves to introduce a new generation of Jewish writers and filmmakers in America. Their work takes seriously the challenge of both defining and living a post-Auschwitz Jewish life. Unlike Job's false friends, who, as Wiesel observes, are held in contempt by God—and the reader— children of survivors do not presume to speak *instead* of the witnesses.[36] Rather, they give voice to the Holocaust's continuing impact on Jewish identity. I then examine the covenant theology of Elie Wiesel, Irving Greenberg, and Richard Rubenstein, as well as Emil Fackenheim's notion of *tikkun* in order to better understand the theological "sequelae" displayed in second-generation artistic works. This examination notes the shift from belief in an interventionist deity to the importance of human action in attempting to build a moral society after Auschwitz. Second-generation witnesses embrace an applied theology. Refraining from adopting traditional assertions of an omnipotent deity, the works of this generation nevertheless suggest the outlines of Judaism's contemporary argument with God.

## THE SEARCH FOR *TIKKUN*

Throughout this study, I note the salient psychosocial elements found in the works of second-generation witnesses as they reflect the centrality of the *Shoah* in shaping contemporary Jewish identity. Issues such as separation anxiety, lack of parental respect for boundaries, a dismissiveness of children's own emotional needs, and fear of hurting the children and the survivors are reflected in many of the second-generation texts and underscore the complexity of survivor parent-child relationships. So, too, does the impact of incomplete or—the reverse side of the same coin—continual mourning on the part of survivor parents.

But the second generation presents a variety of images of survivors. These images range from viewing survivor parents as figures whose Holocaust experience borders on transforming them into holy figures, to viewing parents as damaged people unable and unwilling to let go of the past. Some parents, especially fathers, are silent and remote (especially in the works of Friedmann, Finkelstein, and Raphael). Many are overprotective (this is a common trait reported by the second generation in Fogelman's film *Breaking the Silence*). Most have an inner circle of friends consisting of other survivors. Moreover, it is frequently the case that conflicting images of survivor parents are presented. For example, William Helmreich astutely notes this phenomenon in his important study *Against All Odds: Holocaust Survivors and the Successful Lives They Made in America*:

In one sense [survivor parents] were regarded as all-powerful, indestructible people who had literally made it through hell, notwithstanding
the infirmities they suffered as a result. And yet, this view of seeming
invincibility was often problematic for the child of such parents, for in
their ill-fitting clothes, heavy accents, short height, and unfamiliarity
with American culture, they appeared frail and weak.[37]

Furthermore, second-generation authors display the feelings of uncertainty that result from attempting to discover their own role in the family.
For example, the nameless second-generation protagonist in Wiesel's
novel *The Oath* is overwhelmed by his survivor mother's continued suffering. Unable to understand either the *Shoah* or his mother, the youth is
confused and muses, "Where do I fit in? I suffered with her and for her,
but I could not understand."[38] In addition, children of survivors appear to
know that "something terrible" had happened to their parents. This is a
type of knowledge that may be preconscious. It certainly is present, even
though many survivors' children knew few if any details about their parents' Holocaust experiences. Aaron Hass observes in a recent study of the
second generation that among those he interviewed, "*all* had a sense of
being aware, from a very early age, that they were, indeed, children of survivors."[39]

This book argues that the contemporary children of Job are helping
sensitize society as a whole to the implications of what happened to the
Jewish people and the world a half-century ago. That these second-
generation witnesses were even born, given Nazism's murderous assault
on Jewish existence, is a tale that bears import for all of humanity. The
fact that a second generation exists suggests if not miracle then at least a
sense of awe. Their creative work speaks to the issue of how Holocaust
memory is being shaped in contemporary Jewish and American culture.
Further, this study highlights work by the second generation of those
whom Albert Friedlander terms "Riders Towards the Dawn." These second generation witnesses live in the dawn of "a broken world" while
simultaneously attempting to seek a *tikkun* of both the self and the world.

But readers need to understand that this *tikkun* does not lead to resolution of the *Shoah*. While these creative works articulate the legacy
and lessons of the *Shoah*, they do so always against the background of the
disaster. In this context, it is worth noting the full title of Friedlander's
book: *Riders toward the Dawn: From Ultimate Despair to Temperate
Hope*.[40] The subtitle reflects the enormity of the Holocaust's impact on
Jewish thought and Jewish lives. The United States publisher replaced
the subtitle with one that reveals the characteristically American tendency to ignore history and seek a "happy ending." In this country the
subtitle is *From Holocaust to Hope*. Further, these second-generation
witnesses, like the Holocaust itself, speak both in a particular and uni-

versal voice. Or, rather, the universal message is directly related to the *Shoah*'s Jewish particularity. Moreover, this message sensitizes readers to second-generation Holocaust symbolism and ways of representing the *Shoah* in the lives of those who live in its aftermath. Finally, this study places the artistic work of second-generation witnesses in a theological context that has not yet been adequately explored.

# CHAPTER 2

# *From Pathology to Theology: The Emergence of the Second-Generation Witness*

There was a lot of amateur pop psychology floating around. There were a lot of people talking about "transmission trauma" and the like. Neither I nor other Holocaust survivor children recognized the portrait being painted of us.

—Menachem Rosensaft[1]

Initially, many studies of the second generation tended to pathologize these "replacement" children. Conducted mainly by clinicians, psychologists, and psychoanalysts, these studies were flawed both conceptually and methodologically. For example, they were based on a clinical population that presented itself for treatment. Further, the numbers involved were quite small. In addition, such studies naïvely assumed a homogenous population and therefore failed to recognize the complexity of the situation.[2] More realistically, describing the survivors themselves, Helen Epstein notes that they were "perhaps the most heterogeneous group that had ever made mass migration."[3] They varied in every imaginable way, including prewar places of abode, level of education, type of occupation, degree of religious observance, level of sophistication, age, and Holocaust experience. As with the survivors, so with their children in terms of background. The members of the second generation are united only by their identity as children of survivors. Individual members of this generation in fact constitute a quite heterogenous group, having varying behavioral, religious, and sexual orientations. This book understands the second-generation witness as a specific identity rather than constituting a syndrome in the sense of psychic difficulties experienced by the survivor generation.

Specifically concerning second-generation witnesses and their testimony, it is important to note that their responses tend to vary according to the type of survivor household in which they were raised. Yael Danieli, the clinical psychologist, emphasizes the situational context of intergenerational processes. For example, while noting the frequency of "marriages of despair" among survivors, she distinguishes four major types of survivor families: "*victim* families; *fighter* families; *numb* families; and families of *those who made it*."[4] Each of these types of families has a particular postwar home atmosphere that impacts profoundly on the identity and worldview of the second generation. Most survivors who spent the Holocaust years in concentration and death camps established victim or numb families after the war. Partisans and resistance fighters during the war headed post-Holocaust fighter families. Generalizing, one can observe that in victim and numb families, offspring are less likely to have heard details about the parents' experiences in the *Shoah*. In contrast, children in fighter families heard far more detailed accounts of what transpired during the war against the Jews. Offspring of families who made it, for their part, "report feeling cheated of their heritage."[5] This is because their parents are more assimilated than those in the other types of families and tend to deny the past.

Danieli rightly contends that her taxonomy represents neither "pure and mutually exclusive types, nor [should it] blur the commonality of core issues confronting Holocaust survivors and their offspring."[6] Quite to the contrary, her concern is to counteract the tendency to view survivors and their children as a homogenous group. Rather, their very heterogeneity demands that attention be paid to the specificity of members in both groups. Having said this, it is nonetheless appropriate to note that the novelists whose works this study examines reveal the impact of growing up in primarily victim or numb families. About the offspring of these families, Danieli observes: "Overly concerned not to hurt anyone, keenly sensitive to another's pain and mood changes, the children of victim survivors frequently entered the helping professions."[7]

Rather than pathologize the second generation, it is more realistic—as Helmreich notes—to acknowledge "a basis for detecting trends and tendencies."[8] Lipstadt helpfully suggests that a "complex web of issues" plays a role, "to varying degrees, in the evolution of children of survivors' identity, perception, attitude, and relationship."[9] Among these issues are: (1) separation from frequently overprotective parents; (2) the "phenomenon of the impossible comparison," that is, the feeling that their own problems and lives have less meaning than their parents'; (3) "a need to be superachievers" and thereby somehow undo the trauma of the *Shoah*; (4) "a feeling of loss in terms of a diminished family circle"; and (5) seeking to find a personal mode to express their thoughts about the Holocaust and to "insure continuity with their family's past."[10] I would add to this list a tendency on the part of some second-generation witnesses to achieve a mimesis—in Erich Auerbach's sense of the term—of their parents' Holocaust experience. This is seen most dramatically in the works of Spiegelman and Finkelstein. Collectively, there is a desire on the part of the second-generation witness to "make sense" out of the Holocaust. Their artistic attempts to master an unmasterable trauma have led to a variety of explorations of post-Auschwitz Jewish identity.

The second-generation witnesses have gained perspective on their relationship to the *Shoah*. Childhood anxieties and uncertainties about the Holocaust and their own Jewish identity have yielded to extensive research, readings, membership in self-help groups, extended discussions with parents, and other forms of exploration concerning inheriting the *Shoah* and its impact on forming their Jewish identity. In this context it is appropriate to note Hass's observation that "reports of children of survivors in their thirties and forties are more likely than previous descriptions by younger offspring to demonstrate a valuing of their family's European history."[11] At least in part, this change is due to greater empathy on the part of children of survivors as they gain more knowledge of what their parents survived. This empathy, argues Hass, serves in turn to reduce the "anger the child feels over perceived deprivations resulting from impaired parental functioning."[12] There is as well the recognition on the part of second-generation witnesses who themselves are parents of "the formidable task of raising offspring even under the best of circumstances."[13] Many of the survivors, for their part, have become more familiar with the ways of American culture. Further, this culture now encourages rather than discourages the survivors to speak about their wartime experience. To use a biblical metaphor, the second-generation witness can be seen as learning the lesson of Lot's wife. If one looks back too soon—or engages in confronting the enormity of the Holocaust before the appropriate time—the result may be fatal.

Taking a different turn from the purely clinical studies, Jack Nusan Porter asserts the existence of a "sociopolitical syndrome" consisting of "a wide variety of political and religious action" which, in turn, can be expressed in either particularist or universalist ways.[14] This is a form of Holocaust inheritance that directly involves a *tikkun* of both the self and the world. For example, on the political level the second generation is involved in a variety of activities, including hunting Nazis who went unpunished after the Holocaust, helping in the rescue of Ethiopian Jews, and lobbying the Senate for American ratification of the Genocide Treaty.[15] Referring directly to the psychosocial dimension of the second generation, Eva Fogelman and Bella Savran emphasize a second-generation sense of mission. Survivor offspring view themselves as a direct link with an obliterated past. Therefore, many in the second generation assume a "mission to witness to an event or culture they never really knew."[16] Working in the Boston area in 1976, Fogelman and Savran began children-of-survivor awareness groups whose purpose was to help members of the second generation "work through" the Holocaust by ventilating their feelings about, and sharing their experiences of, growing up in survivor households. Here, as seen in Fogelman's award-winning film *Breaking the Silence* (discussed below in chapter 5), psychosocial issues such as guilt feelings and ambivalence about one's Jewish identity are discussed and become the springboard for authentically confronting one's relationship to the Holocaust and to Jewish history. Neither the Nusan-Porter nor the Savran and Fogelman studies have yet been tested against the newly emergent body of second-generation creative works.

## THE AMERICAN SECOND GENERATION: A BRIEF HISTORY

The existence of second-generation witnesses as a distinct group having a particular purchase on the meaning of Jewish identity after Auschwitz was initially brought to public attention in America with the appearance of two books: *Living after the Holocaust: Reflections by Children of Survivors in America*, edited by Lucy Y. Steinitz and David M. Szony,[17] and Helen Epstein's *Children of the Holocaust: Conversations with Sons and Daughters of Survivors*.[18] Each of these works differed sharply from the pathologizing trend of writing about the second generation in the late sixties and the early seventies. Moreover, both made the point that the second generation's "common origin yields a collective identity," and that while outwardly similar to their nonwitnessing contemporaries, many of whom are third- or fourth-generation Americans, the psychosocial lives of the second-generation witnesses "contrasts sharply with the background of many American peers."[19]

Specifically, *Living After the Holocaust* is a rich collection of fiction, poetry, conversations, and scholarly studies that reflect the *Shoah*'s continuing impact on the lives of its survivors and their children. The contributors' work is united by three themes: the fact that the second generation's lives are shaped by an event not personally experienced; their "duty" to bear witness for their parents; and a "heightened sensitivity to suffering" that eventuates in the fact that many children of survivors enter helping professions such as medicine, psychiatry, psychology, social work, and teaching.[20] Much in the manner suggested by the symbolic names of Job's daughters, this represents an attempt at achieving *tikkun olam* in a world which has lost its moral, psychic, and theological innocence.

Although we have noted the difference between survivors and the second generation, the determination of the latter to inform the world is similar to the wish of survivors. *Living After the Holocaust* articulates the second-generation credo:

> We join in our common background and firm belief that the manner in which the Holocaust will finally be communicated to future generations—through liturgy, education, family rituals, social ethics, and the

stories which will become our heirlooms—is dependent on the knowledge and sensitivities of young people today. To this end, *this book is not
about the Holocaust per se, but about the saving remnant, our parents,
and about their children, us.*[21]

At the time these words were written, there had not yet appeared any second-generation novels and very few films.

The odyssey of Epstein's book reveals much about American culture's changing attitude towards the second generation. Initially, she
could find no publisher for her work. There was simply not enough interest in the topic.[22] Eventually she published a *New York Times* article,
"Heirs of the Holocaust" (1977), that galvanized children of survivors
into a twofold realization: that their distinctive perceptions about the
impact of the Holocaust on Jewish identity were shared by others, and
that there were a large number of second-generation witnesses. One
scholar terms Epstein's work the "real turning point in the evolution of
children of survivors as a communal, emotional, and political entity."[23]
Two years later she published *Children of the Holocaust: Conversations
with Sons and Daughters of Survivors*, referred to by some as "the Bible"
of the second generation. Epstein writes of feeling that the second-
generation witnesses constitute "an invisible, silent family scattered about
the world."[24] She interviews this "family," which transcends geographical
borders, in four countries located on three continents. In addition, her
book also has a chapter concerning details of the earliest psychological
studies of children of survivors.

Epstein finds that the red thread connecting the Holocaust legacy of the
second generation consists of both icons and images. For example, she calls
the faded photos of murdered relatives "documents, evidence of our part in
a history so powerful that whenever I tried to read about it in the books my
father gave me or see it in the films he took me to, I could not take it in."[25]
Further, she writes of the presence of images from the Kingdom of Night
that form her own perceptions. "The Seventh Avenue local," writes Epstein,
"became a train of cattle cars on its way to Poland." Murderers "were
always at large, liable to break up a party or disrupt my class in school or
even take three thousand people out of Carnegie Hall."[26]

This legacy is a knowledge more elusive than systematic, existential
rather than textual, autobiographic as opposed to archetypal. As a daughter of survivors, she movingly describes her legacy in terms of an attempt
to master an unmasterable event. The meaning of the knowledge she
seeks is both omnipresent and elusive. At the center of her identity,
Epstein remained unable to articulate its contents. This knowledge

> had lain in an iron box so deep inside me that I was never sure just
> what it was. I knew I carried slippery, combustible things more secret

than sex and more dangerous than any shadow or ghost. Ghosts had shape and name. What lay inside my iron box had none. Whatever lived inside me was so potent that words crumbled before they describe.[27]

Works of the second-generation witnesses are attempts to unlock this box, share its contents, and, in the process, contribute toward the achievement of *tikkun olam*, something for the "good of the world."

Elie Wiesel's 1984 keynote address at the plenary session of the First International Conference of Children of Holocaust survivors was a symbolic passing of the torch of remembrance from survivors to their children. Linking survivors and their children together, much in the talmudic notion of the chain of tradition, Wiesel underscored the specific and personal relationship that children of survivors have to the Holocaust. For the second generation, he observed, "the war has a face—the face of your father—the face of your mother, her eyes on *Shabbat* or after *Shabbat*."[28] Yet, Wiesel also notes the difference between the first- and second-generation witnesses. The survivors, he attests, had problems with knowledge; their children have "to face problems of the imagination." The link between knowledge and imagination is "inevitably tragic."[29] Privileging survivor testimony, Wiesel notes an inevitable dialectical relationship between the generations. "When knowledge becomes imagination," he writes, "it is as damaging as when imagination assumes the authority of knowledge."[30]

Wiesel's own position concerning the second-generation witness provides both for the sacrality of the task of memory and a recognition that this generation must find its own memorial voice. On the one hand, in his keynote address, Wiesel urges the second generation to "keep our tale alive—and sacred," do not permit its trivialization. Their survivor parents "have shown what they can do with their suffering," the children "are showing what [they] can do with [their] observation of [this] suffering."[31]

On the other hand, while the artistic responses to the *Shoah* are ontologically tethered to survivor testimony, second-generation witnesses speak in their own voices. For example, in *The Forgotten*, Malkiel articulates the nature of this relationship. Thinking of Elhanan, his survivor father whose memory is being consumed by Alzheimer's disease, Malkiel seeks the older man's pardon, saying:

Forgive me, Father. You'll have to forgive me, but I'm going to disappoint you. There is no such thing as a memory transfusion. Yours will never become mine. I can live after you and even for you, but not as you.[32]

Nevertheless, the cultural, psychic, and theological legacy of the *Shoah* is indelibly imprinted in second-generation witnessing and consciousness.

## A NEW GENERATION OF
## JEWISH WRITERS AND FILMMAKERS

Writing in *A Double Dying: Reflections on Holocaust Literature*, Alvin Rosenfeld correctly identified the necessity of developing a "phenomenology of reading Holocaust literature." He appealed for "maps" to guide readers as they "pick up and variously try to comprehend the writings of the victims, the survivors, the survivors-who-became-victims, and the kinds-of-survivors, those who were never there but know more than the outlines of the place."[33] The category of those who while not in the *Shoah* know more than it's outlines, until recently appeared to be a distinction with only limited content. This study suggests that second-generation witnesses know a good deal more than the outlines of the Holocaust. Their creative texts, both written and visual (e.g., films), help provide a more comprehensive phenomenology of understanding the Holocaust's manifold sequelae.

Creative responses by children of survivors began appearing with some regularity in the decade of the eighties. Strongly personal in nature, these works tended to be first novels, films, poems, and so on. As such, they represent a significant point of departure from established Jewish-American novelists and underscore the point made by Ted Solataroff who, writing in a different context, observed, "In rescuing the Holocaust from the banality of repetition, these stories from writers of diverse background provide another indication of the fresh winds of imagination that blow from various sectors of the Jewish scene."[34] In the case of second-generation witnesses, however, it is not a matter of "rescuing" the Holocaust. It is, rather, the *tikkun* of bearing witness to the *Shoah*'s continuing and multidimensional sequelae, of which the second-generation creative works themselves form a significant part. As many of these witnesses are not professional writers and therefore unlikely to be widely known, a biographical statement is provided about each. The transition from works *about* children of survivors to those *by* the second generation marked the appearance of a new social movement in the Jewish and American context. Further, if, as Jacob Neusner contends, the survivors form a new first generation, unlike earlier second-generation American Jews, children of survivors do *not* obey Marcus Hansen's sociological law that states the second generation wants to forget what the first generation remembers. Moreover, as Fogelman notes, the "creative process" of the second generation is a means of both mourning the dead and expressing their own sense of personal loss.[35]

Second-generation texts seek to respond to the ancient question of how to live Jewishly after a catastrophe. For example, the contemporary children of Job are both the last and the first. The second generation is the last one to have intimate contact with survivors as parents. Consequently, they are the last ones to be raised according to the ways of a murdered European-Jewish culture and to hear the languages of their parents' own youth. Some in this generation were, themselves, born in European Displaced Persons camps. Further, this generation is the last one to hear directly the stories of survivors and to have grown up with an extended family that was present through its absence (e.g., photos of relatives murdered in the *Shoah*).

This experience impacted on Jewish identity in a twofold manner. On the one hand, as children many in the second generation were confused and overwhelmed by the Holocaust. Many felt that their Jewishness marginalized them. On the other hand, as adults they have a heightened sense of loss *and* a commitment to their Jewish identity as well as a resolve to learn more of Jewish history. Concerning the latter resolve, it is noteworthy that many of the second-generation witnesses return to the European birthplaces of their parents. Cinematic returns are at the center of Pierre Sauvage's *Weapons of the Spirit*, Myriam Abramowicz's *As If It Were Yesterday*, Saul Rubenik's *So Many Miracles*, and Debbie Goodstein's *Voices from the Attic*. Writers who have returned to their parents' European origins include Melvin J. Bukiet, Helen Epstein, Barbara Finkelstein, Thomas Friedmann, Julie Salamon, and Art Spiegelman.

Second-generation texts constitute a genre that heralds the emergence of a distinctive Jewish voice; one that partakes simultaneously in both the American penchant for ethnic identifiers and the Jewish quest for meaning after Auschwitz. This generation's artistic responses to the *Shoah* display a distinctive angle of vision concerning the relationship between the Holocaust's legacy and Jewish identity in America. These responses acknowledge the pain of antisemitism, the reality of evil, and the impact of witnessing their parents' continued survival. Further, second-generation texts all stand as what Lawrence Langer calls "witnesses to memory."[36] The makers of this art are not "rememberers themselves."[37] Consequently, there is emerging a *paradigm shift* in the shape of Holocaust memory and its representation. Texts written by the contemporary children of Job speak of their own experience of the *Shoah*'s legacy. These texts speak *about* rather than instead of survivors, as this generation seeks to find its own way of shaping the memory and legacy of Auschwitz.

The children of Job are also the first to be born after the Holocaust. Their writings and films reflect both their European legacy and their American environment. Second-generation texts also reveal the richness of Jewish imagination in coping with the Holocaust as well as in serving to renew Jewish literature. Further, these texts emphasize the moral role that literature can play in helping to sensitize audiences to the continuing implications of the *Shoah* for both survivor families and society at large.

Additionally, these texts emphasize the fact that ours is an age of testimony. This testimony is, attests Hartman, heterogenous. "Memory," he writes, "has many shapes [and] deserves to be looked at."[38] Furthermore, these texts reflect the influence of both American culture and Jewish teachings. Concerning the American dimension, it is necessary only to point to the aesthetics of comic books, as in Spiegelman's work; the sensitivity to sexual preference that is seen in Raphael's concern with gay and bisexual issues; and the focus on multiculturism reflected in Salamon's story of second-generation witnesses and second-generation welfare mothers. In terms of covenant theology, each of the second-generation witnesses deal implicitly or explicitly with the altered face of the post-Auschwitz relationship between humanity and God. The human covenantal partner plays a dominant role in attempting to mend the world.

## POST-AUSCHWITZ COVENANT THEOLOGY: ELIE WIESEL, IRVING GREENBERG, EMIL FACKENHEIM, AND RICHARD RUBENSTEIN

A careful reading of second-generation texts reveals the existence of a distinctive post-Auschwitz covenant theology. While attesting to the fact that classical claims of an interventionist Lord of History are no longer credible after the death camps, these texts continue to wrestle with God even when they find the deity guilty. Thus, I find Hass's assertion that "it is toward man, and not God, that the accusation is directed by many children of survivors"[39] only partially correct. More accurate, I believe, is the contention that while the second-generation witnesses' theology of protest cannot accept the Sinaitic covenant, the contemporary children of Job express themselves covenantally in several ways that impact on their Jewish identity. For example, many struggle with the juxtaposition of an omnipotent deity and the destruction of European Jewry. Further, this contending is both explicit and implicit. Overtly, several of the second-generation witnesses declare that the biblical God is no longer credible. Covertly, the fact that the *Shoah* happened itself raises fundamental issues concerning Jewish identity and belief .

Even while concluding that if God existed the Holocaust could not have happened, the second-generation witnesses continue to live their lives Jewishly. They invest apparently secular activities with covenantal implications. This is given clear expression by Eli Rubinstein, a Canadian son of survivors whom Epstein interviewed. Rubinstein speaks for many in his generation when contending that, "I really feel that my raising a family has cosmic significance. I feel I have a sacred duty to have children. I feel it's the only way to respond to the evil of the Holocaust and to assure that the death of my family and the Six Milion was not in vain."[40] The works of second-generation witnesses attest both to the existential nature of post-Holocaust Jewish identity and to the continuing influence of a transformed covenant after Auschwitz. Theirs is an applied theology whose focus is on *deeds*, by which the second-generation witnesses connect both to the Holocaust and Jewish history.

Further, second-generation texts reflect the sense of theological rupture caused by death camps and crematoria. For example, Barbara Finkelstein's novel *Summer Long-a-Coming* speaks of a daughter's theological skepticism as opposed to her survivor father's continued belief. Yet, in facing her own struggle with theodicy, the daughter begins to understand her father, if not God, better. The novel's protagonist, however, begins to view herself in mimetic terms; like her parents she too becomes a witness following the accidental death of her younger sister. A loss of traditional religious faith is very far from precluding one's assumption of Jewish commitment or identity. Nor does it abrogate issues of faith and doubt. Moreover, as noted above by Borowitz, it is the covenant that links this generation with prior Jewish generations.

Second-generation authors for the most part refrain from systematic theological enquiry. Further, they tend not to directly engage in "God talk." Nonetheless, they seek answers to the questions of belief after Auschwitz, the nature of the divine-human relationship, and the meaning of Jewish identity. These writers dramatize a post-Auschwitz and postmodern theological position; one in which the autonomous self has an attenuated relationship to traditional teachings. Yet, the continuing impact of the *Shoah* on their own lives marks these witnesses' determination to seek their own Jewish commitment.

In what follows I outline the features of four important post-Auschwitz understandings of covenant as "maps," in Rosenfeld's sense, to reading the theological context of second-generation texts. While none of the thinkers whose positions are discussed are themselves second-generation members, each sheds significant light on the covenantal stance adopted in second-generation creative works. Two are American-born, two were born in Europe. One is a survivor of Auschwitz, a second was a prisoner in Sachsenhausen, the third and fourth are nonwitnesses. Despite their diverse pasts, each of these thinkers views the Holocaust as a watershed event in Jewish and human history. The *Shoah* calls into question the relationship between God and the world, the post-Auschwitz role of the divine and human covenantal partners, and the credibility of the covenant itself. Elie Wiesel's additional covenant, the voluntary covenant articulated by Irving Greenberg, Emil L. Fackenheim's call for mending the world, and Richard L. Rubenstein's position, which evolved from a death of God abrogating the covenant to a qualified return to covenant, provide theological markers for those wishing to follow the implicit covenantal path outlined by second-generation witnesses. Further, each thinker has significantly shifted the focus of his thought. A direct encounter with the absolute evil of Auschwitz is eschewed. Clearly this evil informs each position, but what now is being articulated is the central second-generation question of how one can live a "Jewish Way" in the aftermath.

## ELIE WIESEL AND THE ADDITIONAL COVENANT

Elie Wiesel's literary works attest to his twofold belief concerning the covenant; it was broken during the Holocaust, and yet it must be reformulated because covenant is the cornerstone of Jewish identity. For example, Wiesel told an interviewer that "during the Holocaust the covenant was broken . . . because of the clouds and because of the fire."[41] On the other hand, even in the darkness of the Kingdom of Night, he observes, the covenant may have been "renewed," although "on a different level."[42] The fundamental point of Wiesel's theological position is, however, the belief that the covenant is the raison d'être of the Jewish people. Each of his many books presents a dimension of the post-Auschwitz covenant. While this is not the place to discuss all of Wiesel's prolific literary *oeuvre*, it is important to note that he has thus far written four novels dealing specifically with the issue of the second-generation witness: *The Oath* (1973), *The Testament* (1981), *The Fifth Son* (1985), and *The Forgotten* (1992). These novels present increasingly developed second-generation characters who gradually assume their role of witness and embrace a specific type of covenant that emphasizes both a particular and a universal dimension. For example, Wiesel's literary second-generation witnesses immerse themselves in studying and teaching about the Holocaust in order to clarify their own inheritance and to bear witness to the Jewish experience in the *Shoah* for the sake of humankind. As I have written about the passing of the literary torch of remembrance in Wiesel's second-generation novels, I will not repeat my conclusions here except to state that for Wiesel the road to God now leads through humanity.[43] Yet it is important to define the dimensions of Wiesel's post-Holocaust covenant.

Carefully analyzing Wiesel's literary corpus, Michael Berenbaum discerns an additional covenant that was forged at Auschwitz. "This covenant," writes Berenbaum, "is no longer between humanity and God or God and Israel, but rather between Israel and its memories of pain and death, God and meaning."[44] Because God is "an unreliable" covenantal partner, attests Berenbaum, Jewish self-affirmation must be "based on our choice to remain Jews and to assume the past of Jewish history as our own and as some way implicated in our future."[45] Further, this self-affirmation involves nothing less than a "covenant with the past of Israel, with its pain, its overwhelming experience of death, and its memories of God and of a world infused with meaning."[46]

Berenbaum emphasizes three characteristics of Wiesel's additional covenant that I view as having specific resonance for the type of covenantal theology attested by second-generation witness texts. These three components are solidarity, witness, and sanctification of life. Solidarity is a normative component of Jewish existence, having roots in both talmudic and hasidic sources. Additionally, Berenbaum notes that for Wiesel this solidarity is "based on a common kinship, a common memory, and a common historical experience."[47] Further, argues Berenbaum, "this solidarity is intensified by anti-Semitism, by a sense of alienation from Western Christian civilization, and by an affirmation of alternate myths and values."[48]

Witness is the second element of the additional covenant. Historically, Jews have been *edim* (witnesses) to the Oneness of God. After the *Shoah*, this witness becomes an essential aspect of the era of testimony. In Berenbaum's words, "Jewish eyes have seen and Jewish ears have heard the awesome revelation at Sinai and the equally awesome (anti) revelation at Auschwitz."[49] For Wiesel, both of these moments are dialectically related. His own writings attest to the dilemma of the witnessing generation concerning the role of Holocaust testimony. Even as this generation speaks, it knows that words betray the experience. Berenbaum rightly points to the metahistorical and transgeographical nature of witnessing in Judaism. Using the Passover seder as paradigmatic, he observes that, understood in the broadest possible way, the role of witness "is not limited to actual victims or actual survivors."[50] Just as Jews in every generation must regard themselves as having personally gone forth from Egypt, "every post-Holocaust Jew must regard himself as though he personally went into the camps and emerged."[51]

This last point is, however, problematic. While it is true that all Jews are survivors, it is true only in a very broad and nonspecific way. Further, with the passage of time and the continued erosion of both solidarity and witness, the persuasiveness of Judaism's formative theological assertions becomes increasingly attenuated. It is precisely here that the second-generation witness stands in a special relationship to the Holocaust. Owing to their parents' experience and the *Shoah*'s continuing legacy in their own lives, this generation can more accurately understand itself as having in some sense, if not gone forth from Egypt, at least been profoundly shaped by the tales of those who have made this (anti-) Exodus.[52]

Sanctification of life (*kedushat haHayim*) comprises the third element of Wiesel's additional covenant. This sanctification, argues Berenbaum, can be understood in one of two ways. On the one hand, it can mean "that the very act of survival is holy."[53] There is, on the other hand, a meaning that more accurately applies to the Wieselian model. This meaning refers to the attempt "to sanctify not merely the very act of survival but the quality of that survival."[54] Here, according to Wiesel, Judaism should work for the sanctification of human existence itself. Wiesel's own dedication to the goal has been recognized by his having been awarded the Nobel Peace Prize. On the level of Jewish particularism, this sanctification is seen in the decision to have children and raise them Jewishly. We have also noted this impulse in the involvement of the second generation on behalf of Jews from the former Soviet Union and Ethiopian Jewry. On the universal level, this notion is expressed by acknowledging the dignity of all human life and working to move the world away from genocidal modes of action.

Wiesel's additional covenant is an all-embracing idea that addresses both believers and nontraditionalists. Berenbaum observes that this covenant "is an additional obligation for those Jews to whom the original covenant is still relevant and meaningful."[55] But, more to the point of this book, Berenbaum notes that Wiesel's additional covenant serves as a continuing source of Jewish self-affirmation even for those Jews who reject, or view as irrelevant, the original, Sinaitic covenant.[56] Although the second -generation witnesses, as we shall see in the following chapters, may no longer view this covenant as relevant to their own lives, each of their works displays aspects of the Wieselian additional covenant, especially in the areas of bearing witness, the sanctification of life, and—with the possible exception of Art Spiegelman—Jewish self-affirmation.

## IRVING GREENBERG AND THE VOLUNTARY COVENANT

Rabbi Irving Greenberg's notion of voluntary covenant, while addressing the post-Auschwitz status of the covenant, sheds much light on the specificity of both American Jews and the second-generation witness. Specifically, the voluntary covenant is an important hermeneutic for reading the theological maps embedded in second-generation texts.[57] For example, Greenberg's notion of covenant transformation following decisive historical crises and his understanding of the masking of holiness by apparently secular activities are twin keys for deciphering second-generation theology. For Greenberg, as for the second generation itself, behavioral issues rather than explicit theological formulations are measures of Jewish identity. For example, he writes that "theology is not a high-priority in the Jewish community."[58] Consequently, adherence to the covenantal way must be determined by what Jews do and not what they say. Greenberg notes that, "for the most part, people have not articulated what they are doing, even to themselves."[59]

Second-generation witnesses' assumption of Jewish commitment assumes new meaning in light of Greenberg's contention that the Jewish people after Auschwitz "volunteered to carry on the mission [of redemption]." Among the generation after the *Shoah*, when there are no illusions about the risks of Jewish identity, Greenberg notes that "the Jewish people did not yield their dream."[60] Rather, this dream and the covenant that it reflects undergo profound transformations in a postmodern age that emphasizes individual autonomy and at best a problematic relationship to tradition.

The lack of overt God-references in second-generation texts needs to be seen against the background of the Holocaust. Divine hiddenness, attests Greenberg, implies that manifest statements (about God) "are less powerful than intimations and signals."[61] On the other hand, a whole range of acts become vehicles for accessing this hidden yet still-present deity. For example, through a variety of rituals and in increasing locations Jews sought God after the second destruction of the Jerusalem Temple. The home and the synagogue took the place of the Temple. Greenberg notes that as prophecy was no longer appropriate after the second destruction, so after the *Shoah* "sacramental and formalistic statements are less likely to be heard today."[62] Rather, expansion is necessary because "in an age of extreme hiddenness God must be discovered everywhere,"[63] in areas ranging from business to politics, to love and to learning. Consequently, Greenberg attests that the State of Israel—an apparently secular state—is in actuality helping usher in the messianic age. Similarly, witnessing to the Holocaust becomes an act of concealed holiness.

Does Jewish history itself provide a paradigm for the type of covenant that is best suited for a postcatastrophic event? In other words, are the creative texts of the second generation following an earlier model? Or are they breaking new ground? The rabbinic covenantal paradigm was Purim, a time of attempted genocide of the Jewish people when human rather than divine agency proved salvific. Here the covenant is less coercive than at Sinai. In fact, God plays no articulated role in this redemptive drama. Quite the contrary is the case. Esther and her uncle Mordecai effectively thwart the genocide. Although neither are Jewishly observant, and Esther marries the non-Jewish king Ahashverosh, Mordecai notes that help will come from another place (i.e., not from divine intervention but from human agency). Together, Esther and Mordecai foil the murderous plans of Haman, Ahashverosh's evil prime minister. Greenberg notes that one of the "deep [secularizing] lessons" of Purim is that one should "never write off assimilated Jews. They come out of the historical closet in the greatest crises and when they are least expected."[64] Further-more, Greenberg views Purim as *the* holiday of the diaspora. The holiday "reflects and affirms the experience of the Jewish people living as a minor-ity outside the land of Israel," and is a blueprint for Jews who plan to "continue living in Diaspora."[65]

Yet, Purim cannot serve as the covenantal paradigm for the second generation. Because the Jewish people were saved from extermination then, the covenant could still be viewed as coercive. But the covenant is, notes Greenberg, "less binding in a world that saw Hitler's murder of six million Jews."[66] Post-destruction Jewish life requires both a new understanding of the covenantal model and new rituals appropriate to living after the *Shoah*.

With Wiesel, Greenberg argues that the covenant was broken during the Holocaust. However, the Jewish people, "deeply committed to the [divine-human] partnership," voluntarily assumed it. Further, this assump-tion of covenantal living was made both by observant Jews and the "vast majority of Jews who heard no commandments but were still so in love with the dream of redemption that they volunteered to carry on the mis-sion."[67] Consequently, from this position there emerge two fundamental assertions. After the *Shoah*, the deity is more hidden than ever, therefore requiring "total Jewish responsibility for the covenant."[68] Secondly, the covenant can no longer be viewed as coercive. In Greenberg's words, "The most horrifying of the curses and punishments threatened in the Torah for failing to live up to the covenant pale by comparison with what was done in the Holocaust."[69]

Creative works by second-generation witnesses attest to the presence of Greenberg's voluntary covenant, especially in its dimension of simulta-neous secularization and Jewish affirmation. For example, the voluntary covenant posits a rich and intimate dialectic between *tikkun atzmi* (mend-ing of the self) and *tikkun olam* (mending of the world). This dialectic also impacts on the second-generation understanding of God. For instance, Greenberg writes that, "Wherever people pursue the covenantal way, there God is present."[70] In short, the covenantal way emphasizes the salvific potential of human deeds. This is reflected among the second generation in a commitment to creating life and to learning more about and bearing witness to the Holocaust. Bearing witness, attests Greenberg, comprises a "new secular Bible."[71] Ritual behavior will include pilgrimages to Auschwitz and to Israel, and "eating potato peels in memory of Bergen Belsen."[72] Ethically, acts that enhance the dignity and self-respect of indi-viduals also comprise the response of the second generation to their Holo-caust legacy. All of these are dimensions of applied theology. The second generation attests the wisdom of Greenberg's view that the appropriate the-ology for our time is one that expresses itself more in terms of life-enhanc-ing deeds than in assertion of theologically sophisticated creeds.

Greenberg's position is clearly helpful in understanding second-generation "theology." For instance, his attestation that one voluntarily bears witness to the Holocaust through a wide range of activities, including those that are apparently secular in nature (e.g., listening to survivor tales, watching films dealing with the Holocaust, and understanding the paradigmatic nature of survivors' lives) goes a long way toward describing this generation. While not restricted to this group, these activities are most clearly seen among the daughters and sons of Job. Despite the heterodox nature of the second generation, Greenberg likens to the convert to Judaism all those who walk the covenantal path. Adherence to Jewish identity is affirmed despite knowledge of the price of such allegiance. Consequently, Greenberg contends that by living as a Jew "one makes all the fundamental affirmations implicit in Jewish existence, even if one does not use the officially articulated way of making one's statements such as bearing witness to creation through Shabbat observance or expressing the messianic hope through prayers such as Aleynu."[73]

Greenberg's voluntary covenant addresses the core issue of the relationship between theology and identity for the second-generation witness. It recognizes both the need for the distinctively postmodern emphasis on autonomy and the necessity of a traditional anchor—the covenant—as the source of Jewish identity. Consequently, in muting the divine role after Auschwitz, Greenberg captures the paradox so frequently seen in second-generation creative works. For example, the increased demand on the human covenantal partner is made by a thoroughly hidden deity. Greenberg writes: "God was saying to humans: You stop the Holocaust. You bring on the redemption. You act to insure that it will never again occur. I will be with you totally in whatever you do, wherever you go, whatever happens, but you must do it."[74] While not each of the second-generation witnesses whose works are examined in this study would agree with Greenberg's contention as to the source of the demand they feel for their sense of Jewish involvement, each does attest both to the existential nature of post-Holocaust Jewish identity and to the continuing influence of the covenant. Further, Greenberg's insistence on the breakdown of the pre-Holocaust distinctions between religious and secular opens the possibility for a new understanding of religion and religious acts as the second generation seeks to define itself Jewishly after Auschwitz.

## EMIL L. FACKENHEIM AND THE SEARCH FOR A POST-AUSCHWITZ *TIKKUN OLAM*

Emil Fackenheim's initial thinking on the *Shoah* led him to formulate a "Commanding Voice" of Auschwitz. This Voice, which spoke both to religious and secularist Jews, called for post-Holocaust Jewish fidelity. This prompted Fackenheim to formulate a "614th Commandment": "the authentic Jew of today is forbidden to hand Hitler yet another posthumous victory."[75] And, indeed, many second-generation witnesses affirm this position. For example, Savran and Fogelman note that by transforming their anger, many children of survivors "have found fulfilling ways of expressing their Jewishness in communal, religious, cultural, or political activities."[76] One son of Job confides that when celebrating the Sabbath with friends by studying ethical texts, he felt close to his murdered grandparents. Participating in his heritage, the young man said to himself, "You see, Hitler, you didn't win."[77] Referring to Fackenheim's formulation, the theologian Richard Rubenstein writes: "Probably no passage written by a contemporary Jewish thinker has become as well known as this. It struck a deep chord in Jews of every social level and religious commitment."[78]

But Fackenheim's "614th Commandment," while striking a deep and powerful psychological chord, is fraught with theological difficulties. For example, those who did not hear the "Commanding Voice" stand implicitly accused of rejecting God and being Hitler's cohorts. Moreover, as Rubenstein notes, the injunction against denying or despairing of God lest Hitler be awarded a "posthumous victory" implies that Fackenheim "[tells] his readers what God has commanded."[79] Despite its religious and existential difficulties, Rubenstein correctly attests that, "It is perhaps best to see Fackenheim's 614th commandment as a cri de coeur transmuted into the language of the sacred."[80] Second-generation witnesses have found that their Jewish identity is not limited to speculation about God.

Fackenheim's more recent confrontation with the *Shoah*'s assault on religious faith, while retaining the idea of the "Commanding Voice" of Auschwitz, speaks more directly of the dimensions of a post-Holocaust *tikkun* in which behavior is more important than creedal statements, and human action more vital than assertion of divine command. As noted in chapter 1, this search for *tikkun* is an important characteristic of second-generation creative work. Therefore, it is appropriate to examine Fackenheim's position in some detail. In the first place, the mending of which he writes will be "at most only a fragmentary *Tikkun*."[81] This is so because of the sheer evil of the Holocaust, which is an epoch-making event in Jewish and world history. The catastrophe means a total rupture with pre-*Shoah* values of Judaism, Christianity, and the Western philosophical tradition. Fackenheim comments that, "because we are situated in the post-Holocaust world," therefore, "We must accept our situatedness. We must live with it."[82] Seeking the foundations of future Jewish thought,[83] he looks to possible ways to mend the rupture of civilizations, cultures, and religions that the Holocaust caused. He finds this in a *tikkun* of the Holocaust "(if a *Tikkun* there is)."[84] Moreover, this mending is "Good news to the world."[85] Philosophical, Christian, and Jewish itself, this *tikkun* has "one universality: that of witness. Its *Tikkun* will be what in Jewish tradition *Tikkun* is always meant to be—*Tikkun Olam.*"[86]

For Fackenheim, a post-Holocaust *tikkun olam* is possible because it was actual during the Kingdom of Night. "A *tikkun* here and now," he contends, "is mandatory for a *tikkun*, then and there, was actual."[87] He cites specific examples of spiritual resistance during the Holocaust that serve as moral beacons for those seeking to achieve a contemporary mending. Moreover, this resistance was manifest in both the Jewish and Christian communities, among the educated as well as those with little formal training. For instance, at Buchenwald a group of hasidic Jews faced a serious moral issue. They were given a chance to buy a pair of phylacteries by a Ukrainian kapo. The price was four rations of bread. However, to give up this bread risked committing the sin of suicide. Nevertheless, the Hasidim "sold" their bread rations. Fackenheim reports a survivor's account which states that the Hasidim "prayed with an ecstasy which it would be impossible ever to experience again in . . . [their] lives."[88] Further, the actions of the fighters in various ghettoes (e.g., Warsaw and Bialystock *inter alia*) in consciously deciding to remain within the ghettoes constitute a "unique affirmation . . . of Jewish self-respect."[89] Rather than abandon parents, the infirm, and children, these fighters stayed and fought. Their battle was hopeless in military terms, but of inestimable importance morally. Moreover, pregnant Jewish women who gave birth at Auschwitz actively resisted the Nazi edict condemning such women to immediate death.

Fackenheim also notes Christian acts of *tikkun* in the form of resistance. Peglia Lewinska, a Polish prisoner at Auschwitz, reacted to the "excremental assault" of the Nazis. She writes: "I felt under orders to live. . . . And if I did die in Auschwitz, it would be as a human being, I would hold on to my dignity. I was not going to become the contemptible, disgusting brute my enemy wished me to be. . . . And a terrible struggle began which went on day and night."[90] Further, Fackenheim discusses the Munich philosopher Kurt Huber and the Berlin churchman Bernhard Lichtenberg. Each man was martyred for publically defending the Jewish people and refusing to embrace the insane logic of the Third Reich's final solution. Huber's act is, attests Fackenheim, an example of the *tikkun* of the idea of man.[91] As mentor to the "White Rose," a small group of Munich students who resisted Nazism, Huber was sentenced to death. For Fackenheim, Huber's importance "lies in his deed more than his thought."[92] Refusing to be silent, Huber consciously chose martyrdom.

Lichtenberg, canon of St. Hedwig's Cathedral, publically prayed for the Jews and other concentration camp victims. He deplored Nazism and was horrified by the events of *Kristallnacht.* Lichtenberg was imprisoned, whereupon he declared his determination to stand with the Jews of Berlin upon his release. He died on the way to Dachau. Lichtenberg's behavior, attests Fackenheim, exemplifies a *tikkun* of the Christian world.[93] Fackenheim distinguishes at least one other type of *tikkun,* that of "ordinary decency," which connotes the acts of the *Hasidei Umot Ha-Olam,* the Righteous Among the Nations or, quite simply, those very few helpers of the Jewish people. Fackenheim's call for a *tikkun* of the world and the self after Auschwitz has the merit of enabling one to speak about religion without implicitly indicting those who hear no "Commanding Voice" yet wish to continue walking on the Jewish path.

The creative works of second-generation witnesses comprise an extension of Fackenheim's call for a post-Auschwitz *tikkun.*[94] Various types of *tikkunim* are displayed in these works. For example there is the *tikkun* of family, in which connections and reconnections are made by now adult offspring of survivors. One thinks here of films such as Debbie Goodstein's *Voices from the Attic* and Danny Fischer's *A Generation Apart.* Also in this category are novels such as Lev Raphael's *Winter Eyes* and Barbara Finkelstein's *Summer Long-a-Coming.* Exemplifying the *tikkun* of ordinary decency are films such as Pierre Sauvage's *Weapons of the Spirit* and Myriam Abramowicz's *As If It Were Yesterday.* Further, acts of the helpers also are reported in Spiegelman's *Maus* and Julie Salamon's *White Lies.* Clearly, each of the second-generation witnesses exhibits the *tikkun* of bearing witness. Furthermore, these witnesses reveal a *tikkun* of the self in their attempts to master the trauma of the *Shoah* even while simultaneously acknowledging that ultimately the catastrophe remains unassimilable. Moreover, the overrepresentation of the second generation in the helping professions can itself be viewed as exemplifying an attempt to heal the world.

## RICHARD L. RUBENSTEIN:
## "GOD AFTER THE DEATH OF GOD"

Richard Rubenstein shocked the Jewish world in announcing over three decades ago that his theological findings led inexorably to the conclusion that "God is Dead." The correlative of this view is the abrogation of covenant. Rubenstein's assertion, widely misunderstood at the time, referred to a *cultural* fact. It was more a statement about man than about God. Rubenstein reached his decisive position in a dramatic encounter with Dean Heinrich Grüber, a Protestant churchman who had risked his life to help Jews during the Holocaust. In Grüber's view, which was based on biblical and rabbinic assumptions about the relationship between sin and punishment, the *Shoah* was God's punishment of the Jewish people. Responding to this assertion of "holy history," Rubenstein said that it would require him to accept the notion that Hitler was God's instrument for punishing the Jewish people. Rubenstein writes: "Unfortunately, I could not affirm both the justice of God and the innocence of the victims."[95] In interpretative terms, attests Rubenstein, the Holocaust is an "unmastered trauma."[96]

Viewing the task of the theologian as "dissonance reduction," Rubenstein writes that "the fundamental question for the religious thinker is not whether the existence of God can be reconciled with monumental historical catastrophe, but how such an event can be understood in the light of God's covenant with Israel."[97] Clearly, in Rubenstein's earlier theological writings the covenant is no longer credible in the face of the extermination of the covenant people. Covenant and election were, argued Rubenstein, no longer able to provide a believable "plausibility structure" for a community that had seen six million of its members exterminated. Several second-generation writers exemplify this conclusion. For example, Art Spiegelman's *Maus*, Lev Raphael's various protagonists, and several of the characters in J. J. Steinfeld's works adopt a "God is Dead" approach.

In recent years, however, Rubenstein has questioned the bleakness of his earlier assertion that men and women live "in a cold, silent, unfeeling universe." While God may be absent or indifferent, humanity still yearns for meaning. He now envisages "God After the Death of God;" one whose divine image is rooted in a variety of sources: Kabbalah, the world of nature, Hegelian thought, and the teachings of Paul Tillich.[98] This deity is not the biblical Lord of History but rather Holy Nothingness, which is to say, no material, personalist deity. "When God is imagined as the Holy Nothingness," writes Rubenstein, "the divine Ground of Being is thought of as beyond all finite categories."[99]

Rubenstein has also modified his view of covenant. In *After Auschwitz*, first published in 1966, Rubenstein observes that he "stressed the punitive and exclusivist aspects of the doctrine of covenant and election. Over the years I have come to appreciate the other side of the picture: humanity's profound need for something like the covenant or its functional equivalent."[100] Rubenstein sees covenant, however, primarily in geopolitical terms as a bulwark, possibly the only such defense, against genocide. But even within particular communities, covenantal—rather than racist—organization is mandatory for harmony. For example, in America—"with its biblical religious heritage and its pluralistic population"—a society organized according to a covenantal basis is imperative.[101] Rubenstein's view of covenant stresses its moral rather than religious component and addresses the issue of an identity based on other

than religious criteria. While few in the second generation share Rubenstein's theological sophistication, this covenantal view is at least implicit
in the work of Art Spiegelman and J. J. Steinfeld.

In the next chapter we begin our discussion by examining those second-generation witness texts—novels and short stories—that deal with
various dimensions of the post-Auschwitz covenant and the *tikkun* of
self. These texts reflect the theological movement outlined above, which
goes from directly encountering the Holocaust, to the "sequelae"; that is,
determining how one can live Jewishly in its aftermath. Further, the second-generation witnesses themselves reflect various elements of the theological positions outlined above. No one theological point of view is completely embraced. Nor do these witnesses self-consciously see themselves
as "doing" theology. Quite to the contrary. Rather, much in the manner
suggested by Greenberg, they reveal the "low priority" of theology in
the Jewish community. However, these works also display the contention
articulated by each of the thinkers whose views are outlined above—that
after the Holocaust, behavior and not formal theological pronouncement
is a more accurate ways of assessing Jewish fidelity. The texts are Jewishly
particularist and seek to understand the *Shoah* as the source for their
contemporary Jewish identity. We pay attention both to the type of
covenantal affirmation and to the rituals associated with second-generation witnesses as they respond to the presence of the Holocaust's shadow
in their own lives.

# CHAPTER 3

# *Second-Generation Novels and Short Stories: Jewish Particularism*

"Remembering the Holocaust" is not an issue for us: we are, in our parents' minds, the answer to the Holocaust. We are, in our own minds, the guardians of a problematic, unique and volatile legacy. We do not need to be reminded of it: rather, we need to find a way of best utilizing it. We need to learn how to translate our consciousness of evil, our skepticism, our sense of outrage into constructive action.

—Helen Epstein[1]

Writing in *Renewing the Covenant: A Theology for the Postmodern Jew*, Eugene Borowitz distinguishes between Jewish modernity and postmodern Judaism. Jewish modernity, he observes, "gloried in a heady universalism," whereas "postmodern Judaism manifests a resurgent particularism."[2] This particularism is especially prominent in the second-generation witnesses whose works are examined in this chapter. Their wrestling with the meaning of Jewish identity after Auschwitz is expressed both in terms of the Holocaust's psychosocial effect on their lives and the event's theological impact. The psychosocial effect is seen in a variety of frequently contradictory ways. For example, as adolescents, the second generation both rebel against and identify with their parents' victimization. Moreover, among the second generation there appears to be both guilt for not having been in the Holocaust and denial that the *Shoah* has any bearing on their own identity. Certain of the second-generation witnesses deliberately place themselves in dangerous situations or imagine doing so in an attempted mimesis of their parents' Holocaust experience. Images of survivors in these largely confessional second-generation works reveal the prevalence of indirect intergenerational communication about the Holocaust.

Survivor parents are portrayed as having flawed parenting skills owing to their Holocaust experience. Deprived of the opportunity of learning to parent because they were either in death camps or in forced-labor brigades, the survivors are described in competing images. For instance, they are both overprotective and remote. Where these novels differentiate between parents, it is the mother who demonstrates compassion. Fathers are emotionally unavailable to their children. Further, the parents are described as being phobic and distrustful of the outside (i.e., non-Jewish) world. Survivors' attitudes toward orthodoxy or traditional Judaism are also mixed. Here an important distinction must be made between belief and identity. The *Shoah* imposed survivors' Jewish identity on them, it did not instill religious belief. Yet, distinctive post-Auschwitz rituals play a crucial role in survivor families examined in this chapter. Consequently, the second-generation witnesses' attitude toward orthodoxy is itself ambiguous. Some reject traditional Judaism and its mythic structure completely. Spiegelman is the primary example of this phenomenon. Others reject orthodoxy but not Judaism. The works of Friedmann and Finkelstein typify this response. Further, certain of the second generation express feelings of anger and rage at Nazism, and a desire for revenge.

These circumstances yield, in turn, significant theological implications. For instance, much in the manner suggested by Greenberg's paradigm, particularist works describe both new forms of Jewish ritual expression as well as new meanings assumed by traditional rituals that are now being re-fused in a post-Auschwitz light. Thus, the daughters and sons of Job embrace the legacy of Jewish fate by becoming socialized according to distinctive sets of ritual behavior. Further, the second-generation witnesses each seek to work through the trauma of growing up in survivor households where the shadows of Auschwitz continue to hover and where the presence of those who are forever absent is felt in a myriad of ways, both spoken and symbolic.

The second-generation witnesses whose works are discussed in this chapter express, either explicitly or implicitly, a theological rebellion. Their theology of protest contends both with a God who permitted Auschwitz and a world that at first condoned the death camps and has by now largely forgotten them. Further, these authors seek to express themselves Jewishly in a manner that displays dimensions of both Irving Greenberg's voluntary and Elie Wiesel's additional covenants. For example, they exemplify Greenberg's notion of people who voluntarily choose the Jewish path. Their actions, while not formally religious, nonetheless betray their determination to remain Jewish.With the additional covenant as described by Berenbaum, these second-generation witnesses attest that Jewish covenantal identity remains a post-Auschwitz possibility. The second-generation witnesses' search for post-Auschwitz meaning involves a *tikkun* of the self that enables them to persist Jewishly.

This chapter discusses the work of six second-generation witnesses: Thomas Friedmann's *Damaged Goods*; Barbara Finkelstein's *Summer*

*Long-a-Coming*; Art Spiegelman's *Maus*; Melvin J. Bukiet's two short-story collections, *Stories of an Imaginary Childhood* and *While the Messiah Tarries*; two of the Canadian author J. J. Steinfeld's short-story volumes, *Dancing at the Club Holocaust* and *Forms of Captivity and Escape*, and Thane Rosenbaum's *Elijah Visible: Stories*. The novels of Friedmann and Finkelstein are each set against the backdrop of the political and social turbulence of 1960s America, with its protests against American involvement in Vietnam and rebellion against establishment forms of religion and government. Although for Finkelstein, the problems of American culture barely intrude in the hermetically sealed life of her heroine, both authors nevertheless invite their readers to contrast the outer turmoil of the nation to their protagonists' inner tumult. Spiegelman's work, for its part, is a tale that literally illustrates the complexity of inheriting memory. His work juxtaposes the naïveté of American culture and the pain of a contemporary son of Job who assumes the ethnic and psychic legacy of Auschwitz.

The short stories provide a different angle of vision concerning the Holocaust legacy of the second generation. For example, Bukiet places his experience in the broader perspective of Jewish history, imagining himself living in the Polish shtetl of Proszowice on the eve of the *Shoah*. The Jews, unaware of the approaching cataclysm, wrestle with the millennial temptations of secular culture that sorely test the proscriptions of traditional Judaism. Switching geographical setting and time, his second volume contains stories that depict the post-Auschwitz response of Jews in America. Steinfeld, on the other hand, addresses a variety of second-generation issues, including revenge, feelings of guilt, and the continuing scourge of antisemitism. Rosenbaum, for his part, focuses on psychological issues and the role of post-Auschwitz theology among the children of Job. Each of these authors voluntarily assume the covenant while stressing the need to bear witness to the Jewish tragedy. Their writings underscore the impact of the *Shoah* on the formation of their own Jewish identity.

## DAMAGED GOODS

Thomas Friedmann was born in Hungary in 1947. His mother survived Bergen-Belsen and Auschwitz, his father was in a forced-labor brigade in the Ukraine. The family fled Hungary during the1956 revolution, arriving in America shortly thereafter. Friedmann subsequently received an M.A. in English from New York University and is currently a professor of English. In addition to his works of fiction, he has written texts dealing with how to teach English. *Damaged Goods*[3] heralds the appearance of second-generation Holocaust witness novels in America. Consequently,

issues that Friedmann raises will appear in subsequent second-generation works. For example, the intermingling of the Holocaust past and the
American present in shaping post-Auschwitz Jewish identity, the complexity of parent-child relationships, the inscrutability of the divine, personal experience of unjust suffering, and elements of post-Auschwitz
Jewish ritual behavior are all dimensions of Friedmann's work .

*Damaged Goods* is, however, distinctive among second-generation
witness novels in portraying life in an orthodox Jewish community. Other
second-generation writers describe the vicinal isolation of survivors and
their offspring, far removed from any Jews or Jewish community. Frequently the young children are raised in rural settings.[4] Friedmann's novel
is, however, set in the thoroughly Jewish context of Borough Park. There
is as well the phenomenon of linguistic insulation that characterizes survivor households. Friedmann's protagonist calls his father by the Hebrew
word *Abba*. The parents speak Yiddish, the language of an annihilated
culture. As the language of the majority of the martyrs of the *Shoah*,
Yiddish conjures images of a religiocultural world that seems oddly out of
place in an American context. It is the language of the old world and of
memory. English is the language of the new world in which history and
memory are not prized. There is a jarring dissonance between these two
worlds.

In Friedmann's work, American popular culture of the late sixties, the
continuing trauma of the Holocaust, and the loosening of Orthodoxy's
hold in the American context are all strands in the web of the protagonist's identity. Consequently, Friedmann's novel, which one critic terms
"an orthodox *Portnoy's Complaint*,"[5] puts the *Shoah* in an American
setting. Antiwar protests, the drug culture, walks on the moon, the 1967
war between Israel and the Arabs, and the trial of the Chicago Eight
merge with the Holocaust's continuing impact, thereby interweaving the
European past and contemporary America. Concerning the protagonist's
difficulties with the Orthodox world, the reader discovers that it can
accommodate neither his *Shoah*-induced sense of guilt nor his personal
feelings.

The novel is in fact a thinly veiled memoir, an insider's description of the precise boundaries and prescriptions of an orthodox world
that the Nazis attempted to annihilate. The rituals of orthodox Jewish
life play a prominent role in *Damaged Goods*. Holy days such as Rosh
Hashanah, Yom Kippur, Shabbat, Shavuot, Pesach, and the Counting of
the Omer become, as it were, characters in the novel. So to do ritual
actions such as wearing a *yarmukah* (skull cap), putting on phylacteries,
*tashlich* (casting away of sins at the New Year), the rite of *kapporah* (a
rooster used as the scapegoat sacrifice), checking for defective *mezzuzoth*
(inscribed parchment with verses from Deuteronomy and the name of

God—*Shaddai*—rolled up and put in decorative cases and affixed to doorposts in Jewish homes), and the rites of mourning. These rituals, while no longer able to compel the protagonist's allegiance, still provide a language of discourse and retain their psychological impact. Thus, Friedmann's novel is simultaneously a story of the protagonist's battle to free himself from the restraints of Orthodoxy and his struggle to confront the meaning of his Holocaust legacy.

Friedmann tells the tale of Jason Kole, who concurrently pursues a graduate degree in English at N.Y.U. ("the Jewish Columbia") so that he may teach literature, and a draft-deferment at Rabbi Baumel's Yeshiva. Jason's life is further complicated when he falls in love with Rachel, a Jewish but nonreligious woman. Halfway through the novel, Jason's mother, also named Rachel, who is considerably younger than her husband, disappears while swimming. Her disappearance leaves Jason without a buffer between himself and his hypercritical father, Mordechai. Although her death is never confirmed, like that of so many Holocaust survivors, she never returns. Rachel's disappearance is the author's way of involving the second generation in discovering the pain of innocent suffering. Following this episode, Jason begins to personally understand the issue of theodicy.

Indirect communication is a frequent phenomenon among survivors of the Holocaust. This exemplifies one aspect of what Robert J. Lifton terms *psychic numbing* or "the diminished capacity to feel." A defense against "overwhelming images and stimuli," this numbing can give rise to later "patterns of withdrawal, apathy, depression, and despair."[6] Mordechai, who never seems to have any personal time to spend with Jason, exhibits a type of behavior that also illustrates the phenomenon of incomplete mourning: never speaking about his first wife and son, who had been murdered in the Holocaust. Yet the father, unlike his son, derives comfort from the rituals of Orthodoxy, which simultaneously act as a barrier between the two.

Like Ariel, Wiesel's second-generation witness in *The Fifth Son*, Jason observes: "My Father speaks to me with silence. He is a nazarite with information, a miser with meaning." For example, the father never speaks directly of his life either before or during the *Shoah*. Rather, he imparts knowledge by indirection. And while this indirection "had become a successful way of dealing with one another," it has traumatic results. For instance, Jason only learns that his father had an earlier family when Mordechai informs him that "he need not say the blessing for the first-born the morning before Passover" (72).

Jason's attempt to separate himself from his father's world assumes the form of a rebellion against Orthodoxy. Yet, he describes himself as "semi-observant, semi-religious." Leaving the Orthodox fold is not easy, and Jason accomplishes this task incrementally. He begins his exodus from the traditional world with small acts of defiance, such as only pretending to ritually wash his hands before meals and silently moving his mouth in "imitation of the blessing" before drinking a glass of water. Eventually, he commits more serious infractions, including going bareheaded. In fact, he explains the meaning of yarmukah in a way that emphasizes religion's constraints: yar = fear, mu = from, kah = God.

Nevertheless, Jason/Yaakov is thoroughly a product of the Orthodox world. (Yaakov, the patriarch, is given the name Israel by a mysterious angel with whom he wrestles throughout the night. This name change means a change of destiny as well.) His very speech patterns reflect the years spent in talmud study. The cadence of his speech is the sing-song recitation of the yeshiva bocher (student). Further, describing his friend Jonesey Kellerman, also a second-generation witness, Jason begins with the formulaic expression found in Gemara: "Come, let us learn" (about Jonesey Kellerman). Yet in terms of adherence to tradition, Jason stands midway between his friends Jonesey, a sexual libertine, and Dov, whose survivor parents are pleased that their son, after qualifying for rabbinic ordination, goes to Israel for further study. While there he also leads the fight against mixed-sex bathing at a public pool in Jerusalem.

Jason's odyssey of self-discovery is blocked by the barrier of the Holocaust. His parents suppress information about their pre-Shoah lives and provide only scant details about their Holocaust experience. Further, Jason lacks both an extended family and grandparents. The absence of both means that there is no one to whom he may turn in order to help bridge the communications gap between him and his parents. Further, grandparents might have helped socialize Jason in the ways of the tradition. Grandparents typically serve as tellers of family lore and as sources of knowledge about the tradition. They are living links in the great chain of Jewish being. As Hass observes, the "absence of grandparents meant that another anchor, source of comfort, and evidence of a secure continuity of life was missing."[7]

Jason articulates one measure of the Holocaust wound inflicted on the second generation when he reflects on the meaning of absent grandparents:

> We Orthodox immigrants, we "Greeners," we lost our grandparents and thus lost the intermediaries who could have absorbed all our curses and resentments with God and tradition. If only I had a toothless but understanding grandmother who ran the family in a foreign tongue or a grandfather on whose kindly knees I could have listened to heroic tales. I could have made love to Rachel [his girlfriend] if I had had grandparents to teach me the sweetness of ceremony and the strength in acceptance. But the people who could have smoothed my transition

from God to Father and from Father to Rachel have been killed off. And so I take on the words of God directly. Call him my remote Grandfather. (53)

But as Jason realizes, remoteness—whether in an emotionally unavailable Father, absent grandparents, or a flawed God—provides neither emotional support nor theological meaning.

Jason's parents communicate only selectively with their son, thereby increasing his difficulty in confronting the Holocaust and achieving a *tikkun atzmi* (repair of the self). For example, the son and his father can only communicate through a system of ritual that emphasizes formulaic expression at the expense of personal feeling. "We were," observes Jason, "too formal for anger, too rehearsed for irony, too unfamiliar for love." Mrs. Kole, on the other hand, expresses love and concern for her son while shielding him from her husband's scorn. Both parents do, however, teach their son survival lessons. Mr. Kole recalls that only those who paid attention to details, "like clean fingernails, and brushing their teeth, and keeping dirt from between their toes" survived forced labor. He concludes that self-sufficiency rather than reliance on God is the primary lesson. Like the observance of orthodox ritual itself, salvation lies in the details.

Mrs. Kole also teaches survival lessons. But she does so by juxtaposing the Holocaust and America. For example, visiting Jason in Far Rockaway, she complements him on his summer tan. His mother shares a secret: women in the camps saved beets, and prior to SS selections, they rubbed the beets on their faces to give them color. Looking healthy could literally save your life. By indirection, the reader is invited to compare the difference between Jason's summer color and his mother's experience with color in Bergen-Belsen and in Auschwitz.

Lack of communication also bears heavily on Jason's subsequent effort to imagine his parents' Holocaust experience. The parents' participation in a "conspiracy of silence" means that the son must fantasize about what happened during the Kingdom of Night. He muses:

> I torture myself with dreams of my mother bidden to do whore's service and Father forced to choose between feeding wife or child with final crusts. But because I don't know them as they were before their transformation into who they are, I see my mother as a child woman being possessed by Father who, after her days at Bergen-Belsen, might have recalled the uncertain safety of her own father. . . . So for me mother remains a victim. (73)

In fact, Jason's imaginings reflect a form of second-generation denial that is common in families where parents do not speak readily of their Holocaust experience. Eva Fogelman reports that therapy with an intergenerational group (child survivors and offspring of survivors), revealed that the second-generation members who had no personal experience of Holocaust loss "shared a need to deny and later to mourn."[8] But this form of denial is different from that of child survivors. Second-generation denial manifests itself in "not wanting to know what happened, in relying on fantasies of what they imagined must have happened."[9] Maurice Blanchot is correct in observing that "the disaster ruins everything."[10]

Friedmann provides a cornucopia of second-generation images of survivors. On the one hand, he distinguishes between survivors and the second-generation witness. For example, in an earlier work he reports on a postwar visit to Debrecen, where both he and his father were born. Friedmann observes: "Only my father's memories were back here. My own memories of this were false, childhood stories that repeated tellings had given the shape of experience. But I didn't know any of this."[11] Following Alain Finkielkraut, Friedmann's protagonist recognizes himself as an "imaginary Jew." In *Damaged Goods* Jason describes himself as "Hardly a witness, I was the ultimate bystander. Somehow I had managed to live through the entire decade on second-hand experiences" (248). On the other hand, the *Shoah* separates survivors and their offspring from other, nonwitnessing Americans, both Jews and non-Jews. Musing on the meaning of the High Holidays, Jason opines:

> What perfect Americans we Jews could be, always optimistic, always forward looking, stripped naked in swaddling clothes three times a year. If only we could forget, if only the baggage on the back and the fear in the heart and the numbers on the arm weren't along to remind us of the past. (178)

This observation clearly illuminates the role played by the *Shoah* in linking survivors and the second generation to Jewish destiny.

Like Wiesel, and unlike Art Spiegelman, Friedmann privileges survivors who, in his second-generation view, formed a "secret society" that admitted no one else. Because they had survived, he muses, "nothing else could shake them." Yet Friedmann does not refrain from speaking about fissures in the survivor community. Hungarian and Polish Jews maintain separate *shuls* and butcher stores. This stems from their respective experiences in the *Shoah*. Polish Jews were being exterminated even as those in Hungary were marrying and raising families. "The Poles," observes Jason/Friedmann, "resenting the Hunks for living, the Hungarians, the Pollacks for being *kapos* or overseers in the blocks" (158). Nonetheless, Jason knows that the survivors "had a dignity, even talking about potatoes, the thought of which had kept Mr. Laufer alive for a year in the Ukraine, that they were not aware of."

Survivors are also presented as modeling very different orientations to Judaism. For example, the elder Koles are deeply divided. Father believes in the minutiae of ritual; he is Rabbi Joseph Soloveitchik's *halakhic* man, one for whom Judaism has become ritualism.[12] For example, after his wife's disappearance, Mr. Kole—"a man of the Law"—remains faithful to detail. Since there is no body, there is no death. Aghast at his Father's willingness to carry on as usual, Jason observes of the elder Kole's fidelity to Orthodox ritual: "Faithful to detail, he manages to forget [his wife's disappearance]. Concentrate [on details]. Forgetting [his wife's disappearance] is better than remembering" (141–42). The son's impression of the impersonality of Orthodoxy is well summarized by his description of his father praying. At this time, the elder Kole—replete with prayer shawl and phylacteries—looks like "an attack bird, a kamikaze plane" (253). This war imagery sharply contrasts with his mother, who tries to engage Jason at the level of feeling.

Survivors, however, cannot undo the past. Jason's mother tells him of a recurring dream that she had in the *lager* (Nazi camp). She envisioned "a great big flood, an ocean [that] would put the fires out and cover everything and I could be happy" (114). After the *Shoah*, however, no fantasies remain. Rather, survivor memories recall every detail. For instance, on the evening of Shavuot (the time of *Mattan Torah*, the giving of the Torah at Sinai, which shaped the Jewish people into a community of witnesses) Jason overhears his parents as they remember the time that the Nazis came for the Hungarian Jews. His mother remembers that apple blossoms fell so thickly that she thought the murderers "were walking through snow." Mr. Kole remembers that when he was rounded up, "dandelion seeds floated like feathers. We slapped them, thinking they were mosquitoes" (58). These are "deep memories" that contrast the harmony of the natural world and the reception of the Torah with the murderous world of Nazism.

*Damaged Goods* articulates how the contemporary children of Job are helping shape memory of the *Shoah*. This shaping occurs in one of two ways. On the one hand, Friedmann reveals the extent to which traditional ritual has become suffused with Holocaust remembrance. The layered texture of these rituals demonstrates both the openness of Jewish ritual and the epoch-making nature of the Holocaust. These are factors that will help determine how the Holocaust is remembered after there are no more living witnesses. It is clear that such commemoration is closely tied to rituals. For example. Greenberg approvingly cites Rabbi Soloveitchik on this matter, claiming that "the master of halacha was correct in insisting that memory must be incorporated into ritual and liturgy in order to become permanent." Extending Soloveitchik's observation, Greenberg contends that after Auschwitz, "halacha was being shaped and was growing within the bosom of the Jewish people, without asking permission from the halachists."[13]

*Damaged Goods* reveals the intermingling of traditional ritual and Holocaust remembrance. Whereas pre-Holocaust Jews lit two Friday evening candles, sabbath preparation at the Kole house includes a five-branched silver candelabra, "each candle a light for life." In addition to a candle for each member of the household, there is an additional candle commemorating the "miraculous events" of the elder Koles' survival during the *Shoah*. The Koles' usage of a menorah (used whenever there are multiple candle lightings) has significance for the development of Holocaust ritual. For example, Greenberg remarks that scholars believe that "the biblical menorah is a stylized tree in tandem with fire; it can be compared to a burning bush."[14] This is an entirely appropriate symbol, Greenberg rightly contends, "for suffering, dying, and yet persisting"; it is the biblical "bush burning in the flames, yet the bush is not consumed" (Ex. 3:2).[15] There is as well the fact that Mrs. Kole disappears around *Tisha B'Av* (late summer), the time that rabbinic tradition ascribes to the destruction of the First and Second Temples at Jerusalem, the Chmielnicki massacres in Poland, and other catastrophes.

Ritual commemoration of the Holocaust dead also occurs during the counting of the Omer, the seven-week period from the end of Passover until Shavuoth. There is sadness at this time for two basic reasons. A plague is said to have carried off twelve thousand disciples of Rabbi Akiva. Another interpretation is that these were the number of people killed during the ill-fated Bar Kohkba rebellion against Rome. The Empire consequently outlawed the Jewish religion, thereby casting doubt over the future of Judaism. In the Kole house, dates are set aside during the Omer "in memory of the concentration camp deaths, particularly the uncharted, hectic cremation during the final days" (29–30). Jason reflects on the the four yahrzeit (memorial) candles burning in his parents' kitchen. They represent his grandfather who disappeared in the First World War and "the vanishing Jews' memories. Bergen-Belsen, Bor, Buchenwald, Grandfather" (30). Concerning the use of memorial candles, Greenberg notes that it is the "single most widespread ritual observance . . . for the six million."[16] For example, returning home one day, Jason discovers the house lit only by memorial candles. In response to his curiosity, his mother simply says, "For my parents, this is the day when the transport arrived" (99). This recalls Dina Wardi's observation that the children of survivors themselves are frequently viewed as symbolic "memorial candles" by their survivor parents.

Friedmann, on the other hand, articulates the specific second-generation witness ritual of studying about the *Shoah*. Jason Kole laments the fact that he "grew up bereft of stories" because the "war against the Jews killed off all the storytellers" (72). In an observation that brings to mind Helen Epstein's reflection, Jason is acutely aware of the fact that his extended family is "preserved only in a few cracked photographs of strangers." "Born in stillness," it is up to the second-generation witnesses to educate themselves about details of the *Shoah*. For example, Jason overhears only "incomplete pieces of conversation." Consequently, he attempts to "match the jagged ends to stories Jonesey occasionally requests from his father" (73). Friedmann wisely implies that post-Auschwitz second-generation identity is comparable to putting together pieces of a jigsaw puzzle. In order to achieve this task, daughters and sons of survivors pursue several paths of self-discovery in an attempt at *tikkun atzmi*. Their parents' testimony serves as impetus to learn more about what happened during the Holocaust, which, in turn, helps this generation better understand itself. The second generation also travel to their parents' European natal cities and villages. They also seek out other second-generation members and support the State of Israel. Finally, they transmit the Holocaust legacy to their own children.

*Damaged Goods* raises a fundamental question about the continuing validity of Orthodoxy after Auschwitz, asking if traditional Judaism is still able to meaningfully address the Jewish people. The image of Orthodoxy is one of triumphalism. For example, orthodox Judaism is presented as a belief that the Holocaust in no way indicts God, and an ideology that makes no provision for religious pluralism. Explaining the intricacies of talmud study to Rachel and her nonobservant friends, Yaakov is reminded that the Orthodox think themselves responsible for the very maintenance of the world. Thirty-six of them (the "lamed-vovnicks") are "mysterious, modest, and remote sages" with extraordinary powers. Orthodoxy as a whole is "the elite among the chosen . . . the last hoop on the barrel containing chaos." Other Jews "who have withdrawn from the Covenant [they] call *goyim*"; they are not distinguishable from Gentiles (46). Jason's friend Dov views religious Jews as barometers measuring the presence of societal antisemitism. He observes that when religious Jews are mocked, "start packing, the gas is not too far behind" (172–73).

Yet Friedmann's novel challenges both the superiority and the validity of Orthodoxy in two ways. Overtly, the protagonist slowly but steadily leaves the orthodox world. By novel's end, he moves out of his father's house and in, at least temporarily, with Rachel. Orthodoxy lacks a credible plausibility structure for him personally. Even more ruinous, however, is the unstated challenge to faith running throughout the novel. If Orthodoxy has all the answers, and if halakha is the true guide to Jewish perfection, why the *Shoah*? One cannot separate the catastrophe that befell the Jewish people from Orthodox explanations of God, the world, and theodicy. Quite the contrary is true. Jason articulates the nature of his own twofold Jewish legacy. For example, he is convinced that his permanent seat in shul, his *pisgah* (observation post), is "confirmed, down to the installation of a small metal name plate, by the fact that [he is] the intimate of a people who have survived both Bergen-Belsen and a Ukrainian death march" (248).

With Greenberg, Jason Kole's stance is that after Auschwitz, prewar distinctions between the sacred and the profane are no longer secure. After Auschwitz, the minutiae of traditional ritual fail to provide either psychological or theological coherence. The "triumphs" of Orthodoxy, such as preventing construction in Jerusalem of a pool that permits mixed bathing, fail to address Jason Kole's attempt to shape his post-Auschwitz Jewish identity. More significant for Jason and the other second-generation witnesses in this study is the ritual of hearing their parents' tales, reading about the Holocaust, and learning their own family history. All of these rituals lead to an expression of solidarity and witness, two of the pillars of Wiesel's additional covenant.

Jason reflects on the intermingling of biblical and Holocaust litanies, commenting on their relevance for the second generation. Listening to an intonation of the names of biblical generations, "the begetters and the begotten," he attests that he loves the sound: *Cain who begot Enoch to whom was born Irad who begot Mehujael who fathered Methusael who begot Lamech, these the generations of the accursed Cain the Wanderer*. However, Jason articulates a second-generation witness consciousness in observing the following:

> the modern litany of lost generations, the roll call of Auschwitz, Dachau, Maidenek [sic], and Buchenwald, Sobibor, Treblinka, and Birkenau, camps of no begetting, have the same effect on me as the drumbeat of Biblical generations. (84)

Jason's identity as a son of Job derives both from the Bible and from Auschwitz.

Mrs. Kole's disappearance is the novel's turning point and initiates Jason more fully into his role as a second-generation witness. "I knew nothing," he exclaims, "I was unprepared and unlettered in death" (132). In fact, Jason is "obscurely relieved" at the manner that his mother had chosen to disappear. Unlike Spiegelman who, as we shall see below, rages against his mother for her suicide, Friedmann's protagonist is vaguely thankful that his mother "had decided to relieve me of the special set of circumstances . . . which would have forced me back into the Orthodox camp" (147). He is clearly upset and confused at his mother's disappearance, but the manner of her departure permitted him to mourn in his own, non-orthodox way.

Jason's father, for his part, cannot believe that his wife is dead. Rather, he takes Jason to a grocery store where an obscure Yiddish-speaking cashier who mysteriously appeared one day was hired. He believes the woman's story exemplary. Anything is possible in America he tells Jason. Rachel can start again. Mr. Kole then teaches Jason his survivor's philosophy of Jewish identity. "A Jew," he says, "can be anybody because we can hide anywhere. We can disappear into blue eyes and white skin and straight noses." "They can kill us," exclaims *Abba*, "but we don't kill ourselves. We survive. We're supposed to" (264–65).

The novel's title is, itself, symbolic. Damaged goods has a wide range of referents. For example, Mr. Kole quizzes Jason about what may be offered as a sacrifice at the Jerusalem Temple. Only animals, goods, and people without blemish can serve there. Applied to the secular world of America, the list grows longer. For example, according to orthodox Judaism Jason's friend Rachel is damaged because she is a non-observant unsupervised young woman whose parents live in Florida. Jason himself is damaged because he refrains from wearing his yammie (yarmukah) continually. Further, Rachel and Jason as a couple are damaged. Areas outside the Orthodox *eruv* (enclosure) are also damaged. Idiomatically, *damaged goods* is a term that applies to divorced people. In the context of Friedmann's novel, however, his parents and their survivor friends are damaged by the *Shoah*, and their offspring bear their own Holocaust-induced wounds.

*Damaged Goods* sets the stage for other Jewish-American writings by children of survivors. The continuing trauma of the Holocaust as seen in issues of engagement, overprotection, and separation among family members are distinctive dimensions of what Danieli terms *victim families*. Jason's search for post-Auschwitz Jewish identity transcends the confines of Orthodoxy, yet refrains from embracing the nebulous and ever-shifting stance of secular culture. Rather, his second-generation identity emerges from a complex interaction of factors. American culture, ritual and non-traditional forms of Jewish expression, as well as his own pursuit of Jewish and Holocaust knowledge all shape Jason Kole's identity as a second-generation witness. He embodies dimensions of both Greenberg's voluntary covenant and Wiesel's additional covenant. With the former, Jason Kole rejects mandated or imposed identity. Instead, he voluntarily seeks his own Jewish ground. With the latter, Jason's concern is less a relationship to God than it is a search for a personal connection to his parents and to Jewish history, and a determination to bear witness to memories of death, pain, and suffering.

Moreover, Jason's preparation for a career in literature implies that he is committed to teaching and writing about the *Shoah* in hope that his witness will perpetuate the memory of Auschwitz and impel his students, if not all of humanity, to act in a manner that leads away from genocide. These actions constitute both a *tikkun atzmi* and a *tikkun olam* in Fackenheim's sense of bearing witness in a secular world.

## SUMMER LONG-A-COMING

Barbara Finkelstein is an American-born daughter of Job. She comments on the dual effect of her Holocaust legacy, observing that the "*Shoah* is not [her] center, it's [her] shadow, like footsteps walking up behind [her]."[17] On the other hand, she also notes the clear presence of the Holocaust in her own life, contending that the "Holocaust casts a shadow too wide for [her] to escape."[18] She is keenly aware of the fact that "the Holocaust robbed [her] of a family history and robbed [her] family history of its complexity."[19] Consequently, her life is shadowed by absences. For example, in Russia her elderly uncle terms Finkelstein "a potato from exhausted soil."[20]

Finkelstein articulates the difficulty of "creating a story out of History." "In trying to write about the Holocaust," she says, "I had to make it smaller; bring it down to me."[21] She accomplishes this task in a twofold manner. For example, actual tales of her parents' Holocaust experiences are told in the form of depositions that each give to a Yad VaShem oral historian. These stories are factual oral histories "because," attests Finkelstein, "I did not know how to fictionalize the Holocaust."[22] Consequently, she does not attempt to imagine what happened during the *Shoah*. Further, by utilizing Yad VaShem, Israel's Holocaust memorial museum and archive, Finkelstein underscores the significance of collecting survivor oral histories. These histories are precious human documents that personalize a world-historical event while providing insights into the nature of human endurance and the reality of evil.[23] Secondly, she tells of the Holocaust's continuing effects on her family.

*Summer Long-a-Coming*[24] is the story of the Szuster family. The novel is narrated by Brantzche (Brenda) Szuster, a perceptive fifteen-year-old who tells the reader:

> Scraping my nails on the past, testing my foothold in the future, was habit with me by the time I was ten. All I needed was a personal holocaust to twirl around in my mind, and then I could carry my parents' obsessiveness with me into my generation. That's what my fifteenth summer gave me. And now it seems all I ever do is live in 1968. (8)

In brief, Finkelstein depicts the post-Auschwitz life of Rukhl and Yankl Szuster—pious Jews who operate Jake's poultry farm, located on the outermost rim of the Jersey pine barrens in a town called Long-a-Coming—and their three children: Sheiye (Steven), Brantzche, and Perel (Pearl). Sheiye, the eldest, is mediocre in all that he attempts, with one exception. His one talent is that he is attracted by and commits evil. Brantzche and Perel are inseparable. They invent and speak to fictional characters and are united in their dislike of Sheiye. During the summer of

Brantzche's fifteenth year, Sheiye accidentally runs over Perel in his pickup truck. Brenda claims that she warned her brother. He contends that she never signalled him. While this tragedy of innocent death symbolically links Brenda to her parents' Holocaust experience, it also drives a permanent wedge between them. She is ostracized and, one year later, the parents move to Israel.

Shunning the outside world, the parents derive spiritual sustenance from orthodox Jewish practices. Yet their family is dysfunctional. The Szusters are insulated and isolated from the outside world. The family speaks Yiddish, practices Jewish rituals including *davening* (prayer), and observes Shabbat. Finkelstein's novel in fact provides the most sustained and systematic look at a religious response to Auschwitz among the second-generation works in this study.

Further, her novel underscores the emergence of new post-Holocaust rituals in Jewish practice. For example, the adolescent Brenda wonders why her father eats potato peels every July, which is the yahrzeit (commemoration of the deaths) of his family murdered in the *Shoah*. This ritual act recalls Greenberg's contention that, "in the decades and centuries to come, Jews and others who seek to orient themselves by the Holocaust will unfold another sacral round. Men and women will gather to eat the putrid bread of Auschwitz, the potato peelings of Bergen-Belsen."[25] The elder Szusters also continually speak about the chronology of the war. Throughout the novel, the parents' incomplete mourning leads to them dismissing their children's emotional needs and demands as insignificant in relation to what the parents endured during the Holocaust. About her family's emotional health, Brenda observes that "the Szusters refused nourishment from the outside world, so naturally they began to devour each other" (123).

Theologically, *Summer Long-a-Coming* is an unrelenting encounter with the post-Auschwitz problem of theodicy. This encounter may best be understood as a question: How do members of the second generation inherit the memory of evil and give shape to this memory in their own lives? Finkelstein offers several responses to the theodical question. On the one hand, her novel suggests, much in the manner of Isaac Bashevis Singer's work, that evil is cyclical and unending. For example, Herman Broder, the protagonist in Singer's *Enemies, A Love Story*, observes: "Cain continues to murder Abel. Nebuchadnezzer is still slaughtering the sons of Zedekiah and putting out Zedekiah's eyes. The pogrom in Kesheniev never ceases. Jews are forever being burned in Auschwitz."[26] Similarly, observing her parents' devastation following Perel's fatal accident, Brenda comments that "Perel's death only proved that their children didn't compensate for the murders of the previous generation but, rather, reenacted them" (207). Brenda even contends that Perel's death is a "new holocaust in the Szuster family—or, more accurately, it extended the old one" (205). Yet, this is not Brenda's final theological response to her Holocaust inheritance.

The parents communicate their Holocaust experience by indirection, exhibiting many manifestations of the survivor syndrome. For instance, their children are each supposed to be high achievers, thereby compensating for their murdered aunts and uncles. The household also manifests specific survivor rituals. For example, the elder Szusters "reinvented" the war in the kitchen. Chronological accuracy was gauged by the year specific people had been murdered. In addition, the telephone receiver is habitually turned upside down in its cradle where, attests Brenda, it "looked like a squat, obese, plastic creature carrying a dead child belly up in its two dwarfish arms" (131). Further, the elder Szusters continue their pattern of incomplete mourning, rarely speaking to their children about those who had been lost in the *Shoah*.

Moreover, the parents display an obsessive concern for health while overprotecting their offspring from the outside world. Like Jason Kole, Brenda deeply resents this "protection," observing that her parents "mined [the chicken farm] with Orthodox Judaism, exploding little bombs of Sabbaths and Passover, incapacitating their children so they couldn't function properly anywhere outside the farm" (12). Brenda views her parents first and foremost as habitual hiders. They hid in Polish woods from the Nazis and the Christians. Now they are hiding in America. Moreover, hiding from her own connection to the Jewish catastrophe comprises at least part of Brenda's own Holocaust legacy.

The elder Szusters betray their Holocaust legacy in a variety of behavioral and ritual ways. Like Friedmann's Kole family, the Szusters light yahrzeit candles. In fact, mourning is one of the central rituals in *Summer Long-a-Coming*. These memorial flames have an enormous impact on Brenda. For example, she attests that the cabinet full of empty memorial glasses causes her to believe that "*yurtsaht* [sic] represented yet another Jewish holiday whose celebration was whimsical and whose meaning was indecipherable" (133). The association of Jewish identity with the Holocaust yahrzeit candles is so great in the Szuster home that Brenda attests:

> I would not have been surprised to learn that no one else on earth knew
> a thing about this candle, and assumed that my father had designed a
> new holiday to remind us that we were Jews. (133)

Further, Brenda herself is a symbolic memorial candle, having been named after her Father's older sister who was murdered during the *Shoah*.

As a young girl, Brenda strives to comprehend the Holocaust and its impact on her parents. She has a clear image of her father becoming "enfeebled" on the yahrzeit of his family. He tells Brenda, "Twenty-eight years ago today, the Nazis gassed my mother and four sisters." "And?" the daughter asks. "There is no and," he replies (134). Brenda is angry and confused. She wants an explanation. Her father responds by emphasizing ritual: "The only explanation is that I want you and Perel to daven!" (134). Unsatisfied, Brenda seeks a rationale for the outrage of the *Shoah*. Challenging her father on a topic that may prove more tractable, she asks how he knows the anniversary since he has no calendar. Subsequent events provide a sobering response to Brenda's queries.

Like many second-generation witnesses, Brenda has conflicting views about her parents. William Helmreich, as noted earlier, stresses the predominance of this phenomenon. On the one hand, Brenda views her parents as incredibly strong. They survived the Holocaust when so many others did not. She observes of her parents: "To my mind, they were indestructible: Even Nazis couldn't kill them. Lesser tragedies could vanquish me" (247). On the other hand, she views them as vulnerable people forever marginalized. Brenda recalls seeing her parents before they moved to Israel. She describes her perceptions:

> Mama and Papa . . . looked shrunken, reduced by their dated fancy clothes once more to cast-off refugees. They would never look like ordinary citizens lulled into complacency by defensible borders, the longevity of geneological lines, and the tacit approval of divine providence. No matter where they lived, they would look like wayfarers whose code of conduct prepared them only for crisis. (247)

The novel's remaining chapters deal with Brenda's life after her parents leave, and the increasing intensity of her own search for ways of connecting to her Holocaust legacy. Initially, she stays with Sonia and Laybl Kichner, Long-a-Coming's other survivor family. Brenda and Sonia have a mother-daughter relationship that the teenager missed with her own biological mother. Further, Sonia speaks to Brenda about the Holocaust. At the Kichners, she discovers that they, too, engage in the post-Auschwitz Shabbat ritual of looking at family photos. Book two of the novel describes Brenda's life in Greenwich village, where she plays the piano at a bar and attempts to deal with the deep emotional scars left by Perel's death. Visting Steven on Perel's fifteenth yahrzeit, she discovers that he has constructed an elaborate series of lies about the past. Married, he names his daughter after his deceased sister, whom he contends died of leukemia. Steve's counsel is to forget the past.[27] Brenda, for her part, urges remembrance. Ceasing her own mourning after a final visit to the farm, Brenda begins to come to terms with Perel's death and is thereby enabled to begin to come to grips with the magnitude of her parents' Holocaust pain.

Brenda's images of her father are intimately associated with an orthodoxy that does not address her own spiritual needs. On the one hand, she describes her father in terms reminiscent of Friedmann's Jason Kole. "I had watched [my father's] wretched figure," she writes, "embalmed in *talis* and *tfilin*, rock back and forth in prayer, engaged in a monologue to God, his grief silent at all costs" (89). Her use of the word *embalmed* symbolically equates Orthodoxy with death. Yet, Brenda articulates two conflicting notions of Shabbat. To her parents' outstretched arms, "Shabbos offered a banquet of fruit and flowers from the World to come, wrapped in a smell they compared to the cherry orchards in the Polish towns of their childhood" (24–25). But for Brenda herself, seeking her own American identity, Shabbat is an unwelcome reminder of an unwelcome past. "What was Shabbos," she queries,

> but a claustrophobic memory set upon me, citizen of a new world with too many tantalizing diversions? The weekday motored me towards adulthood and choice; Shabbos parked her charabanc alongside my parents' chevy and tapped out a message on my forhead that I could never elude the past; that I wasn't traveling forward at all, but had gotten thrown back into the rubble of ancestral commitments. (26–27)

Nevertheless, the teenaged daughter looks forward to Shabbat because on that day her mother tells parables and occasionally reveals bits of information about her Holocaust experiences. This *tikkun* of storytelling is supplemented by an additional ritual consisting of viewing old family photographs. Stored in an old leather bag, these photos were "too sacred for the ordinary photograph album" (30). Irreversibly bound to the past, Brenda's mother becomes "part of the photographs in her lap, moving her lips silently to respond to the pictures' questions" (31). Prewar family photos are, as Epstein notes, visual documents of a powerful history that resists being fully comprehended.

Brenda Szuster engages in a sustained second-generation *din Torah*. Following the well established Jewish tradition of arguing with God, she wonders about the deity's role in her parents' lives.[28] From Uchan, her Father's birthplace, to Long-a-Coming, "it had all been reckless destruction, as if God had faltered in His capacity to distinguish between the wrongdoers and the blameless" (212). Like its millennial predecessors, this contemporary version of the question of innocent suffering has no answer. Rather, it serves to stimulate further questions and additional reflections. In Brenda's case, responses run the gamut, from the classical position of self-blame (*mi pinei hatainu*) to a working through of her Holocaust inheritance. She gradually comes to terms both with her parents' suffering and the meaning of the loss of innocence.

If Brantzche is angry with God, her parents' position is Jobian. This is especially the case with Yankl Szuster who, in the face of epic catastrophe (the Holocaust) and personal tragedy (Perel's death) utters Job's statement of faith: "Yea, though He slay me, in Him will I trust" (Job 13:15). Brenda, for her part, rebels against the unshaken faith of the pious. Seeking mastery and meaning, she discovers that the *Shoah* is unmasterable. Brenda observes of her father that "the murder of his family and his world hadn't challenged his belief in God." Nor does his traditional ritual life diminish. The elder Szuster instinctually, or so it seems to his daughter, obeys Jewish law and interpretation. For example, after Perel threatens to commit suicide, following what she perceived to be her mother's insulting comparison between herself and Sheiye, Yankl beats the young girl. Brenda observes of this incident: "one unwritten tenet formed the foundation of my father's Judaism: Thou shalt not die out. There was no God-given commandment more elemental than that" (126). In this case, Papa exemplifies Fackenheim's "614th Commandment." Following Perel's punishment, the daughters only pretend to pray.

Although no philosopher, Brenda's father tells the Yad VaShem oral historian his religious point of view. Both Rukhl who had hidden in barns and joined the partisans and Yankl who, like Jason Kole's father, had been in a slave labor camp, refused to allow their experience to subvert their faith. In Jewish history the choice has always been between a theological empiricism where historical events threaten to overwhelm faith in the covenant, and a response to history that upholds Jewish teachings even while acknowledging the impact of historical events that offer countertestimony to those teachings. Yankl Szuster chooses the path of traditional faith. He responds to the interviewer's query about his continuing faith after Auschwitz:

> You ask me why I believe in God, how I can still *daven* to Him three times a day in light of the senseless destruction of my family. You know, you can start out at point "A" and head off in twenty-five different directions. You can wander down strange roads for years, but eventually you have to come back to who you were—to who you are. I believe in God because I have no one else to believe in. (182)

For Yankl, the ways of God with humanity are inscrutable. The father describes himself as a "simple man" who looks to the wisdom of the learned and to Jewish history for attestations of God's existence. His own task is simpler and more immediate. As his mother and father before him, Yankl is a Jew and that is the only way that he knows to be human. Here Yankl embodies the point of view of Dodye Feig, Elie Wiesel's maternal grandfather and a disciple of the Wishnitzer Rebbe. The epigraph to Wiesel's *A Jew Today* contains the words that his grandfather spoke to the young Wiesel: "You are Jewish, your task is to remain Jewish. The rest is up to God."[29]

The father also responds to the question of how he survived. Unlike the Koles in *Damaged Goods*, who emphasized self-reliance rather than dependence on God, Yankl Szuster attributes his survival to two things: strong faith and some good friends among the Poles. He concludes with a parable showing the non-Jewish world's enmity towards the Jews. A farmer, according to Mr. Szuster, discovers an ant infestation on his property. He kills most of the ants, exterminating them with pesticide. Some ants escape and develop an immunity to the spray. The farmer buys a more powerful pesticide. But it is impossible to kill the entire ant population. The Jews, concludes Yankl Szuster, were the ants while the world was the farmer. This pessimistic view is understandable in a survivor, yet leaves little or no room for contact with the outside, non-Jewish world.

Yankl's theological position reflects a centrist Orthodox response to the Holocaust. Specifically, the *Shoah* is an indictment of humanity. It reflects nothing about the goodness of God or Judaism's traditional belief in messianism. On the contrary, the Holocaust reveals the moral bankruptcy of modernity and the spiritual hypocrisy of Christianity. This position is articulated with great learning and passion in the writings of Rabbi Eliezer Berkovits and Professor Michael Wyschogrod. Both of these European-born thinkers acknowledge that the Holocaust was an enormous *human* catastrophe but that it adds nothing new to the discussion of theodicy. Further, too much emphasis on the *Shoah* is dangerous because the event is still capable of causing Jews to lose their faith.[30]

Yankl Szuster adheres to his faith. On the first anniversary of Perel's death, he and Mr. Berg the *shohet* (ritual slaughterer) study traditional commentaries (*Mishna* and *Gemarah*) all evening. At day break they chant "*Eli, Eli, Lomo asawtoni?*" (My God, my God, why have you forsaken me?) (246). Brenda imagines her father asking God why, after all his Holocaust losses, he had to lose Perel, an innocent child. Universalizing her father's imagined pleadings, Brenda wonders if he thought he had sinned or, perhaps the Jews—following the model of Isaiah 53— suffer for the sins of the world. Put as a question, this latter point of view reads: Can the Messiah come without suffering? In Wiesel's *The Gates of The Forest*, the protagonist contends that it is too late for the Messiah to come. After Auschwitz, Jewish salvation depends on human action. It is, however, unclear whether these are the father's questions or Brenda's projections. In any case, the questions remain questions.

Brenda is a second-generation witness who refuses to theologically "normalize" the Holocaust. Quite the contrary is the case. She is angry with God, alternately blaming the deity and the Nazis for her parents' behavioral irregularities (36). Following Perel's death, Brenda links God to historical events in observing that "History wasn't finished abusing us" (198–99). But Brenda's image of God undergoes several transformations. Initially, her understanding is naïve, appropriate to an adolescent point of view. For example, immediately following Perel's death, Brenda seeks to hear God's voice by going to the middle chicken coop where, every Sukkot, her father built a *sukkah* (a temporary structure symbolizing the fact that the Israelites wandered in the desert for forty years and had no permanent dwellings). The *sukkah* symbolizes as well the dwelling of the *shekhinah* (divine presence) among the Israelites. Brenda, however, does not hear the divine voice. Rather, she sees another image of suffering in the person of a severely deformed young girl. This experience confirms her belief that God's mercy is absent. Later on in the novel, Brenda's view changes as she comes to understand one of the central points of both Wiesel's and Greenberg's positions: as God becomes increasingly enfeebled or hidden, it is up to humans to take a more active role in maintaining the covenant.

The remainder of the novel chronicles Brenda's slowly evolving theological and psychological maturity. The steps she takes are manifold and involve a recognition of her mimetic enactment of her parents stance vis-à-vis the world, an awareness that she never really understood her parents, a slowly dawning appreciation of her relationship to the Jewish tradition, and an articulation of a second-generation mission to seek the *tikkun* of bearing witness.

Specifically, *Summer Long-a-Coming* portrays Brenda's mimesis of her parents' Holocaust experience in several ways. For example, initially her parents want her to accompany them to Israel. She, however, is opposed. Prior to negotiating her remaining in Long-a-Coming, Brenda thinks that she will live in the woods if she has to: "My parents had done it, and so could I" (241). Similarly, as her parents endlessly rehearse the events of the war, so too does Brenda continuously review the circumstances of Perel's death. Later in the novel, the daughter of Job mentally compares herself to her parents, listing specific points of contact between them: she and her parents were "bereaved and ignored witnesses of murder"; since *they* had no family, neither should Brenda; as their families died violently, so should hers; post-Auschwitz life did not matter to them, and life without Perel did not matter to Brenda (259). These comparisons compel Brenda to an awareness of how emotionally and intellectually crippled her life was after Perel's death, a death for which she received her parents' implicit blame. Nonetheless, she articulates the *fate of the witness*, telling Sheiye: "I can't figure it out . . . all I did was witness. I lived to tell, the way [our parents] did" (287).

Brenda's depression begins to dissipate as she enrolls in City College. Like Jason Kole, she studies American Literature, writing an M.A. thesis on Ellen Glasgow. Glasgow is a transitional writer in Southern American literature whose works analyze many themes pertinent to Brenda's own experience as a daughter of Job, including the conflict between traditional culture and modernity. Frederick McDowell describes Glasgow's work in terms of its characteristic themes for modern Southern fiction. These include "a diffused disenchantment with human experience and an acknowledgement of the reality of evil; an emphasis upon isolation and frustration as conditions inherent in man's existence; a realization of the ambiguities and the complexities underlying moral and philosophical issues; and a tragic view of experience that is often modulated by the grotesque, the incongruous, and the ironic."[31]

Hearing her parents' Yad VaShem tapes compels Brenda to realize that she could never have possibly understood her mother and father. The elder Szusters present an image of continual mourning. Further, their lives continue to revolve around slaughter. Yankl especially does not want his daughters to watch as the chickens are prepared for market. Emotionally unavailable to their children, the parents act, live, and think according to the ways of a murdered culture. Brenda's emotional healing and her quest for a positive Jewish self-identity (*tikkun atzmi*) begin as she listens to the tapes.

Listening to survivor testimony is itself a second-generation witness ritual. In addition, Brenda juxtaposes this act with others whose practices are more deeply rooted in the tradition, thereby enhancing its legitimacy. Her description of this new ritual deserves full citation:

> Every few weeks I listen to the tapes the way observant Jews listen to their rabbi's sermon on Shabbos. I pore over the stories and their possible interpretations, flicking on fast forward and reverse, just as yeshiva boys burn their eyes out over *Pirke Avot* [*Ethics of the Fathers*]. (69)

Survivors' tales are gates through which the listener can come closer to the *Shoah*, although without ever really being able to comprehend it. Further, the experience situates Brenda within Judaism in a manner that the more formal Orthodoxy of her parents could never achieve. For example, she no longer resents Yiddish as the "language of death tallies," and Judaism itself as restrictive and world-negating.

Her parents' testimony yields conflicting images for Brenda. On the one hand, it serves to humanize them. Brenda tells her brother that she is "insanely jealous" of the oral historian for drawing "real personalities out of Rukhl and Yankl." Consequently, Brenda wants to get to know her parents, she likes them. But she also contends that her memories of being a daughter of Job include "deranged" parents who flew around like demons and slaughtered chickens. One of them prayed three times a day and the other gave lectures. They are the people who passed this lunatic judgment on me! I survived something horrible like they did. Do they pass judgment on themselves?" (298)

These are the reflections of a thirty-year-old woman who is addressed both by the pain of her childhood and the admiration that she is now able to feel for her parents as a mature person. These two parts of second-generation identity are explored more fully in chapter 5.

*Summer Long-a-Coming* is at its best in accounting for the contemporary children of Job's coming to grips with the issue of innocent suffering. The Holocaust links the identities of parents and their offspring. Like the mysterious disappearance of Mrs. Kole in *Damaged Goods*, Perel Szuster's accidental death causes Brenda to realize that she is not as free from history as she had formerly believed. Further, she begins to understand that she is not as different from her parents as she had imagined. Instead, Brenda realizes that she cannot "view apocalypse without crumbling under its fallout." Specifically relating Perel's tragedy to her own reaction to hearing her parents' Holocaust tales, Brenda observes that:

> Up until that moment my parents' tales of survival had done little more than fuel my self-emancipation fantasies of entrapment and escape. At best, staying alive was a question of odds, of monitoring the whereabouts of a predator, and sidestepping it in the nick of time. With Perel gone, I had the sickening realization that survival meant coming out the victor by chance, not by destiny or individual cunning. The Szusters were merely like the other creatures on the farm—chickens, earthworms, dogs—who, on suspending their vigilance for a second, succumbed to a greater, more confident power. (203–4)

Brenda's realization, which brings to mind Terrance Des Pres's insight concerning the loss of innocence for those born after Auschwitz, is the first step on her road to accepting her Holocaust legacy. Her personal experience of unwarranted evil and suffering links Brenda to the historical experience of the Jews in Europe. Significantly, the novel's dust jacket portrays sheep going to slaughter. The implication is twofold: that Jews passively went to their deaths, and that there was a purpose to the process. Sheep, after all, are a source of food and clothing. The case was entirely different with the Jews of Europe. After Perel's accidental death, Brenda now begins to understand that Jews were murdered simply for having been born, and not for any special action they undertook or refrained from undertaking or any belief that they affirmed or denied. In Rabbi Joseph Soloveitchik's terms, the Jews of Europe were murdered because of the covenant of being rather than the covenant of doing.

Finkelstein's heroine consciously articulates her second-generation mission.³² Brenda Szuster is nearly thirty before she believes that she "has the right to exist." But assuming that right, she gives herself permission to end her piano career, another form of hiding, and to pursue her quest to discover more about her parents and the Holocaust by travelling to Poland in order to meet the "few people who had sheltered my parents during the Nazi occupation," thereby revealing the *tikkun* of ordinary decency. Further, "terrifying as it was," Brenda realizes that she can have a child, hence a new generation to whom she can teach the lessons and legacies of the *Shoah*. Brenda may not be able to undo the Holocaust past, but she comes to realize that "at long last [she must] undo the damage of [her] parents' judgment on [her]" (262).

The complexity of Brenda's feelings towards her parents is focused in the mother-daughter relationship. On the one hand, the adolescent Szuster sisters are fascinated by their mother's femininity. They watch as Rukhl puts on lipstick. Brenda views it as a privilege when her mother asks her to loosen the clasp of her too-tight bra; she pretends her own body was "ample and pliant, instead of bony" (153). The young girl, betraying the Orthodox ambience of the Szuster household, witnesses her mother changing from farm clothes into a dress and compares the effect to lighting candles on Friday night: "The ordinary work week put on royal garb and became Shabbos" (154). Further, both young girls ask their mother details of personal hygiene. How, they wonder, did the mother wipe herself in the woods during the war. Rukhl told her daughters that she used *bletlakh* (large leaves). This dimension of the mother-daughter relationship is positive and affirming, enabling the two to draw closer together.

Yet, on the other hand, Ruhkl Szuster frightens Brenda, who, although not as cerebral as Jason Kole, is far more expressive. Her intimate feelings about her mother reveal the psychological weight of the second generation's Holocaust legacy. For example, Brenda recalls that at public occasions she and her mother are in on a secret, but the daughter does not know what it is. Equally devastating is Brenda's anger at her mother's past. The daughter has a fantasy of rolling her mother into a tiny ball and throwing her through time and space to 1942 Poland. These examples demonstrate that the *Shoah* remains an unmastered and unmasterable trauma even for the generation born after.

By the end of the novel, the farm has given way to a convenience mini-mart. Despite her childhood loathing of the poultry business, Brenda now realizes that it represented her parents struggle: "to live, to produce, to improve." Further, Brenda embraces a position that reflects certain dimensions of Wiesel's additional covenant. For example, her theological protest remains a protest from within. While unable to affirm traditional theological assertions about God vanquishing evil, she neither abandons nor refutes Judaism. On the contrary, she recognizes the salvific importance of memory; the novel's last line is "*Gedenk* . . . Remember. . . ." Visiting the site of their old farm for the last time, Brenda has a "seance" with the dead Perel in which her younger sister's soul releases Brenda from the obligation of returning. Reminiscent of the work of Isaac Bashevis Singer, this scene establishes the power of the dead in the lives of the living. Unlike her parents, however, Brenda is able to work through her grief and guilt by means of this contact and thereby achieve a *tikkun atzmi*.

Upholding Wiesel's additional covenant, Brenda assumes the role of witness although she realizes the difficulty of this task. Acknowledging that she will have a child means that Brenda upholds the sanctification of life, a central tenet of both the Greenbergian and the Wieselian ideas of covenant. Finally, Brenda's implicit covenant resides not with God, who has proven an unreliable covenantal partner. Rather, it depends on Brenda's self-affirmation to remain Jewish and to assume the past of Jewish history as her own. A major part of this self-affirmation is her identity as a daughter of Job whose covenant is with "the past of Israel, with its pain, its overwhelming experience of death, and its memories of God." Finally, unlike her parents, Brenda stakes out a specifically second-generation position concerning post-Auschwitz Jewish identity. Based neither on texts nor traditional Judaism, Brenda's *tikkun atzmi* comes from relating to her parents' tales and her own experience of suffering. Yet, unlike her parents, she does not use suffering to define and exclude the world. Rather, the second-generation witness seeks to transform suffering without denying its impact.

Brenda comes to terms with her second-generation identity by integrating two primary sources. "Between literature and my parents' oral histories," she writes, "I have come to accept one truth about my past and future: I am not that different from Mama and Papa. Like them, I live without hope of settling scores yet love life unreasonably, and will until the day I die—even though I cannot reclaim what I have lost" (262). Brenda's choice of life over (psychic) death places her firmly in the Jewish fold. Even though *Summer Long-a-Coming* is cognizant of the ambiguity of Jewish existence in America—the survivors either move to Israel or are dying, one son of survivors divorces and then remarries a non-Jewish woman, and Brenda's own brother chooses not to remember—Brenda herself is a *zahker* (rememberer). Like Jason Kole, Brenda will teach literature and thereby transmit the legacy of the Holocaust to succeeding generations.

## MAUS

Art Spiegelman is a professional cartoonist, editor of *Raw* magazine, and formerly a contributing editor of the *New Yorker*. Born in Stockholm three years after the *Shoah*, his books on the second-generation witness are the most widely known of this genre because of his use of animal figures. Jews are portrayed as mice and Nazis are cats. This imagery is both chilling and evocative. Other participants in the Holocaust and World War II are also depicted as animals: Americans are dogs, a French non-Jewish prisoner in Auschwitz is a frog, Poles are pigs, Swedes are reindeer. Additionally, a fish is a jeep driver, and there is a butterfly fortune teller. The widespread cultural impact of Spiegelman's work is attested by a Pulitzer Prize for *Maus: A Survivor's Tale*,[33] his two-volume comic book/novel, and by the fact that several of the book's cartoon panels comprised an exhibit at the Jewish Museum. Moreover, there is an interactive CD-ROM that contains the entire history of the *Maus* project, including tapes of Spiegelman's interviews with his father, Vladek.[34]

Spiegelman reports that the Holocaust is his own point of entry into both Jewish history and Jewish identity. Unlike the protagonists in the works of Friedmann and Finkelstein, however, Spiegelman recalls that in his mid-teens he "often thought life would be a lot easier if [he] were not Jewish."[35] The Jewish fate seemed too overwhelming to be borne. But this attitude began to change during the decade of the seventies. Then, he attests, "whenever an article would appear that had anything to do with the Holocaust I would find myself reading it."[36] Here Spiegelman, like Brenda Szuster, exhibits a second-generation identification with his parents' victimization, thereby opening the possibility of exploring fully his own Holocaust legacy. In preparation for *Maus II*, which deals with survivors' post-Auschwitz survival, Spiegelman told an interviewer that he read "as many survivor accounts as [he] can get hold of and [is] looking at the scraps of film footage and handfuls of photographs that survive."[37] What he found most useful, however, were "drawings and even paintings made by survivors within the camps."[38] Vladek's tales help Spiegelman understand who he is as a son of Job, serving as his "shoehorn with which to squeeze [himself] back into history."[39] Yet, as will become apparent below, Spiegelman's Jewish self-understanding reflects Rubenstein's view that it is an existential and ethnic rather than a covenantal identity.

*Maus* is simultaneously biography and autobiography that reveals the second generation's desire to know about its Holocaust legacy. Spiegelman accomplishes this by sharing his parents' (Vladek and Anja Zylberberg Spiegelman) prewar, Holocaust, and post-*Shoah* narrative. *Maus I: A Survivor's Tale* outlines the author's growing concern to learn more about his parents' Holocaust experience and, consequently, his own identity. The second volume, *Maus II: And Here My Troubles Began*, contains a more detailed account of both the Holocaust and post-*Shoah* experiences of his parents, while portraying Spiegelman's attempts to learn as much as he can from his ailing father before it is too late. Detailing the survivor's continuing survival reveals the depth of the trauma of the *Shoah*. In this context it is important to note Lawrence Langer's report of his interviews with Holocaust survivors. One survivor, asked to describe his feelings upon liberation, responded, "Then I knew my troubles were *really* about to begin."[40] Langer astutely observes that this answer "[inverts] the order of conflict and resolution that we have learned to expect of traditional historical narrative."[41]

The survivors' continuing survival is a saga of unhappiness; physical and psychic pain mar their lives. Anja commits suicide while Spiegelman is an undergraduate. Vladek, for his part, finds coping with the mores of American culture difficult and unattractive. Like Mordechai Kole and the Szusters, Anja and Vladek's parenting skills are deeply flawed. Further, like Mr. Kole and the elder Szusters, Vladek is unable to permit his son his own psychic space. Instead, he psychically overwhelms the young Art with the horrors of the Holocaust, including the indifference of the bystanders, the suffering of the victims, and the brutality of the murderers. Later, when Art is older, Vladek reveals the existence of a small number of non-Jewish helpers in the Kingdom of Night.

The *Maus* volumes are also Spiegelman's own story of being a child of Job. He tells a painful tale of growing up in Rego Park in a house where the dead are a haunting presence among the living. The *presence of this absence* is constant. Like Elie Wiesel's Ariel and Thomas Friedmann's Jason Kole, Spiegelman is a second "only" son of his parents. Richieu, the Spiegelman's European-born son, had died in the Holocaust. An enlarged photo of Richieu hangs like a ghostly icon in his parents' bedroom. Following his marriage, Art confides to his wife Françoise that "it's spooky having sibling rivalry with a snapshot" (*Maus II*, 15). Spiegelman's statement recalls Wiesel's question about the children of Job: "How could they live in a house filled with tragedy?" The *Maus* volumes provide an in-depth look at the psychosocial themes that define family dynamics in many survivor households. For example Spiegelman, like Friedmann, tells the story of an enmeshed and psychically crippling father-son relationship characterized by the father's emotional unavailability. With Finkelstein, Spiegelman also reports his own feelings of guilt and anger as well as acknowledges the pain he feels at the realization that he is not permitted to think his own problems matter. Moreover, all three of the novelists reflect an inability to adequately understand either their parents or the Holocaust.

On the other hand, Spiegelman echoes a common second-generation theme in observing that writing *Maus* enabled him to "continue [his] relationship [to his] father."[42] Consequently, the *Shoah* is both barrier and bond between father and son. For Spiegelman, linking himself to a world-historical event means an inescapable confrontation with his own Jewish identity as well as an attempt to distill what he believes are the lessons of the Holocaust. Yet, this identity is more imposed than fully embraced or negotiated. Unlike either Jason Kole or Brenda Szuster, Spiegelman defines his own Jewish ground in a largely negative manner. He interprets his confrontation with evil as leaving him no other option. In this sense he resembles the character of Jake Brody in Hugh Nissenson's novel *My Own Ground*, in which the protagonist contends that evil has defeated both God and humanity.[43]

Spiegelman's story is inextricably bound to and illuminated by its format. Genre defines the message. The author confides to an interviewer that he views comics as co-mixing "together words and pictures."[44] While this is not the place to trace the role of the comic book in American history, it is worth noting that the American comic strip is the result both of "the natural evolution of graphic humor" and "quirks of American history" that include a "high percentage of the population that was either semi-illiterate or illiterate."[45] Commenting on the profound transformation of comics in more recent history, Spiegelman observes that in the 1960s comics became "avant garde," drawn for their own sake and "not simply to sell newspapers."[46] Further, he contends that there is an "increasing visual literacy that comes from and through the culture."

*Maus* combines both American and Jewish components. For example, the American dimension of Spiegelman's work is seen in the popularity of comic strips such as Walt Disney's *Mickey Mouse*, *Bugs Bunny*, and *Porky Pig*. Specifically concerning the use of comics as a medium for reflecting on matters of serious concern for ethnic identity, one can point to the efforts of Aline Kominsky-Crumb, one of the first women whose work appeared in underground comics. Her feminist *Wimmen's Comix* deals with issues of Jewish feminism.[47] Spiegelman's own earlier work is also relevant to the discussion. In 1972 he drew a cartoon strip with mice "who were obviously Jews, wandering around a ghetto, and cats dressed in S.S. uniforms."[48] Spiegelman based this cartoon on remembered childhood stories.

Spiegelman attests, however, that he views Franz Kafka's "Josephine the Singer, or The Mouse Folk" as fundamental to *Maus*. Kafka's tale deals with a rodent people (the Jews) who live precariously in a world devoted to their extirpation. After reading this story, Spiegelman "began pursuing the logic and possibilities that that metaphoric device [cats and mice] opened up."[49] Additionally, he notes a film class taught by Professor Ken Jacobs at SUNY–Binghamton that focused on both racist and cat-and-mouse cartoons. *Maus* is, however, distinctively the result of the confluence of Spiegelman's Holocaust inheritance and his special artistic ability.

Spiegelman's own considerable research into the Holocaust, a common second-generation theme, yielded a direct association between Nazi antisemitism and the mouse image. Specifically, the epigraph to *Maus II* is taken from a newspaper article of the mid-1930s in Pomerania, Germany. The article denounces Mickey Mouse as "the most miserable ideal ever revealed." Further, in a macabre example of art anticipating life, the writer continues: "Healthy emotions tell every independent young man and every honorable youth that the dirty and filth-covered vermin, the greatest bacteria carrier in the animal kingdom, cannot be the ideal type of animal." The author concludes with an exhortation to his readers: "Away with Jewish brutalization of the people! Down with Mickey Mouse! Wear the Swastika Cross!" This would be extremely amusing if it were not so deadly.

The genre issue deserves further attention. Owing to the nature of the Holocaust itself, the comic book format was bound to create difficulties. While Spiegelman's work was applauded by many, others questioned its appropriateness. Obviously a work in the postmodern mode, part of the initial difficulty arose over how *Maus* should be categorized. Was it a best-seller in the fiction or nonfiction category? The *New York Times* put *Maus* first in one and then in the other category. But this was merely the tip of the interpretive iceberg. Terrance Des Pres and the literary critic Lawrence Langer speak for those who hail Spiegelman's work in terms of both literary-critical studies and genre. Des Pres viewed *Maus* as a "family romance, replete with guilt and unresolved complexities caused by the hold of the past upon the present, a kind of knowledge-as-suffering that cannot be dismissed, but only shared in the 'survivor's tale' before us."[50] Specifically concerning the cat and mouse imagery, Des Pres wrote of the first volume that "it seems clear that the cat and mouse fable, together with its comic-book format work in a Brechtian manner to alienate, provoke, and compel new attention to an old story."[51]

Similarly, Lawrence Langer wrote a laudatory review of *Maus II* that appeared in the *New York Times Book Review*. Spiegelman's book, attests Langer, "is a serious form of pictorial literature, sustaining and even intensifying the power of the first volume. It resists defining labels."[52] With Des Pres, Langer contends that the use of animals aids the viewer in the painful task of Holocaust interpretation. "The meaning," writes Langer, "is in the effort, not the results, and the animal characters create a distancing effect that allows us to follow the fable without being drowned in its grim, inhuman horrors."[53] Finally, Langer pays tribute to Spiegelman's art. "Perhaps no Holocaust narrative will ever contain the whole experience," writes Langer, "but Art Spiegelman has found an original and authentic form to draw us closer to its bleak heart."[54]

More recently, Geoffrey Hartman suggests that Spiegelman's use of animal characters bears great symbolic weight in attempting to define the human condition. Combining "the folkloric beast fable with American popular cartoons" permits Spiegelman to comment insightfully on the nature of the post-*Shoah* human condition. For example, Hartman writes that *Maus*'s "metamorphosis of the human figure recognizes that the *Shoah* has affected how we think about ourselves as a *species* (the human? race)."[55]

A very different response to *Maus* is given by Hillel Halkin. Allowing that Spiegelman's comic book format was intended with all seriousness, Halkin and others are concerned that readers will be distracted from the doom of European Jewry. For example, Halkin points to the troubling fact that drawing people as animals "is doubly dehumanizing, once by virtue of symbolism and once by virtue of graphic limitations."[56] What Halkin means by graphic limitations concerns the great difficulty of personalizing animal faces. In addition to all looking alike, cartoon faces hide rather than illuminate discreet feelings and emotions. With the passage of time and the disappearance of all who actually survived the Holocaust, what cultural and pedagogical role is *Maus* likely to play in teaching about the catastrophe of European Jewry and its aftermath? This debate is likely to continue with even greater intensity as the *Shoah* becomes an increasing focus of American culture in both its high and low forms of expression. At the very least, Spiegelman's work should provoke a rethinking of the role of comics as a medium for high seriousness. *Maus* will, however, likely be viewed as a watershed event in the shaping of post-Holocaust memory.

Spiegelman's drawings utilize specific images to reveal significant information about the psychological state of survivors both during and after the *Shoah*. To cite but one example, as Vladek labors on his exercycle he recalls some of the terrible events of the *Shoah*. His memory includes two particularly dreadful episodes: the decision *not* to hide Richieu with a Polish family; and the hanging of four friends whose corpses were displayed for a week in the town square as a warning. Spiegelman deftly portrays Vladek as exhausted physically by his workout and drained psychically by his memories (*Maus I*, 81 and 91). Another drawing portrays Vladek and Anja before their deportation walking on a swastika-shaped path leading nowhere (125). All Jews, whether believers or atheists, were condemned to death by the Nazis. There has never been a more comprehensive—and deadly—definition of Jewish identity.

Emphasizing the theme of the presence of an absence, Spiegelman portrays the *Shoah*'s continuing effects on the second generation. The illustrations are especially effective at this point. For example, he draws himself seated at his cartoonist's board. Juxtaposing significant dates of Vladek's Holocaust experiences and events in his own life, he portrays the presentness of the European past in the life of an American second-generation witness (*Maus II*, 41). Further, by drawing himself as a child both at the board and in the office of his survivor-psychiatrist, Spiegelman graphically portrays his inner feelings of being overwhelmed by the enormity of the Holocaust (43–46).

*Maus I* contains a separate unnumbered four-page segment entitled "Prisoner on the HELL Planet: A Case History," which deals with Anja's suicide. This segment is a powerful portrayal of the nature of second-generation guilt. This guilt needs, however, to be distinguished from the phenomenon of survivor guilt. Among second-generation witnesses, guilt arises from several sources. For example, many feel guilty for not having been in the *Shoah*. Others feel guilt, quite undeservedly, for the fact that their parents' suffered during the Holocaust. Still others feel a sense of guilt for not being able to comprehend the meaning of their parents' suffering and their own Holocaust legacy. Additionally, this segment reveals Spiegelman's estrangement from and ignorance of covenantal Jewish identity.

The "Prisoner" portion begins with a photograph of Anja and Art at age ten. Spiegelman next draws himself in prison garb. As prelude, it is necessary to know that when the author was twenty, Anja committed suicide, without leaving any note. Shortly before this occurred, Spiegelman had been released from a state mental hospital with the proviso that he live at his parents' home. Returning later than usual, he saw a crowd at the house. Taken to the neighboring home of a physician, Art is told of his mother's death. Her suicide is another way that Spiegelman recognizes the survivor's intense psychic pain and depression. At her funeral Art reveals his own distance from Jewish ritual. He recites verses from the *Tibetan Book of the Dead* while Vladek recites the traditional *kaddish* (prayer for the dead).

Leaving the funeral parlor early, Art is berated by a survivor-friend of his parents for waiting until after Anja's death to express his feelings. During the *shiva* (seven-day mourning period), friends visit the Spiegelman home. Their words of solace are drawn in the same balloon as their indictments of Art. Spiegelman next draws three discreet memories. The first contains four epitaphs: "Menopausal Depression," "Hitler Did It," "Mommy," and "Bitch" written in capital letters. Each epitaph is accompanied by an appropriate image: Anja's heavy, nude body lying in a bathtub; a tangled pile of corpses lying in front of a swastika-festooned brick wall; Art as a ten-year old, dressed in a prisoner's uniform, lying in bed while Anja reads to him; and Anja herself slitting her Auschwitz numbered wrist. It is clear that Spiegelman realizes that the suffering in his parents' lives and his own stems from the ontic wound of the *Shoah*. His is a second-generation witness identification with parental Holocaust experience that he begins to assume as his own.

Spiegelman's second and third memory panels focus directly on the theme of second-generation guilt. Drawing himself in a prison cell, he recalls that the last time he saw his mother was when she had come into his room late one night asking if he still loved her. Resentful of the way she "tightened the umbilical cord," Art dismissively mumbles, "sure Ma." His mother leaves the room, closing the door behind her. Anja's separation anxiety only serves further to alienate her son, and is reminiscent of the difficult intergenerational communication between Brenda Szuster and her mother.

Art "congratulates" Anja for committing the perfect crime. He exclaims, "You murdered me mommy and left me here to take the rap." Juxtaposing the historical naïveté of nonwitnessing Americans (the other prisoners wishing to sleep who tell Art to "pipe down") and second-generation witnesses who are both the "first and the last," Spiegelman underscores the fact that the planet that "hosted" Auschwitz is by definition a "Hell planet," and his own emotional state as well as that of his parents is tantamount to living in a psychological hell. This scene metaphorically portrays the difference between those who seek the *tikkun* of bearing witness to the continuing trauma of the Holocaust and those who are indifferent both to the catastrophe and its continuing ramifications.

Like Friedmann and Finkelstein, Spiegelman shows that for survivors, what Lawrence Langer calls "deep memory" is the framing memory. Deep memory is completely focused on the *Shoah*. It refrains from obeying the usual sense of chronological time. Opposed to this is "common memory," which restores the self to pre- and postwar life.[57] Such "deep memory" is often employed by survivors in the form of Holocaust "lessons" that are offered to the second generation as guidelines for their own lives. For example, Vladek tells Art several such survival "lessons." When his ten-year-old son is abandoned by friends after he had fallen while roller skating, he sobbingly tells Vladek what happened. The survivor responds with a *Shoah* "lesson." "Friends? Your Friends?" he sarcastically queries in the cadence of his refugee English "if you lock them together in a room with no food for a week. . . . Then you could see what it is, Friends!" (*Maus I*, 5).[58] Further, Vladek also recalls that working as a cobbler and a tinsmith at Auschwitz, both skills self-taught in the camp, saved his life. Vladek tests all assumptions about human behavior against the merciless yardstick of Auschwitz.

The *Maus* volumes bear graphic witness to the process by which the second generation inherits Holocaust memory and how, in turn, this memory shapes identity. This process involves both voluntary and involuntary actions on the part of survivors. We have noted above Vladek's survival axioms. But there is more. For instance, attesting to the psychic impact of hearing about German cruelties, Art and Françoise listen to

Vladek tell of Jews being burned alive while their body fat further fuels the fire, she sobs, Art exclaims, "Jesus" (*Maus II*, 72–73). There are in addition Vladek's involuntary actions. For example, the couple hear him moaning in his sleep. Françoise is alarmed by this, but Art is used to hearing the sounds of survivors' nightmares. He recalls that as a child, he "thought that was the sound all grown-ups made while they slept" (74). Moreover, Art confides to Françoise that as a young boy he had recurring Holocaust-related nightmares; in one of them, S.S. men dragged away his classmates; in another he fantasized about zyklon B—the poison gas used to murder the Jews—coming out of showers. These images confirm the observations of both Helen Epstein and Robert M. Prince concerning the role of Holocaust imagery in the lives of the second generation.

Second-generation identity includes feelings of guilt for not having experienced the Holocaust. Ellen Fine writes of this phenomenon among the French second-generation. She observes that, "if he dares to speak the name of the dead, the post-Holocaust writer must bear the burden of guilt for inventing memories that are not his own."[59] In its American context, second-generation guilt assumes various forms. For example, it can lead, as in the case of Al Singerman, who was born in a displaced persons camp in Germany, to placing oneself in an extremely dangerous situation. Volunteering for Vietnam, Singerman thought that he, like his parents, could prove himself a survivor.[60] In the literary sphere, Thomas Friedmann's protagonist refers to himself as "the ultimate bystander," suffering from an event that he has not personally experienced. Barbara Finkelstein's heroine, for her part, fantasizes about "rolling her Mother into a ball and throwing her back to 1942 Poland;" her own guilt lies in not being able to understand or master the *Shoah*.

Spiegelman responds to the issue of second-generation guilt in a manner that combines aspects of the positions taken by Al Singerman and Finkelstein's Brenda Szuster. For example, Spiegelman appears to agree with Singerman's response. The cartoonist comments to an interviewer that some survivors' children put themselves in extreme situations such as mental hospitals in order to experience what their parents lived through. Pursuing the mimetic response of Brenda Szuster, Spiegelman observes that during his own stay in a mental hospital, he felt that he "echoed" his father's experience. Art symbolically imitated Vladek, "collecting scraps of string . . . in case they would come in handy later."[61] This mimesis reflects another dimension of voluntarily accepting the legacy of the *Shoah*.

Second-generation guilt also emerges in conjunction with the very act of attempting to write about the Holocaust. For instance, Art acknowledges to Françoise that he has a dual sense of unease. In the first place, he feels that his attempts to reconstruct the reality of the Holocaust are totally inadequate. Further, Spiegelman himself is troubled by the genre issue; he is relying on a *comic strip* (*Mans II*, 16). He underscores his own misgivings by drawing himself surrounded, and harassed, by the media and advertisers who wish to sensationalize and thereby trivialize the *Shoah* (42).

Spiegelman portrays the useful role that psychiatry played in helping him fully assume his Holocaust legacy. Unable to work and feeling blocked creatively, he seeks help from Pavel, a survivor psychiatrist who helps him in three important ways. First, he places Spiegelman's own childhood into context. Art, attests Pavel, is the *real* survivor. Why? Because as a child he had survived Vladek's endless ridicule, which the mental health professional attributes to the father's own feelings of survivor guilt. Further, Pavel believes that no lessons have been learned from the *Shoah*, except perhaps the lesson that nations can get away with it. This position echoes the view outlined by Primo Levi in *The Drowned and the Saved*, where he writes:

> After the defeat, the silent Nazi diaspora has taught the art of persecution and torture to the military and political men of a dozen countries. . . . Many new tyrants have kept in their drawer Adolf Hitler's *Mein Kampf*: with a few changes perhaps, and the substitution of a few names, it can still come in handy.[62]

Pavel also assists Spiegelman is coming to grips with the fact that the Holocaust remains an unmasterable trauma. For example, attempting to explain what Auschwitz felt like, the psychiatrist frightens Art by screaming "BOO!" (*Maus II*, 46). Auschwitz, attests Pavel, felt like this all the time. There are, after all, limitations to the second-generation's identifying with and understanding what happened to their parents. Implied by this action is the question of whether the *Shoah* eludes all artistic response. Perhaps the eternal horror and silence of Eduard Munch's *The Scream* is the only appropriate artistic response to Auschwitz. On the pragmatic level, Pavel also provides physical details about the tin shop in which Vladek worked that enable Spiegelman to complete his book.

Spiegelman dramatically portrays the endless mourning of his father as well as his own second-generation pain. On the last page, Vladek lies in bed exhausted. He is telling Art how he and Anja were reunited after the *Shoah*. In Vladek's account, their post-Auschwitz life is one of happiness and contentment. Drained, and no longer able to speak, Vladek tells Art to turn off the tape recorder. The continuing *presence of the* [Holocaust] *absence* is underscored when Vladek calls his second-born son "Richieu." This is "deep memory," and it emphasizes the fact that Vladek continually mourned his firstborn son. The book's final panel is in fact the end of one saga and the beginning of another. His parents' tomb-stones are juxtaposed with the dates 1978–1991, when he began and completed the *Maus* volumes. This second bar mitzvah (thirteen years), unlike his earlier one, was neither coerced nor foreign to Spiegelman. Quite the contrary is the case. Now he voluntarily explores the meaning of his Holocaust legacy and how it defines him as a post-Auschwitz Jew.

The theological stance of *Maus* is camouflaged, but gives credence to Greenberg's contention that apparently secular deeds may mask holiness. Further, the connection between generations—itself a crucial dimension of Jewish identity—plays an important role in Spiegelman's story. For exam-ple, in *Maus I*, Vladek reports a dream he had while in a German prisoner of war camp. His dead grandfather, who had been a religious man, appears wearing a *tallit* (prayer shawl) and *tefillin* (phylacteries). The grandfather serves as a seer who both predicts Vladek's release from the camp and links it with the reading of a particular Torah portion (*parsha Truma*). Moreover, the reader is aware of the fact that many other rites of passage are associated with *parsha Truma*. For instance, at this time Vladek and Anja were married; Art was born and later became a bar mitzvah at the time of this Torah reading. Nevertheless, Vladek recognizes the radical countertestimony of the Holocaust as he tells Art that "here [in Auschwitz] God didn't come." Like the Koles in *Damaged Goods*, Vladek contends that "We were all on our own" (*Maus II*, 29).

Spiegelman's work, however, does bear witness to Greenberg's con-tention that the voluntary covenant describes Jewish affirmation in the age of Auschwitz. For example, Vladek's own tales attest that his survival involved both religious and secular factors. For instance, Vladek's coping skills and resourcefulness were instrumental in his staying alive. His vol-unteering for various tasks, including teaching English to a kapo, provided Vladek with food and better treatment. Yet, this is only one part of the story. The "theology" of *Maus* involves other considerations as well. Specifically, it is the applied theological action of a "righteous helper," one of the *Hasidei Umot Ha-Olam* (The Righteous Among the Nations), that helps Vladek survive. Like Yankl and Ruhkl Szuster, Vladek owes his life to a caring Christian. One of his fellow inmates in Auschwitz was a priest who one day came upon a weeping Vladek. The priest, who knew Hebrew and *gematria*, or number mysticism, comforts the Jewish prisoner by pointing out that his tattoo equals the Hebrew word for life (*Hai*). Fur-ther, the priest tells Vladek that the first two digits of his tattoo are equiv-alent to *k'minyan tov*, another good sign. The last two digits equal thir-teen, the age of becoming a bar mitzvah. Vladek attests that, although never seeing the priest again, the man's intervention sustained him during an especially bleak emotional period of time. Moreover, Vladek met a French, non-Jewish prisoner, to whom he taught English. Able to receive food packages as a non-Jew, the prisoner sustains Vladek with both food and friendship.

Specifically concerning the voluntary covenant, *Maus* reveals several important points. For example, the biblical paradigm of an intervening deity and a coercive covenant are no longer credible. Nor is the assertion that "we are punished for our sins." The rabbinic paradigm of Purim, for its part, is also inappropriate when dealing with the relationship between God and Auschwitz. Unlike in ancient Shushan, where Mordechai prophesied that "relief and deliverance will come to the Jews from some other place," in Auschwitz help came from no place. If God was hidden in the death camps, human actions were also under close scrutiny. However, like Mordechai Kole, Vladek may have been too quick to dismiss God. The logic of theology permits or, better, demands that one not stop looking for God based solely on empirical evidence and that the nature and function of the deity assume different form according to a particular historical cycle.

Perhaps more accurate is Wiesel's observation that in Auschwitz God was not a theological topic but, rather, the "extra bowl of soup, pushed at you or stolen from you, simply because the man ahead of you is either stronger or quicker than you."[63] In Auschwitz, Wiesel continues, "God . . . cannot be found in humble or grandiloquent phrases, but in a crust of bread."[64] The existence of extermination centers and death camps impoverishes both humanity and God. The God of the voluntary covenant, attests Greenberg, neither commands nor intrudes in human history. Quite the contrary is true. If God was in Auschwitz, then God was "starving, broken, humiliated, gassed and burned alive, sharing the infinite pain as only an infinite capacity for pain can share it."[65] Rather, the burden of the covenant now shifts to humanity and human action. Moreover, Vladek insists that Art have a bar mitzvah, thereby validating the importance in his own Post-Auschwitz life of the centrality of this Jewish rite of passage. In addition, Françoise converts to Judaism in order to honor Vladek's wishes.

I contend neither that Spiegelman is a theologian nor that he is a practicing Jew. His own attestations indicate a very different conclusion. With Richard Rubenstein, he believes that Auschwitz destroyed the possibility of believing in God. Consequently, *Maus* functions on one level as Spiegelman's *din Torah*. With Finkelstein, he puts the notion of a covenantal deity on trial. Unlike Finkelstein, however, Spiegelman assumes that all the evidence is in and that God is guilty. Thus, Spiegelman's definition of Judaism is distinctly contemporary; having nothing to do with either *halakha* or classical texts. Rather, his second-generation identity is imposed with brutal clarity by the Holocaust. For instance, the author of *Maus* contends that he is "very completely a Jew and that of course has been driven home by having to understand what happened to my parents."[66]

Spiegelman bears second-generation witness despite his own feelings of ambivalence about the tradition. Unlike either Friedmann or Finkelstein, each of whom attempts to affirm a positive sense of the meaning of being Jewish after Auschwitz, Spiegelman feels that this type of identification is parochial. For example, he strenuously rejects the label of Jewish writer and appears estranged from traditional Jewish rituals. Further, he views his Jewish identity as a "kind of diaspora alienation that comes with this peculiar imposition of an identity."[67] Yet Spiegelman is clearly a son of Job. His own witness forms a link in the chain of Holocaust transmission. For example, he dedicated *Maus I* to Anja, and inscribes *Maus II* to the memory of Richieu and his own daughter Najda, the third generation.

*Maus* tells a particular tale but its message is universal. For example, the cat and mouse format strikes a resonant cross-cultural and international chord. But Spiegelman's work is rigorously particularistic in graphically depicting the results of history's deadliest example of Jew-hatred. Further, his work focuses an unblinking eye on the continuing suffering imposed by the *Shoah* on its survivors and their offspring. Although Spiegelman contends that he did not intend his work to be a corrective to various forms of nationalist antisemitism, he is "grateful that it's perceived as having some social use."[68] If, Spiegelman opines, *Maus* "makes people rethink that moment [the Holocaust] and the consequences of that one moment in recent history, I'm glad for that."[69] But Art Spiegelman's work is less a crusade against antisemitism than it is a personal testimony of how the Holocaust both shapes and is shaped by second-generation identity.

## SHORT STORIES: A BIOGRAPHICAL NOTE

Melvin Jules Bukiet, J. J. Steinfeld, and Thane Rosenbaum are three sons of Job who have written short stories reflecting the impact of the Holocaust on their identity as second-generation witnesses. Bukiet, formerly literary editor of *Tikkun* magazine, was born in New York City and grew up among Polish survivors. His father survived Auschwitz, while his mother was born in New Jersey. A freelance writer, who teaches creative writing at Sarah Lawrence, his *Stories of an Imaginary Childhood* won the 1993 Edward Lewis Wallant Award. Following this he published a second collection of short stories entitled *While the Messiah Tarries*. J. J. Steinfeld is a Canadian writer. He was born in a Displaced Persons camp in Munich. Both his parents were Polish Jews; his mother was in Auschwitz and his father survived in hiding. Steinfeld won the 1990 Creative Writing Award from the Toronto Jewish Congress Book Committee. Thane Rosenbaum teaches Jewish literature and the Holocaust at the New School for Social Research as well as a course in Human Rights at Fordham University Law School. Born in Washington Heights, Rosenbaum left his position as an attorney, where he was significantly involved in his firm's pro bono service, to pursue writing and teaching. Neither his mother, who had been in Maidanek, nor his father, who survived Bergen-Belsen, spoke about the Holocaust when the author was a child. Consequently, he views writing as a "compensation for the years of childhood silence."[70] Although their writings differ in style and tone, each author is rigorously particularist in confronting the issue of their Jewish identity after the *Shoah*.

## STORIES OF AN IMAGINARY CHILDHOOD AND WHILE THE MESSIAH TARRIES

Melvin Jules Bukiet's stories seek to retrieve a "golden age" in Jewish life by writing about the shtetl of Proszowice. Bukiet reports that his father "spoke of the shtetl constantly."[71] Thus, as a child, he thought that Proszowice, along with London, Paris, and Rome, was one of Europe's four major cities. But this collection of stories, which the author wrote because of and for his father, is not an attempt to recreate the shtetl. Rather, Bukiet attempts to inscribe his life as it might have been in a Jewish world now vanished. In so doing, he retrieves a portion of that world, with all its hopes, illusions, and prayers. His twelve stories, narrated by a nameless but perceptive twelve-year-old boy, emphasize the innocence of Europe's Jews on the eve of the *Shoah*. Unknowingly poised on the edge of a precipice, the Jews of Proszowice speak across the abyss of time and murder.

Bukiet's is an imaginative as well as a literary achievement. Unlike the other second-generation witness writers, his work deals not with the aftermath of the *Shoah* but rather with its prologue. As such, it pays homage both to survivor memory and second-generation imagination. Consequently, *Stories of an Imaginary Childhood*[72] recreates a Jewish world lived largely under the sacred canopy of tradition. Far from sentimentalizing or idealizing this world, however, Bukiet's tales reveal that under this canopy there lived a variety of Jewish people whose ethical and moral standards were neither better nor worse than those of their neighbors. These shtetl inhabitants include con men, such as Isaac the Millionaire; prostitutes, including the three-hundred-pound Rebecca; Isaac, the philosophical gravedigger; and the shrewish Shivka Bellet. All of these people were destined for extermination.

Bukiet renders their descriptions in a manner that recalls the work of I. B. Singer. Demons and dybbuks are every bit as real as trees and grass.

Bukiet's tightly written prose evokes biblical themes and Yiddish curses, ancient faith and modern skepticism. Rabbinic wisdom is pitted against the lure of emigration to America. As the nameless narrator nears his bar mitzvah, he experiences conflicting feelings of allegiance; ancestral teachings compete with the attractions of assimilation. "Torquemada," the last story in Bukiet's collection, is a complex dream-tale. Unlike the dream of Joseph, however, this story details centuries of Jewish persecution while claiming that Christians hate Jews because Jews hate themselves. Awaking from his frightening dream, the narrator is comforted by his father, who naïvely states: "it's the twentieth century of civilized man. . . . What harm could possibly come to us in 1928?" Unlike the father, Bukiet's readers can supply the answer to that question.

Bukiet, like many second-generation witnesses, goes on a pilgrimage to Auschwitz. Accompanying his father and other survivors on this journey, the author writes about his experience:

> Seeing and thinking about the Holocaust may be as difficult as living it, not the hurt of the body, not in the specific searing memories, but in having to face a universe that will allow such evil. Life is not as it used to be once it contains Auschwitz.[73]

Bukiet's observation, like that of the other authors in this study, focuses attention on the loss of innocence after Auschwitz. The earth has indeed become what Spiegelman calls a "Hell planet."

My remaining remarks will focus on the issue of this son of Job's attempt to more fully comprehend his Jewish identity. Bukiet's work is a literary expression of the necessity of delving into Jewish history in order to more fully know one's heritage. Mindful of the impossibility of imagining the *Shoah*, Bukiet instead attempts to articulate how the legacy of pre-Holocaust Jewish life informs his own sense of Jewish selfhood. Impelled by his father's Holocaust history, the author seeks to explore the calm before the storm; as such, his work is a variant of Finkielkraut's imaginary Jew.

This attempt to imagine a pre-Holocaust Jewish consciousness distinguishes Bukiet's second-generation writing. Yet he articulates a distinctively second-generation lesson concerning remembrance. "The deliberate remembrance, the refusal to forget," he writes, "the commitment this entails for creating a life worth living in a better future, whether this means America, Israel, or something within the individual self, is the only free choice we have to make."[74] With Wiesel, Bukiet views memory in salvific terms. It is nothing less than the path to achieving a *tikkun atzmi*.

Bukiet's second collection of short stories, *While the Messiah Tarries*,[75] is a superbly written collection of short stories whose protagonists collectively struggle to seek meaning in the face of an anomic and spiritually empty world. The purpose of these struggles, although unknown to the protagonists, appears to either hasten the coming of Messiah or to reveal precisely the power of evil that delays this coming. Furthermore, the title itself bears a twofold significance. It refers on the one hand to Maimonides' twelfth principle of faith: "I believe with perfect faith in the coming of the Messiah. Even though he may tarry, despite this I believe." Additionally, as Bukiet notes in the epigraph, this messianic credo was "recited by some European Jews entering the gas chambers."[76]

Two of the collections's nine stories deal specifically with the Holocaust. Although ostensibly neither is directly concerned with second-generation issues, both "Himmler's Chickens" and "The Library of Moloch" provide distinct angles of vision concerning responses to the *Shoah*. "Himmler's Chickens" treats two crucial themes: the role played by the Holocaust as a source of Jewish identity, and the ease with which the *Shoah* can fade from *Jewish* consciousness. Both have implications for the second-generation witness. Edgar Kahn is a middle-aged attorney whose life is defined by mediocrity. Unlike his immigrant father, Kahn is only marginally Jewish. As a ten-year-old child, however, he recalls seeing newsreel footage of Bergen-Belsen so savage that it compelled him to "slam his eyes shut." Forty years later, Kahn is a bill-collector whose office is in a rundown section of Passaic, New Jersey. He is irresistibly drawn by an advertisement in the Military Mans' Bookshop offering to sell a home movie of Heinrich Himmler, Hitler's second-in-command, killing his barnyard chickens near the end of the war. This sets in motion a chain of events that Kahn knows "has to do with God." Kahn's subsequent dealings with the Nazi who sells the film, and who has a miniature death camp in his home, serve both to sicken the attorney and to enhance his sense of Jewish identity. Concluding his purchase, Kahn rushes out of the house and fights evil the only way available to him: by throwing the film into the polluted waters of the Passaic river.

"The Library of Moloch" is an exquisitely wrought piece that raises questions about the role of oral history archives and the subsequent tendency to "package" (i.e., desanctify) survivor testimony. Originally established as a public relations gesture by a university "eager to balance the scale of public opinion" after one of its faculty members had been exposed as a wartime collaborator, the library "sought no less than a moral explication of the universe." The stories of the witnesses "were equivalent to their souls." Yet, the library itself is described in terms of death; it is a "mausoleum" whose librarians are "gravediggers." What of the survivors themselves? "The hell with them."[77]

The tale's dénouement comes in an encounter between a female survivor and the director of the library. The two literally live in different worlds. While she was in Auschwitz, he grew up in Bala Cynwyd on Philadelphia's main line. Her deep cynicism undercuts the director's self-righteousness. She questions the library's fundamental assumptions, e.g., that survivor testimony will prevent future genocides and that all survivors want to remember. Further, the woman objects to the very term *survivor*, as it suggests personal ability as opposed to luck. Rather, she prefers to think of her peers as "merely remainders, or the remains." Additionally, the interviewers are "jackals" feeding on the "last tasty flesh" that sticks to the bones of the witnesses. Echoing the mishnaic warning about tampering with forbidden matters (*Hagigah* 14b), the mysterious woman survivor tells the director, "There is only one sentence for those who tamper with forbidden mysteries" (194).

Alone, the director falls asleep; his cigarette sets the room ablaze. Restating the talmudic legend attesting that when the Jerusalem Temple was in flames the priests threw the keys heavenwards, Bukiet describes the tapes of testimony afire: "the words of the witnesses escaped." The story ends when the director, himself engulfed by flames, watches his recently completed interview of the woman. Earlier she had told him that there are two inviolate realms, one of which is memory. Now, in response to the director's frenzied query, she responds that the second such realm is theology. Bukiet echoes the position of Wiesel in drawing attention to the sacrality of survivor testimony. Those who deal with this testimony are required to recognize that "the ground on which they stand is holy." Fire can purify or it can destroy. Unlike the director, second-generation witnesses do not assume that they can analyze, catalogue, and classify survivor information and by these actions fully understand their parents experience. On the contrary, like Fackenheim, Greenberg, and Wiesel, they view survivor testimony as sacrosanct.

## DANCING AT THE CLUB HOLOCAUST
## AND FORMS OF CAPTIVITY AND ESCAPE

J. J. Steinfeld is a Canadian second-generation witness whose stories are especially strong in their grappling with the *Shoah*'s psychic legacy, detailing the emotional pain of those who inherit the Holocaust. Unlike Bukiet's father, Steinfeld's father remained silent about the Holocaust.[78] The Canadian writer's protagonists are children and grandchildren of survivors. Most are portrayed as writers, professors, or graduate students; some are artists. Many are divorced, some are separated. Despite their societal roles, all share two characteristics: they live on the margins of society and they are consumed by their Holocaust legacy. In fact, many seem trapped in and by the past. Further, Auschwitz casts a heavy pall over the protagonists' Canadian existence. In one protagonist's words, second-generation Holocaust memories are "inherited like eye colour or facial features" ("Starring at Auschwitz," 138).[79]

All of Steinfeld's protagonists share the dilemma of the witness. As articulated by Primo Levi, this dilemma involves the tension between the need to testify and the realization that no one is listening.[80] For example, the rage and anguish of the second generation stands in sharp contrast to the docility of the Canadians with whom they interact. Steinfeld underscores this rage by employing language that is jarring and culturally discordant, a searing indictment of the dissonance that exists between the Holocaust and the indifference of Canadian culture. His second-generation protagonists utilize words like daggers that rip at the heart of complacency.

Several second-generation themes emerge in Steinfeld's Holocaust stories. As with the novelists whose works we have examined, he treats the second-generation experience of the death of the innocent ("The Funeral") and the experience of growing up in a home where "deep memory" effectively silences communication between survivors and their offspring ("The Coinciding of Sosnowiec, Upper Silesia, Poland, 1942, and Banff, Alberta, Canada, 1990"). Further, the issue of second-generation guilt is a common theme in his work ("Ida Solomon's Play"), as is the mimetic replication of survivor parents' Holocaust experiences ("Academic Freedom"). On the theological level, many of the survivor parents embrace Fackenheim's notion of the "614th Commandment," seeing in their children's accomplishments a triumph over Hitler and Nazism ("The Star of David").

The issue of second-generation guilt plays a large role in Steinfeld's work. Some of his protagonists feel guilty for not having been in Auschwitz; others wish that they could have taken their parents' place. Further, some feel that after the Holocaust Jews can never be at ease in history. Still others believe that the Holocaust is too crushing a burden; they lose their minds. Steinfeld's second-generation protagonists differ, however, from their American counterparts in one important respect. Unlike the latter, the Canadians are intent on revenge. Many of Steinfeld's characters fantasize about burning, shooting, or otherwise destroying Nazis, German sympathizers, Holocaust deniers, and locations that serve as gathering spots for antisemites.

Such vengeance is dramatically portrayed in "Dancing at the Club Holocaust." Here, a psychiatrist believes that his second-generation patient is fantasizing about a club in New York City that caters to Nazis who ritually humiliate those of their members designated as "Jews." The analyst wants to refer his client to another specialist. But more than that, the client's chaotic and violent imaginings stand in sharp contrast to the analyst's orderly world. The reader discovers that the club actually does exist, at least for the patient, whose mother, a dancer before the war, was tortured by the Nazis and is unable to use her legs. In keeping with the flames of the *Shoah*, the protagonist torches the nightclub. Unlike Wiesel, for whom memory itself is a form of vengeance, Steinfeld's protagonists advocate a physical act of violence against German Nazis.

Vengeance of a different type appears in the short story entitled "History." This tale is in the volume *Forms of Captivity and Escape*, which the author dedicates to the memory of his parents, and deals with the second-generation wish to undo history. Set in 1927 Germany, it tells of a failed assassination attempt on the life of Hitler. The assassin, who kills a body-guard rather than his intended target, tells his companions that there were just too many guards. Steinfeld's brief story is also an attack on the intellectuals who did not take the threat of Nazism seriously. For instance, the failed assassin is derisively termed the *thinker*. As the mans' companions beat him, he claims that he will kill Hitler the next day. History, however, cannot be undone.

"Because of the War" is arguably the best crafted and richest story in Steinfeld's collection. He creatively portrays how the Holocaust legacy is inherited by succeeding generations, deftly juxtaposing the traditional ritual of bar mitzvah and the continuing impact of the *Shoah* on the third generation. Matthew is the son of a mixed, and now failed, marriage. Nearing the time of his bar mitzvah, he receives a large package bearing no return address. Opening it, the youth discovers two disparate types of gifts that underscore the dual nature of Matthew's identity: he is Canadian, and he is a grandchild of Job. On the one hand, the package holds dozens of valuable hockey cards, and a book of poems by Robert Service. The other gifts are a Yiddish book, a black yarmulke (skullcap), and a large illustrated spiral notebook containing the words "I am an earthworm Jew."

Speaking with his mother, Matthew learns the history of these gifts and his own Holocaust legacy. His uncle Bernie is the sender of the package. Tova, the boy's mother, explains that their father had given the Yiddish book to her brother when he was about Matthew's age. Further, Bernie had worn the yarmulke at his own bar mitzvah. Although the boy has not seen his uncle in the nine years since his grandmother's funeral, the youth hopes that he will attend his bar mitzvah, as there is no possibility of his Christian father so doing.

Matthew learns about the *Shoah* by indirection. Tova's sharing of her own childhood links the boy to his grandparents and, through them, to the Holocaust. He learns that his grandfather, a reticent man, read from the Yiddish book every evening, explaining to Tova and Bernie that it told about Polish Jews before Auschwitz. The father only commented that the book's author had probably died in a concentration camp. Steinfeld indicates the *Shoah*'s painful psychic legacy for both its survivors and their offspring. He describes the youth's grandmother as having a worn body that always seemed to say: "Enough pain, enough pain . . ." (259). As for Bernie, four days before his bar mitzvah he "already considered himself a man. A man going crazy at twelve years old" (259). The stress of being a son of Job leaves the youth with tension headaches "and a yearning to live under the ground, protected like an earthworm. 'I am an earthworm Jew' he wrote over and over in a large spiral notebook" (259–60). Like Finkelstein's Szuster family, Bernie attempts to hide from the Holocaust.[81]

Unlike the survivors in the novels of Friedmann and Finkelstein, however, Steinfeld's survivors in "Because of the War" are neither Orthodox nor religious. But they are unmistakably Jewish and eagerly embrace this identity. Steinfeld describes them in terms that bring to mind Spiegelman's parents. He writes: "The parents were not religious, but they would not allow their children to forget they were Jewish. Life had taught them that lesson" (260). Thus, the parents' Jewishness is based primarily on Fackenheim's 614th commandment. As children of survivors, Bernard and Tova remember that their earliest recollections were of the tattooed number on their mother's arm. All of Bernard's attempts to learn about the Holocaust, about his parents' ill health, and why he had no living grandparents were met with the same response. "Because of the War."

In school, Tova and Bernard respond differently to their Holocaust legacy. The young girl draws pictures of, and writes stories about, her mother's tattoo, for which she receives good grades. Bernard, on the other hand, eschews the cerebral. Those annoying him he calls "Nazis." Moreover, his quick temper and mood swings are further indications of the youth's anger. Bernard also bears the burden of carrying the name of his father's older brother, who was murdered by the Nazis. Although he recites his *haftorah* (prophetic) portion flawlessly and subsequently becomes a well-known sports announcer, Bernard remains deeply troubled by the continuing impact of the *Shoah*.

Steinfeld ends his story symbolically. Emerging from the synagogue after his bar mitzvah, Tova and Matthew see a man sitting in a car. Recognizing her brother, Tova shouts his name. But he drives away. Responding to her son's query about why Bernard did not stay, Tova surprises herself by uttering the phrase "Because of the War." She thinks perhaps her brother may someday find a place where everyone was safe and no one would have to say that phrase. But it is clear that Bernard has not yet achieved a *tikkun atzmi*. This tale is important on a variety of levels. It reveals that the Holocaust is not an event that ceased effecting people in 1945. Additionally, Steinfeld is one of the few writers who attempts to deal with the third generation. In so doing he reveals both the differences in knowledge between generations as the *Shoah* recedes in time, and the fact that the Holocaust still addresses, even if in a more oblique manner, the third generation, who must now begin their own means of shaping memory of the catastrophe. Finally, like Friedmann's juxtaposition of biblical begetting and death-camp names, Steinfeld's linking of biblical and Holocaust legacy underscores the concern of the second-generation witness to seek appropriate ritual modes in order to transmit the tale of the *Shoah* to succeeding generations.

## ELIJAH VISIBLE

Thane Rosenbaum's stories comprise a carefully crafted series of reflections on the psychological legacy of the *Shoah*. The nine tales in this collection sensitively probe issues of loss and mourning that accompany the attempt of a second-generation witness to come to terms with his Holocaust inheritance. Viewed through the eyes of Adam Posner, the protagonist in each of Rosenbaum's stories, the continual *presence* of the Holocaust *absence* is portrayed at various stages of Posner's life cycle and in different geographical locations. In one story, "The Little Blue Snowman of Washington Heights," he is a kindergarten pupil whose hypervigilant survivor parents constantly warn him about the dangers of the outside world. The school nurse comments on the effects of their continual drilling the youth for catastrophe: "The parents have turned this poor little boy into a concentration camp survivor, and he wasn't even in the camps!"[82] In another tale, "An Act of Defiance," he is a professor of Holocaust studies obsessed with the *Shoah*. Yet he feels guilty for *not* having been in Auschwitz. Like Friedmann's Jason Kole and several of Steinfeld's protagonists, Adam Posner realizes that "[he] wasn't there, in Poland, among the true martyrs. Everything about [his] rage was borrowed" (59). The protagonist is also portrayed as a New York City attorney, an abstract expressionist painter, a prep school sophomore, and a 10-year-old. Geographically, he lives in Atlantic City, Miami, and New York City. By means of this post-modern aesthetic that collapses time and space, Rosenbaum illustrates the continuing impact of the Holocaust on the children of Job.

Born in 1960 in Washington Heights, Rosenbaum notes that his parents moved to Miami when he was 8 or 9 in "a conscious decision to get away from refugees and survivors."[83] Unlike many of the other second-generation witnesses in this study, the author observes that most of his friends were not children of survivors. Yet, now married and himself a parent, he attests that his second-generation legacy makes him "part of an army where there is no possibility of draft-dodging."[84] The continuing impact of the Holocaust on the children of Job is visually portrayed on the dust jacket and the book's inside cover. A young man, presumably Rosenbaum, chin in hand, is clearly perplexed. Dressed partially in a suit and partially in the stripped garb of a death camp inmate, the son of Job is framed both by a *magen David* and a motorcycle. One foot has a shoe, the other is bare. Like Spiegelman's image of the Nazi guard's rifle pointing at the author's head, this drawing attests to the impact of the *Shoah* on contemporary Jewish identity. Further, it re-enforces the sense of loss felt by the second-generation. The book, however, also exemplifies the search for *tikkun atzmi*. For example, Rosenbaum attests that writing *Elijah Visible* was an attempt to know his deceased parents better.[85]

Rosenbaum casts a relentless eye on key second-generation concerns. For instance, flawed parenting and the death imprint form the core of "The Pants in the Family," "Bingo by the Bungalow" and "Lost, in a Sense." The latter story also deals with the issue of unwarranted suffering and untimely death. Cancer claims the life of the father of Adam's best friend. Neither of the boys are ever the same following this "premature, cruel, and uncalled for" loss. Like Finkelstein's Brenda Szuster and Art Spiegelman in this chapter, and Julie Salamon in chapter 4, Rosenbaum's protagonist confronts the issue of the death of innocents and theodicy thereby being initiated into the world of gratuitous pain and suffering; a universe that victims of the Holocaust inhabited without surcease. "Cattle Car Complex," for its part, illustrates the power of the *Shoah* in the unconscious life of the second-generation. In this avatar, Posner is an attorney trapped in an elevator. The elevator car metamorphizes into a cattle car. Adam calls for help, but his condition grows progressively worse; physically, his glasses break, his suit rumples, and he soils himself. Psychically, he becomes undone. Imagining himself a Jew in war-time Europe, Posner delivers soliloquies in which he outlines Jewish suffering and berates the Germans. Finally freed from his physical prison, he remains a psychological captive. As the elevator doors open, he wonders, like the doomed souls in Auschwitz, whether to stand in the line at the left or the right. Similarly, in "An Act of Defiance," Adam is a teacher of the Holocaust whose second-generation status leaves him phobic and pessimistic about the human condition. Mourning and loss continue long after the *Shoah* as an historically anchored event has ended.

*Elijah Visible* also explores the process by which the Holocaust is transmitted between generations while articulating both the second-generation mission and various images of survivors. Adam Posner believes that his legacy is transmitted genetically. Beyond, or, in addition to verbal means, the children of Job are biologically informed about their patrimony. Rosenbaum writes: "Parental reminiscences had become the genetic material . . . passed on by survivors to their children" (5). Again, in keeping with the genetic image of inheritance Adam Posner muses: "My DNA may be forever coded with the filmy stuff of damaged offspring, the handicap of an unwarranted inheritance" (63). Moreover, the author confides that while he was not "paralyzed as a child" [by the Holocaust], he "soaked in [and absorbed the pain] in some mystical way."[86] While the second-generation mission is to bear witness, there is a recognition of the difference between survivors and the children of Job. For example, musing on his relationship to his uncle, Adam Posner the teacher observes: "Haskell was the last one. The lone survivor. The passer of the torch. And then there was me, filled with fear of a fumble" (62). Rosenbaum portrays a variety of survivor images. For instance, survivors are, as noted above, "damaged goods." Yet, they are also portrayed as life-affirming. Uncle Haskell, for his part, adopts a type of Fackenheimian "614th Commandment" in observing: ". . . my life, with all the riches and pleasures that I allow myself, is an act of defiance." Unlike his phobic nephew, Haskell vigorously embraces life. He exclaims to his nephew: "I am an assassin to their mission" (66). These conflicting survivor images are reminiscent of Helmreich's observation cited above in chapter 1 and underscore the complexity of psychosocial dynamics in survivor families.

Rosenbaum's work also explores the corrosive effects of modernity on Judaism. Post-Holocaust Jewish life in America teeters on the edge of oblivion. The attenuation of the tradition is seen in a variety of ways: the loss of God; ignorance of Hebrew; and not knowing how to pray. However, much in the manner of Greenberg and Wiesel, the author links bearing second-generation witness to the revitalization of Judaism. "Romancing the Yohrzeit [sic] Light," "The Pants in the Family," and the title story place these issues in focus. Focusing briefly on "The Pants in the Family" the reader sees both the deterioration of Judaism and intimations of continuity. After learning that Mrs. Posner is terminally ill, Adam and his father go to a little used shul, "a memorial to the rituals of the past. . . ." Neither Posner can read Hebrew. Nor do they know which prayers to say. Nevertheless, the survivor conducts his own *din Torah* by "roaring like a wounded lion" (47). Shouting at God is a protest, but one that comes from within Judaism. Furthermore, following his mother's death, Adam and his father grow closer emotionally and the survivor begins sharing his Holocaust experiences with the youth thereby insuring the continuity of witnessing to the *Shoah* and its aftermath.

"Elijah Visible" specifically links survivor testimony and the role played by Elijah the prophet. Like Elijah of antiquity, survivor testimony is holiness in disguise. Both the biblical prophet and Auschwitz survivors, suggests Rosenbaum, bear a salvific message. Although the theological position of this story is more implicit than overt, Rosenbaum draws the reader's attention to crucial post-Auschwitz issues for the children of Job. Adam Posner appears in this tale as a teacher who attends his cousins' Passover seder. Appalled at their indifference to ritual, Adam calls the seder a "sacrilege, a disgrace, a *shande.*" The real cause of tension, however, is a letter from their cousin Artur, a survivor who lives in Belgium. While the American cousins had been raised in "calculated silence" about the past, recalling Helmreich's observation about the "curtain of silence," Artur sends a list of all their relatives murdered in the *Shoah.* Further, the survivor charges them with a mission: "You must live a life that gives meaning to their death, and comfort to their souls. We must learn the lessons from the fire" (96–97).

Artur's letter receives two vastly different interpretations. Adam's cousins, Sylvia and Miriam, believe that the old man wants to extort money. Adam, for his part, understands that Artur is "trying to save us all." Adam then tells his cousins stories that their parents had withheld: Adam's father saved their father's life in the camps; Artur, a child in Auschwitz, had been marked for selection on several occasions; Sylvia and Miriam's father was married before the war. The Nazis murdered his first wife. This last piece of news unnerves Miriam. After showing them a picture of the first wife, silence descends on the room. The cousins begin carefully reading Artur's letter, like a sacred scroll, although it is hard news to take. While Elijah did not come to the Posner home that evening, the next day Artur purchased a plane ticket so that he could visit his cousins.

Rosenbaum intentionally sets the tale at Passover, a time of liberation from oppression. In this case, it is the oppression of silence about, and ignorance of, the *Shoah* from which the cousins are to be liberated. Further, while the traditional Elijah does not appear—the wine cup from which the prophet drinks remains full—Artur is on the way. This linking of the two figures is crucial. For one thing, Rosenbaum's story suggests that through silence and ignorance the chain of transmission of the *Shoah* is in danger of being broken. Therefore, owing to the precariousness of the situation, it is necessary that Elijah, or Elijah-like figures shed the traditional role of invisibility.[87] Further, as Greenberg notes, tales of the witnesses constitute a secular Bible. Bearing witness to these tales is an act of holiness. Moreover, Rosenbaum adopts a Wieselian position in implying that listening to a witness makes of one a witness.

Rosenbaum explicitly engages the theological dimension of post-Auschwitz Judaism in "The Rabbi Double-Faults." Rabbi Sheldon Vered is apparently an apostate; playboy, unscholarly, and avid tennis buff, he seems indifferent to the Jewish religion. Aside from women, his passion is tennis which he plays wearing a black arm brace. Surprising his congregants, Rabbi Vered introduces his twin brother, Rabbi Joseph Rose from Israel, at a Shabbat service. Unlike his Florida twin, whom he has not seen in 30 years, when Rabbi Rose delivers his *derash* (sermon), he cites biblical and talmudic sources. His reverence for God and the tradition is clear.

Rabbi Rose informs the congregation of his family history. A staunch Zionist, he left Poland in 1936 to settle in Israel. Shortly thereafter the Nazis murdered his family and sent his twin brother to Auschwitz. Prior to the Holocaust, Sheldon was the most brilliant student in school, passionate about learning and about God. Thinking all his family had been killed, Joseph Rose "decided to return to God" and became a rabbi. Joseph Rose tells the congregation that a rabbi's job is "always to give his congregation a sense of God's presence" (139).

The tale's theology is articulated in a wager made on the tennis court. Unlike the wager argument of the French philosopher Pascal, however, the stance of Rabbi Vered challenges a deity weakened by the Holocaust. Vered invites Adam, who has recently become a bar mitzvah, to join him, his brother, and another person for a game of doubles. The youth is to team with Vered's brother. Although Adam has reservations about Rabbi Vered, his parents are delighted that a fellow survivor wants to include their son. They tell him: "In a way you are related to [Rabbi Vered]." As the match wears on, the weather grows increasingly worse. Dark clouds gather and a severe storm threatens. The weather is, however, no match for the theological storm that rages between the two brothers. The survivor is set apart from his twin by virtue of the Holocaust. He no longer believes in God, and rejects the Jobian model of unquestioning obedience. He taunts both God and his brother, telling Rabbi Joseph: "You speak as a rabbi who knows God but doesn't. I don't speak of God because I'm afraid I do know him" (146).

The agreed upon wager deals with the role of theological skepticism after Auschwitz. If Rabbi Vered and his partner win, then Joseph must re-vision God. No longer the deity who intervenes in history, lacking omniscience and in no way omnipotent; God is diminished (Wiesel and Greenberg), or on vacation (Martin Buber's "eclipse of God"), or absent (Rubenstein's "death of God"). In other words, Joseph must show his congregation "a different side of God," the one that his survivor brother saw in Auschwitz. If, on the other hand, Rabbi Rose and Adam win, then it must be Rabbi Vered who re-visions the role of God, returning the deity to the synagogue and reading from the Torah.

The foursome agree to play a tiebreaker. As Rabbi Vered serves, his armbrace falls away revealing the Auschwitz number tattooed on his arm. His brother stares at the number in horror. It is Joseph's turn to serve. He double-faults. Rabbi Vered wins and the heavens open. Alone on the court, Sheldon Vered begins a hasidic dance, "mumbling Hebrew words of revelation, spinning joyously in the luminous rain" (155).

Rosenbaum's exploration of the possibility of faith after Auschwitz leads to several important, if tentative, conclusions. Both brothers have an epiphany; Sheldon Vered's occurs in Auschwitz, his brother's illumination comes on the tennis court when he witnesses Vered's tattoo. With Wiesel, both men come to understand that God must never be justified at the expense of humanity. The deity must be constantly interrogated. Further, both brothers implicitly agree with Greenberg's observation: ". . . it is not so critical what position one takes after the Holocaust, as long as one is ashamed of it."[88] Moreover, Rabbi Vered's "Hasidic dance" at the end of the story is a continuation of his argument with God. But his defiance is one of profound disappointment, calling to mind Wiesel's observation that on Rosh HaShanah in Auschwitz he "had ceased to plead" (with God). "I felt very strong. I was the accuser, God the accused."[89]

Specifically concerning the second-generation attitude towards faith and doubt, Adam's witness will now incorporate an interrogation of God as part of his own Jewish identity. Too young for theological sophistication, it had been he who suggested to Rabbi Rose that his brother be made to introduce God and Torah in the services, Adam learns that Auschwitz fundamentally calls into question basic assumptions about the relationship between God and historical events, chosenness, and covenant. Adam's lesson is one that emerges from Greenberg's voluntary covenant; after Auschwitz, Jews cannot be compelled to accept the covenant. Rather, the Jewish people voluntarily agree to live their lives Jewishly. Moreover, this son of Job takes several steps that bring closer his embrace of Jewish self-affirmation; one of the dimensions of Wiesel's additional covenant. For instance, he becomes a bar mitzvah; he is told of the connection between survivors and the second-generation - thus opening the possibility of achieving solidarity between the generations, another characteristic of the additional covenant; and the tennis match reveals the complexity of the post-Auschwitz relationship between God, historical events, and Jewish identity.

## CONCLUSION

This chapter has shown that the contemporary children of Job who pursue a particularist response to the *Shoah* seek to clarify their own relationship to Judaism and their Jewish identity. All have undertaken an odyssey that led them to more fully explore the Holocaust and their parents' experience during the *Shoah*. Whether growing up in an urban environment (all but Finkelstein's protagonist did this) or on a farm, each of the particularist second-generation witnesses began with the knowledge that his or her parents were survivors. But this knowledge initially serves more to obfuscate rather than clarify each witness's own identity. The protagonists in these works are profoundly disappointed in God. Rather than rejecting Judaism, however, they seek a *tikkun* of the self and the tradition by means of adopting post-Auschwitz ritual forms and, with the possible exception of Spiegelman, display a (largely unarticulated) voluntary commitment to sojourn on the path that perpetuates Judaism after Auschwitz.

We turn next to an examination of second-generation novels that treat the *Shoah*'s universal lessons. These novels speak in terms of a mission to improve society (*tikkun olam*) and the necessity of teaching the world compassion.

# CHAPTER 4

# *Second-Generation Novels and Short Stories: Jewish Universalism*

We know only too well that Auschwitz, Treblinka, and Bergen-Belsen represent the ultimate consequences of anti-Semitism as well as all other forms of racial, ethnic or religious hatred. It is therefore *our* obligation—as much as if not more than anyone else's—to fight against these phenomena whenever and wherever they occur. For it is only thus that we can justify our existence as human beings and Jews in the aftermath of the Holocaust.
—Menachem Z. Rosensaft[1]

Second-generation writers whose works are examined in this chapter emphasize what they perceive to be the *Shoah*'s universal message. Their universalism, however, does not deny their Jewish identity but rather fulfills it. Collectively, their novels are an appeal for a type of *tikkun olam*—a repair or mending of the world—in which all forms of antisemitism, homophobia, and racism are abolished. Moreover, these second-generation witnesses also seek to achieve a *tikkun* of the self whereby they bear witness in a manner that is healing. This distinguishes them from many of the protagonists in J. J. Steinfeld's work, who appear unable to relate to either nonwitnessing Jews or to the non-Jewish world at large. Further, in an attempt to transform their Holocaust legacy and to understand their parents' experience, many children of survivors—as Jack Nusan Porter observes—embrace a "wide variety of creative political and religious action."[2] These activities may be either particularist or universal in nature.

As we saw in the preceding chapter, the particularist writers focus on issues of post-Auschwitz Jewish identity, family relations, images of survivors, theological rebellion, and the continuing threat of antisemitism. The authors of the short story collections speak, respectively, of a "back to the future" endeavor whose goal is to imagine a different legacy (i.e., living one's life in a shtetl on the eve of the Holocaust); the role played by the *Shoah* in contemporary Jewish life; the dominance of Holocaust imagery in the life of the second-generation witness that leads in turn to a quest for vengeance; and the feelings of loss and mourning coupled with an implicit second-generation theology.

Universalist writers, for their part, raise similar questions, but in the context of articulating the broader societal implications of antisemitism and the *Shoah*. For example, this *tikkun* of witnessing reflects a moral mission. Recalling Eliezer Ben-Yehuda's definition of *tikkun olam* as "something for the good of the world," the universalist second-generation authors seek the *tikkun* of ordinary decency. This decency is expressed in a variety of ways: Carol Ascher's *The Flood* speaks out against American racism; Julie Salamon's *White Lies* deals—at least in part—with a deeply flawed and morally corrupting political system that yields second-generation welfare mothers; while Lev Raphael's *Dancing on Tisha B'Av* and *Winter Eyes* link antisemitism to the phenomenon of homophobia on the one hand, and, on the other hand, reveal the psychological devastation wrought by the Holocaust on the lives of its survivors and their offspring.

These second-generation writings have, in addition, great theological resonance. For example, they underscore the breakdown of pre-*Shoah* distinctions between sacred and secular in understanding what constitutes religious acts. Further, these novels reflect Irving Greenberg's contention of the need for an applied theology. After Auschwitz, it is not sophisticated creedal statements but rather actions taken to enhance human dignity that matter. This assertion is embedded in Greenberg's paradigm of the voluntary covenant. With Elie Wiesel, these second-generation witnesses appear to embrace dimensions of an additional covenant, with its emphasis on the post-Auschwitz role of solidarity and the sanctification of life. It is, however, important to emphasize that the Jewish perspective of the second-generation witnesses is rooted neither in classical texts nor formal theological training. Rather, it emerges as a response both to their parents' continued survival and the impact of the *Shoah* on their own lives. Nevertheless, like their particularist counterparts, the universalist writers are engaged in discovering more about themselves by learning first of all about their parents' Holocaust experience, and through this more about Jewish history. The protagonists in the works of the universalist writers, however, are more extensively involved with issues and themes of American culture than their particularist counterparts.

## THE FLOOD

Carol Ascher, author of *The Flood*,[3] was born in America and trained as an anthropologist. In addition to writing fiction and essays, she also is a research analyst dealing with issues concerning minority education. Her mother fled Berlin in 1937, going to England where—in a refugee camp for children—she met her husband-to-be, a Viennese-born psychoanalyst. Ascher recalls that as a young girl her religious education "was pretty much limited to not denying my being Jewish" and simultaneously "being rather ashamed of those who were conspicuously Jews."[4] Consequently, she differs radically from the protagonists in chapter 3. Both she and her sister are married to non-Jews. Yet Asher claims that this has served to heighten her Jewish feelings and "given [her] the awareness that the responsibility for Judaism in the family is [hers]."[5] Not formally religious, she nonetheless feels "deeply connected" to Judaism's "rich and complicated religious and cultural tradition." Further, she celebrates most holidays with her Jewish friends. She observes that "*The Flood* expresses fictionally many of the themes of identity, assimilation, and responsibility in the new land."[6]

*The Flood* is one of the few novels written by an American-born author that focuses on the lives of refugees. Unlike Lore Grozsmann Segal's *Other People's Houses*, which was written by a Viennese child refugee who escaped on the *kindertransport*,[7] Ascher's novel is set entirely in America. Specifically she tells of events during the turbulent summer of 1951 in Topeka, Kansas. The Hoffmans, who are secular Austrian Jews, and a small cadre of other European exiles are affiliated with the Menninger Clinic. David and Leah Hoffman have two daughters, six-year-old Sarah and her precocious nine-year-old sister Eva, the novel's narrator. The safety and comfort of her parents' pre-Holocaust lives is a measure against which the reader understands the mother's moral anxiety and the father's cynicism as he discusses the meaning of the Holocaust and American racism with his colleague and fellow refugee Mordecai. Unlike Dr. Hoffman, Mordecai is a religious Jew who refuses to abandon God. In reality, the two psychiatrists agree on nothing, including the goal of psychotherapy.

The novel's title alludes to a natural disaster, in response to which the Hoffman's open their home to a family, the Willigers, who are "refugees" from the deluge only to discover that their guests are deeply racist and antisemitic. Eva, for her part, rejects racism and begins to embrace her identity as a Jew. There is also a humanly caused upheaval in the form of the landmark *Brown v. Topeka Board of Education* decision abolishing segregated schools. Dr. Hoffman and Mordecai discuss the issue of racism in comparison to the *Shoah*.

Several second-generation themes appear in *The Flood*. In common with the particularist novels, Ascher paints a portrait of her heroine's mother as a compulsive worrier. Mrs. Hoffman worries about issues ranging from health to the appearance of uniformed police. Further, the Hoffmans are both isolated and insulated, having lost home, family, culture, and language. The elder Hoffmans speak German, although Mrs.

Hoffman is ambivalent about the language. For example, while denouncing German as "Hitler's language," she frequently speaks and therefore thinks in her native tongue. Further, refugees share with survivors the feeling of being out of (cultural) place. Dr. Hoffman cynically expresses his otherness in response to being called to help sandbag the banks of the flood-swollen river. Now, he observes, he can prove his *usefulness* as a citizen. Further, the Hoffman's passion for culture—they and a survivor couple play chamber music—attests to their European origin and appears dissonant amidst farmers and manual laborers.

Universalist motifs are seen in a concern for others in need, such as flood victims, whom Mrs. Hoffman insists on terming refugees; an emphasis on the healing professions, in this case psychiatry; and a passion for justice. The latter is expressed by the elder Hoffman's unease over the Willigers' racist remarks. It is also seen in Eva's physical response to racism. Like Finkelstein in *Summer Long-a-Coming*, Ascher's heroine discovers the repugnant presence of a deeply ingrained American racism. She physically reacts against this moral disgrace. With Bukiet's *Stories of an Imaginary Childhood*, Ascher writes from a child's perspective in attempting to formulate the lessons of the Holocaust. Unlike Bukiet, her novel moves towards implementation of these lessons, although in an unsophisticated and attenuated manner. Finally, the protagonist's Jewish self-understanding is clearly universalist in tone and content.

The core of *The Flood* is Eva's coming to terms with her post-Auschwitz Jewish identity. This identity, as with other second-generation writers in this study, is an amalgam of her parents' European experience and her American milieu. At age nine, her understanding of identity and responsibility are greatly shaped by her parents' conversations and by her own talks with Mordecai. Unlike the Koles in *Damaged Goods*, the Hoffmans are very far from traditional Judaism either in practice or belief. Yet they, like the Szusters in *Summer Long-a-Coming*, Vladek and Anja in *Maus*, and the Justs in *White Lies* (see below), want their children to have a firm Jewish self-understanding. For the Hoffmans, Jewish identity includes neither davening nor candle lighting nor the incessant telling of refugee tales. Nor is it to be found in other forms of ritual practice, whether traditional or post-Auschwitz in nature.

Rather, *The Flood* articulates a distinctively modern definition of Jewish identity as coming not from within (i.e., the study of classical texts or the living of a traditional life), but from the ambiguous impact of antisemitism on the Jewish psyche. The historian Michael A. Meyer perceptively comments on this phenomenon, noting that, on the one hand, "antisemitism may produce (among some Jews) mild or severe negations of self." On the other hand, Meyer writes, "it may have entirely the opposite effect, resulting in a renewed affirmation of Jewish identity."[8]

The fact that this identity may be almost entirely without content is a phenomenon of modernity. Meyer notes that Jews who refused to convert but who remained alienated from the tradition retain a *"Trotzjudentum,* a Judaism of defiance or spite."[9]

Mrs. Hoffman's anxiety over Eva's Jewish identity crystallizes in an incident at a local church. The church's basement is a collection center for food and clothing needed to help flood victims. Eva is infatuated by the church's beauty and wishes that she could pray there. The young girl's mother is stunned into observing that she should take her daughter to a synagogue because the youngster clearly does not "understand what it means for someone not to know they are Jewish" (102). Consequently, she tells Eva that there were two types of children in the British refugee camps; those who had no idea what their Jewish identity meant, and those who did. Those who did reflected different orientations to the tradition. For example, those "who had been given a religious or Zionist training, or who knew they were Jewish by other means were all right." Although they suffered too, "they had some real understanding of why they had come to this strange place" (104). The fact that her mother's story made Eva "feel dizzy and weak in the knees" indicates that the young girl is far from being indifferent to either Judaism or the Holocaust. Rather, in the culturally homogenous and decidedly Christian context of 1951 America, it is simply easier to "fit in," to be universal rather than particular.

On the level of post-Auschwitz theology, Leah Hoffman teaches her daughter an important lesson of the voluntary covenant. After the Holocaust it is not eloquent theological formulations that matter, as we have seen in Wiesel's attestation about the meaning of God in Auschwitz. Rather, the only post-Holocaust theology that matters is one that recognizes the importance of compassion. For instance, after Eva naïvely exclaims "wouldn't you like to go to a church like this?" her sobbing mother says that the church "doesn't look very religious," and, further, she believes "more in what they are doing downstairs" (101; the basement houses supplies for flood victims). Ascher's story dramatizes Greenberg's contention that the crucial post-*Shoah* religious act is "to recreate the image of God. In an age of divine hiddenness, the most credible statement about God is the creation of an image of God which, silently but powerfully, points to the God whose image it is. Qualitatively, this means to feed a starving child, to heal a sick person."[10] And, we may add, to help restore the dignity of those who suffer from natural disasters such as floods, hurricanes, and earthquakes.

Further, pre-Holocaust distinctions between religious and secular are, as we have noted, no longer meaningful. Human behavior rather than theological discourse is the measure of any position. In Greenberg's words, "to leap in and pull a child out of a pit, to clean its face and heal its body, is to make the most powerful statement—the only statement that counts."[11] Ascher's novel starkly reveals the unpleasant but common coexistence of religion and prejudice: Christian ministers who preach that segregation is God's will; churchgoing racists; the Willigers, who are antisemitic and anti-black, but who "give the Lord His due" (pray before eating). These are powerful statements emphasizing Greenberg's point that post-Holocaust religious life consists of an entire range of apparently secular acts, such as giving material aid to flood victims, housing evacuee families, fighting for social justice—all of which restore human dignity.

Ascher specifically comments on her sense of responsibility to help improve the world. Her view of *tikkun olam* deserves full citation.

> *Bei uns* (Among our kind—refugees) there was a sense of responsibility to make the world better. Gradually, I came to believe that this was also a way of showing that we were not victims—that we had sufficient resources to watch out for others, worse off than we.[12]

But the Ascher family paid a steep price for their desire to improve the world.

> In every neighborhood where we lived, a tree in our yard was invariably chopped down by some neighbor enraged at my mother's activities for racial integration.[13]

Further, at least part of this rage was based on anti-Jewish feeling. Ascher continues:

> I remember being taunted by neighborhood children for not believing in a Christian heaven and hell. They couldn't accept that, relieved of the fear of hell, I wouldn't be a liar and a thief. My certainty that I lived by a secular morality that was every bit as demanding as any of their religious morality—that was, in fact, not merely driven by the self-interest of going to heaven or not going to hell—gave me a secret pride.[14]

Ascher's recollection clearly illustrates the phenomenon of *Trotzjudentum*.

Like Job, the refugees in Ascher's novel confront the age-old issue of innocent suffering—*zaddik ve-ra lo*. Mordecai explains the complexity of the problem by telling Eva the variety of Jewish theological responses to the Holocaust. His own father had been a pious Hasid who praised God even as he entered the gas chamber, much in the manner implied by the title of Bukiet's collection *While the Messiah Tarries*. On the other hand, Dr. Hoffman cannot abide the dissonance between the classical claim of Jewish theology that God is a redemptive deity and what happened to the Jews of Europe. Nor, for that matter, can he tolerate the situation of

Blacks in America. He contends that even if God exists, he—Dr. Hoffman—could not pray to Him.

Theologically, the views of Dr. Hoffman and Mordecai's martyred father represent two opposing points on the Jewish post-Auschwitz theological continuum. Like Yankl Szuster, Mordecai's father expresses a centrist Orthodox view that faults man and not God for the evil of the *Shoah*. The question for the centrists is best stated by Eliezer Berkovits. He contends that "Why the Holocaust?" is the wrong question. Rather, one needs to ask "Why the World?" Berkovitz writes that God made the world such that humanity has free choice. Further, although God is slow to anger, the deity will ultimately intervene; each step along the path of history brings the Messianic era closer. Berkovits affirms the prophetic position that God is a redeeming deity.[15]

The problem of theodicy, however, appears irresolvable in traditional terms to Dr. Hoffman. His is a death-of-God view similar to that expressed initially by Richard Rubenstein. With the talmudic heretic Elisha ben Avuya, Rubenstein contends that there is "neither Judge nor judgement" (*Let din ve-let dayyan*).[16] The historical evidence of God's absence, contends Rubenstein, is overwhelming. Consequently, we live in a time that is "functionally Godless."[17] The complexity of the situation is underscored by Mordecai's observation that both positions may be correct. Walking with Eva on the grounds of the clinic, they speak about the relationship between Jewish identity and theodicy. After the young girl confides that she doesn't feel proud of being Jewish, Mordecai tells her he does and speculates about the ways of God with the world. For his part, Mordecai resembles Yankl Szuster in adopting a Jobian stance; the psychiatrist tells Eva that there is no answer to the problem of evil and suffering. Rather, this problem is an endless cry echoing across the centuries.

Ascher juxtaposes natural and humanly caused disasters—the flood and the Holocaust. Both bring suffering in their wake. The flood, however, is something that the people of Topeka can fight against. Further, they unite in attempting to help its victims. Betraying an inability to distinguish both historical circumstances and the uniqueness of the Holocaust, Mrs. Hoffman views the plight of Jews in Europe, flood victims in Topeka, and Blacks in America as a seamless web. This is an ersatz universalism, one that blurs rather than clarifies the situation. For example, despite her experience, the mother uncritically adopts a type of Jewish self-hate or, at the very least, a tendency to accept the belief of antisemites that the Jews required further "improvement" before being fully accepted into German society.[18] For instance, she criticizes Hasidism, an eighteenth-century Jewish mystical-pietistic movement originating in Poland. Hasidism is distinguished by its religious fervor and intensity of ritual practice. In her view the hasidim failed to acculturate, thus bringing down the murderous wrath of Nazism upon the entire Jewish people. Mrs. Hoffman's view is clearly divorced from reality in at least two fundamental ways: she blames the victims for the crime, and she fails to comprehend the fact that Nazism's raison d'être was to make the world *Judenrein*.

How is one to account for Mrs. Hoffman's bizarre understanding? One way is to examine the impact of antisemitism on the German-Jewish community at the turn of the century. Meyer writes of the new anti-semitism in late-nineteenth-century Germany that served as a divisive force. He observes that "it inclined German Jews to find scapegoats."[19] These scapegoats were varied and included *Ostjuden*, Jews from eastern Europe whose appearance, speech, and mannerisms were most clearly unassimilated. Reform or liberal Jews were, on the other hand, blamed by the Orthodox for the new antisemitism, which the Orthodox considered—in the biblical manner—as an expression of "God's wrath." Orthodox Jews were in turn blamed by liberal Jews for "remaining too visibly different."[20] Confirming Meyer's observation, Mordecai tells Eva that in his father's shtetl the orthodox Jews blamed assimilationists for Hitler's growing power. From this, one can see the degree to which Mrs. Hoffman's own sense of Jewish identity had been shaped by German antisemitism, as well as the futile and woeful misreading of their situation on the part of both the orthodox and liberal Jews. This misreading of their historical situation is typical of Mrs. Hoffman's generation and underscores both the uniqueness and ferocity of the Holocaust.

The issue of post-Auschwitz theodicy and Jewish identity is a complex phenomenon. When seen from the perspective of a nine-year-old girl, even one as precocious as Eva Hoffman, distortions inevitably occur. She naïvely asks Mordecai if God wants there to be suffering. Unable to deal yet with the subtlety of theological reasoning, the young girl wishes to take concrete steps to fight bigotry. For example, the wrongs of history can be either set right or at least temporarily overcome by personal actions. After hearing Mr. Williger utter classical antisemitic stereotypes (the Jews own all the stores, Jewish agencies in New York are going to reimburse all Jewish losses incurred by the flood, etc.), Eva is determined to seek her own form of post-Auschwitz justice. Unsatisfied by Mordecai's response to theodicy that "people have to live with the pain of what they see everyday" ( 176), the young girl physically acts to thwart prejudice. Jolie, the Williger's young daughter, and Sarah are in the Hoffman's backyard playing in an inflated pool. Comparing this location to the municipal swimming pool, Jolie says, "here we got to swim with Jew-Niggers. And they don't allow none there" (186). Sarah responds by telling Jolie her remark is "not nice." Earlier, Jolie had displayed her prejudice to Mrs. Johnson, the Hoffman's cleaning woman. Eva, for her part, overturns the pool shouting "Why? Why?" The young girl's attempt to set things right leads her to temporarily run away from home. Her odyssey takes her to the banks of the flood-swollen river where, in a symbolic act, she helps an old black man retrieve some objects from the receding river. Eva's symbolic gestures are meant both on the level of personal empathy and as an attempt to achieve at least a partial *tikkun olam*. Further these gestures confirm Rosensaft's observation about a second-generation mission and anticipate the quest for societal improvement on the part of Jamaica Just in Julie Salamon's *White Lies*.

The title of Ascher's novel is also symbolically important. She offers four different interpretations for understanding the meaning of the flood. For example, she employs Theodore Roethke's observation as an epigraph: "Surround yourself with rising waters: the flood will teach you how to swim." Roethke's psychological point of view implies both that humans will assume responsibility, and the necessity of survival amidst a dangerous environment. In contrast, the biblical point of view understands the waters as divine punishment: humanity has taken too much responsibility or, rather, arrogance, and—in the process—has violated divine imperatives not to shed blood and to live on the earth in peace. Yet, the two characters who maintain that the flood is a divine punishment are Reverend Thomas, a racist preacher who contends that God sends the waters as a warning to those who seek integrated schools, and Lillian, a severely disturbed inmate of the Menninger Clinic who is certain that the flood is the result of human evil. Mrs. Johnson, the Hoffman's black maid, for her part, is convinced that the flood has been brought on by the interference of white rainmakers.

The most traditional interpretation of the flood is offered by Mordecai. His is a covenantal view that stresses the fact that God's post-flood covenant with Noah, symbolized by a rainbow, is universal in nature (Gen. 9:8–17). God promises to refrain from destroying the earth. The fate of the planet is now in human hands. Each one of us is responsible for the other: Jews, whether refugees from Hitlerite Europe or the target of American antisemitism; evacuees from the flood; and black victims of discrimination need to work collectively against evil and suffering. Further, the biblical flood is both destructive and cleansing; the saved remnant makes a new covenant with God. *Tikkun olam* is expressed as social justice in Ascher's novel. Eva Hoffman is a contemporary Jemimah. Like her sister of antiquity, she seeks to elevate and enoble humanity.

## WHITE LIES

Julie Salamon is a daughter of Holocaust survivors who, much in the manner of Nadine Fresco's image of the amputated hand that one never had, views the Holocaust as an omnipresent fact of her life and identity. Born in Seaman, Ohio, she earned a B.A. at Tufts and a law degree at New York University. Initially working as a freelance writer whose articles appeared in the *New York Times*, *Vogue*, and *Moviegoer*, Salamon was for 11 years film critic for the *Wall Street Journal*. She contends that the *Shoah* is primal, "especially for somebody whose parents are survivors." The event, continues Salamon, is "at the core of your being."[21] As in the case of Ascher's *The Flood*, Salamon's novel *White Lies*[22] interweaves Holocaust narrative with the innocence and bigotry of American culture in portraying dimensions of second-generation identity on these shores. Unlike the novels of either Friedmann or Ascher, Salamon's story refrains from commenting on the tumult created by America's social protests. Rather, she focuses on the second-generation mission to bear witness by attempting to morally improve the world. Salamon told an interviewer that in her view the Holocaust's legacy should be "a cry for justice."[23]

*White Lies* combines particularist and universal themes. For example, Salamon sensitively depicts a mother-daughter relationship that enables the protagonist to learn from her mother. Unlike Finkelstein's portrayal in *Summer Long-a-Coming*, Salamon describes a loving mother and an emotionally responsive daughter. Like Finkelstein, however, and with Friedmann and Ascher, Salamon also articulates a theology of protest in the face of the death of an innocent. The novel's universal concerns are seen in a quest for social justice, a desire to mend a deeply flawed world, and a commitment to the *tikkun* of bearing witness.

Salamon tells the story of Jamaica Just, a newspaper reporter and daughter of Job, who believes that her writing assignments bear universal weight; they are "crusades for betterment." She and her older sister Geneva live with their parents in a small Ohio village. The parents Eva and Dr. Pearlman—he changes his name to Just, in honor of his European birthplace—exemplify two different survivor responses to the *Shoah*. Eva speaks without passion about the Holocaust. Her understated stories of the *Shoah* mask the horrific details of her own and her husband's experiences. Dr. Just, unbeknownst to his daughters, lost his first wife and child in Auschwitz and was the medic for a resistance group in his small Hungarian town. Subject to dark moods of depression, his fierce quarrels with Eva—in their native Hungarian tongue—frighten the young Jamaica, who hides in a closet.[24] Neither parent, however, develops the ability to mourn. Consequently, Eva cautions the children not to say anything that will upset their father, whose episodic rage overwhelms the entire family and evidences the continuing presence of the memory of the absent Holocaust dead.

Criticized by her Jewish but highly assimilated managing editor for taking the world's evils so personally, Jamaica steers her own course.

Her family name itself symbolizes Jamaica's determination to seek a *tikkun olam*. On the one hand, as noted, Just is the name of a small Hungarian town that is her father's natal village. Her mother gives this name to immigration officials as the family name because, the survivor attests, the word carries such a "noble meaning" in English. Jamaica's surname also identifies her second-generation task. Like the prophet Amos, she seeks to "let justice roll down like waters, and righteousness like an ever-flowing stream" (Amos 5:24). The difficulty of achieving this task is, however, graphically portrayed—on the hardcover edition—by the engraved image of a Don Quixote figure.

Jamaica pursues her search for justice amidst the impersonal and violent landscape of New York City, which presents both a tremendous obstacle to—and great opportunity for—achieving a *tikkun* of the social order. Among her assignments, three stories provide the framing narrative for Jamaica's identity as a second-generation witness. One of her stories is autobiographical, the other two are pieces of investigative reporting. She writes an article on children of Jewish Holocaust survivors, one on second-generation welfare mothers, and a feature article on "news junkies," individuals who habitually write letters to the editor. Each of these tales are symbolically linked. For example, Jamaica perceives a kinship between second-generation Holocaust witnesses and second-generation welfare mothers. Further, Jules Marlin, the news junkie about whom she writes, is himself a survivor who knew Jamaica's father prior to the Holocaust.

Assigned to write about second-generation witnesses, Jamaica experiences the ambivalence common to this generation. While it is true that the Holocaust is the most important event in the lives of this generation, it is also the case that it happened before their birth. How can one respond to this situation? The case is further complicated owing to the fact that the editor assigns the story not on the basis of interest, but rather for commercial reasons: it will sell newspapers. The situation causes Jamaica to wonder if she is entitled to speak. Here it is helpful to recall Ellen Fine's observation concerning the difference between survivors and the second generation. The survivors question how to speak of the unimaginable, whereas the second-generation ask, "Do I have the right to speak?" Jamaica is troubled both by the fact that she had been "untimely born" and by the fact that she also feels alienated from those Jews who "were made uncomfortable by the ugly scar on her past." A major part of her own identity is as a woman who is "an out of context American Jew" (33). Jamaica is a young woman torn between forgetting and remembering the Holocaust. This typifies the second-generation struggle between not wanting to remember that their parents were helpless victims, yet experiencing the legacy of the losses daily. Jamaica is a second-generation witness, one of those who, in Wiesel's haunting phrase, have "inherited the burden but not the mystery." She wanted to forget, but "it was her birthright to remember" (28).

Jamaica's is an inherited memory of the *Shoah*. Humbled by the knowledge that nothing had directly happened to her, she nonetheless— like all the contemporary children of Job—lives in the shadow of the *Shoah*. For second-generation witnesses, it is the desire to know their parents lives better that serves as a vehicle for understanding the impact of the Holocaust on their own existence. "For me," writes Lucy Steinitz, "the Holocaust has been the most determining factor in my life because it was the most determining in my parents'."[25] Jamaica Just's self-image as a second-generation witness is framed in her self-perception as a "phoenix child, rising out of the ashes of both death and destruction" (29). It is imperative for a fuller understanding of her identity that she attempt to achieve a more coherent understanding of the chaos that preceded her birth and to which she is forever attached.

Yet this Holocaust knowledge frequently leads to feelings of being unworthy in comparison to what parents had suffered. In Jamaica's case, the young woman constantly expresses her fear of not measuring up. Feelings of unworthiness stem from two major sources. On the one hand, there is the crushing psychological burden placed on the children by their parents to be "memorial candles" for those who perished. On the other hand, members of the second generation believe that their own problems are insignificant in comparison to what their parents experienced during the *Shoah*. Such feelings are specifically expressed by Jason Kole in *Damaged Goods*, Brenda Szuster in *Summer Long-a-Coming*, Art Spiegelman in *Maus*, and several of the Adam Posner protagonists in Rosenbaum's *Elijah Visible*. For Jamaica, this concern runs the gamut from questions asked her widowed mother—"Mom? How big a disappointment am I?" (76)—to ruminations about her deceased father: "She didn't know what his expectations were for her, but she was certain she wasn't living up to them" (166).

The issue of second-generation guilt is a complex phenomenon. While far from being found among all children of survivors, or from being the determining factor in the life of the second generation witness, among those it does affect, the results are clear. For example, as we have seen in Brenda Szuster's case, the survivor parents employ their Holocaust experience as a form of control; for example, Mrs. Szuster is annoyed by the triviality of her offspring's rivalries and feelings, and so informs them. So, to, does Vladek Spiegelman. For Salamon's Jamaica Just, the mechanism is more subtle. The daughter is not directly accused by her mother. Rather, both Jamaica and Geneva *imagine* that their mother indicts the triviality of their childhood concerns. Jamaica muses:

> In moments of anger, her daughters thought their mother was conspiring continually to make them feel guilty. How dare they worry about not making the cheerleading squad, pimples, flab? Had they been in concentration camps? Had their parents been murdered? (79)

The despair is only compounded by the fact that these questions were *not* asked. Stifling her questions serves to create distance between Jamaica and her parents. Not wanting to hurt them, she ends by hurting both her parents and herself. "Why didn't anyone ask them these questions," thinks Jamaica, "so they wouldn't have to ask them of themselves?" (79).

Feelings of guilt are, moreover, frequently fused with jealousy for not having been in the camps. As noted earlier. this is a prominent theme in Canadian and French second-generation writings, and also emerges in the American second generation. For example, Jamaica feels not only shame but "a weird form of jealousy" about being unable to confront her parent's experience. A similar feeling is evoked in Finkelstein's novel, when Brenda and Perel are in the woods and wonder if they could have survived the *Shoah*.

Yet even in the same family there may be very different second-generation reactions. Jamaica, for example, insists on protesting—she dislikes unfairness—while Geneva remains largely passive: acquiescing to all her parents' demands, she becomes adept at avoiding arguments and scenes. This variety of response is also noted in Finkelstein's novel. Brenda Szuster is impelled to remember, while her brother Sheiye wishes to forget. William Helmreich notes this phenomenon. Focusing on the film *A Generation After* (sic) (see below, chapter 5), he writes:

> resentment is expressed by one son in a family at the "guilt trip" transmitted from parents to children, while a second son views his parents with awe and "forgives them for the pain they have caused him."[26]

Further, many children of survivors wonder whether they could have survived the Holocaust. Consequently, they attempt to replicate their parents' Holocaust experiences in a variety of ways, ranging from hoarding diverse items such as food and string, to placing themselves in great danger. Here it is relevant to recall Spiegelman's report that, during his confinement in a mental ward, he subconsciously replicated one dimension of Vladek's experience by collecting and hoarding scraps of string. We have also noted earlier an extreme version of this mimetic phenomenon as expressed by Al Singerman, who volunteered for the Army to fight in Vietnam, thus proving that he, too, "could be a survivor."

Like Job of antiquity, Jamaica is doubly alienated. Unlike her biblical counterpart who feels unjustly accused both by God and the community, Jamaica's sense of isolation is primarily psychological rather than theological. On the one hand, she is clearly different from non-Jewish

Americans. Yet she deeply resents Jews who are indifferent towards or ignorant about the *Shoah*. Even those Jews with whom she presumably shares much in the way of culture, history, and ritual practice serve only to underscore her own sense of apartness. For example, upon meeting Sammy, her American-born future husband, they both feel comfortable with their shared Jewish heritage, including close families. This close-ness proves, however, illusory. The son of nonwitnesses remembers the humorous anecdotes his parents—who had spent the war on an airbase in Texas—told him as a child. Visiting Jamaica at Thanksgiving, Sammy hears tales of the Holocaust from her aunt. She tells him that she had been in Auschwitz and should not even be here today. "Why," Sammy politely asks, "is that?"

The differences between children of survivors and those of non-witnesses are seen on every level. Those who are raised in the shadow of Auschwitz have different psychological markers. Their socialization imagery involves associations beyond the experiential realm of the second generation of nonwitnesses. This is seen in the very association given to common words such as *tattoo*, *grandparents*, and *camp*. For example, Jamaica recalls college bull sessions where the "tragedies" of American life are compared to the *Shoah*. Her classmates spoke of divorced parents, suicides, adultery, and noncommunicative parents. Listening to these sto-ries, Jamaica would think:

> Had any of them [her friends], their parents, been tattooed and shaved, turned spooked and deranged? Were their grandparents murdered? Did their mothers talk cheerily about girlhood chums they went to camp with and mean Auschwitz? (85)

Jamaica's childhood memory is different. She confides her belief that all Jewish parents spent World War II "in concentration camps or in hiding" (34). This recalls Art Spiegelman's childhood belief that all adults had nightmares. Unlike Brenda Szuster, Jamaica is in awe of her mother; she views Eva as a heroine—"the only reminder that survival is a form of hope" (182). Jamaica's perception underscores Eva Fogelman's con-tention that despite their great diversity, what unites the members of the second generation is their identity as children of survivors.[27] This identity both unites them as a definable group while simultaneously distinguishing them from children of nonwitnesses.

The vicinal isolation from other Jewish people that characterizes Jamaica's childhood deserves further consideration. A common theme in second-generation writings, this phenomenon underscores a basic para-dox among survivor families. On the one hand, many of them live among non-Jews. Jamaica grew up in a small Ohio town where she and her fam-ily were the only Jews. Despite being crucial as the town's only physician, the family is viewed as "glamorous oddballs." The Justs are *other* in a twofold sense: as Jews and as survivors. Yet, on the other hand, understandable distrust of the non-Jewish social world characterizes certain victim families. Hass reports that the world for children of survivors with whom he came in contact "is clearly a hostile protagonist."[28] Yet, as implied in Nusan Porter's observation, children of survivors frequently transform this mistrust into a mission to better the world.

Reminders of the Holocaust's legacy come from the surrounding culture as well as from within the family. For instance, none of Jamaica's childhood friends knew about the *Shoah*. Moreover, she recalls that her fifth-grade teacher, who was "only partly antisemitic," assigned the class a genealogy project; the youngsters were to trace their family tree. Asking her father for help, the young girl is told that her family tree "has been pruned." Dr. Just's cynical response masks his own rage and teaches his daughter nothing about either her heritage or her parents. Yet, this remark also calls to mind Helen Epstein's observation that her "family tree had been burnt to a stump."[29] Unable to comprehend her father's cynicism, Jamaica copies her teacher's family tree, which is "leafy with ancestry." This act expresses both the young girl's wishes as well as her shame and denial of loss. She is mystified when Eva, seeing the borrowed genealogy, begins sobbing.

The survivors' reticence to share their experience with their daughters is both understandable and paradoxical. While wanting the world to remember the Holocaust, Eva and her husband attempt to protect their daughters from this dreadful experience. Thus, Eva invents tales about herself. Retrospectively, Jamaica highlights the difference between families of nonwitnesses and survivor families in observing: "While other kids' parents were shyly not telling them about sex, her parents were studiously not telling her about surviving death" (28). Specifically, her mother's consequent acts of invention help explain the book's title. For example, Jamaica opines about her mother, "she wasn't a liar," simply "a woman of imagination."

At age nine, Jamaica reads Leon Uris's *Exodus*. Lacking the sophistication to analyze the novel's prose, she is profoundly disturbed by the detailed descriptions of torture and the camps. Echoing Prince's contention that the Holocaust is a "psychosocial event of the first magnitude . . . simultaneously a real event in the outer world and is also an inner event, indelibly marking our consciousness with metaphors," Jamaica recalls having dreams of mangled Holocaust corpses that bore the faces of her parents. Inheriting Holocaust imagery is a shared second-generation trait, one that is especially prominent in Spiegelman's work. Reflecting the child's point of view found in Ascher's novel, Jamaica becomes staunchly anti-German, refusing even to eat German chocolate cake, although Eva tells her that all the ingredients—except the Swiss chocolate—are made in America.

Jamaica's role as a second-generation witness evolves in stages. As a young girl, she and her sister knew that their parents survived the Holocaust. But this knowledge was only a "vague fact" to the daughters, comparable to their awareness that their mother "grew up in an unknowable—and unspellable—place called Berecszacz" (34). Yet, confirming the testimony in *Living after the Holocaust: Reflections by Children of Survivors in America*, Jamaica recalls that even as small children she and Geneva were aware of the Holocaust. "For us," she muses "'the war' always meant World War II, *as though we'd been born a generation earlier*" (my emphasis, 34). As children, the little that the Just daughters knew about the *Shoah* was communicated nonverbally, or in fragmentary and parsimonious statements, a phenomenon widely reported in the documentary films discussed below in chapter 5.

Unlike some survivors, who either converted or raised their children as Christians in order to shield them from another Holocaust (for example, the story of Gabriela Korda in Epstein's *Children of the Holocaust*),[30] the secular Justs raise their daughters Jewishly. But with few of the tradition-sustaining rituals that one typically associates with Judaism. Quite to the contrary, Jamaica's second-generation identity—not totally unlike that of Art Spiegelman—appears imposed by her parents' experience during the *Shoah*. A pre-Holocaust assimilationist, Dr. Just came from a town whose Jewish population identified with German Jewry rather than the ghettoized *Ostjuden*. This bit of history makes Jamaica aware of a twofold reality: Nazis made no distinctions between believers and nonbelievers, all were to be exterminated; and the *Shoah* sustained her parents' Jewish identity if not their belief.

Dr. Just instills in his daughters both a Jewish and an American identity. Yet the former appears in large part a reaction to the youngsters' Presbyterian Sunday-school education that teaches Jamaica a song about Jesus, which her father hears her sing. Shortly thereafter, he gives the young girls two versions of the Hebrew Bible: a comic book and a double record album. This is reminiscent of what Meyer terms the "Judaism of defiance" that also appears in Ascher's novel. In addition, Dr. Just insists that Eva light Friday-night candles. This is so, attests Jamaica, "our Presbyterian surrounding wouldn't obliterate the yellow stars engraved on our souls" (77). Dr. Just's actions reveal his determination that his daughters stay connected to Judaism, despite the Holocaust and despite his own inability to believe.

The American component of Jamaica's identity is no less complex. She remembers her father always telling her and Geneva that "they were Americans first, Jews second." Retrospectively; Jamaica muses that her father's gratitude for being in America caused him to deliberately lie in order "to repay an unwritten debt."[31] When Jamaica and Geneva begin dating, their father gives them money and tells them to pay their own way so that they owe nothing to anyone. Looking back, Jamaica imagines her father feeling "more burdened than usual by the gift of a second life. It cost too dearly" (83). Telling his children nothing, Dr. Just at the same time does not want the world to forget.

The next stage of Jamaica's second-generation identity becomes more fully articulated in college. Here she begins to assume personal responsibility for bearing witness. Reading Jerzy Kosinski's *The Painted Bird*, she is physically sickened by the phrase "the Jews going to slaughter." Angered, she begins to realize that the Holocaust involved *people*, who had their own hopes and dreams, aspirations, fears, and desires. Jamaica is moved to observe that:

> Those Jews aren't nameless, pitiable beings to me, yesterday's swollen bellies, a 40 year-old magazine cover. They are my mother, my father, my uncles, my aunts, my cousins. They are me. (37)

Her assertion that she is one with the Jewish victims links the second-generation witness to the obligation of testifying on behalf of survivors. Her realization, although less traumatic than that of Finkelstein's Brenda Szuster, is no less crucial. Further, she underscores the central point that the second-generation witness understands: the Jewish catastrophe destroyed families, communities, an entire world. People, rather than numbers, images or statistics, need to be the central focus for students of the Holocaust.

Bearing second-generation witness carries its own complexity. For example, although she must bear witness, Jamaica worries especially about the inevitable trivialization of the event as it enters popular culture. The Holocaust, she muses, has become "the pop metaphor for evil" (30). This infantilization extends even to the selling of "I survived Auschwitz" T-shirts sold at Holocaust conventions. Nevertheless, the knowledge of these distortions quickens Jamaica's resolve to perpetuate the memory of the crime in order to remember its victims and to help save the world from itself.

Jamaica's efforts at achieving *tikkun olam* occur on both the familial and communal levels. She universalizes the lessons of the Holocaust by meditating on what she herself learned as a daughter of survivors. Jamaica's universal emphasis is important and deserves scrutiny. Reflecting on what she will pass on to her unborn children, she thinks:

> I want my children, when I have them, to know what happened during World War II. I don't want them to think their birthright is privilege and ease. I hope they have those things. I have. But I want them to know that

such things are a matter of luck and circumstance and should be appreciated. My mother, too, was a child of privilege for the first eighteen
years of her life. I guess I will make my children feel guilty, even though
that isn't my intent. (44)

Her intention to reveal the story of the Holocaust to the third generation
clearly distinguishes Jamaica from both the "white lies" approach taken
by Eva and the dark rages of her father. Further, as noted in chapter 1,
the desire to tell their own children—the third generation—about the
*Shoah* is "one of the few discrete traits held in common among children of
survivors."[32]

Jamaica's wishes clearly conform to the second-generation themes
set forth by Prince.[33] She seems especially concerned to stress the political
dimension of the *Shoah*'s legacy and links it to ethical behavior in observing that she wants any children that she may have to learn certain Holocaust lessons:

> I make an effort to be decent because I have some understanding of
> what happens when decency doesn't exist. I try to keep aware of what
> the government is doing because I have some understanding of what
> happens when governments turn evil. I try to be good to my family and
> friends because I have some understanding of what it's like to have
> family and friends taken away (44).

*White Lies* attempts to come to terms with post-Auschwitz theodical
issues such as the death or disappearance of innocent victims and the
continuing presence of evil. In this sense Salamon's work shares the second-generation concern expressed by Friedmann, Finkelstein, and Ascher.
In the process, Salamon's heroine begins to confront the issue of suffering
in her own life, thereby enabling the second-generation witness to attempt
to understand at least some of the trauma experienced by her survivor
parents.

Seeking meaning in the accidental death of her high-school friend,
Jamaica turns first to a pantheistic explanation by reading *Moby Dick*.
Next, she turns to her parents, seeking an explanation from those who are
intimately acquainted with pain and suffering, evil and death. Their subsequent discussions reveal much about communications between survivors and their children. Like Jeremiah of antiquity, Jamaica asks why
the innocent suffer. Older than Ascher's Eva Hoffman, Jamaica engages
her parents in discussion of theodicy. Eva Just speaks in a personal tone,
confessing to her daughter that she does not know the point of the suffering of the innocent. Referring to her experiences in Auschwitz, Eva
confides to Jamaica that in the camp she felt as if she was "floating above
it all," as if she "wasn't there," and she never felt like she was a part of it.
Eva's response displays a type of behavior that Robert J. Lifton describes

as "psychic numbing." Lifton defines this phenomenon by comparing Auschwitz and Hiroshima survivors. He writes: "a central feature of anyone's encounter with death, most characteristically during massive holocaust, is a cessation of feeling, a desensitization or psychic numbing."[34]

Yet in this context it is important to note that psychic numbing could take one of two forms. It could, as Lifton observes, assume the form of the *Muselmänner*, or walking corpse, about whom Primo Levi writes, "One hesitates to call them living: one hesitates to call their death death."[35] This type of numbing led inevitably to death. On the other hand, numbing may be "an aid to survival" among "privileged Jewish prisoners" who "know nothing and act as if death does not exist."[36] There was, of course, overlapping of these psychological conditions. Eva, for her part, tells Jamaica that in Auschwitz the dead were smelled—as their bodies burned in the crematorium—not seen. Eva does recall that after her liberation she saw the corpses of German soldiers by the roadside. This sight filled her with joy.

Jamaica's discussion with her father is less personal but causes her more anger. Dr. Just maintains the psychic distance between himself and his daughter by speaking theologically rather than personally. Yet, ironically, unbeknownst to the young teenager, Dr. Just is himself gravely ill. Consequently, his responses to her queries assume an even more urgent tone. Although estranged from the teachings of normative Jewish theology, Dr. just initially embraces a Jobian response: the ways of God are inexplicable. Interestingly, however, he does not take the next step and follow Yankl Szuster's total embrace of Job: "Though He slay me, in Him I will trust." Pushed by his daughter as to whether he believed in God, Dr. Just at first endorses Melville's fatalism.

Still unsatisfied, Jamaica again asks her father about God's role in an individual's life and, by extension, in history. At this point the elder Just responds in a twofold manner: he contends both that all the laws are in the Bible and that God or some higher being gave the Ten Commandments, and it's better not to ask too many questions. Her father's evasiveness and her own sense of grief prompt the teenager to angrily question Judaism. She sobbingly accuses Judaism's "tough" God, the tradition's lack of forgiveness, and the absence of a heaven. What, she wonders, is there to look forward to?

This theological discussion achieves its dénouement with two "revelations." Dr. Just rejects any possibility of an interventionist deity, an afterlife, or earthly justice. He tells his daughter to "do her best—and be a good girl—on this earth." Rejecting belief in God, he adopts instead the scientist's dispassionate view, death is part of life. Jamaica's friend learned this lesson early. Hurt by her father's seeming callousness, Jamaica wonders if the fact that her late friend was not Jewish excluded him from her father's concern. The young girl is angry at both God and her father; both represent a Judaism that she neither understands nor desires. As she matures in her understanding of the relationship between her Holocaust legacy and her Jewish self-understanding, however, Jamaica's universalism will stem directly from her own firm sense of Jewish identity.

As is characteristic in survivor families, it is the mother from whom Jamaica hears tales of the *Shoah*. Eva tells her daughter of the Nazi "logic of destruction,"[37] astounding Jamaica with the claim that Dr. Mengele—the infamous Angel of Death at Auschwitz—saved her life. Unlike Yankl Szuster, Eva does not resort to prayer as the response to the Holocaust. Rather, she tells Jamaica what happened. Selecting Eva to live and her mother to die, Mengele had done the younger woman a favor because, she explained, Jamaica's grandmother could never have survived the wretched conditions that existed in Auschwitz. Further underscoring the madness of the Third Reich's kingdom of death, Eva recalls the story of Judy, a beautiful young woman from Just who took special care of herself in Auschwitz, "wasting" her share of margarine by rubbing it into her skin. Judy wanted her skin to be smooth when she was liberated. As an aside, it is important to note that this attention to personal cleanliness and hygiene is characteristic of many women's response to Auschwitz.[38] Eva, for her part, tells Jamaica that at one selection Mengele noted a tiny rash on Judy's back and condemned her to death. Within a week, the victim's mother died and her sister went mad. After that episode, Eva began hating the Angel of Death. Eva reports these stories in the same tone of voice that she used to tell Jamaica about mundane problems ranging from domestic issues to her own tennis game, thus enmeshing the Holocaust past in American culture.

Jamaica learns more about the *Shoah* and her own family history from Jules Marlin, himself a survivor and "news junkie." Jamaica feels a twofold kinship with Jules: he is a survivor—therefore like her parents—and he shares her passion for moral justice. Concerning the former, Jules reveals that he also lived in prewar Just, was also a secular Jew, and had hoped to study medicine. Further, Jules's brother had been Dr. Just's best friend, whereas Jules himself had been in love with the doctor's first wife, who, along with her infant daughter, was murdered in Auschwitz. Dr. Just's postwar rages stem from this "deep memory" of loss. He responds in two basic ways to the anger caused by his feelings of helplessness. In addition to periodic rages, he frequently drives the family car in a suicidal manner. Dr. Just's postwar response underscores the role played by murdered siblings in survivor households. The consequent emotional weight adds to the psychic burdens born by the post-*Shoah* generation. This devastating presence of the absent was seen in Friedmann's *Damaged Goods*, where Jason Kole is the "second born 'only child';" Wiesel's *The Fifth Son*, whose protagonist Ariel is named after his murdered sibling; and *Maus*, when Spiegelman tells his wife that it is "spooky" having sibling rivalry with a ghost.

Like other second-generation witnesses, Jamaica also learns a portion of Holocaust history through the ritual of listening to survivor tales. Jules Marlin, for example, tells a story that emphasizes the helper theme. He survived the Kingdom of Night owing to the help of Christians.[39] Jules tells Jamaica that a conductor enabled him to board a train leaving Just, and a peasant woman permitted him and a young Jewish couple to hide in her cellar. Jules's tale illustrates the mystery of good, which is far greater than the mystery of evil. Amidst the millions of active or passive accomplices to murder, there existed a few individuals whose actions serve as moral beacons. Their stories need to be heard first of all because they are true. Secondly, they prove that one person's actions can literally save a life. Finally, although there can be no equation between the numbers of people who either murdered or passively acquiesced to murder and those who helped, the actions of the helpers convey a vital message to the second generation: Not everyone in the world wants the Jews dead. Further, as Emil Fackenheim attests, a *tikkun* of the world is possible now, because it was actual then (during the Kingdom of Night).

Striving to achieve social justice is a hallmark of universalist writers. The second-generation Holocaust legacy includes a recognition that society will not truly be just unless all of its segments are treated equally. Social justice is Jamaica's ruling passion. In fact, she sometimes feels that "the only people left in the world who *cared* were her and Jules Marlin" ( 13). The survivor's letters to the editor evince a deep concern about America's lack of moral focus. Jules and Jamaica embody what Wiesel terms "mystical madness," a commitment to empathy and compassion in a world that prizes neither. Responses to Jamaica's article on the Holocaust, for example, carry the clear message that most people are tired of hearing about the *Shoah* and that antisemitism remains a strong social force in American culture. Jamaica muses that not only "cranks and lunatics" believe the Holocaust "was a good thing;" even "otherwise normal people" may share that view in the privacy of their homes.

In contrast, Jules and Jamaica are committed to bear witness; they are still "capable of feeling outrage." Both the first- and second-generation witnesses adopt a Wieselian position concerning the indifference of the world. Silent public approval only gives warrant to the executioner. Indifference and social justice cannot simultaneously abide. Wiesel recalls that in the early days he shouted to change man. Now, however, he shouts in order to prevent man from ultimately changing him.[40] Bearing witness to the unredeemed state of the world is a step toward achieving a repair of the world. Jamaica, for her part, universalizes the *Shoah*'s lessons, extrapolating a mission to fight against racism, poverty, and all other forms of societal inequity.

Jamaica's "shout" for justice also extends to include a rejection of the anomie that characterizes much of her generation. For example, she opposes cultural fads in literature, reacting strongly against post-modernism, with its contention that no text is privileged (e.g., a novel, a newspaper article, and a laundry list bear the same moral equivalence) and that meaning can be supplied only by the reader. The very fluidity of meaning associated with the term *postmodern* easily gives rise, in the worst cases, to a type of academic and intellectual game playing.[41] Jamaica is angry because her editor drops all of her criticism from an acerbic piece that she has written on postmodern fiction, of which he is a devotee. Jamaica views postmodernism as sanctioning moral and ethical irresponsibility. As a daughter of survivors, she is sensitive to the fact that this movement may lead down a slippery moral slope that condones anarchy, anomie, hatred, and eventually murder.

*White Lies* portrays the second-generation witness in terms of social responsibility. Jamaica as a writer and Geneva as a physician work for the improvement of humanity. Placing this type of concern within the framework of post-Auschwitz Jewish-African-American relations, Hass observes that:

> Children of survivors frequently identify with and feel compassion toward other groups who have been discriminated against because they too are seen as being out of the mainstream, in a way not a part of the gentile world. Children of survivors may have fought for the rights of blacks during the civil rights movement because blacks were not perceived to be a part of the gentile majority, but a group marked for oppression by a gentile society, as Jews had been at other times and in other places.[42]

The universal dimension of Jamaica's second-generation mission is vividly seen in her efforts on behalf of second-generation welfare mothers. Embodying the book cover's Don Quixote image, Jamaica writes about an individual "bravely trying to fight the system." Yet her concern is autobiographical and deeply personal. She identifies with Lonnie, a young welfare mother about whom she writes, seeing striking parallels between the two of them. She speaks of this comparison to her barely comprehending husband, telling him that:

> It's hard to explain. I guess I have this image of myself as a martyr once removed, that somehow I've been victimized by the Holocaust even though that was my parents' show, not mine. In a weird way, I guess I related to Lonnie, stuck where she is because of her parents. (71)

Jamaica's compassion may in fact be viewed as an attempt to undo a contemporary injustice. Unable to effect a similar undoing of the Holocaust past, she transforms this legacy into a mission to mend the social evils of the present. Additionally, and much in the manner of *The Flood*'s Eva Hoffman, Jamaica is outraged by American racism. The attitude of both of these protagonists supports Hass's contention about compassion for those who are seen as out of the mainstream.[43]

Salamon's novel is as well a study in contrast of attitudes towards survivors. On the one hand, Jamaica, as noted, views her mother in heroic terms, as a model of hope. Eva Just's survival is exemplary and bears salvific meaning. On the other hand, certain mental health professionals are unable to view survivors in other than clinical terms. Asked to analyze the motif behind Jules Marlin's compulsive letter writing, a psychobabbling television psychologist responds in the following manner:

> I would say that writing letters would be that person's way of gaining control. You could call it "undoing," performing a meaningless, purposeless ritual that is meant to erase guilt but that doesn't really accomplish anything. It's on the neurotic, not the psychotic end of the spectrum. (165)

This pigeonholing of survivors is reminiscent of Cynthia Ozick's depiction in *Rosa*, where a psychiatrist pursues Rosa in order to study (rather than learn from) her.[44] Further, this response is antithetical to Spiegelman's depiction of Pavel, the survivor-psychiatrist whose help enables Art to complete *Maus*.

As children, the Just daughters keep secrets concerning their Jewish identity. Unlike the authors in chapter 3, this identity is expressed much in the manner of Marrano Jews (crypto Jews of the Iberian Peninsula, forced to convert but who maintained Jewish rites and rituals in secret). Jewish rites and rituals are practiced in hiding. For example, bottles of kosher wine hidden in the closet, candles that the family lit on Friday night in the master bedroom, trips to out-of-town synagogues, and Hebrew lessons from Berlitz records.[45] At the time, Jamaica believes that their parents did not want them to feel embarrassed in front of their friends. Later, however, a psychiatrist treating Geneva contends that the girls were being "prepared for another Holocaust." Jamaica, for her part, thinks that "psychiatrists [are] full of shit" (119). The different second-generation perceptions of psychiatry mirror the great disparity in empathy and competence among members of the mental health profession. What Geneva's psychiatrist fails to realize is that the Justs are more than perpetual victims. Rather, they are survivors of a watershed event living in a world that has learned little from the *Shoah*.

Salamon's novel offers no closure to the tension between the second-generation witness and other, nonwitnessing Americans. Jamaica's marriage is failing; Sammy is unable to deal with her compassion and empathy for others which, he feels, overwhelms their own relationship. However, the triad of Eva, Geneva, and Jamaica is functioning well. Although physically separated, Jamaica and her mother speak frequently on the telephone, meet often, and display the strength of mutual family support characteristic of many survivor households. Further, Jamaica continues her ritual practice of listening to stories about Auschwitz and the Holocaust.

## DANCING ON TISHA B'AV AND WINTER EYES

Lev Raphael was born in New York in 1954. He received an M.F.A. in Creative Writing from the University of Massachusetts at Amerherst and a Ph.D. in American Studies at Michigan State University. He now devotes himself to full time writing. His work, including the short-story collection *Dancing on Tisha B'Av* and the novel *Winter Eyes*,[46] treats the author's coming to grips with his threefold identity as a gay son of Job. Raphael's writing has earned much recognition, including the 1990 Lambda Literary Award and the Harvey Swados and Reed Smith prizes for fiction. Like the other authors in this study, both of his parents survived the Holocaust. Unlike any of the other authors, however, they explicitly reject Judaism and he becomes a bar mitzvah only at age thirty. Unlike Spiegelman, Raphael adamantly views himself as a Jewish writer. Further, he sees at least part of his second-generation mission as bridging the gap between the straight and gay Jewish communities. Raphael's position is one of tension. On the one hand, his gayness is seen by many as an obstacle to full inclusion in the Jewish community. Yet, on the other hand, as a second-generation witness his works bear directly on the complex issue of the relationship of the Holocaust to contemporary Jewish identity.

Raphael's work treats issues of identity that arise in coming out as a Jew and as a gay. He sees a threefold question emerging from both types of coming out: "What will people think? Will I be exposed? Will they still like me?"[47] Initially, Raphael feared confronting his own "demons": his "fear of being gay" and his own Jewish self-hatred. Specifically concerning the second-generation witness, his writings explore the tensions that exist both within families and within Judaism itself concerning being gay and Jewish. Linking the threefold nature of his own identity, Raphael's writings emphasize the importance of ending all forms of prejudice. Consequently, his work implicitly stresses both the pluralism of Greenberg's voluntary covenant and the dimension of solidarity and witness that play crucial roles in Wiesel's additional covenant. Like the work of Ascher and Salamon, Raphael's writings may also be viewed as a quest for repair of the social order. Unlike the other two writers, however, he specifically links antisemitism and homophobia.

Raphael articulates the *Shoah*'s effects on second-generation identity in psychosocial terms that raise as well theological issues. For example, his writings reveal many themes associated with the "death imprint" among survivors, such as alternating periods of rage and silence, depression, incomplete mourning, and abandonment of Jewish faith owing to rejection of classical theological claims. In the process, his second-generation characters are profoundly shaped by the presence of an absent memory. Further, like Thomas Friedmann, his work depicts a distant father-son relationship, the vast gulf that separates survivors and their offspring, an awareness of vulnerability in terms of omnipresent antisemitism and gay-bashing, and a compulsion to read about and bear witness to the Holocaust.

Reflecting on his own experience, Raphael attests to the Holocaust's direct effects on the second generation. Echoing Friedmann, he comments on the role typically played by grandparents in socializing a grandchild. Raphael observes that the *Shoah* "robbed" him of his grandparents and, therefore, severed a "living connection" with his parents' European past. Consequently, lacking grandparents and having parents who are reticent about speaking of the *Shoah*, Raphael recalls feeling psychologically estranged both from his heritage and from American culture. This, in turn, results in his initial rejection of Judaism. "I grew up," he confides, "with an early knowledge of the absolute worst things about humanity anyone could ever imagine. Is it any wonder that it also affected how I felt about myself as a Jew? I wanted to belong, but I also felt ashamed of Jewishness. It took years to work that out."[48] Raphael's case illustrates a general issue for second-generation identity. "Fear," observes Hass, "is perhaps the most prevalent problem in children of survivors."[49]

*Dancing on Tisha B'Av*, winner of the 1990 Lambda Literary Award, is a collection of short stories that explores a variety of issues concerning the Holocaust, gayness, and Jewish identity. The collection's Holocaust short stories portray a variety of survivor images. Some are harsh and rejecting, while others attempt to teach lessons to the second generation. These contradictory images are reminiscent of Finkelstein's Brenda Szuster, who holds conflicting images of her own parents whom, as we recall, she sees as both heroes and misfits. Further, the reader learns of the difference between survivors and their offspring. "Witness," which Raphael writes from the perspective of a daughter of Job, describes the protagonist's mother as "a woman for whom loss was not a memory but a shadow hanging over everything she did" (197–205). Much in the manner that Spiegelman describes his father's "bleeding history," the narrator in "Witness" observes of her mother: "she would suddenly blur for me as a woman, as my mother, and seem a figure burdened by history." Yet, again like Finkelstein's and Salamon's protagonists, the narrator describes her mother as "a monument to a different vision of being a woman." Moreover, one of the stories—"Fresh Air"—raises the issue of survivor revenge, which, as we have noted earlier, is raised directly only by the Canadian writer J. J. Steinfeld. Both male and female survivors in Raphael's stories are psychologically remote from their children and, consequently, inflict great emotional pain on their offspring. The results of this Holocaust-induced flawed parenting are noted by Hass, who perceptively writes:

> the consideration for the children of survivors, therefore, is whether their Holocaust background will debilitate and constrain them or will be transformed into positive intrapersonal qualities and interpersonal concerns. The answer to this question . . . is equivocal.[50]

In the same tale, Raphael describes the mother in a manner that presents her as literally bearing Lifton's death imprint while simultaneously revealing the difference between witnesses and their offspring. The mother is slightly injured after unsuccessfully attempting to run down a former camp guard whom she saw crossing the street in Queens. Convalescing at home, the mother keeps opening windows in order to let in fresh air. Finally, she confides to her son that this air is needed to dispel the stench of the death camps, about which he could never know: "the filth, the piles . . . worse than death. The smell. Books can't tell you, film is nothing" (114). Sobbing, she tells the boy that the smell is now on her and she cannot get it off. The second-generation witness, however, is bound to observe—and not experience—his mother's suffering. Rather, his is the task of finding his own voice with which to bear witness to his mother's continuing anguish.

Certain of Raphael's stories deal with the issue of whether to have children after Auschwitz. This is fundamentally a theological issue.[51] Should the Jewish people continue to exist as Jews? If not, what meaning does this have for all those who throughout history have lived as Jews? Survivor responses are contradictory. For example, in "Fresh Air" a survivor refuses to have a postwar abortion because so many Jewish children had already been murdered. Yet, in "The Life You Have," the survivor mother supports abortion precisely because of the murder of one and a half million Jewish children. The world cannot accept Jews. Yet, Raphael is willing to indict the mother's homophobia no less than Nazism's murder of the Jews. For example, upon discovering her son's gayness, she writes him a note regretting that she had not aborted him. This seems a heavy-handed authorial technique. No matter what one's personal views, on phenomenological and historical grounds there is no valid comparison between the Holocaust and abortion.

Raphael does, however, write feelingly of the emotional burden placed on children of survivors. The narrator son in "Fresh Air" observes that he "was a child of necessity, of duty to the past, named not for just one lost relative but a whole family of cousins in Lublin: the Franks." The son, interpreting his first name—Frank—as a memorial, begins to understand that this fact "perhaps . . . explained [his] mother's distance, [his] father's rage—how could you be intimate with a block of stone?" (109). Generalizing from this phenomenon, Hass notes two relevant points. First, survivor powerlessness to protect loved ones during the war frequently is manifested as postwar rage displaced from the persecutors towards the survivor's children. Second, survivors overvalued their children, "perceiving them to represent murdered relatives, if not European Jewry as a whole."[52]

Like all of the second-generation writers in this study, Raphael is acutely conscious of the difference between survivors and their offspring. His protagonists echo Wiesel's earlier-cited observation about the distinction between memory and imagination. The second generation can speak for but not in place of the survivors. For example, Raphael's narrator in "Fresh Air" muses: "But then I had not survived bombings, beatings, typhus, near-starvation, and the death of all my friends, so what did I know?" Similarly, in "War Stories" Raphael describes the difference between a survivor mother—who told of her experiences—and her son Marc, who listened. In the process, he distinguishes between words and comprehension. The words made sense, but "slowly strung together, the pictures they created crushed Marc." "How," asks Raphael, "was he to deal with the unimaginable?" (24).

I have chosen to focus on three Holocaust short stories in *Dancing on Tisha B'Av*, two of which also shed light on the relationship between Jewish identity and sexual orientation. A common thread running throughout the stories is the "conspiracy of silence" in which many survivors, including Raphael's parents, engage. Noted by all the authors in this study, who as children hear only isolated vignettes of their parents' Holocaust experience, Raphael's example is an extreme form of the situation. Owing to his parents' finding their past too difficult to talk about, the Holocaust becomes a barrier between the generations. This phenomenon is strikingly present in the second-generation documentary films discussed below in chapter 5.

"Inheritance"[53] begins with the narrator's comment that he was lucky when his mother died; being alone in another state he did not know that she had willed him "the German money." Ostensibly, this tale deals with German reparation payments to survivors, the so-called *Wiedergutmachung*, or "making good again." Under this plan, the government of what was formerly West Germany agreed to pay compensation to Jewish prisoners of the Third Reich. This compensation could only be paid for the prisoners' slave labor. There is no way that one could be compensated ethically, morally, psychologically, or theologically for the Holocaust.

In fact, *Wiedergutmachung*—a particularly questionable word in this context—raised a profound emotional and moral crisis in the survivor community, and formed part of the community's legacy to their offspring. Some survivors believed it proper to accept such payments. Benjamin Ferencz, an international lawyer who played a vital role in establishing material claims against Germany on behalf of Holocaust survivors, writes that these payments "made [survivors'] lives just a little bit easier. To some it meant a new start in a new direction."[54] However, others felt that accepting such money would dishonor the memory of the dead. One pious survivor of the I. G. Farben slave labor plant at Buna-Auschwitz refused payment. He wrote that "his conscience dictated that he should accept no money from the sadists."[55]

The narrator of "Inheritance" recalls the family's emotional tumult when his mother reluctantly agrees to the requisite medical examinations and legal work to receive reparations. But the money remains unspent. While the mother was alive neither the German money nor her years in concentration camps were spoken about. In fact, there was very little emotion expressed in the home. Wondering why his mother had left him the money—was it a test?—the narrator recalls that his mother had treated him "like a poor relation she'd taken in out of pity" (178). The distance between mother and son stands in striking contrast to the closeness of Friedman's Jason Kole and his mother. Yet, as we have seen, distancing is a common phenomenon among survivors. While it may help them avoid confronting their own pain, it also immeasurably increases the pain of their children.

The tale concludes with two memories and a realization. In the process, Raphael underscores the feeling reported by many second-generation witnesses that, as (replacement) children, they often felt "invisible" to their parents. Wiesel writes about this phenomenon in two of his second-generation novels, *The Oath* and *The Fifth Son*. Similarly, the narrator of "Inheritance," who is the oldest, most intellectual, and emotionally stable of the family's three children, feels that none of them had ever been "quite real" to their mother. Having lost everything: home, country, people, and family—the mother did not even possess any photographs—she held on to the past "through silence." (As an aside, Raphael told an interviewer that—when younger—he would read about the Holocaust "to try to pass through my parents' silence, to try to understand them."[56]) In "Inheritance," the narrator recalls that his mother's silence in fact spoke volumes and was expressed through her frequent nightmares. Like Spiegelman, Raphael's narrator remembers hearing his parent's nightmares. Yet, much in the manner of Eva Just, who warned her children not to provoke their father, in this tale the narrator's father would give his children an admonishing look in the morning that signaled them not to mention the nightmare. Nonverbal cues served both to communicate the survivor's continued suffering and to thwart the children's natural sense of curiosity. Stifling their desire to know more about their mother led, in turn, to further the distance between parent and children.

The narrator is in fact claimant to two inheritances. Materially, he receives the *Wiedergutmachung*. Yet this money will remain unspent. He also inherits memories of watching his mother's continuing survival. For example, in addition to hearing her nightmares, he recalls his mother sitting alone at night softly speaking Yiddish. As if to underscore the vicious madness in her world, she would frequently utter the word *Shaydim* (malicious spirits). With his mother's death "howling" inside him, the son finally understands that his mother left him "the German money" to ensure that he will remember the Holocaust. He learns his mother's final Holocaust lesson; "compensating" for the *Shoah* means forgetting the crime.

In "Caravans,"[57] Raphal underscores the complexity of second-generation identity by portraying the narrator's desire to assume both his Jewish religious heritage and his sexual preference as a gay man. By juxtaposing the suffering of a survivor and the presence of homophobia, Raphael implies that all forms of hatred and prejudice are destructive. The story also emphasizes the feeling of kinship that exists among members of the second generation, calling to mind Helen Epstein's observation: "There had to be people like me, who shared what I carried, who had their own version of my iron box." The nameless narrator's remote father feels that his whole life is cursed. Speaking in Yiddish, he exclaims that his life is "empty" (*leydig*), "nothing" (*gornisht*), and "dead" (*toyt*). Hypercritical and impossible to please, the father rejects both Judaism and his own son, whom he refers to as a "faggot" (*feygeleh*). The father's thoughts about his son were communicated to the boy, "like news bulletins" (73), by his mother. To underscore the estrangement between father and son, Raphael describes the son and father as "boarders renting rooms in the same house" (73). The fact that the son is gay further exacerbates the gap between them.

Jewish identity is the topic of the only important discussion between father and son. The narrator's father tells his son the reason that the family has abandoned Jewish religious and ritual practice; the boy was not circumcised because "that's how they *knew*" (72). The father tells his son that he spoke perfect Polish and German and had blue eyes. But one could not hide *that*. Contrasting the innocence of America and the experience of Europe, Raphael's narrator exclaims, "This is America." The father responds to the son's naïve outburst much in the same fashion as Vladek Spiegelman does when ten-year-old Art reports being abandoned by his friends. In this case, the narrator reports that his father "nodded, contemptuous, knowing, his tragedy crushing my unthinking optimism" (72). The father draws a theological lesson as well from Auschwitz. Ridiculing the boy's hope to become a bar mitzvah, the survivor observes, "You don't need all that *chazerai*, its *bubbeh mysehs*, nonsense, junk." Adopting the position of Dr. Hoffman in *The Flood*, and Dr. Just in *White Lies*, the father tells his son, "There's no God, no Torah; it's only lies. All I learned in *cheyder* [religious school], those hours chanting and sweating to be close to God, what did they get me? Tell me that" (73). The survivor's theological rage is bearable neither to himself nor his son. The paradox here is that the second generation wants to belong to the Jewish people, whereas the survivor rages at his suffering caused by belonging.

The son's feeling of psychic pain and social isolation are ameliorated by his friendship with Bonnie Rosenthal, a daughter of survivors. "Talking to Bonnie," he opines, "was like Robinson Caruso discovering footprints on his island: I was not alone" (75). Invited to the Rosenthals for an *'erev Shabbat* (Friday evening) dinner, he meets Bonnie's father—a college professor and a widower—and her younger brother. Her father had been in several camps and had an extensive library on the Holocaust; Bonnie tells the narrator that her father "never left": "He's there every day. You know when you talk to him." Unlike his own father, however, this survivor is willing to speak about his experiences and encourages the narrator to explore further.

Exposed to the richness of Jewish ritual life in the form of a Friday night candle-lighting that reveals his own lack of Jewish knowledge, the narrator is prompted to expand his search for a usable Jewish past. He thinks that, perhaps, "the truth of the man I didn't know [his own father] would be clearer if I searched for him through our shared Jewish past, the tradition he had completely abandoned and refused to pass on to me" (78). Thus, the second-generation witness seeks to learn more about his father by voluntarily embracing the legacy of Jewish history. The Holocaust, while obviously the teenager's point of entry into Judaism, will not be his last stop. As we have seen, his inability to understand his father symbolizes the difficulty that members of the second generation experience in attempting to communicate with their parents and to understand them.

There can, however, be no reconciliation between father and son. While at the Rosenthal's apartment the narrator sleeps with Bonnie's brother. According to kabbalistic tradition, the union of male and female on earth simulates and stimulates that of God and the *Shekhinah* (female aspect of the deity) above. Friday evening is an especially auspicious time for this ritual activity, which, when performed with the correct intention, brings about a *tikkun* of the world. Raphael mentally invites the reader to make this comparison. At the tale's conclusion, the son remembers his parents' horror over the three-day Stonewall riots, which occurred in 1969 at a Greenwich Village gay bar. While homosexuals were beaten by police, the Stonewall riot also launched the gay rights movement in America. Comparing this to events in Nazi Germany, his parents are outraged. The son mistakenly assumes that they are referring to the police beatings and harassment. He is shocked when his father equates homosexuals and Nazis. "They did that too," the father said; "they were *parshiveh baheymehs*: filthy beasts" (81).

Confirmed in his suspicion of his son as a *feygeleh*, the survivor despises both the boy and himself. He continues to think that his life is cursed; first Auschwitz, now the news about his son. Unlike the father's friends, who will have wedding pictures and grandchildren, the narrator's sexual preference will force his father "outside that circle of simple continuity." His father is unable to confirm either the son's sexual preference or his Jewish identity.

"Abominations"[58] is a strong and well-written story that universalizes the *Shoah*'s lessons by explicitly linking antisemitism and homophobia. The setting and the story combine to strengthen Raphael's message. Homophobic graffiti has been sprayed on a bridge located on the Michigan State University campus, which symbolizes Midwestern culture and American values. The sentiments sprayed on the bridge—"KILL ALL FAGS, DEATH TO HOMO QUEERS, GAY? GOT AIDS YET?—voice the feelings of many university groups, including students, faculty, and campus police. This situation conjures up images of public reaction in Germany and throughout Europe both shortly before and during the Holocaust. One does not need a bomb, a gun, or a knife to be a murderer; silent, or not-so-silent, public approval are equally effective. Raphael is, in fact, restating Wiesel's point dealing with the guilt of bystanders, a point that Wiesel dramatizes in his novel *The Town Beyond The Wall*. Further, by focusing on the relationship between siblings of nonwitnessing parents, Raphael underscores the continuing impact of the *Shoah* on succeeding Jewish generations. Interviewed by a reporter for a campus newspaper, Brenda, a professor, unintentionally "outs" her gay brother Nat.

*Abominations* alludes to the biblical prohibition of homosexuality (Lev. 18:22 and 20:13). The textual references read, respectively, "You shall not lie with a male as with a woman; it is an abomination [*to'evah*]"; and "If a man lies with a male as with a woman, both of them have committed an abomination; they shall be put to death, their blood is upon them." While the precise meaning of *to'evah* is far from clear, historically the Book of Leviticus is cited as warrant against homosexual acts. Raphael's use of the title, however, invites readers to consider whose actions are abominable, the gays or the gay-bashers.

Further, the tale—through comparisons with certain acts that transpired during the *Shoah*—links gay-bashing with the millennial abomination of antisemitism. *Abominations* refers to still a third issue: homophobia *within* the Jewish community. Seen leaving a gay bar, Nat and his lover Mark are expelled from an orthodox congregation. This expulsion has serious religious ramifications. For example, Mark is an accomplished *ba'al koreh* (Torah reader). Further, his presence at the small orthodox *minyan* (communal gathering for prayer) is also vital as he is the tenth person, ten being the requisite number for public prayer. Raphael's story illustrates that it is no less an abomination after Auschwitz for Judaism to discriminate against Jews. Raphael contends that "the measure of Judaism is whom it includes, not whom it excludes."[59]

Raphael's contention is clearly a challenge to traditional Judaism. Can the tradition accommodate the pluralism of American Jewish life, including sexual preference? In other words, must the choice be between Judaism and homosexuality? Or can one find a Judaic home despite one's sexual orientation? Answers depend upon denominational ideology. For example, reconstructionist and reform Judaism freely ordain both gays and lesbians as rabbis. The left wing of Judaism has made the greatest accommodation to American pluralism. On the right wing, orthodoxy distinguishes homosexuality from the homosexual. Condemning the former, it is concerned with the latter. Yet, such distinctions seem not to influence behavior towards homosexuality.[60] Conservative Judaism on this issue—as well as others—adopts a position somewhere between the two extremes, frequently distinguishing between halakhic and metahalakhic views of homosexuality.[61]

Globally speaking, gay rights is part of the general challenge that modernity poses to classical Judaism. The tension between traditional teachings and contemporary realities, while nothing new in revealed religion, is now being expressed in intense ways. In a similar manner, can the second-generation witness serve as a bridge between the survivors' experience and the nonwitnessing world? In other words, can the experience of witnessing the witnesses be translated into a message that addresses the concerns of a great variety of people? This question is, finally, one of how appropriately to universalize the Holocaust and its legacy. Michael Berenbaum and Edward T. Linenthal have written insightfully on this issue as it was confronted by the United States Holocaust Memorial Museum.[62]

"Abominations" is, however, fundamentally Brenda's story. She, in turn, is a cipher for the attitude of "straight" Jews toward gayness. It is she who must come to terms with her own feelings about homosexuality, her brother, and her family. She accomplishes this by analogy to the *Shoah*. A colleague who expresses homophobic sentiments is identified as one who believes that the *Shoah* receives too much attention. After being outed, Nat tells Brenda that his dorm room has been torched. She, in turn, remembers seeing films of Germany in the thirties that show the early stages of Nazi violence against Jews: Jewish shops on whose storefronts had been written "JUDEN RAUS" (Out with the Jews), synagogues ablaze, and orthodox Jews being murdered. The fire leaves untouched only Nat's gay liberation pink triangle button.

Although earlier in the story Brenda resented gays appropriating Holocaust symbolism, she now has a change of heart because senseless violence has touched her brother. She thinks of what European Jews had lost: "homes and apartments . . . that had been looted, burned, destroyed, trainloads of plundered bloody goods snaking their way back to the Fatherland: mattresses, pianos, candelabras, coats" (229). Like Julie Salamon's Jamaica Just and Carol Ascher's Eva Hoffman, Raphael's Brenda believes that the Holocaust teaches a lesson of universal tolerance. Unlike Thomas Friedman's Jason Kole and Art Spiegelman, Raphael believes that this lesson is slowly being learned. At the end of the story, Brenda wears the gay liberation button as she drives Nat and Mark home to tell the parents the truth about their relationship. This is pertinent to the second generation because Raphael is suggesting that a *tikkun* of the self can be achieved.

Raphael's story is, on one hand, a clear message about the evil of homophobia. With Wiesel, Ascher, and Salamon, he is telling his readers to stand with the victims of prejudice and hatred. In this way, "Abominations" sensitively universalizes the Holocaust's legacy. His portrayal of Brenda's growing empathy with her brother is a sign that the tensions generated within a family over the discovery of a homosexual (or lesbian) member can be resolved. This is a *tikkun* of family life. Further, the tale is testimony by a second-generation witness that the *Shoah* plays a powerful role in the lives of all Jews, including daughters and sons of nonwitnesses. In addition, Raphael's tale reveals that gays can be committed Jews with valid religious needs. They deserve no less respect than heterosexual Jews. Gay Jews' religious sensibilities are legitimate.

"Abominations" does, however, have conceptual problems and raises historical concerns. For example, Brenda "remembers" that the king of Denmark elected to wear a yellow star in solidarity with Danish Jews. Consequently, she dons Nat's gay liberation button. But the problem here is that Christian X, the Danish King, in fact did not wear a yellow star. Nazi Germany never imposed the Nuremberg laws, which mandated wearing this star, on Denmark.[63] Clearly, King Christian and the majority of Danes served as helpers and rescuers of their Jewish citizens.

Theirs is a record of national moral distinction. But the issue here resides in bearing true witness. If the second-generation witness is to be authentic, then it will have to reflect both what the Holocaust was and the nature of Jewish fate during the *Shoah*. The Holocaust was a *novum* in history because birth itself was a capital offense. Gays were persecuted, tortured, and murdered. They and Nazism's many other victims deserve to be remembered. The point here is not to engage in an obscene study of comparative suffering.[64] How, after all, would one quantify this? Jews were murdered for being Jews, not for any acts, religious or sexual, that they either performed or refrained from performing.

The question that needs constant asking is why the Jews? This question does not imply disrespect for any of Nazism's many victims. Rather, it is to recognize that Nazism built a kingdom of death. The Third Reich's circle of victims kept increasing, but Jews were always at the center of this circle. The historical, interpretive, and phenomenological questions assume even greater urgency in light of the recently opened National Holocaust Memorial Museum in Washington, D.C., as well as the impact on popular culture of Steven Spielberg's film *Schindler's List* and the phenomenon of Holocaust denial.[65] The second-generation witness has a moral obligation to attest with precision to the facts of the Holocaust and to the event's continuing impact. This is one reason that members of the second generation immerse themselves in books about the *Shoah* and why they do not substitute their imagination for their parents' memory.

The question of Brenda's "conversion" is also problematic. Raphael's description of this process is flawed. For example, he merely hints at, without providing adequate detail, the conflicts that Brenda must feel. Does she now love her parents any less? Is she suddenly able to accept Nat and Mark's relationship? What of her own heterosexual feelings? Has she instantaneously resolved all of these issues? Further, how realistic is it to assume that the dorm fire served for her as a functional equivalent of St. Paul's "Damascus Road" experience? Meant to link the victims of antisemitism and gay bashing, the story does not sufficiently distinguish between the two examples.

"Abominations" is linked to two crucial Jewish holy days. The first is Yom Kippur, the solemn Day of Atonement, which occurs in the fall. Ritually, on the Day of Atonement one seeks to do *Tshuvah*, or penance. *Tshuvah* literally means *turning*: turning toward Torah and turning away from sin. A public reading from the Book of Leviticus occurs on Yom Kippur. Hearing the portion read, Brenda muses that, according to the sacred text, her brother and Mark are abominations. She also remembers that this was the time she first brought Nat and Mark home to meet their parents. Further, by not telling the parents about the relationship between the two men, she feels duplicitous.

The tale concludes with a second trip to the parents' home that occurs in the spring, which is the time of Passover. Now Nat and Mark disclose their gayness. Theologically associated with the Exodus from Egypt, Passover marks a liberation from bondage. Further, the Passover seder symbolizes the shedding of not only the physical but the psychological impediments of slavery. Despising oneself, as Raphael once did, for being both a Jew and gay, is the worst form of oppression. For example, like Spiegelman, Raphael discloses that while an undergraduate, he came to the realization that he had a poor self-image as a Jew and that he did not particularly like Jews.[66] Thus, on the level of symbol, Raphael's story describes the liberation of Nat and Mark from the oppression of hiding their gay identity. This is clearly a turning point in their personal lives. Further, on the collective level, American public rituals and events such as gay pride parades and the gay games serve to openly announce that gayness is nothing about which one should be ashamed. Nevertheless, how valid is the implication that by publically proclaiming oneself a survivor or a second-generation witness one will be liberated from oppression. The suicide rate among survivor writers is staggering. There is more than a hint of gay triumphalism in Raphael's story.

*Dancing on Tisha B'Av* does, however, make a significant contribution to understanding second-generation witness identity. Raphael intelligently explores the tensions involved in his various identities; Jewish, second generation, and gay. Each of these identities is a minority within a majority culture. Moreover, the tension inherent in being Jewish and gay is real. For example, the very title of the book is significant. *Tisha B'Av*, the ninth day of the Hebrew month of *Av*, is the day that tradition assigns to the time of the destruction of the Temple in Jerusalem (both in 586 B.C.E. and in 70 C.E.). In commemoration of this somber time, traditional Jews fast, attend worship services, sit on low stools as a sign of mourning, and read from the Book of Lamentations. In contrast, Raphael is dancing on this date. Doubtless, he is suggesting that conventional—and oppressive—traditional norms such as the biblical warrant for homophobia must be overturned in order to achieve freedom from persecution.

Initially fearful of his identities, Raphael ends by embracing them. Further, he views writing itself as a potentially salvific act. Books can change the way people think, believe, and behave. Writers sensitize people to tragedies and, in the process, galvanize their audiences to seek justice. Responding to a question about the writer's role in sensitizing people to tragedies ranging from the Holocaust to AIDS, Raphael depicts writers as "messengers." Pointing to the examples of Emile Zola and Harriet Beecher Stowe, each of whom in his or her own fashion sought to achieve at least a partial *tikkun olam*, Raphael—in Wieselian fashion—observes that "writing does change the world."[67] To the extent that this change occurs, one can discern the beginnings of a *tikkun* of a world still deeply flawed by hatred and oppression.

Raphael's evocative novel *Winter Eyes* pursues and sharpens some of the themes in his earlier writing. Thus, survivors' silence about their Holocaust experience, denial of Jewish identity, and anger with God figure prominently in the work. Yet, *Winter Eyes*—the title derives from the young protagonist's mishearing of the German *Die Wintereise* (winter journey)—is also a coming-of-age novel that explores the protagonist's encounter with his Jewish and gay identities. Stefan Borowski is a precocious child of survivors whose parents conceal the youth's Jewish identity from him. Max, his father, is a university professor, while Anya, his mother, works in publishing. Like the Hoffmans in Ascher's *The Flood*, both parents know many languages and are highly cultured, especially in the realm of music. Further, this love of culture is the only discernable aspect of their Jewish identity. Divided into three unequal segments— "Lessons," "Separate Lives," and "Connections"—the novel follows Stefan's growing awareness of his gay identity and his anger at discovering that he is Jewish. In the process, Raphael reveals the degree of Jewish self-hatred that Stefan's flawed upbringing has inculcated. Like Ascher, Raphael begins by adopting a child's point view in which innocence and confusion are blended.

Unlike the stories in *Dancing on Tisha B'Av*, the novel is set in New York City during the sixties. Like Friedmann, Raphael employs the student protest against American involvement in Vietnam as a backdrop for his protagonist's own inner turmoil. The youth wonders why his remote parents rarely speak to him about the family's history or any other personal issues, and why his mother exclaims that she should not have had a child. Further, his Uncle Sasha, who teaches Stefan to play the piano and is the one adult in his family who expresses tenderness toward him, is reluctant to speak about the past. Raphael underscores this conspiracy of silence in several ways. For instance, all of Sasha's allusions to the Holocaust end in unfinished sentences. On those rare occasions when they do speak of the past, it is always about the war. This causes the young boy to petulantly muse, "The War [was] always coming in . . . couldn't they ever forget it? (51). Stefan's outburst calls to mind J. J. Steinfeld's short story "Because of the War."

Raphael's novel deftly examines certain themes that commonly appear in second-generation writings. For example, he treats the absence of an extended family and the singularity of survivor families. As in the case of the youthful Jamaica Just, Stefan's questions about an absent extended family are met with evasive responses. For instance, when Stefan asks why he—unlike everyone else at school—has no grandparents, Sasha simply says, "They died." Again, as in *White Lies*, Stefan's parents frequently quarrel in a foreign language behind locked doors. Stefan discovers a pre-Holocaust photo in his uncle's bedroom. Of the four people pictured, he can identify his parents and uncle, but not the fourth person, who is his mother's sister, Eva; The youngster thinks that she looked like his mother. And like him. He attempts unsuccessfully to discover the identity of his murdered aunt.

Stefan feels surrounded by secrets; the past is a secret, the adults keep secrets by speaking to each other in Russian or Polish, and his emotional life is a secret. Stefan's gayness, which he describes as "the biggest secret he ever had" (122)—at the time—is expressed in a variety of ways that culminate in his initial experience with Louie, an older boy who lives in the same apartment building. His parents' divorce further complicate the youth's emotional life. After suffering a heart attack, Stefan's father reveals the truth about the Holocaust, the parents' survival, and the youth's own Jewishness. At this point, Stefan is enraged and feels anger toward his parents, his uncle, and his own identity. In response to his son's angry query about how the parents could do this to him, the father says that they wanted to "save him from the past." Unlike either Salamon's Jamaica Just or Art Spiegelman, Raphael's protagonist neither heard "bits and pieces" of Holocaust tales nor had any awareness of himself as a Jew. The news about his own identity and his parents' Holocaust experience overwhelms him. Moreover, Stefan's image of survivors differs considerably from Salamon's heroic view. For example, he "feels ugly about his parents. Like when he couldn't stop looking at a man or woman without a hand or leg; his father had told him never to stare but he always did when he saw a broken person" (83).

Stefan inherits no memory of a Jewish past. Consequently, he does not know who he is and keenly feels this lack of a coherent autobiography. He is able to fill in neither the "many blanks" nor to account for the omnipresent inconsistency between what his parents say and how they behave. For instance, although his parents and uncle always denigrate America as vulgar in comparison to Europe, they also sometimes hate the Old Country. When he expresses a desire to learn Polish and visit the country, Sasha tells Stefan not to go because the country is a graveyard. The boy's confusion extends also to the religious realm. On the one hand, his parents are visibly upset by the sound of church bells. Further, Louie is surprised that Steven—although nominally Christian—knows so little about either the Bible or about Christianity. Yet, on the other hand, the elder Borowski's intensely reject Judaism. For example, like Dr. Hoffman in *The Flood* and the nameless father in Raphael's *Caravans*, Professor Borowski is a militant atheist. He tells Stefan that "There is no God. . . . It's all lies" (41). Anya, for her part, derides the Bible as a book responsible for millions of deaths. Stefan is deeply perplexed by these utterances.

Stefan's uncertain identity is further shaken when he hears Louie utter antisemitic sentiments (e.g., that the Jews killed Jesus). Although Sasha had explained to Stefan that the Romans executed Jesus, when Louie cites biblical sources Stefan is too embarrassed to admit never having read the Bible. Like the child-survivor and lesbian activist Irena Klepfisz, Raphael raises the issue of antisemitism in the gay movement.[68] As committed to human dignity and freedom as the gay and lesbian communities appear to be, many in these communities are also are stigmatized by the millennial scourge of Jew-hatred. Moreover, Raphael implies that even while agitating for gay rights—a distinctly contemporary phenomenon—certain members of the gay community rely on the false teachings of antiquity to condemn others. Addressing this issue elsewhere, Raphael speaks of himself as being doubly an outsider: a gay in Judaism and a Jew in the gay community.[69]

Second-generation Jewish identity is a complex issue. Raphael illuminates this complexity by introducing its ethnic component. The outbreak of the 1967 Six Day War between Israel and the Arab states yields parental responses that surprise Stefan. He is puzzled at the fact that his family seems drawn closer by the dramatic events. His confusion intensifies when Anya says, "We need to be together at times like this" (107), and his father, who after divorcing Anya now teaches at the University of Michigan, calls Stefan in New York City. Why this sudden concern for Israel? What possible connection do the Borowski's have to the Jewish State?

Focusing on American Jewish identity, Raphael describes the doomed high-school romance between Stefan and Jenny. Uncomfortable with her sexually, Stefan is equally disturbed that Jenny's Vietnam protest is sterile and vapid. Juxtaposing types of violence, Raphael's protagonist is mugged on his way to a protest. While Raphael's portrayal of the loss of innocence is not as dramatic as the portrayals of the other second-generation writers in this study, his protagonist is made to experience unwarranted suffering. Following this incident, Stefan begins getting in touch with Holocaust history. Reading about the camps he imagines the filthy bodies of his parents and Sasha and discovers Poland's deep-seated antisemitic attitudes. He further distinguishes between the "safe and untouched" Vietnam petition signers like Jenny and "the simple brutality" of his own mugging. He is able to utilize his his own experience of physical pain as a point of entry into his parents' Holocaust world. His experience of physical pain is coupled with Stefan's psychic distress at his mother's remarriage. Yet it is this second marriage that rekindles a Jewish spark in Stefan's mother and, consequently, stimulates him to explore his own identity.

The novel's dénouement occurs when Stefan meets and falls in love with Marsha, a bisexual Jewish woman. Fleeing New York City, Stefan enrolls at Syracuse University in order to come to grips with his multiple identities. Like Bonnie Rosenthal in *Caravans*, Marsha is the only female able to make Raphael's protagonist comfortable with his identity. In fact, Stefan and Marsha have travelled a similar path. Their experience of American Jewish cultural diversity leaves both of them wounded. Yet, their behavior exemplifies aspects of Greenberg's voluntary covenant. Raphael, again like Klepfisz, illustrates some of the difficulty that Jewish feminists have concerning traditional Jewish teachings and orthopraxis. For example, Marsha confides to Stefan that, as a young girl, she felt ritually excluded from Judaism. Marginalized by the Conservative synagogue services, she is made to feel that she "wasn't as good as them" (235), Marsha stopped going altogether after leaving home. Yet, Marsha's is a form of "dissimilation";[70] she rejects that which is oppressive in the tradition, but not the tradition itself. For example, she reads books on Jewish history and the Holocaust, attempting to seek her own connection to her Jewish identity.

Stefan's Jewish self-hatred prompts a long discussion between him and Marsha. He tells her about his lonely and unhappy childhood, including his discovery of a No-Jew Club at his school. Stefan befriends one of his classmates, himself marginalized and ridiculed by the other boys, only to discover that his friend is also antisemitic. The list of hurts piles up: his parents' divorce, finding out from his father that his parents and Sasha had lied to him, "being Jewish and too ashamed and betrayed to do anything about it" (233). Stefan's is a classic example of those whose feelings of self-loathing come from internalizing negative societal images of Jews.[71] A consequence of the Jewish encounter with the Enlightenment, this self-hatred paralyzes interest in discovering more about oneself Jewishly. For example, he feels like throwing up at the sight of Hasidim (distinctively garbed pious Jews). Echoing Mrs. Hoffman's unstated fear in Carol Ascher's *The Flood*, Stefan thinks, "Its like, that's me! They look so gross" (234). Further, he embraces additional antisemitic stereotypes: Jews are pushy, loud, and love money. He also wonders if his nose is "too Jewish." Nevertheless, Stefan invites Marsha to New York to meet his mother and stepfather. Furthermore, he wants her to accompany him to Michigan to attend his father's wedding. Thus, despite the Holocaust and his own feelings of Jewish self-doubt, Stefan's actions betray his desire to be connected to Judaism.

Both Stefan and Marsha voluntarily embrace the covenant. Marsha's reading about Jewish history, including the Holocaust, reveals that she is connecting with her identity. Stefan's own sense of being a covenanted Jew is more problematic. He begins to accept his second-generation identity, the legacy of the *Shoah*, and his own bisexuality through his relationship with Marsha. Both of them embody Greenberg's criterion that those who voluntarily embrace the covenant "make certain commitments and express certain beliefs."[72] Greenberg compares the situation of the post-Auschwitz Jew to that of the convert in writing that the convert "testifies that although the Jews are driven, tormented and persecuted to this very day, the convert still wants to be a Jew, that is wants to offer the testimony of hope anyway."[73] After Auschwitz, Greenberg attests, "the survival of the Jewish people in a world full of enemies, where the model of the Holocaust is circulating, is in itself testimony to the existence of a hidden God whose awesome, if invisible, force is evidenced in the ongoing life of the Jewish people."[74] Raphael's novel portrays the confusion and difficulty of embracing the ethnic and sexual aspects of his second-generation identity; yet his voluntary, if incremental, assumption of Jewish identity is the thread that stitches these components of selfhood together. His Jewishness is a "testimony of hope."

*Winter Eyes* is a provocative but flawed novel. Raphael's book does reveal the psychic devastation wrought on the second generation by survivor parents who do not share their experiences with their offspring. Moreover, certain survivors hope to "protect" their children by raising them as non-Jews. As noted earlier, this was the case with Gabriela Korda, the South American daughter of survivors who was raised as a Protestant by her parents, who had identified with the aggressor. Korda's father changed his attitude dramatically, however, with the advent of the Eichmann trial.[75] Yet, it seems odd that Stefan, despite his precocity, never reads about the Holocaust on his own. Moreover, his Jewish self-hatred seems greater than his unease about being gay. Finally, there appears to be a spirit of gays excluding from their world all straight people. This detracts from the novel's solid contribution to understanding the Holocaust's universal dimension.


## CONCLUSION

The works of Ascher, Salamon, and Raphael reveal several important dimensions of second-generation identity and the quest for *tikkun olam*. These writers all focus on the Jewish tragedy but use it as a springboard to assert universal lessons about the necessity for seeking social justice, the importance of tolerance, and the ability to achieve a *tikkun* of the self. Stories that convey the continuing impact of antisemitism and other forms of racial hatred may educate audiences, thereby helping to eradicate or at least diminish this type of behavior. Moreover, each of the authors views writing as accomplishing several crucial goals. Writing is first of all a protest against injustice. Secondly, these authors are attempting to "turn history into story," thereby hoping to come to grips with what remains an unmasterable trauma. Finally, by writing the story of their parents' survival and its impact on their own lives, these second-generation witnesses hope to share the message of common human vulnerability, thereby helping to prevent Holocaust modes of thought from operating in the world.

We turn next to documentary films made by members of the second generation. These works treat both the psychosocial and theological dimensions of being a second-generation witness while providing a model of "working through" the effects of the *Shoah*.

# CHAPTER 5

## *Second-Generation Documentaries and Docudramas: Jewish Particularism*

> Only by learning about the past can we have some appreciation of what was lost, destroyed. And, perhaps, only through knowledge of the Holocaust and our parents can those in the second generation fully understand themselves.
>
> —Aaron Hass[1]

The films of second-generation witnesses focus on psychosocial issues that played a prominent role in the filmmakers' lives as children and adolescents. These films are significant in visualizing an important transition in the lives of second-generation witnesses. As young adults they are now prepared to confront the anxiety, pain, and uncertainty of growing up in survivor households. Issues such as the survivors' "conspiracy of silence," parents who wanted either to micromanage their children's lives or who, conversely, were emotionally unavailable, and feelings of being unworthy emerge with great frequency. Yet, these second-generation films reveal attempts at a *tikkun* of self, of family life, and of society on the part of the contemporary children of Job who themselves are either married or have partners, and many of whom now have families of their own.

The films discussed in this chapter collectively deal, on the one hand, with a "working through" of the trauma of the participants' Holocaust inheritance. Saul Friedlander writes that "*Working through means confronting the individual voice* in a field dominated by political decisions and administrative decrees which neutralize the concreteness of despair and death."[2] As these films demonstrate, the second-generation witnesses have confronted the individual voice of survivors in an intense manner. On the other hand, these films are creative efforts to mourn their own losses—for example, abbreviated or lost childhoods, murdered grandparents, and lack of an extended family. Additionally, these works help give shape to the type of Holocaust memory that members of the second generation will transmit to their own children.

Eva Fogelman observes that the framing question of her film *Breaking the Silence* is "What does it mean to be Jewish after the Holocaust?" This query animates all of the second-generation films discussed in this chapter. Some in this generation recall rebelling against their Jewish identity as youngsters. Like Lev Raphael, they remember being frightened that what befell their parents in the Holocaust would be their own lot as well. Others report the psychologically stifling atmosphere of their childhood homes. In an important study, Ilana Kuperstein observes the dynamic at work as the Holocaust impacts on the Jewish identity of the adolescent children of Job:

> Many experience conflicts regarding their Jewish identity. The fact that their parents were victimized purely on the basis of their race has many different effects on the parent and the child. Whether the adolescents reject Judaism or not, in most cases they have a very strong sense of being Jewish, because of their parents' experiences, and almost regardless of their religious convictions. These adolescents may rebel against religion, yet they usually come back to see themselves as Jews, and those who are not devoted in the religious sense still retain cultural ties to their heritage. Some become supporters of Zionism and of Israel. It is almost as if Hitler's persecution has singled their families out as Jews, and made them forever aware of being Jewish.[3]

As they mature, however, the second-generation witnesses seek to define themselves as post-Holocaust Jews who have a distinctive Holocaust legacy. Further, this legacy leads to a definition of Jewish identity that involves dimensions of Greenberg's voluntary covenant, focusing on the noncoercive nature of post-Holocaust Jewish affirmation.

Second-generation films consist of several genres. First are documentaries, in which children and parents relate their own experiences. But the term *documentary* in this case indicates a new type of genre. Annette Insdorf astutely observes that these documentaries are "a new form—neither documentary nor fiction—that shapes documentary material through a personal voice."[4] "Certain filmmakers," she writes, "have been able to transform the documentary into a personal genre, closer to the memoir or journal."[5] Next, there are docudramas, which utilize actors, although not necessarily professionals, in order to *dramatize* both second-generation issues and particular events that happened to survivor parents during the *Shoah*. Third are films dealing with the *Hasidei Umot Ha-Olam* (Righteous Among the Nations), non-Jewish helpers who at great risk to themselves and their families assisted Jews. This genre is discussed in chapter 6.

Important examples of the documentary genre include Gina Blumenthal's *In Dark Places* (1978), Miriam Strilky Rosenbush's *The Legacy: Children of Holocaust Survivors* (1980), Steven Brand's *Kaddish* (1983), Jack and Danny Fisher's *A Generation Apart* (1983), Eva

Fogelman's award-winning *Breaking the Silence* (1984), and the Australian film *Angst* (1993). A related subgenre combines the documentary format with experimental techniques, best exemplified by Abraham Ravett's *Half-Sister* (1985), *Everything's For You* (1989), and *In Memory* (1993). These films share several features: they contain archival footage, their discussions portray Jewish life prior to the *Shoah*, and each encapsulates the intense nature of survivor—offspring relationships, including the effects of survivor inability to mourn, sublimated rage, and prolonged grieving. The films of Blumenthal, Brand, and Fogelman include reflections by scholars who attempt to place the Holocaust and its aftermath in philosophical, psychohistorical, and theological contexts. For example, Susan Sontag speaks on camera in Blumenthal's *In Dark Places*, Robert Jay Lifton and Edward Mason offer observations on the second-generation in Fogelman's *Breaking the Silence*, and Brand's *Kaddish*, while not interviewing scholars on camera, credits three Holocaust scholars; Yael Danieli, Yaffa Eliach, and Randolph Braham.

## THE DOCUMENTARIES

Among the documentaries, I have chosen to discuss *Kaddish*, *Breaking the Silence*, *A Generation Apart*, Ravitt's trilogy, and *Angst*. Each film depicts various aspects of the Holocaust's legacy for second-generation identity. Psychosocial themes that effect the second generation include separation anxiety, distancing between survivors and their offspring, difficulty in communicating about the *Shoah*, and second-generation witnesses' anxiety about their connection to the Holocaust and to Judaism. In certain of the films, survivors and their offspring learn to speak to each other, thereby freeing the emotional logjam that impeded the development of their relationship. In addition, these films speak of a second-generation mission in terms of the *tikkun* of bearing witness on behalf of their parents. Further, *Breaking the Silence* articulates a universal dimension in speaking about a moral mission to alleviate suffering and improve the lot of humanity. On the theological level, each of these works makes either an explicit or implicit statement about the meaning of Jewish identity. Why did my parents suffer? And why do I suffer the consequences? are both ways of asking about the role of God, the credibility of the covenant after Auschwitz, and the task of seeking to mend the world.

## *KADDISH*

Steven Brand's *Kaddish* traces the stages of Jewish identity in the life of Yossi Klein. Brand himself is a son of Viennese Jews who fled Austria in

1939. His film was made over a five-year period and deals with the complex father-son relationship between Yossi and Zoltan Klein. The film opens in Jerusalem's *Har Ha-Menuchot* Cemetery with Yossi saying *kaddish* for Zoltan.⁶ Yossi recalls his father's emphasis on his survival and the fact that the Kleins (parents, Yossi, and his sister Karen) are a survivor family, although Mrs. Klein and the children are American-born. Yossi emphasizes the difference between survivors and nonwitnesses in observing that Zoltan told him bedtime stories of the Holocaust, whereas his mother would read him Dr. Seuss books. Since his father's death, Yossi watches home videos of Zoltan narrating his own Holocaust experience. Cinematagraphically, scenes from the present are shot in color whereas both prewar and Holocaust stills are in black and white, thereby simultaneously distinguishing time periods while revealing the inexorable *presence of the absence* in the lives of survivors and their children.

Yossi's embrace of his Jewish identity comes only at the end of a very long and painful path of self-discovery. He recalls that as a child he experienced anger toward and fear of family rituals, such as the lighting of candles on Friday evening. Echoing Lev Raphael's feelings, Yossi observes: "The rituals disturbed me because I saw our family as reenacting something that had been murdered. Yarmukah, teffilin (phylacteries), shul, Shabbes, the whole thing had been wiped out. I was very frightened. If this is what happened to millions of Jewish families who lived exactly as we did, then what was going to happen to us?" This position reminds viewers that, as children, many offspring of survivors display great anxiety about their Jewish identity .

These feelings intensify when Yossi discovers he is named after his grandfather—"Somebody who," he observes, "got murdered because he was Jewish." Like Isaac Bashevis Singer's Herman Broder and Masha in *Enemies, A Love Story*, Yossi worries about America being overrun by Nazis. Indeed, Insdorf observes that "Yossi's obsessive Judaism [is] inseparable from paranoia."⁷ Yet, his response also confirms Prince's observation about the role of Holocaust imagery in the lives of the second-generation. For example, Yossi wonders if people would hide him, and reports a dream in which the Nazis invade Coney Island and kill him as he eats cotton candy. Yossi embraces this apocalyptic stance early on when, at the age of eight, he literally begins writing Zoltan's story, viewing his father as a monument.

Yet later Yossi exhibits the effects of intergenerational tension, observing that he had to get out of the house and break from his father's legacy: "I wanted to be normal and an American." Like Julie Salamon's Jamaica Just, Yossi notes the perplexity of the second generation when he observes, "Nobody ever tried to kill *me* because I am Jewish." Yossi's apparent denial of Holocaust impact on his identity is subsequently abandoned in favor of a more mature and nuanced understanding of the relationship between his father's past and his own present. How, then, is the second generation connected to the *Shoah*?

Yossi has many discussions with Zoltan about Jewish identity and the *Shoah*. Initially following Rubenstein's early distinction, Zoltan embraces ethnic identity while rejecting the traditional view of God as an interventionist deity. Thirty or forty years ago, observes Zoltan, they (Nazis) proved that anyone born a Jew cannot be made safer by denying or disowning Judaism. Yet when Yossi asks Zoltan if he prayed to God in the bunker in which he had been buried for five months, the older man shakes his head no. "Later," Zoltan says, "we forgave God and prayed again." The trial of God is a theme that emerges among many Holocaust survivors. Wiesel, for example, notes that such a trial occurred in Auschwitz in 1944. Three scholars, he writes, "convened a rabbinic court of law to indict the Almighty." The verdict was guilty. "There was a silence," writes Wiesel, "that could be compared only to *Mattan Torah* at Sinai, which the Talmud describes as a special silence." But after "a minute or an infinity of silence," one of the judges "shook himself, smiled sadly, and said, 'And now let us pray *Maariv*' [the evening prayer]."[8] Zoltan is a knowledgeable but nonpracticing Jew. In the film he wears a *yarmukah*, but the viewer discovers that this is because Breindy, his wife, agreed to marriage only if he would consent to become Orthodox. Zoltan's Holocaust experience and the horrors of recurring nightmares in which he imagines ways that his parents met their deaths destroyed all vestiges of traditional attitudes towards God and faith.

However, like nearly all survivors, Zoltan is firmly committed to the importance of Israel.[9] The camera emphasizes this point by focusing on Zoltan's face, which shows both animation and dignity as he discusses the Jewish state. It is clear that he is in full agreement with the view of Rabbi Joseph Soloveitchek that Israel is "a knock on the door of history." Zoltan no longer feels secure in America and contends that Israel is the future for his childrens' generation. At this point, the camera cuts to an Israel Day parade in New York City. Yossi's definition of Jewish identity, on the other hand, lacks even the comfort of Israel. "A Jew," he observes, "is one who is constantly on the verge; on the verge of annihilation, on the verge of revelation, constantly on the verge." Like Spiegelman, Yossi's Holocaust legacy leads him to seek therapy.

Yossi's search for his second-generation identity and his relationship with his father are framed by politics. The son is an activist on behalf of the Jews in the Soviet Union, and edits a Jewish newspaper. Arguing at an *'erev Shabbat* dinner, Yossi refrains from eating while contending that the Jewish people need a post-Holocaust Judaism. Zoltan, wiser and with a humor born of agony, asks, "You can't eat boiled chicken in the post-

Holocaust Judaism?" Shortly afterwards, Yossi's parents attend an unveiling in Israel, where Zoltan dies. The camera juxtaposes Yossi saying *Kaddish* in Israel and a Purim celebration, black-and-white photos of Anne Frank and Zoltan, and a color shot of Israel. By this method Brand suggests the unity and continuity of Jewish history while emphasizing the centrality of both the *Shoah* and the reborn State of Israel.

Now the head of the Klein household, Yossi reflects on the tender aspect of his relationship with Zoltan. Although Yossi contends that "when you grow up with death you're just not stunned by it," the camera shows a different reality. His face is masked in sadness. Recounting the things he will miss about his father, Yossi articulates both the survivor's fear of politicians and the social world and a heretofore unacknowledged warmth and compassion. Concerning the former, he recalls Zoltan announcing in a doctor's office that Kissinger is worse than Hitler. Yet Yossi also confides, "I miss kissing him. We used to kiss all the time when I was a kid." Extending the bounds of his personal loss, Yossi speculates that the loss of survivors "is also a Jewish loss." Like certain of Raphael's survivors, after the war Zoltan had not initially wished to bring Jewish children into the world. In a mimetic extension of this sentiment, Yossi tells the viewer that he is afraid of living in, or bringing children into, a world bereft of Holocaust survivors.

The camera shows three different interpretations of post-Auschwitz Jewish identity. Karen, Yossi's sister, is expecting a baby, thereby symbolizing Jewish continuity. Yossi is now wearing a *yarmukah* and "trying to extract what is eternal in Judaism" because there is no certainty in our time. His ideological stance impedes him from exploring the possibility of marriage and children, thereby cutting off a Jewish future. His mother, concerned with preserving that future, observes that Yossi is really not yet ready for marriage. Yossi is convinced that (in the late seventies and early eighties) conditions are ripe for another Holocaust. The camera cuts to a still of Hitler, then focuses on New York City, returning at last to mounds of human remains and ovens. Echoing Susan Sontag's concerns, Yossi reflects on the fact that both the word itself and images of the Holocaust have been appropriated and diminished by American culture. Further, he is concerned about the unbridled growth of materialism, which he links to the emergence of apocalyptic violence.

Concerning the phenomenon of apocalypse, Susan Sontag opines in Blumenfeld's *In Dark Places* that people are in search of extreme sensations and that "Holocaust" has become an all-too-convenient shorthand. In *Kaddish*, Zoltan's voiceover is heard saying "When we came back" and is played against the backdrop of a desolate and gutted New York City. Yet Zoltan never abandons his belief in Jewish peoplehood. The camera cuts to Yossi interviewing Zoltan. Yossi's father, reflecting the views of Eliezer Berkovits and Irving Greenberg, opines that "history proves there is something special about this little people, the Jews." Refraining from formal belief in God, Zoltan's Jewish identity is confirmed by the continued existence of the Jewish people itself.

Yossi's breakthrough in relating to his father and to his own Jewish identity occurs when he goes to Jerusalem in 1981 to attend the World Gathering of Jewish Holocaust Survivors, where he interviews survivors. Amidst tales of great personal loss, the camera cuts to the interior of Yad VaShem and pictures of young Jewish children with numbers on their arms. Yet Yossi is tired of the "same old rhetoric." Instead, he wants something enduring about the meaning of survival for the Jewish people. As if to emphasize the dissonance between words about the Holocaust and the experience of living in a survivor household, the camera cuts to survivors and the president of Israel making speeches at the gathering. Yet on the last day, Yossi is touched by words that emphasize the fact that the burden of bearing the Holocaust legacy is now passing to the children of survivors.

On camera, Wiesel eloquently states the relationship between the *Shoah* and Israel. He observes, "Our pain is only bearable because we are meeting in Jerusalem." This love for Israel (*Ahavat Yisrael*) is precisely what Zoltan Klein attempts to infuse in Yossi. Listening to Yemenite Jews blowing the *Shofarot* (rams horns), Yossi thinks it sounds like the "heralding of redemption," and he weeps uncontrollably. He is jealous of the sons and fathers who share the experience at the World Gathering. He knows that Zoltan would have seen it as "the culmination of everything." The World Gathering enables Yossi to transcend all emotional and psychic barriers in seeking a positive Jewish identity. He views those present at the conference not as victims but as survivors. The distinction is crucial. Yossi comes to see that "Jews would not have survived [historical onslaughts] if, after every catastrophe, they had dwelled on [them]." A survivor is one who is able—in some measure—to transcend tragedy. Yossi articulates his own moment of transcendence near the end of the film when he abandons the apocalyptic and embraces a prophetic view of Jewish identity in observing that "I believe a godly spirit infuses Jewish history." Yossi's position is, in fact, remarkably similar to the observation Zoltan makes about the relationship between history and Jewish identity.

At film's end, the viewer discovers that Yossi Klein fulfills his father's prophecy. The son lives in Israel, is married, and works as a writer. Brand's film underscores a crucial dimension of second-generation identity. The *Shoah* and Israel are the two epoch-making events of twentieth-century Jewish existence. Scholars debate the relationship between Israel and the Holocaust; some view the Jewish state itself as a child of the *Shoah*. What is clear is that the two are inextricably linked in Jewish consciousness. Moreover, the very title of the film suggests the altered state of the post-Auschwitz Jewish theological dynamic. The act of saying kaddish itself attests to Jewish determination to walk the covenantal path in spite of the Holocaust while emphasizing the role of the human covenantal partner.

## A GENERATION APART

*A Generation Apart* is another "personal documentary" that raises important questions about how the *Shoah* impacts on second-generation identity and intergenerational communication. The film, produced by Danny Fischer and directed by his brother Jack Fisher, opens with a family traveling in a car. A voice-over states that *'erev Shabbat* was not a big deal when the Fisher children were kids, but now that they have children themselves, the event assumes crucial significance. Eleven people come to Alan and Esther Fisher's home every Friday evening. Structurally, the film consists of a series of interviews and discussions: between the Fisher brothers; between them and their survivor parents; between the brothers and three other second-generation members; and between the bothers and two other survivors. Contemporary scenes are in color whereas stills of Auschwitz and other Holocaust situations are shown in black-and-white.

The film treats second-generation identity within the context of reactions to parental expectations and the crucial distinction between experience and imagination. Responding to the older brother Joe's suggestion that the Holocaust might have effected the boys' lives, Danny tries to imagine his parents as children before the war. Interviewing them, he elicits a story from his mother, an Auschwitz survivor. The one thing on her mind all these years is not knowing *when* her mother died. Did she and Mrs. Fisher's little sister and brother get taken to the gas after ten minutes? Or after one hour? Or two hours? Like Jamaica Just in *White Lies*, Danny recalls that he has always known about the camps, but that he never used to think about it too much, thus distinguishing himself from survivors. However, he also recalls his mother's various references to the "hard times" she has gone through, and that she does not want any more "hard times" with him. It is clear that "hard times" is Mrs. Fisher's shorthand way of referring to what Langer calls "humiliated memory."[10] This memory, writes Langer,

> is an especially intense form of uncompensating recall. Instead of restoring a sense of power or control over a disabling past (one of the presumed goals of therapy—and perhaps of history too), it achieves the reverse, reanimating the governing impotence of the worst moments in a distinctly non-therapeutic way.[11]

Mrs. Fisher's frequent references to Hitler are accompanied by photos of Auschwitz and jarring music.

The film then focuses on specific interviews with second-generation witnesses from various countries, thus calling to mind Epstein's contention that children of survivors comprise an "invisible, silent family scattered about the globe." Initially, these interviews are prefaced by a frame showing Danny with his young son. The second-generation witness wishes that he had spoken more to his parents about their Holocaust experience, the implication being that he would then be better able to transmit this legacy to his own child. Danny's interviews with other children of survivors reveal what and how they learned about the Holocaust from their parents. Shelley Gelfman, an artist whose mother survived Bergen-Belsen, where she met Anne Frank, echoes the feeling expressed by Brenda Szuster, Jamaica Just, and Art Spiegelman in reporting that as a child she thought everyone had been in the *Shoah*. Yorum, an Israeli actor, thinks it is much too soon to deal with the Holocaust and contends that he never thinks about his parents' experience when he is acting. He admits that it "feels good" to play an S.S. man, whose diary he reads in order to prepare for his role. However, Yorum is unable to recall the name of a concentration camp survivor whose part he once played. Yorum's relationship to the Holocaust is one of denial. On the liturgical and theological levels, his attitude corresponds to that of the *tam*, the simple one who at the Passover seder is unable to grasp the enormity of the meaning of the Exodus.

Peter, an Australian physician, contends that he has made peace with his parents. Like Yossi Klein in *Kaddish*, Peter makes *aliyah* but loses his medical license for prescribing narcotics for himself. Following a suicide attempt—he apparently has not made peace with his *Shoah* legacy—Peter works at a home for the retarded. He is married and has a family. Teaching people how to relate to one another, a *tikkun* of human relations, makes him happy. Despite their geographical, vocational, and linguistic differences, these second-generation members seem at ease with one another while revealing the kinship of second-generation witnesses.

The film reports a common phenomenon among children of survivors: the pressure of living with their parents' expectation that they become superachievers. "If one does not succeed," observes Peter, "the guilt is tremendous." Hass comments on this issue:

> For survivors, their children were symbols of rebirth and restoration. These parents may have harbored unconscious magical expectations that their offspring would undo the destruction of the Holocaust and replace lost family members, provide meaning for their empty lives, and vindicate their suffering. Survivors' children may also have provided the justification for their survival, thereby expiating survivor guilt. The

direct or indirect communication of these overwhelming expectations created a need in many children of survivors to achieve a great deal in order to compensate for their parents' deprivations.[12]

The relentless presence of the *Shoah* in the lives of survivors clearly manifests itself in child-rearing practices. Moreover, although these practices vary greatly, all relate to the parents' experience under Nazism. For example, David Mittleberg reports that "children of survivors share a commonality of experience that derived from their specific process of socialization."[13] The Fishers, much in the manner of *The Testament of Job*, always viewed Joe as a "replacement" for murdered family members. His subsequent anger causes Joe to tell Danny that "the Holocaust has always been used against us as an instrument to make us feel guilty."

Mr. Fisher neither understands nor accepts his older son's artistic vocation. Joe, who was born in a detention camp in Cyprus, recalls the burden of his parents' unrealistic expectations for him. We see a picture of Joe as a five-year-old dressed as Moses and crowned by a *Magen David* (Star of David). Like Yossi Klein and others, Joe feels that such expectations thwarted his childhood. In fact, his father, Alan Fisher, remembers that Joe's birth gave us a new beginning, but the most telling comment is Joe's observation: "When they had me, they had something else in mind, an ideal baby." The tension between father and son is underscored as the camera crosscuts between them, Mr. Fisher saying, "Yes, he represented all the murdered of my family," and Joe's painful comment that his father "does not understand that I want to be my own person instead of what he wanted me to be."

Shelley's experience is different. Telling her mother why she left home, she observes, "You did not push me around. You just put down everything I did." This prompts a wrenching confession on the older woman's part. "I was not there for you," she tells Shelley, "because I was not ready mentally or emotionally." Afraid of losing everyone she loves, as she did in the camps, Mrs. Gelfman tells her daughter that she purposely kept her at a distance. The mother adopts a coping strategy of depersonalization: pychologically removing herself from her daughter. In a scene of strong emotional force following this disclosure, mother and daughter kiss and embrace. Mrs. Gelfman poignantly observes, "I think I owe all my children an apology." Sighing, she concludes on a note of great pathos. "I do not know," she says, "who owes me an apology."

Mrs. Gelfman tells Joe a tale that reveals much about how her Holocaust experience constricted her relationship with her children. A three-year-old blind boy from Lodz cries in the transport to Auschwitz. Mrs. Gelfman's father gives him some bread. Immediately upon arrival, the boy is gassed. He died hungry and cold, she observes, "just as he came into the world." Mrs. Gelfman then makes a startling admission: "I always see that little boy whenever I look at my children." Reflecting the apocalyptic position adopted by Yossi Klein in the early parts of *Kaddish*, Shelley states that she expects another holocaust. Mother and daughter then appear on camera and Mrs. Gelfman asks if Shelly fears that the *Shoah* can reoccur. "I do not want to feel I put a load on you," the mother says. In response, Shelley speaks with great emotion in observing, "Well you did. You did put a load on me."

The film's most focused comments on the issue of inheriting the Holocaust come in a series of exchanges between Danny and Joe. Their remarks illustrate the fact, noted earlier, that even among siblings in the same family there can be vastly different perceptions of their Holocaust legacy. For example, a highly agitated Joe exclaims to Danny, "You never saw it. You never went through it. What does their experience have to do with you?" With Shelly Gelfman, Joe views the Holocaust in terms of guilt. Reflecting his own experience, Joe wishes not to perpetuate the sense of guilt. He concludes that the brothers only *imagined* the parents' experiences. The older brother contends that Danny is really talking about "a holocaust of the mind." In response, Danny wisely observes, "But I grew up in a house with Holocaust imagery." The continuing *presence of the absence* serves to weave together the multilayered texture of memory in survivor families.

In fact, the positions of both brothers need to be taken into account in assessing the phenomenon of inherited memory. As Wiesel's *The Fifth Son* so powerfully demonstrates, children both are, and are emphatically not, their parents.[14] Joe's point of view is correct insofar as the Holocaust as a historically anchored event is over. But Danny's position reflects the reality, noted in chapter 2, that what unites all children of survivors is that they are "witnesses to memory." Danny confides to his brother that his own understanding of the role of the Holocaust in his life has changed dramatically. Initially, he thought that the *Shoah* had nothing to do with his life. Now, he says, he thinks about it on a daily level. Joe is unconvinced and reminds Danny that the survivors' experiences belong to them. Danny, however, responds in a manner that draws universalist implications. Clearly, it is correct that the experience belongs to the survivors. But he observes that "everyone has parents and everyone has problems with them." Danny's understanding of the family dynamic universalizes the issues in a manner that encompasses intergenerational communication.

Danny's position is also important theologically. His identity is bound to the *Shoah* even while transcending the event. For example, in a statement that illustrates dimensions of Fackenheim's earlier "Commanding-Voice"-of-Auschwitz position, Danny observes: "The biggest blow I can give to Hitler's intention is to live my life to the fullest and to get as much joy out of life as I can. My parents survived. I have children. They will have children. The Jewish People survived." Danny's affirmation begins with the personal and ends with *k'lal Yisrael. Am Yisrael Hai*—the Jewish People lives—is both a statement of fact and a statement of faith.

Yet, the survivors in *A Generation Apart* model a different understanding of post-Auschwitz faith. For example, Shelley's uncle Ziggy recalls that the Nazis would not permit him to accompany his father to Auschwitz. The young man fell to his knees and prayed that God would miraculously intervene. Nothing happened. The camera then cuts to Alan Fisher who, for his part, observes that he had to help himself and not depend on God. This point of view echoes that of the Koles in *Damaged Goods* and *Maus*'s Vladek Spiegelman. It is revealing, however, that each of these survivors as well as Zoltan Klein in *Kaddish* and Alan Fisher continue the ritual aspect of Jewish existence despite their lack of belief in God. This practice reflects two essential features about the dynamics of contemporary Jewish identity. First, most survivors commit themselves to raising their children Jewishly even after the *Shoah*. Secondly, much in the manner suggested by Wiesel, Greenberg, and Shlomo Riskin, having Jewish children after Auschwitz is itself an act of faith similar to accepting the covenant at Sinai.

The film's final scene shows how the *Shoah* infuses traditional ritual practice with new meaning even while affirming the role of the family in transmitting the legacy of the Holocaust. The Fishers celebrate Hanukkah with their grandchildren and sing *Ma'oz Tsur Yeshuati* (O Mighty Rock of My Salvation), the hymn traditionally associated with this ritual moment. While not found in the Hebrew Bible, Hanukkah has special significance in the post-Auschwitz context. Hanukkah (dedication), symbolizes the victory of the few over the many and the miracle of the one-day supply of oil that burned for eight days. The lighting of candles is accompanied by a blessing that reminds those present of God's miracles. The *Hallel* said at this time speaks of both miracles and wonders that served to preserve Jewish existence and identity during the time of the Hasmoneans. By implication one thinks as well of the saved remnant of European Jewry and their descendants. *Ma'oz Tsur*, for its part, is a recapitulation of God's mighty saving acts in history that preserved the Jewish People against those bent on its destruction. Moreover, it is customary to publically advertise the miracle of the lights by placing the candles in a window so that all may see. Observed by the Fishers, and others who survived the Holocaust, and taught their grandchildren, Hanukkah is a visible sign of Jewish perseverance.

## BREAKING THE SILENCE

Eva Fogelman is a daughter of Job whose adult life has been spent working with and writing about children of survivors. The awareness groups that she and Bella Savran began over two decades ago in Boston have subsequently spread throughout the country. Fogelman is a psychotherapist, social psychologist, and filmmaker. She is a cofounder of the Jewish Foundation for Christian Rescuers and codirects Psychotherapy with Generations of the Holocaust and Related Traumas at the Training Institute for Mental Health. Fogelman recently wrote *Conscience and Courage: Rescuers of Jews During the Holocaust* (1994).

*Breaking the Silence* deals with the results of living in a survivor household ruled by the "conspiracy of silence." Undertaken to "protect" their offspring from the Holocaust, this vow proved dysfunctional and psychologically thwarting. Fogelman writes about her impetus for making this film: "as a child of survivors . . . when I discovered that parental silence about the Holocaust was a barrier which prevented young Jews from connecting with their rich heritage that was destroyed by the Nazis, my impulse was to bring them together." The film is set in the context of a nine-member second-generation discussion group that meets to reflect on their Holocaust inheritance. In addition to Eva Fogelman, other second-generation members who speak in the film include Helen Epstein, Moshe Waldoks, Menahem Rosensaft, and Samuel Norich. Scholarly perspective is provided by Robert J. Lifton and Dr. Henry Gruenbaum. Directed by Edward Mason, *Breaking the Silence* portrays the second generation's attempt to connect with Jewish history, their parents experience, and their own identity. Fogelman's important film, a rich and provocative exploration of the psychological aspects of the Holocaust legacy, portrays individuals shedding their dependent status. Initiating discussion with their parents about the Holocaust reveals important things both about the survivors and their offspring.

Linking the film's survivors is their display of elements of the "death imprint." The corrosive and destructive nature of this phenomenon, portrayed so vividly in the novels, is clearly seen in the relationship between Regina, a survivor, and her daughter Yolanda. Regina speaks about seeing her own mother taken to be gassed. Finally beginning to share the agony of this trauma, Regina comments, "even after thirty-six years . . . I could really never tell my daughter." The survivor asks how it is possible to tell another human being that the Nazis took millions of humans and gassed them. "My mother," she continues, "was the most important person in my whole life. And possibly she still is today." "What," she asks, "happens to my pain? It will never go away." The camera shot heightens the fact of Regina's psychic isolation by showing her seated alone, while her American-born husband and Yolanda are seated close together.

But since Regina is also a mother, how does she relate to her daughter? What messages does Yolanda receive about her mother's past and about her own identity? Yolanda recalls that, as a young girl around five years old, she went into the bathroom as Regina was exiting. She said to her mother, "You were in a concentration camp, Mommy?" Yolanda vividly remembers that Regina's face got hard and stern. The mother said, "Yes, I was," and put her head down. Yolanda reports knowing from this response that she was not supposed to ask about the topic. The subject was not raised again for the next dozen years, but in the interim Yolanda began reading voraciously about the Holocaust. Fragmentary or nonverbal communication is in many ways even more frightening than silence to young children; it sends the message that survivor parents are not to be questioned, thereby closing off avenues of communication. In addition, the lack of parental testimony can lead to preoccupation with the question of how parents survived. This is clearly the case in the novels of Friedmann, Finkelstein, and Spiegelman. Commenting on this issue, Fogelman writes that some second-generation members "suspected that their mothers were sexually abused and that their fathers stole food from other inmates."[15]

This episode reveals much about the quandary of both the survivors and the second generation. As we have seen, parenting skills are severely flawed by the Holocaust experience. Inability to mourn leads many survivors to perceive life as an enormous burden. The demands made by children seem intolerable. This typically results in poor intergenerational communication. Parent and child attempt to protect each other and both feel misunderstood: the other party simply cannot understand their pain, let alone attempt to alleviate it. For example, Yolanda observes: "I had a lot of burden. And I could not get angry at her. And there is so much to be angry about." The mother wants her daughter to "respect [her] resignation." Yolanda, for her part, wants Regina to "respect [her] search." What are we to make of this seeming impasse?

At first blush, this exchange confirms the chasm that exists between those present in the Kingdom of Night and those who were not. Survivors carry emotional scars, whether visible or not. Blocking access to their memories clearly does not stop transmission of the death imprint. Memory itself, as Primo Levi observes, "denies peace to the tormented."[16] Yolanda's curiosity about her mother's past is the natural curiosity any daughter has about her mother. And their relationship is far more open than the one between Brenda and Rukhl Szuster in *Summer Long-a-Coming*. Like *White Lies'* Julie Salamon, Yolanda wishes to know not only for herself but for her unborn children. She worries about transmitting the legacy of the Holocaust to the third generation. If my children do not know, Yolanda observes to Regina, "then what happens to the memory?" The second-generation witness thus emerges as a vital link in the chain of memory. Yolanda tells Regina, "We have to talk about your mother so that I can tell my children about her."

Yolanda then articulates a position that reveals the role of the second-generation witness, as she rightly tries to separate herself psychologically from her mother. However, she does not stop here. She takes the next, crucial step in observing that "I am trying to hold (my mother's) experience within me. But in my own way." This second-generation way or, more accurately, these ways are the topic of this book. An artist and potter, Yolanda feels that the knowledge of her mother's experience gives her own work an "extra feeling and force." In effect, Yolanda's work tangibly expresses Reb Nachman of Bratslav's observation that "there is nothing so whole as a broken heart." Confronting the psychic pain of her mother's tale and its impact on her own identity, she transforms this knowledge into a passionate aesthetic that infuses her work with meaning. Yolanda's art is, in fact, a distinctively second-generation testimony.

In a very emotional scene, one of the survivors, surrounded by his children and grandchild, says, "Let them remember. Forever. If they have kids, let the kids remember. Forever and ever." The pathos of this moment is heightened by the camera's focus first on the survivor, who, overcome by emotion, wipes his eyes with a handkerchief, then on his daughter comforting him, and finally on his infant grandson drinking from a feeding bottle, thus visually uniting the three generations but emphasizing that third-generation inheritance will be at an even greater remove from the *Shoah* than the second generation, which at least saw, and heard, the survivors. The third generation will have to develop its own way of preserving and shaping Holocaust memory. This shaping will, in turn, reflect the influence of the second generation, which, as Hass observes, "can exert more regulation over the transmission process than did their parents, whose nightmares, and anger often intruded involuntarily, spasmodically."[17]

*Breaking the Silence* combines both immigrant and survivor experience. One son of Job remembers that in high school he felt ashamed that he was not an American. A female member of the group recalls that she was an antisemite in high school, totally rejecting her parents' background and her own identity, feeling that if she was not Jewish, she would be safe. The woman's comments recall those of Raphael, Spiegelman, and Klein, all of whom attest to feeling uneasy about their Jewish legacy during their adolescent years and beyond, until they begin to work through their Holocaust inheritance. Further, ambivalence towards Judaism is also displayed by Mrs. Hoffman in *The Flood*. The second-generation group helps this daughter of Job confront both her parents' experience and her own identity. Here the *Shoah*'s initial legacy is one of self-loathing. Other group members attest to the anger they felt because their parents were not well, because the children had no living relatives, and because of the "general anger [felt by] immigrant children [when] your parents do not fit in."

Specific clinical issues raised by the second generation deal with their parents' separation anxiety, their distrust of the outside world, and, perhaps the most unbearable burden imposed on the contemporary children of Job, their expectation that their children will serve as "replacements" for murdered siblings or parents. Present in many of the novels, this issue is clearly stated in *Breaking the Silence*. The camera focuses on a young woman who says, "I felt that I was the image of my mother's mother. I was supposed to be her." However, she clearly rejects this role, telling her colleagues in the group, "I do not want her (my mother) to make me her mother." A second woman reports her reaction to this type of expectation. "It was so sad," she recalls, "I was too little to take it. It was too much of a demand."

Moshe Waldoks, at that time a professor of Jewish history, views this as the juncture at which the trauma of survivors passes on to their children. He observes that "parents told their children they should be compensations." The enormity of living to be a "compensation" is overwhelming. This feeling of debt or loyalty, observes Dr. Gruenbaum, "skews" the lives of the second generation. Alongside this, members of the second generation frequently heard that the social world should not be trusted.[18] A young woman in the group reports that because her own mother feels people cannot be trusted, the survivor pushed her away. Another female group member reports being haunted by the feeling that anything she loves will be taken from her. Both of these observations are similar to Mrs. Gelfman's position in *A Generation Apart*.

Against this background emerges the second generation's quest for a *tikkun* of self and family relations. Eva Fogelman observes, for example, that "some of us identify with the suffering because it is something we just cannot get past." Although both parents and children wish to protect each other, the group enables the second generation to accept their own feelings while coming to understand that, as Fogelman observes elsewhere, "survivors are generally not damaged by the discussion of their painful pasts."[19] Moreover, by speaking to their parents about Jewish life before the Holocaust, second-generation members receive a "sense of historical continuity." Both survivors and their children at this point engage in the timeless process of transmitting and receiving memory, which characterizes the Jewish historical experience.

*Breaking the Silence* also focuses on the universal dimension of the second generation. Helen Epstein notes that in the last decade children of survivors go from being invisible to being visible. Taking this theme one step further, Lifton contends that there is nothing less than a "social movement by children of survivors toward being heard." The second generation, he opines, insists "upon feeling, being true to, confronting their own history." The works examined in this book strongly support Lifton's contention. The parents' Holocaust history is the point of departure for the second-generation witnesses' relationship to the Holocaust past and to their own lives in the present. But how does the second generation shape its own "memory" of the *Shoah*?

The contemporary children of Job have a pedagogical mission, both in the classroom and beyond. For example, Ruth Bork, a daughter of Job, accompanies her parents when they speak at various schools. The camera powerfully reveals the societal impact of the *tikkun* of bearing witness. Crosscutting between the faces of the schoolchildren and those of the Borks conveys two messages: the link between generations, and the fact that the Holocaust and its lessons are being taught to non-Jews as well. This latter fact is emphasized as the children discuss various issues, including societal indifference toward Jewish doom during the *Shoah*. The children articulate their strong feelings that such indifference must never be repeated. Perhaps they are influenced as well by tales concerning the *tikkun* of ordinary decency.

Much in the manner of Salamon's Jamaica Just, members of the second generation portrayed in Fogelman's film also pursue a commitment to the moral improvement of society at large. This goal emerges from the realization that, as Waldoks observes, "children of survivors are particularly sensitive to the fact that civilization failed." This realization may, of course, lead either to nihilism or to altruism. Frequently, the response will be somewhere between the two extremes. In the case of Waldoks and others in this film, the impetus moves towards altruism. For example, Waldoks articulates the second-generation task in the form of a question. "Can we after the Holocaust," he wonders, "inculcate humanness into the world again?" To do so would necessitate, at some fundamental level, undoing much of modernity, which, as Zygmunt Bauman notes, is the time when morality and rationality move in opposite directions.

Menachem Rosensaft, as we have seen, views the second-generation movement as the coming together of formerly isolated individuals whose work "coalesces around human rights issues." For Rosensaft, the second generation represents a "moral point" whose task is to deal globally with human rights issues. This point of view stands in sharp contrast to the perspective of the authors whose work is discussed in chapter 3, thereby illustrating the diversity extant among the children of Job.

*Breaking the Silence* concludes on a hopeful note for the future. At least certain of the group members reconnect to their survivor parent(s). As Dr. Gruenbaum notes, "The group enabled and empowered the participants to go home and talk to their parents in a unique and different way." Moreover, by breaking through the wall of silence, these second-generation witnesses also learn about and embrace Jewish history and their own Jewish identity. Formerly viewed solely in terms of existential pain, second-generation identity is considerably broadened by belonging to and sharing with the group. Perhaps the most important particularist lesson learned is that Judaism is far more than the name given to a long and uninterrupted history of pain and suffering. In other words, the group members heed the warning of the late Professor Salo W. Baron to avoid what he terms "the lachrymose conception" of Jewish history. Helen Epstein emphasizes this point in observing that once one works through the issues involved in being a child of survivors, it is then possible to study what happened prior to the *Shoah* and immerse oneself in the richness and diversity of Jewish history. Against the background of six broken candles and shots of the group and survivor parents, members of the second generation sing the Partisan song "We are Here" (*mir szeinen doh*).

## HALF-SISTER, EVERYTHING'S FOR YOU, AND IN MEMORY

Abraham Ravett was born in Poland in 1947, and currently teaches film at Hampshire College. Yiddish is his mother tongue and German his first language. Raised in Israel, he learned English when his parents came to America. The influence of his early peripatetic experience is clear in Ravett's autobiographical films. Moving from continent to continent, he reports, meant that "documents were an important part of our lives."[20] His parents also adopted a "conspiracy of silence" about the Holocaust, yet he recalls that they wept at television shows depicting the *Shoah*. Like Friedmann, Ravett acknowledges that the Vietnam War impacted greatly on his work. He reports that he began to work on his parents' lives in 1974, attempting to discover what it means to be a survivor.[21] Ravett's films constitute an experimental response to his second-genera-tion identity and determination to bear witness. He portrays the frag-mentary nature of post-Auschwitz memory for the daughters and sons of survivors. Further, this memory tends to be associative rather than chronological: various documents and images such as letters, photos, and dolls trigger the filmmaker's attempt to connect to the Holocaust. Consequently, Ravett's "memory" is simultaneously an attempt to recon-struct lost lives from remnants and a ritual of mourning.

*Half Sister* is a film that treats Ravett's reaction to discovering the secret that his mother had a daughter who was murdered during the Holocaust. Like Friedmann's Jason Kole, Ravett had been raised as an only child. An aunt in Israel, whom his mother is visiting, sends her nephew a picture of Toncia, his half-sister. The film is one of silences: the silence of the absent sister, the lack of narration, and the silence that fol-lows in the wake of the catastrophe of the Holocaust. Toncia's absence becomes a constant presence for the filmmaker. Yet the film also speaks to the audience in a variety of ways as Ravett, unlike Bukiet, tries to imagine not what his own life could have been like before the war, but rather what his half-sister's life could have been. First of all, there are a plethora of second-generation Holocaust icons: dolls, photos, children's shoes, railroad tracks, the face of an anonymous woman at different ages (the stages of a life from which Ravett's half-sister was so cruelly cut off?). These icons are a point of entry into knowing about the Holocaust for the second generation. In addition, the silence provides room for the viewer to fill in. Further, silences are discomforting, involving the audience even while making it uneasy. The filmmaker himself attests that there is a "rhythm and a sound in the silence."[22]

Ravett also utilizes facts of Holocaust history in his attempt "to work out the dilemma of my upbringing."[23] For example, there is a color shot of a woman urinating. Ravett wants the audience to recall that in the forced marches, one could not stop. People had to urinate while standing. Further, he juxtaposes the face of a little girl and dismembered body parts. This theme of physical dismemberment prefaces the filmmaker's psychic dismemberment. Icons of memory, however powerful, can never eventuate in a complete knowledge of the Holocaust. Quite the opposite appears to be the case: the more pieces of the memory puzzle that one has, the less sense the *Shoah* makes.

*Everything's For You* explores several crucial themes: Ravett's tortuous relationship with his father, which is quite similar to the one portrayed in *Maus* and *A Generation Apart*; the discovery of three previously hidden photos of his father's first family gassed in Auschwitz; his growing realization of how the *Shoah* crippled his father; and his determination to pass the story on to his own young children. This concern for the third generation witness is, as we have seen, articulated in Salamon's *White Lies*, and is also emphasized by Yolanda in *Breaking the Silence* and Danny Fisher in *A Generation Apart*. Ravett interviews his father in English, Hebrew, and Yiddish. The fact that the interviews dissolve into a blank screen, and that Ravett keeps asking questions of his now dead father, reveal the fact that the Holocaust remains an elusive presence in the lives of the second generation.

Technically, the film contains a mélange of devices. There are drawings by Ravett's young daughter, computer animation that enables the filmmaker to show action or movement within a particular frame, split screens, digitized images, and, in Wieselian fashion, dialogues real and imagined. Yet, as in *Half Sister*, silence is Ravett's most successful device. The film captures the silences between father and son as an integral part of their dialogue, sometimes spoken and more frequently unspoken, between survivors and their offspring.[24]

The film opens with an invocation of the father's name. Chaim, the Hebrew word for life, is dead. The name is repeated on screen four times, but Chaim is only one of the senior Ravett's names. How he was called depended upon who was doing the calling. For example, the viewer learns Chaim's wife called him Henyek, whereas to people in New York he was Herbert. "I called him Pop," says Ravett. Each name indicates the degree of intimacy between those involved. Ravett interviews his father, asking him about his prewar family. At this point Ravett's cinematic discourse takes over: split screens, visual blips of Jewish faces and groups in Europe; an animated segment of a father spanking his son who had broken a key in the lock of their home's front door is captioned by a question: "Pop, why did you hit me so hard?"

Speaking in a repetitious, almost ritual, incantatory tone, Ravett beseeches his dead father in English, Hebrew, and Yiddish. His anger is clear as he asks, "Now that I need to talk to you, where are you?" The screen next shows a still of Chaim sitting and staring out the window. It is only now that the father responds to his son's earlier question. The survivor last saw his family in 1944. In broken English Chaim states, "They kill right away the women and children." The camera focuses on Chaim's face, which is a mask of sadness. The scene cuts to Jennifer Ravett, Chaim's granddaughter, reading from a story that she wrote and illustrated. The little girl's tale is also about danger—a wolf is banging at the family's door. But unlike her grandfather's tale, Jennifer's ends happily. The wolf goes away and Jennifer has cookies and milk.

Abraham Ravett's repeated questions to his father—"What did you do on the day they sent you out of the ghetto?" "What did your wife say?" "What did your children say?"—underscore his quest to fill in the missing pieces of his own identity. The relationship of the Holocaust past to the American present—and future—is confirmed when the scene cuts to the Ravett grandchildren talking to their tense and preoccupied grandmother. Abraham also asks his father specific questions about the nature of Jewish identity; for example, why was Chaim so upset when his son brought home a non-Jewish girlfriend. Chaim has difficulty articulating a response. The camera shows his face looking over his left shoulder, perplexed. Perhaps he is struggling to find the correct words. Or perhaps he is incredulous that, after the *Shoah*, any Jew would want to interact with any Christian. The disjointed narrative indicates that Chaim's own life has been brutally interrupted and irretrievably ruptured. Chaim speaks with bitterness about the Polish people who murdered the Jews and about the *goyim* who betrayed his mother's hiding place. The camera then focuses on Mrs. Ravett, who tells how their relationship originated. Contrasting her husband's post-Holocaust physical and emotional debilitation, his wife remembers that he was so strong (before the war): "How could you know," she asks, "that someday this man he was going to be so sick?"

By the end of the film, Abraham begins to understand some of Chaim's many secrets. Why, for example, he could not stand to wait in line (it reminded him of Jews lined up to be gassed); why a hot meal meant so much to a man who lived on the verge of starvation; and why a potato was so precious to him. Abraham abandons his earlier anger at Chaim—"everything was a secret, you never told me anything." The son discovers three photographs of Chaim's first wife with their two children. Addressing his dead father, Ravett says "now I see everything." But this seeing reveals the difference between the witnessing generation and their offspring. Abraham understands that he "cannot know anything." Yet he can love his father. "All the time," he confides to his absent father, "I'm looking for someone who looks like you, who speaks Yiddish like you."

*Everything's For You* reveals the *tikkun* of bearing witness as an ineluctable legacy of the Holocaust. Ravett, for example, muses, "I have two children now Pop, just like you did." Moreover, Abraham is shown as a loving and involved father. He takes showers with his young son, changes his diapers, and speaks to him. The film itself ends with a shot of a blank screen and Chaim being interviewed. Responding to a question, Chaim says, "I marry in 1931 . . ." This is followed by silence and the credits. His father's story must constantly be told, and retold. It has ended but has no end. Ravett's children, in their turn, must discover, internalize, and find their own language and icons with which to shape Holocaust memory.

*In Memory* is the most directly theological of Ravett's films. By juxtaposing traditional mourning rites with archival footage from the Lodz Ghetto and Beit Lochamei HaGetaot (the Museum of the Ghetto fighters in Israel) the work invites reflection on the relationship of God to Auschwitz and the relationship of the Jewish people to God. The film opens in the dark with a cantor chanting *El Male Rahamim*, (God, full of Compassion), a prayer for the souls of the dead. The solemnity of this prayer and its association with remembering the dead is emphasized by the fact that it is recited as part of the *Yizkor* (memorial) service on Yom Kippur. Additionally, *El Male Rahamim* is recited at the time of yahrzeit and upon visiting parental graves. The film's locale is Poland, itself a vast Jewish graveyard. Ravett's film in fact commemorates this dead world. The film ends the way it began, with one exception: the Hebrew of *El Male Rahamim* is translated on the screen.

Ravett's trilogy moves between the poles of self and history. His is an interrogation of God no less than an inquiry into his own identity. For example, *In Memory* centers on the words "God full of compassion," but the viewer is left with the unanswered—and unanswerable—question about divine compassion during the Holocaust. Ravett attests that his parents were proud of being Jewish, although they were not religious in any formal sense of that word.[25] Nevertheless, the filmmaker's works demonstrate that listening to survivor testimony is tantamount to a new post-Auschwitz ritual. Like Brenda Szuster, Art Spiegelman, Adam Posner, and Jamaica Just, Ravett emphasizes the centrality of being a "witness to the testimony." His utilization of silence serves to remind the audience of the brokenness of second-generation memory. Although this generation lacks a coherent narrative of the *Shoah*, they still seek to achieve a *tikkun atzmi*.

## ANGST

*Angst* is a recent film that tells the story of three Jewish comedians who are children of Job. What strikes one immediately about this film is the apparent dissonance between the title and the fact that the performers are comics. Their jokes and routines are quite amusing. But their personal stories are not at all funny. In reality, their humor is a mask for the angst that they feel as inheritors of their parents' Holocaust legacy. Humor in this case is a way of simultaneously distancing from and dealing with the absurdity of the *Shoah*. As the film cuts between various comic routines and the comics' personal observations, the viewer comes to understand the wrenching nature of this dissonance.

The three performers are Deb Filler from New Zealand, Sandy Gutman (a.k.a. Austen Tayshus) from Australia, and the American Moshe Waldoks. Each confides several things that together comprise a second-generation gestalt. For example, memories of a lonely or unhappy childhood are recounted. Moreover, none of these children of Job yet understands the Holocaust. Further, each confesses to a sense of bewilderment as children, being unable to understand either the tensions within the family or their own sense of guilt. Others who appear in this film include Helen Epstein and Arnold Zable, who was born to refugee parents in New Zealand and whose memoir *Jewels and Ashes* movingly recounts his 1989 pilgrimage to Poland. Ruth Nathan, a psychologist, addresses the inaugural Australasian Holocaust Descendants Gathering and, like Joe Fisher, contends that what is transmitted between generations is "the holocaust of the mind."

In the film's serious moments, the children of Job reflect the impact of the Holocaust on their Jewish identity. The second generation experiences both pain and anger. For example, Deb Filler weeps while speaking of the Holocaust to her father. She confides that the Holocaust is "part of who I am. It's really a big part. And I have to acknowledge it." Sandy Gutman becomes enraged when thinking about the gassings of Jews, the role of the educated in planning and carrying out the murders, and the death of Jewish culture. He turns away from the interviewer, saying, "I'm going to have to go now." Moshe Waldoks, for his part, is asked if there is an appropriate response to Auschwitz. He replies by screaming. This immediately brings to mind the response of Pavel, Spiegelman's survivor psychiatrist who, when asked by his patient what Auschwitz felt like, screams "BOO!" He tells Spiegelman that Auschwitz "felt a little like *that*. But *ALWAYS!*"

Watching *Angst* recalls the power of Holocaust imagery in the lives of the second-generation witnesses and illustrates the uses to which humor is put. Moreover, the film involves the audience on a variety of levels. Some of the jokes, those that are not Holocaust related, are funny. One does not hesitate to laugh. Those that refer to the *Shoah*, however, make one uneasy. Some are used to illustrate the apartness of young children of survivors from their peers. For example, Deb Filler recalls that as a schoolchild she heard stories of rabbits tunneling under farm fences. "But," she thinks, "the fences weren't electrified. There were no watch-towers, no German Shepherds." Others reveal distinctive second-generation behaviors, as in Filler's characterization of a conversation between two children of survivors: exaggerated fear of danger, elaborate details, many "escape" or alternate plans, fears about explosions on subways, uttering "God forbid" after conjuring certain dreadful scenarios, and spitting over one's right shoulder. Holocaust routines strike with sledge-hammer force. Again, Filler tells her audience that last summer her dad took her on a holiday tour of Eastern European death camps, "And," she adds, "being a comedian I decided to do a show about it." She concludes by asking sardonically, "Is everybody happy?"

Psychologically, humor is a means of coping with that which is beyond one's ability to master. Drs. Seymour and Rhoda Fisher contend that the world itself is an absurd place and that humor provides a means of managing terror.[26] The second generation has, in fact, shown great ingenuity in coping with its Holocaust legacy. The use of humor is a way of dealing with that which is irretrievably lost and that which is beyond one's control. For these second-generation witnesses, humor is the reverse side of rage. Humor is both the defining characteristic of their identities as children of Job and simultaneously a way of dealing with the pain of that identity. Confronting the enormity of the *Shoah*'s continuing legacy means a resort to a certain type of gallows humor that permits them both to accept their helplessness to undo the past and also to explore their relationship to their parents' experience and to the Jewish tradition.

The film underscores humor's tragic dimension in detailing a conversation between Gutman and Auschwitz survivor Abraham Cykiert, a Yiddish poet and radio broadcaster who lives in Melbourne. Cykiert survived as a comedian writer, "writing gutter poetry for the camp hierarchy." When Gutman asks him for an example, the survivor responds with the following "joke": "If we take all the men in this camp, ass to prick, all those who've gone through the chimneys, it would be the greatest fuck-up since humanity started." With Wiesel, Cykiert believes that the *Shoah* has become desanctified. "Experts" who know nothing are followed by "people who do not distinguish the real soul from idol worship."[27] The camera then cuts to Gutman performing in a Sydney comedy club, his voice-over saying, "Sometimes when I go on stage I feel like I'm going to the electric chair."

*Angst* also makes clear, however, that these three second-generation members are "Riders towards the Dawn." They seek ways of confronting the Holocaust yet continuing as Jews. Two of the three are married: the Waldoks (Moshe and Anne) are the parents of two daughters; Gutman is a newlywed. Filler is both protective of her father and gives voice to his experience. She is the co-writer of a play about the second-generation entitled *Punch Me in the Stomach*. Waldoks recognizes that although the "pain of the *Shoah* is never going to be repaid," it is "not fair to make [our children] into a symbol of something else."

Each of these children of Job articulates what we may term a *second-generation lesson*. This lesson is twofold: the necessity to bear witness to the Holocaust, and the importance of striving to achieve a *tikkun* of the self. Perhaps Sandy Gutman best summarizes the impact of the Holocaust's legacy on the second generation. He confides that he always wanted to "climb inside" his father's head in order to more fully comprehend the Holocaust. Unable to do this, he voices what he perceives to be the relationship between survivors and the second generation while extrapolating a mission. The experience of the Holocaust, he notes, "can only live through the survivors and the children of survivors who are interested enough and can utilize it and distill it and make it relevant to this generation and the following generations. That's what I'm trying to do."

## THE DOCUDRAMAS:
### *THE DR. JOHN HANEY SESSIONS* AND *OPEN SECRETS*

Mention should be made of two docudramas by Own Jay Shapiro, a film professor at Syracuse University. Shapiro, who is married to a daughter of survivors, produced a film project entitled *Alinsky's Children*, which is composed of two docudramas, *The Dr. John Haney Sessions* and *Open Secrets*. The scripts, written by Thomas Friedmann, are composites of tales of survivors and their offspring.[28] These works differ from the documentaries in the nature of their cinematic discourse and by the fact that they utilize actors. For example, the docudramas refrain from employing archival footage of either prewar Jewish life in Europe or horrifying Holocaust images from ghettos and death camps. Rather, these films make use of "ordinary" items such as yahrzeit candles, calendars, and photos of murdered relatives as distinctive second-generation markers for denoting the *presence of the absence.*

Friedmann's scripts for these two color films utilize traditional ritual and classical talmudic tales even while revealing their post-Holocaust transformation. For example, the four questions asked at the Passover seder, and the talmudic tale of Kamtza and Bar-Kamtza frame the films' second-generation quest. In effect, these films portray the contemporary children of Job as both distinctly American and singled out as Jews much in the manner described by Kuperstein's earlier-noted observation. Both films raise questions that have crucial implications for Jews living in multicultural America. For example, these works reflect ways American culture at large views Jews and the Holocaust. Further, they make explicit the role played by the *Shoah* in helping shape contemporary Jewish identity.

*The Dr. John Haney Sessions* sensitizes viewers to the relationship between the Holocaust and personal identity in the context of a second-generation therapy group. Dr. Haney, the psychiatrist, is a Christian married to a daughter of survivors. Technically, the film opens with a mélange of images and sounds that seem connected despite their obvious differences. Four faces and four voices appear in kaleidoscopic fashion. Various techniques, including the use of audio blips, visual intercutting, fade-ins, fade-outs, sub-titles, white lights, and side-to-side movement, suggest the alienation and separation felt by members of the second generation. Faces that partially go off the edge of the screen create tension between the visual images and the soundtrack, heightening the audience's awareness of the brokenness of the post-Auschwitz covenant. Moreover, it soon becomes obvious that audio-blips occur each time a death camp name is mentioned. This heightens the sense of personal and historic disruption caused by the Holocaust. While this technique is innovative, it also has a tendency to compete with the tales that are being told.

The four second-generation members relate how their own lives reflect the continuing effects of their survivor parents' Holocaust suffering. For example, the four tell of the difficulty their parents experience in trying to relax, their food obsessions, their aggressive behavior, and their problems with intimacy and trust.

On the mythic level, the reaction of each of the four group members corresponds to the approaches to history embodied by the four questioners of the traditional Passover seder. The *haham*, or wise one, understands the enormity of the Holocaust and its continuing impact. A thoughtful speaker, he retells his parents' survival stories, although wisely discerning the distinction between survivors and their offspring. "What can I tell you?" he asks. "It's her story; it's her memory. I have no control of the faces in my dreams." The *rasha*, or wicked one, is portrayed by the cynic who expresses his rage through tasteless jokes. Moreover, the *rasha* is the one who in the Passover seder asks why *you* (rather than *we*) suffered and were oppressed, thereby separating himself from the identity and destiny of the Jewish people. The *tam* is the simple one who is blind to the epoch-making nature of the Holocaust. This figure is portrayed by an actress who reflects on a role that she has been offered, observing, "I've had pretty good luck with World War II you know." Her response is similar to that of Yoram, the Israeli actor in *A Generation Apart* who "feels good" about playing an S.S. man. In both cases, narcissism masks denial. The actress, for instance, asks the other group members to "pretend that I'm not even here." The fourth character at the seder is the child, the figure who lacks the capacity to inquire and is unable to grasp the Holocaust's significance.

These four attitudes or models are fluid. They emphasize types of reactions on the part of the second generation. Moreover, all four characteristics may be present in any child of survivors. These four attitudes may also be seen as psychological stages through which a member of the second generation may pass. On the universalist level, it is also important to note that these four interpretive categories may be broadened to society at large. In other words, changing images of survivors and societal reactions to the Holocaust may also reflect these four models.[29]

*The Dr. John Haney Sessions* raises a variety of issues concerned with inheriting the Holocaust. For example, on the universal level, a fundamental civilizational question is how a society that has learned to kill with impunity or be indifferent to murder can act morally. At the level of Jewish particularism, one must inquire about the relationship of God to the death camps and the suffering of His chosen people. Is it still credible to believe in God? What is the relationship between ethnic and religious identity after Auschwitz? What is the rate of intermarriage among second-generation witnesses?[30] Unlike *Breaking the Silence*, *A Generation Apart*, and *Kaddish*, *The Dr. John Haney Sessions* comes to no dramatic or narrative resolution. Rather, it reveals that second-generation identity is an evolving process. The questions remain as questions. Nonetheless, by utilizing the Passover seder as paradigmatic, viewers are invited to recall the Exodus, which commemorates redemption from bondage and is a foundational tale for Jewish identity.

*Open Secrets* reveals a particularist view of the complex and tender way in which religious survivors transmit their legacy. Employing a more conventional narrative form than *The Dr. John Haney Sessions*, *Open Secrets'* eleven sections challenge viewers to enter the moral universe of Jews and others who care deeply about the future of humanity. Focusing on the family as central transmitter of Jewish identity, the film also emphasizes the continuing importance of classical texts as guides to post-Auschwitz Jewish life.

The title of the film is itself a metaphor for the *presence of the absence* in the lives of the second generation. In this case, Eliezer (Elie) Joseph Alinsky is a ten-year-old child of Job troubled by an antisemitic "joke" concerning Jewish nose size and stinginess that he hears on a bus. Through a variety of interactions with his parents, whom he calls by the Hebrew titles *Imma* (mother) and *Abba* (father), Elie becomes increasingly aware of the meaning of the rituals in his home. For example, the survivors' distrust of the social world means that the doorbell must be rung in a special way to gain entrance. Further, a locked china cabinet filled with Hebrew books and Jewish ritual objects reveals the "open secret" of Elie's Holocaust legacy. So, too, do hidden photos of family members lost in the *Shoah*, and calendars with yahrzeit dates.

In contrast to the young-adult second-generation members in the documentaries, Elie's youth prevents articulation of a mature philosophy of history or a coherent definition of Jewish identity. His position is much closer to Eva Hoffman, the nine-year-old daughter in Carol Ascher's *The Flood*. Both youngsters possess a child's naïveté concerning the triumph of good over evil, and both strive for an unambiguous moral clarity. Yet he begins to understand his Holocaust legacy when he unlocks the glass door of the china cabinet and when he pushes his finger through the flame of the yahrzeit candle.

The Alinsky family is portrayed as a loving and caring unit. Elie suffers few of the psychic wounds revealed in the documentaries. His mother teaches him about the Holocaust on the personal level, showing the youth photos of their murdered extended family, revealing her own pain when lighting the memorial candles, and by discussing with him the central Jewish phenomenon of memory. Elie wonders how long the yahrzeit candle will burn, and why his mother does not light separate candles for each of her parents. *Imma*'s understated response—"How many candles can I light?"—indicates the sheer enormity of the destruction caused by the Holocaust. Elie reveals his anger and confusion by petulantly asking, "If it [the candle lighting] makes you feel bad, why do you light it? And if it doesn't make you feel bad, why do you have to lie down?" Responding, his mother wisely tells Elie not to be angry with the candle, because it did not do anything. Referring specifically to the yahrzeit dates, the mother tells Elie, "You don't think about it, but suddenly you just know." This is reminiscent of Rukhl Szuster in Barbara Finkelstein's *Summer Long-a-Coming*, with the crucial exception that Elie's mother is more invested in telling him about the *Shoah*. The cinematography powerfully represents the Holocaust inheritance by fading the mother's face into that of Elie's.

Elie now discusses the antisemitic episode with his father, who allows Elie to measure his nose. Discovering that his father's nose is several inches from his head, Elie asks if it is too big. The father responds with a joke of his own: "It doesn't block my eyes, so it's just the right size." The two then discuss whether nose size could prevent one from serving at the ancient Jerusalem Temple. *Abba* is proud that Elie remembers this talmudic discussion from their study together. He exclaims in Yiddish, "Ah *Ahn eisene kopf!*" (an iron [smart] head). Reassured about his father's nose size, Elie wonders about his own. The father again responds in a joking manner, telling the boy to take a deep breath, allowing him to hold it for what seems a very long time, and then telling him to let it out. Since Elie's nose "worked" all right it is, attests the father, "just the right size." Elie, still perplexed, tells his father he is trying to free the air better. This is the boy's imperfectly remembered version of the joke's punch line. The father now understands the "joke."

*Abba* reacts as observant Jews have always responded in times of crisis, by seeking guidance from traditional sources. He tells Elie to bring the talmudic tractate *Gitin* so that they may together study the issues involved in Elie's question. Obeying his father, the boy goes to the study and removes the volume from the shelf. Staggering under the tractate's enormous size, Eli returns to his father. The two study the intriguing tale of Kamtza and Bar Kamtza, which deals with a mistakenly extended dinner invitation that leads to the destruction of the Jerusalem Temple. The host wishes to invite his friend Kamtza, but the man's servant brings instead his enemy Bar Kamtza. The latter is ordered out of the banquet, although he offers to pay for the entire party. Blaming the rabbis who were present but did not protest his treatment, Bar Kamtza betrays rabbinic Judaism, allying himself with the Roman Empire and intentionally rendering ritually unfit a calf that the emperor offers for sacrifice at the Jerusalem Temple. One interpretation contends that the Temple was destroyed because of "causeless hatred" (*sinat hinam*).

But the tale of Kamtza and Bar Kamtza serves as the father's way of teaching Elie how to think Jewishly about second-generation issues such as the place of forgiveness, the role of vengeance, and the post-Auschwitz credibility of rabbinic teachings themselves. The boy rightly protests that he does not understand. This is the beginning of wisdom. Mr. Alinsky rehearses some of the rabbinic responses to the story. He then makes a startling confession: there is no real answer. We do not know, he tells Elie. Only the prophet Elijah can clarify the situation. This assertion refers to the belief that at the end of time, Messiah will come and resolve all difficulties that now appear irreconcilable.

Cinematographically, *Open Secrets* powerfully conveys the relationship between pre- and post-Auschwitz Jewish identity. Part of the recitation of the Kamtza and Bar Kamtza story occurs in the dark; Alinsky's voice is heard, but neither he nor Elie are seen. Here the film indicates that although the past is no longer literally present, it remains really present and serves to help shape second-generation memory of the Holocaust. Further, the Alinskys keep a traditionally Jewish home, which itself impacts on their son's identity. Viewers see a cut-glass wine decanter and other ritual objects such as *mezzuzoth*. Consequently, Elie's identity is shaped both by traditional symbols and the omnipresence of the *Shoah*.

Elie's learning about his Holocaust legacy is accomplished as much by observing as by asking questions. In a poignant scene, his parents, alone in their bedroom, recall the time they were rounded up for deportation to death camps. Unknown to them, Elie listens at the door. Because the family is together but unaware of this fact, this revelation occurs without realization. Nevertheless, the secret is now open. Elie closes the door and returns to his bedroom. Unable to sleep, he goes downstairs, takes the yahrzeit candle and walks to the mysterious glass cabinet. He unlocks the doors, removes several books, and begins reading. The film ends with the screen-filling image of an open book whose upside-down photo (a visual reminder that the *Shoah* itself overturned the moral universe) shows Jewish children wearing the *Magen David* being sent to death.

Elie's initiatory path takes him from being the butt of an antisemitic joke to a hidden auditor of his parents' testimony. Now he must himself come to grips with the Holocaust's meaning for his own second-generation identity. He assumes the dimensions of his identity only gradually. Elie's odyssey involves him on an increasingly deeper level with his parents. He learns both from their words and their silences. More approachable than Reuven Tamiroff, the father in Wiesel's *The Fifth Son*, and more likeable than Valdek in Spiegelman's *Maus*, Mr. Alinsky resembles instead Elhanan, the father in Wiesel's *The Forgotten*. Nevertheless, he refrains from revealing everything. He and his wife take refuge in their silence. They are, however, sympathetic and understanding, encouraging questions in the traditional expectation that these queries will lead to a deeper awareness of the meaning of their son's identity as a contemporary child of Job.

## CONCLUSION

This chapter revealed the variety that exists among the children of Job. The documentary films focus on psychological issues viewed through the prism of parent-child relationships. These relationships bear the *Shoah*'s indelible stamp: incomplete mourning and its opposite, unending mourning; parents who are either overprotective or afraid to love; and children whose identity is formed by a trauma they never personally experienced. Yet, these children of Job are committed to working through their Holocaust legacy, achieving a *tikkun* of the self, and to bearing witness by giving voice to their parents' experience. The docudramas, for their part, illustrate a highly stylized response to the psychosocial dimensions of the Holocaust's legacy for the second generation.

Both genres implicitly raise theological issues as well. They ask about the meaning of second-generation Jewish identity, articulate specific rituals for affirming that identity, and advocate the necessity for distinctive images and rituals with which the contemporary children of Job can express themselves. Further, these films reveal that the second-generation witnesses voluntarily embrace their identity and seek their own form of Jewish commitment. Much in the manner suggested by Greenberg's model, many live Jewish lives even while refraining from specific theological formulation. Moreover, in their determination to bear witness, to express solidarity with Jewish history, and to sanctify life, the contemporary children of Job model Wiesel's additional covenant.

We turn next to films that deal with the acts of the *Hasidei Umot Ha-Olam*. Acting in secret and in a deeply hostile environment, the deeds of the helpers and rescuers of the Jewish people dramatically reveal the universalist impact of the Holocaust, raising questions about human obligation and ethical action.

# CHAPTER 6

# *Second-Generation Documentaries and Docudramas: Jewish Universalism*

> To understand all the people who stood by, you need to understand the few who didn't.
>
> —Pierre Sauvage[1]

"When one saves a life," says the Talmud, "one saves an entire world" (Sanhedrin 4:5). Formulated centuries before the *Shoah*, this talmudic dictum recognizes both the sanctity of human life and the moral imperative to intervene on behalf of its preservation. It stands in the sharpest possible contrast to Nazism's rational planning for, and systematic implementation of, the Final Solution. This "solution" aimed at first degrading Jews, then murdering them, and then destroying them a second time by effacing their memory. Nazism reversed one tenet of the Talmud. Yet the action of the murderers is also addressed by the sacred text that reads "Whoever destroys one life it is as if he destroyed the entire world" (ibid.). However, a small group of people scattered throughout the Kingdom of Night and acting in accordance to diverse motivations displayed the "courage to care" about the Jewish plight. The salvific acts of the *Hasidei Umot Ha-Olam*, the Righteous of the Nations, constitute applied theology in its most sublime expression.

The acts of non-Jewish helpers and rescuers stem from a variety of complex and contradictory sources. Raul Hilberg distinguishes between "selective helpers," those who wanted to save specific individuals or categories of individuals, and "those who willingly assisted almost any Jews, including total strangers."[2] For example, some helped out of religious conviction. Yet other helpers were nationalists and antisemites. Still others were Judeophiles. Some helped because of their own sense of morality. Frequently, there were multiple motivations.[3] Moreover, as we shall see from the films discussed in this chapter, the framework of this help varied greatly. On the one hand, there were elaborate networks of rescuers. Belgium stands out in this category. There is also the example of the French village of Le Chambon-sur-Lignon which, while lacking organization, was committed to helping those in need. On the other hand, there were acts of isolated individuals working in an intensely hostile environment. This was especially the case in Poland.[4]

The deeds of the helpers shed light on the meaning of religion. Further, in risking their lives and those of their families, these individuals extend our notion of what constitutes the essence of religious behavior. The fact that certain of the rescuers were atheists who renounced all formal religious belief reveals the diversity of the sources of moral motivation during the *Shoah*. The actions of atheists and others with little or no formal religious commitment saved thousands of lives. One thinks immediately of Oskar Schindler, although there are other less well-known examples.[5]

By definition, films dealing with rescuers have universal implications. Or rather, these films put in stark terms the relationship between particularism and universalism that existed during the *Shoah*. Was one a Jew, and thereby subject to murder? Or was one a gentile and thus able to blend into the amorphous group of murderers and bystanders? Fackenheim terms the situation a two-dimensional abyss "torn up in the decade between 1935—the Nuremberg laws—and 1945—the end of the Holocaust." He writes:

> One abyss is between "non-Aryan" Jews robbed of choice and eventually doomed to a choiceless death, and "Aryan" Christians cursed and blessed by the gift of a choice—that between acquiescing in their "Aryan" designation and rejecting it, this latter if necessary unto death.[6]

The second abyss, he continues, is between Jews and Christians, on the one side, and the respective Bible of each on the other. The questions during the Kingdom of Night were starkly simple. Was a Jew human? Should one bother to save a Jewish child's life? During the Holocaust the majority answered these questions negatively.

The second-generation mission to tell stories of the helpers and rescuers is part of the universal legacy of the Holocaust. By making these stories part of the fabric of Jewish history, second-generation witnesses accomplish several vital tasks. First, they participate in the act of *Hakarat HaTov* (recognition of goodness), which is an intrinsic good. Further, they keep alive the memory of the deeds of the righteous as a perpetual reminder that moral behavior during the *Shoah* was possible. That so many failed to act in such a manner serves as an eternal condemnation. Because the few did act to achieve a mending of the world under such horrific conditions, this mending remains a post-Auschwitz possibility. In Fackenheim's words, "in the Holocaust world there occurred a *Tikkun* of ordinary decency. Those that performed this *Tikkun* may insist that they did nothing unusual. However, a post-Holocaust Jew—and the post-Holocaust world—can never cease to be amazed."[7] Deeds of the non-Jewish helpers serve to educate future generations about human responsibility in the face of evil. Further, as Eva Fogelman notes, these stories "illustrate the complexities inherent in making moral decisions."[8] Finally, as with everything connected to the Holocaust, deeds of non-Jewish helpers assume an intensely personal meaning for second-generation witnesses, who would not even have been born if the lives of their parents had been lost.

Viewing these "personal documentaries," one is struck by several common themes. First of all, there is an attempt to reveal and perpetuate the deeds of the helpers. Second, each of these films centers on what Insdorf calls a "cinematic return," a journey to Europe in order that the survivors may revisit, and their offspring see for the first time, the rescuers and the places where Jews were sheltered. Seeking to understand both their survivor parents' experience and their own identity, the now adult children of survivors interview the rescuers. One is also struck by the enormity of the rescuers' deeds and their refusal to think of themselves as heroes. What we did was nothing, say the helpers. The people whose lives they saved believe differently.

Moreover, their actions challenge and frighten us far more profoundly than the deeds of the murderers. For example, each of us is able to feel morally superior to those who killed and those who passively watched. The actions of the killers and the bystanders fill us with revulsion or shame. They do not challenge us. The deeds of the righteous do. Uncomfortable questions, accusations really, present themselves when watching and listening to these people. For example, writing about the villagers of Le Chambon, Pierre Sauvage observes that "the challenge for us now is to learn to understand this 'banality of goodness' even during the Holocaust—and to recognize that to care about other people is also to care about yourself."[9]

My discussion focuses on four personal tributes: Myriam Abramowicz and Esther Hoffenberg's *As If It Were Yesterday* (1980), Pierre Sauvage's *Weapons of the Spirit* (1987), Saul Rubinek's *So Many Miracles* (1987), and Debbie Goodstein's *Voices From The Attic* (1988). These films elucidate the *Shoah*'s universal impact by helping to educate about goodness and moral behavior. Additionally, they help sharpen our angle of vision on the mission of the second generation. Further, these films seek to articulate the manifold implications of the *tikkun* of ordinary decency. Making these films the second-generation witnesses encounter the mystery of goodness which is far greater than the manifold expressions of evil which shaped their parents' Holocaust experience.

## AS IF IT WERE YESTERDAY

*As If It Were Yesterday* (*Comme Si C'était Hier*), directed by Myriam Abramowicz and Esther Hoffenberg, is an eighty-six minute black-and-white film with English subtitles. Abramowicz is an American photographer, and Hoffenberg a French artist. Neither had ever made a film. The genesis of the film was Abramowicz's meeting with the Belgian woman who had hidden her parents from the Nazis.[10] She was joined by Hoffenberg, the film's narrator, who "felt herself implicated in the stories of survival."[11] Her own parents had been hidden in Poland. *As If It Were Yesterday* focuses attention on the phenomenon of hidden children and the impact of the *Shoah* on their identity.[12] The film consists of a series of interviews, almost exclusively with gentiles, and has multiple dedications. First, it honors all Belgian people who aided the Jewish population persecuted during the Nazi occupation. Second, the work memorializes those men and women who were deported with the Jewish children they hid. Finally, it is also dedicated to the filmmakers' parents. In Hilberg's terms, the film deals with helpers who "willingly assisted almost any Jews, including total strangers."

Accompanied by the haunting music of the female singer Neige, the film opens with a woman seated in a chair reflecting on the madness of the Holocaust. She remembers the day years ago that Myriam, a young Jewish classmate, did not come to school. Facing deportation, Jewish children had to hide. The speaker found it shocking that Jews wearing the yellow star were like "branded animals." Reflecting on the question that still haunts us today, the woman remembers her reaction so many years ago: "I said, 'It isn't possible that human beings suffer such things. Why . . . ?'"

Utilizing historical footage, the film describes the process by which Belgium's Jews were identified, isolated, and persecuted. Following the German invasion on 10 May 1941, this process was buttressed by the enforcement of increasingly severe antisemitic restrictions. The camera shows stills of soldiers rounding up Jews in Fort Dossin at Malines, as well as mass anti-Jewish demonstrations in Liège. The camera then cuts to the rescuers, each of whom tells a vignette of his or her experience. Twenty-eight "ordinary" people from all walks of life—dressmakers, teachers, priests, physicians, housewives, merchants, nursery directors, social workers, agency administrators, postmen—saved the lives of four thousand Jewish children by placing them in homes, institutions, and convents. Abramowicz reports that when the film premiered in Belgium, people suddenly discovered that their next-door neighbors had hidden Jews.[13] The primal issue at stake is perhaps best described by Andrée Gueulen, a social worker, who observes, "It was a race between us and the Gestapo. Who would get the children first?"

During the interviews, the camera catches the emotions of the rescuers as they recall the traumatic events of those days. Elisa Robson, a dressmaker in Antwerp, nervously folds and unfolds her hands. Madame Brat, a homemaker in Antwerp, describes how very difficult and emotional it is to recall the events of long ago. She tells of the time that her son witnessed the Gestapo arresting the parents of a young woman hiding in the Robson's home. Describing the daughter's reaction to her parents' arrest, Mrs. Robson says, "The girl was completely shattered." The viewer sees Mrs. Robson place her hand on her breast and hears her voice quiver with emotion as she recalls the events. Father Père Capart tells of the German nurse who threw an infant's feeding bottle to the ground saying, "There is no need for that. They will all get what they need." The children were subsequently put in vans and gassed. The priest also remembers "the distress of many among the boys in the Marollen Quarter who knew that they would never see their parents again." Father Capart observes that he "always respected Jewish religious attitudes." He appreciated the Jewish origin of Christianity and states that "in any case, we never tried to make them become Christians."

Discussions between helpers and the helped form the heart of the film. For example, Nana Ruyts, a Brussels dry goods merchant, and Lea Abramowicz, Myriam's mother, speak about her rescue. After outwitting the persecutors, Mrs. Abramowicz calls Nana Ruyts who, with her husband, comes for the Abramowiczs and takes them to their apartment. The Nazis then sealed the Abramowiczs' apartment. The camera shows a close-up of Lea holding Nana's hands while saying "Thanks to you . . . many times . . . we are here today." Nana Ruyts hid up to twenty-three persons.

One of the terrible ironies surrounding the issue of hidden children is that their own mothers posed a great danger to them. For example, Maurice Heiber, responsible for the orphanage at the AJB,[14] observes that this danger consisted in the fact that if the mother knew where the child was hidden and went to see him or her as he or she was moved from place to place, she could be followed. "There were," he recalls, "raid units all over Brussels. And generally you could easily spot Jews. So my first rule was no visits of children by mothers." For the victims it was heartbreaking. For the Nazis, it was the perfection of a system. Heiber's observation also underscores the existence of widespread collaboration in Belgium. Fernande Nonneman, an office clerk, remembers the unspeakable pain of taking an infant away from its mother in order to save the baby's life. She vividly recollects the pathos of the moment, observing, "Taking away that child from its mother who had only given birth fifteen days before . . . I'll never forget that image." At this point she sighs and continues: "I am a mother myself and I understand how that woman suffered. Giving me her child with the hope I would save him."

Through the pathos of the individual tales, there are moments of occasional humor. Maurice Heiber tells of the time that a family wanted to return the five-year-old Jewish boy they took in because he was a thief. Heiber asks the family what happened. Laughing at the memory, he recalls being told that the boy stole the little Jesus icon from the crèche they had given their daughter for Christmas. Heiber took the boy aside and spoke to him "as an adult," saying, "you know the Nazis want to kill us all. And here you are with good people trying to save you. Why did you steal?" The boy confesses after Heiber reassures him that nothing will happen to him. He took the Jesus icon because he knew "that Jesus is a Jew. The Germans could take him so . . . I had to save him." Heiber tells the story to the parents, who were simple workers. "When I told them," he says, "they began to cry. They held the child." Heiber concludes by observing, "These are the kinds of memories which stay alive."

During the *Shoah*, however, there were few happy endings. The camera swiftly moves from humor, to sadness, to death. Following Heiber's story, the viewer next hears from Fela Herman, a member of the Jewish Solidarity organization. Herman's activities underscore the existence of *Jewish self-help* during the *Shoah*, a phenomenon only now beginning to receive increased scholarly attention.[15] She recalls placing two young brothers with a Christian family. Although receiving money and food ration cards, the "helpers" refused to bring in the children to verify that they were being treated well. Finally the brothers were brought in, their bodies covered with infections. The camera then shows Heiber, who recalls the time he had to tell a Jewish family that their hidden daughter had died of diphtheria. "Your child is dead," I said to the mother. "She is a soldier who fought the Nazis just as we do." The reaction was tragic. "The grandfather hit his head against the wall. The father fell numbed, and the mother was screaming."

The names of those who helped deserve repetition. In addition to those already mentioned, there are Dr. Christine Hendrickx; Yvonne Blaze, a homemaker in Huizengen; Yvonne Nevejan, Director of O.N.E. (the National Childrens' Fund); Marie Henriette Coulemans, Director of Jourdan Nursery, Yvonne Jospa, a social worker; Judith Van Montfort, an office clerk, and herself half-Jewish; David Ferdman, a businessman; Félix, a postman in Namur, who intercepted and delayed letters denouncing Jews or their rescuers; and Thérèse and Marcelle Lacroix. Each of them played heroic roles, although each denies that what they did was anything out of the ordinary. While space forbids detailing their deeds in this chapter, each determined that saving the lives of Jewish children was the most important response they could make against the extermination policy of the Nazis and their many collaborationist allies. The actions of the helpers dramatically exemplify what Greenberg terms the central religious testimony after Auschwitz; saving human life and enhancing its dignity is the only appropriate response to Nazism.

Most of the four thousand Jews saved in Belgium remain there today, are married, and have children of their own. Many keep in touch with those who saved their lives. Near the end of the film, the camera shows a reunion between Jerry Rubin, one of the hidden children, and Andrée Gueulen. The two embrace warmly. Rubin, now married, is himself a father. While the camera focuses on Gueulen's face, Jerry Rubin speaks off camera, telling her how much she represents to him for having hidden both him and François, his younger brother, whom the Rubin family was reluctant to give up, yielding only after Andrée pleaded with them. A close-up of Jerry and Andrée shows him telling her that during those years she meant reassurance to him.

The scene ends by echoing the theme of the trauma of Jewish mothers forced to give up their children in order to save their lives. Andrée asks Jerry to imagine how his mother must have felt giving up her two-year-old child. "Can you imagine," she continues, "anyone today saying 'Here's a child, two years old. If they find him, it's death.'" The camera focuses on Andrée's face as she wonders if anyone can know what it means to a mother to be separated from her child. "Giving him to total strangers. . . . That," she concludes, "was the most dramatic of all." The film effectively humanizes the plight of the Jewish people by focusing on Jewish mothers and children. Further, it also highlights the prominent role of women in rescue efforts. Esther Hoffenberg comments on this phenomenon: "Only they could walk on the street holding a child's hand and not attract attention, or hide false identity cards under bunches of leeks in a shopping bag. Their mutual help network was extraordinary."

Several of the hidden children share their own memories of terror and uncertainty. Betty Kichelmacher, Willy Bok, Fanny Filosot, and Ida Hollander all reflect on the impact on their identity of being hidden during the *Shoah*. Ida, who lived in Holland, remembers staying inside all the time. Because she was unable to go to school, her hosts' children brought her library books to read. On the other hand, Willy Bok and his sister lived in a small village in Belgium and went to school with their non-Jewish peers. But life was complicated for these young Jewish children. Gustave Collet, an assistant to Father André Namur, recalls the common problems that the hidden children shared. For example, they were worried about their parents, about their own false identity, and about dissimulating their personality. Collet remembers one child who "couldn't remember his own name. He had changed it so many times."

Two of the hidden children emphasize the permanence of their psychological scars. Betty Kichelmacher, who nervously clasps and unclasps her hands when speaking, found out at the age of twelve that her parents had been deported and gassed in Auschwitz. She also lost two brothers as well as cousins and uncles. An aunt emigrated to America and never contacted Betty. The camera shows a still of Betty as a young girl, while in a voice-over she states that she stayed in various homes until the age of seventeen.[16] She specifically recalls sitting in a train, wearing a coat with a number on it, and being surrounded by strangers. When the train stopped, others got in, and "I saw . . . I was in another family." Asked by the interviewer what image of her parents she retains, Betty responds that her father must have been a religious man. She describes leaving her parents house at age three. Her mother came downstairs with her. "She held me so tightly. I remember her face was bathed in tears. . . . And," Betty concludes, "I wondered why."

The post-*Shoah* path was neither easy nor uniform for the hidden children. Betty recalls that some ended in psychiatric hospitals and are still there today. Some children succeeded while others did not. It depended on several factors: loving foster parents, tutors, education. She herself had no one. Consequently she, and others like her, had no chance at a career. Fanny Filosof, another of the hidden children, tells of the Holocaust's impact on her identity. At the age of ten she was separated from her parents forever. Her consequent idealizing of her parents had serious emotional consequences. For example, she continually rejects families who wish to integrate her into their lives because these families, she attests, "appeared like usurpers of my parents." Acknowledging that families who took in children during the war were not always rewarded for their generosity, Fanny reflects on the terrible trauma to identity caused by this upheaval. "Maybe," she observes, "they didn't know how difficult it is for a child to invent himself new parents and to accept them as such. On the contrary, children often resent being made to belong."

The film concludes with testimony from the rescuers in response to the question Why did you help the Jews? Their statements stand in the sharpest possible contrast to Nazism's contempt for Jewish life. For example, one of them contends that the Jewish children "simply had to be saved." Another, responds, "You cannot remain idle when you know children are being slaughtered and taken to Germany to be gassed." A third, who was arrested three times during the war, said that if she was going to be arrested anyway, it might as well be for a specific act of resistance. Yet this woman is quite undramatic about her actions. She reports that if not the Jewish children, it might have been the parachutists, members of the secret press, or something else altogether with whom she could have been involved. Further, she confides to being constantly afraid—not of being caught, but of not knowing how she would react under interrogation. Everyone, she philosophizes, had the same fear. This fear made some collaborate and others resist. A nurse attests that she never really thought about it, but that every human being has the instinct to protect someone who is being attacked. I helped the Jewish children, she says, "for humanitarian reasons and to resist the occupation ."

Perhaps the most complex and heartbreaking phenomenon associated with the hidden children is their identity confusion. For example, Fela Herman attests to the fact that the "children clung to the places where they were hidden." This frequently caused great anguish when those parents fortunate enough to survive the Holocaust came to retrieve their children. Often the children did not wish to leave the safety of their foster homes. Herman states that it took a long time before the children accepted their natural parents again. It was, she observes, "a new tragedy for these people." This observation is certainly different from the experiences reported by Betty Kirchelmacher and Fanny Filosof. But in fact, it is well attested in the literature. An extreme example is a nine-year-old girl's claim: "The Jewish God killed my parents. He burned my home. Jesus Christ saved me."[17] Doubtless these reactions reflect what the children heard in their new environments and underscore the complexity underlying rescuer motivation.

Today Myriam Abramowicz, born in Brussels in 1946, believes that *As If It Were Yesterday* has broadened its scope and assumed a distinctly post-Auschwitz universal role. The film can, she attests, bring together African Americans and Jews.[18] People who have been or are imperiled may identify with the plight of the Jews. Abramowicz feels that the non-Jewish audience is brought closer to the entire situation by being able to identify with the rescuer in the sense of thinking, "*I* could be that person."[19] So-called revisionists, who are in fact not revisers but deniers of the Holocaust, and other Jew-haters are also unmasked by the testimony given in the film. If the *Shoah* never happened, what are the helpers talking about? What can the demagogues do about the testimony of the non-Jewish righteous?

The reaction of Jewish audiences to *As If It Were Yesterday* is more complex, ranging from those who learn to those who "refuse the film."[20] Some Jewish viewers wonder how Abramowicz can make such a film when they, themselves, lost family members in the Nazi genocide. Others contend that what was done was not enough. A third response is typified by those Jews who feel wonderful. For Abramowicz the film helps clarify the historical record of the Kingdom of Night. She reminds her audiences that she is here only "by the grace of these people." From this highly personal observation, Abramowicz draws a twofold lesson for the entire Jewish people. *As If It Were Yesterday* serves as a reminder to the Jews that they were not completely abandoned during the *Shoah*. In addition, she views the film as a "way of learning trust." Further, Abramowicz herself planted the seed that sprouted a decade later in the convening of the Hidden Child Meeting held in New York in 1991.[21]

## WEAPONS OF THE SPIRIT

Pierre Sauvage's *Weapons of the Spirit* asks why the five thousand villagers of Le Chambon-sur-Lignon helped save the lives of five thousand Jewish people. The film is prefaced by a quote from Albert Camus's *The Plague*; itself a parable on Nazism, the novel was written in a farmhouse near Le Chambon. Camus's words put the Chambonnais' actions into perspective: "There always comes a time in history when the person who dares to say that two plus two equals four is punished with death." "And," he continues, "the issue is not what reward or what punishment will be the outcome of that reasoning. The issue is simply whether or not two plus two equals four."

Sauvage's film is both history and journey of self-discovery. Like Finkelstein's Brenda Szuster, Sauvage confides that he was "raised in hiding" not only during the last year of the *Shoah* but in the postwar years as well.[22] He interviews the now elderly rescuers in French. English translations are provided. The Chambonnais' responses reveal a clear understanding of human obligation that recognizes the need for applied theology. The rescuers' testimony reflects Greenberg's sense of the voluntary covenant, which emphasizes human responsibility and respect for the sanctity of human life. For example, Henri and Emma Héritier attest that helping the Jews was "just the right thing to do." Like Abramowicz's film, *Weapons of the Spirit* portrays helpers whose behavior is described in Hilberg' s second type, those who help even total strangers.

The film opens with a shot of an old train traversing the countryside. Unlike the Nazi trains of death, however, this train leads the viewer on an extraordinary journey of hope and life. Sauvage's voice-over tells the viewer that he is a Jew, born in Nazi-occupied France in 1944. Many of his extended family were murdered during the *Shoah*. Against the background of prewar photos, the viewer learns that Sauvage's mother lost her mother, younger brother, sister, brother-in-law, and little niece. Later, Sauvage reports that Dr. Roger LeForestier, the physician who delivered him, was subsequently murdered by the Nazi thug Klaus Barbie. Yet, in the midst of this unparalleled evil and massive indifference, the deeply religious peasants of Le Chambon opt for prosocial behavior. Moreover, this response is viewed as natural. For the Chambonnaise, saving Jews was the moral equivalent of daring to say that two plus two equals four.

Historically, the Chambonnais, Huguenots in a Catholic country, have themselves experienced persecution. They well understand the experience of being marginalized or placed outside the majority culture's universe of human obligation. For example, in 1936 the Chambonnnais also provided a haven to refugees from the Spanish Civil War and others whose lives had been tossed about in the turbulent historical sea of that time.

Specifically concerning the villagers' response to Nazism, Pastor André Trocmé, a conscientious objector, is a pacifist whose Christian belief compels him to resist Nazi oppression. His assistant pastor, Édouard Theis, shares Trocmé's views. They are a minority of two who first warn, "We must not *fight* the Germans and, second, we must not *collaborate* with the Germans." In a Sunday sermon preached the day after Marshal Pétain's puppet government signed an armistice with Nazi Germany, Trocmé admonished his congregants that "the responsibility of Christians is to resist the violence that will be brought to bear on their consciences through the weapons of the spirit." Trocmé, whose cousin Daniel was murdered in Maidanek, was himself imprisoned and later released.

*Weapons of the Spirit* cuts back and forth between the Holocaust past and the present in telling of French collaboration and the villagers' resistance. The past is portrayed in black-and-white. Archival footage shows the Vichy government's capitulation to Nazi Germany. There are scenes of Pétain and Hitler, an antisemitic exhibition that warns of the great peril Jews posed to France's national life, and other similar antisemitic displays. Eighty-five thousand French Jews, ten thousand of them children, were deported under the Vichy regime. A camera smuggled into Rivesalt shows a chilling view of a deportation. This shameful tale of French collaboration contrasts vividly to the actions of the Chambonnais. The villagers were neither cunning nor organized in a special manner. In stark contrast to the Belgian experience, Magda Trocmé, André's widow, ironically notes, "If we'd had an organization, we would have failed." How then is one to account for the altruistic behavior of Le Chambon?

One of the remarkable features about the Chambonnais is that they base their actions solely on the biblical ethic and represent the clearest example of an authentic religious response to the Jewish situation. Even fundamentalist Christians, who elsewhere in Europe displayed such hostility to the Jewish people, in Le Chambon became their protectors. Marie Brottes summarizes the attitude of Le Chambon's fundamentalists towards the Jews. Even though they (the Jews) did not accept the Gospels, she observes, "for us they were the people of God, the neighbor to love as yourself." And the Jewish people had truly "fallen among thieves" (Nazis and their French helpers). Madame Brottes recalls that one of the villagers would arrive and say, "I have three Old Testaments" (Jews). "And," she recalls, "an old Christian took them." It is left to the theologically unsophisticated Marie Brottes to articulate the primary difference between true and false Christians during the Holocaust. "Your faith is in vain," she observes, "if works do not follow." Moreover, the entire village, including a Catholic minority, participate in the rescue effort, establishing orphanages and group residences where food and provisions are shared.

The actions of the villagers of Le Chambon give meaning to the true sense of ecumenicism. Marc Donadile, a Protestant pastor who worked with the French rescue group *Cimade*, recalls that "the Jews felt close to us because of our ties to the Old Testament, and we felt close to them because they were the people of God." "The prophets," he states, "nurtured us in our struggle against the Nazis."[23] Acts of resistance ranged from Pastor Trocmé's refusal to reveal names of hidden Jews—"It's not the role of the shepherd to denounce his flock"—to the commonsense farmer who recalls hiding forged identity papers in (empty) beehives because he knew that the Nazis would not place their hands inside.

As with Abramowicz's film, watching Sauvage's film creates the desire to commemorate all the names of the rescuers. The Trocmé's American daughter Nelly Trocmé Hewitt recalls that the "Jews were part of the community just like we were." Emile Seches directed the Jewish boarding school adjacent to German headquarters. Roger Darcissac, the public-school director, told the Germans that there were no Jews in his school because "it was the human thing to do." Roger Bonfils, an innkeeper, was forced to convert his business into a convalescent home for wounded German soldiers. He denied the soldiers' contention that "the place was full of Jews." He said, "They are tourists." Georgette Barraud, whose boarding house sheltered many of the Jews, speaks for her fellow Chambonnais in stating, "It [the rescue] happened so naturally. We cannot understand the fuss."

Like the prophets of antiquity, the people of Le Chambon think themselves unworthy. Pierre Sauvage notes elsewhere that the villagers were "very reluctant" to speak to him about their wartime help. "They believe," he writes, "that to appear to trumpet your deeds is to devalue them."[24] Although the villagers of Le Chambon were hesitant to speak about their actions, these life-saving activities reveal a profound knowledge about the difference between good and evil. For example, Édouard Theis states that "for the Pétain regime [they] had nothing but contempt." The Chambonnais' was an applied theology that empowered the villagers to stand with and assist the victims.

Sauvage's interviews with some of the rescued Jews elicits their complex emotions. Unlike the Jews of Belgium, none of those rescued remain in or near Le Chambon. Moreover, few return to visit after the war. "It is not that I wasn't grateful," attests Joseph Atlas, one of the rescued. "But," he continues, "I first had to surmount the tragedy of the Jewish people's experience." The pathos of this situation becomes even clearer during Suavage's interview with Marguerite Kohn, an Orthodox Jew who kept kosher for the duration of her stay in Le Chambon. She recalls going to church services from time to time, and sending her children to the village school except on Saturday. The Chambonnais were extremely kind to her and her children. But she also recalls living in constant fear of being caught by the Germans. Madame Kohn's own family suffered terribly during the *Shoah*. Recitation of her Holocaust dead is accompanied by various photos. For example, the fact that her husband was gassed on 25 January 1944 is synchronized with a black-and-white shot of their wedding photo. A color shot of a hanukkiah (menorah) provides the backdrop for the information that her brother, the father of three children, was deported in 1943. Similarly, black-and-white photos of family members plus color shots of Jewish ritual objects are shown as Madame Kohn reports that her sister-in-law was deported in January of 1944 along with her husband and four children. Many cousins, to whom she was very close, were deported with their husbands and children, as were aunts and uncles. Asked by Sauvage how many returned, Madame Kohn utters one word: "None."

The film really tells two stories: one is the remarkable tale of an unpretentious group of peasant farmers, the other is the filmmaker's attempt to come to grips with his own identity. The first story is both a testimony and an accusation. For example, why did some people who call themselves Christians act in an altruistic fashion, while the overwhelming majority of Christians acted as apostates? At this point, it is well to recall the observation that "apostasy is the religious equivalent of treason."[25] The actions of the Chambonnais underscore the nearly omnipresent treasonous actions of the majority. The issue really focuses on the normative content of the Christian message. What allowed the majority to acquiesce to, or willingly participate in, the murder of the Jews, yet at the same time commanded the people of Le Chambon to save them? As Sauvage himself asks, "What did the peasants and villagers of Le Chambon understand that so tragically eluded their Christian brethren from the Pope on down?"[26]

A different perspective on Le Chambon is offered by Lesley Maber, an Englishwoman who moved to the village shortly before the Holocaust and taught school there for thirty years. Much in the manner of the Deuteronomist of antiquity, she posits the notion of choice. "Humanity," she observes, "is fundamentally good, with the possibility to become fundamentally bad." Lesley Maber contends that "any community anywhere has the choice to make and can choose right." She concludes by observing that "people who seem like ordinary people can do great things if given the opportunity."

Sauvage also theorizes about the actions of the Chambonnais, contending that their deeds were contagious. He believes that the Jews survived because of what he terms a "conspiracy of goodness." For example, both Robert Bach, the Vichy Préfect for Le Chambon, and Julius Schmähling, the Wehrmacht Major stationed in the village, underreported the Jewish presence. Sauvage wonders if Bach was influenced by Trocmé's example, or whether it was because the Préfect himself was of Heugenot descent. Sauvage wisely notes, however, that in the context of Le Chambon it was easier for Schmähling to go along with the villagers. In another context, observes Sauvage, "he might have just as easily murdered."[27] The camera's focus on pen-and-ink drawings of children being marched off to deportation centers, accompanied by jarring and discordant music, attests to the ease with which so many aided and abetted in the murder of the Jewish people. While Sauvage's theory of a "conspiracy of goodness" is morally attractive, there appears little evidence to document it. Daniel Trocmé's observation that "Le Chambon is a contribution to the reconstruction of the world" does not have a resonant echo in the majority of France where there was no comparable effort to achieve either a *tikkun olam*, or a *tikkun atzmi*.

*Weapons of the Spirit* also chronicles Sauvage's journey of Jewish self-discovery. Reminiscent of Lev Raphael's *Winter Eyes*, Sauvage's parents only reveal his Jewish identity to him when he is eighteen and about to embark for Paris in order to attend school. Obviously he did not become a bar mitzvah, nor did he learn or study anything about Judaism. He recalls being "raised with taboos," and that his parents had cut their ties to Judaism long before the war.[28] He told an interviewer, "I was deprived of memory, and that probably generated an almost compulsive need to reconstruct a part of a past that I was not raised with."[29] Sauvage attests that his re-entry into Judaism is attributable to two factors: returning to Le Chambon at a key moment, and the birth of his son. The latter serves as a reminder that Sauvage "belonged to a chain of generations, and of the importance of rootedness to the past."[30] Unlike Spiegelman, Sauvage feels that this past continues to address him. While for both these sons of Job the Holocaust is the point of entrance into Jewish identity, Sauvage does not stop with the *Shoah*. His sense of Jewish rootedness is manifested both in the telling of the story of Le Chambon and in the fact that he marries endogamously and raises his children as Jews.

Sauvage's film also reveals the variety of *Jewish* response to Nazi persecution. He distinguishes three basic types of such response. First of all, there is the example of the steadfast faith of the Orthodox and their messianic waiting. This model is personified by Marguerite Kohn. There is as well a Jewish resistance group that is active in and around Le Chambon. When members of the group are shown on screen, the Yiddish Partisan Song (*mir szeinen doh*) is sung in the background. Giora Freidman's klezmer music also enriches the narrative.[31] Like Abramowicz, Sauvage also shows the example of Jewish self-help. Madelaine Dreyfus, a Jewish woman relief worker, arranges for children to be housed with the peasants and farmers of Le Chambon. She recalls that teenagers were more difficult to place than younger children. But even so, revealing that the two fourteen-year-olds with her are Jewish prompts a helping couple to respond, "Why didn't you say so?" The teenagers are taken by the couple. Moreover, the viewer learns that in the woods of Le Chambon, Jews danced the Hora. These activities were in addition to study, learning, and the observance of traditional holidays. While not an articulated theme of Sauvage's film, many Jews hiding in Le Chambon displayed their own weapons of the spirit.

Sauvage's film has clear universalist implications. The filmmaker himself believes that *Weapons of the Spirit* makes a contribution to defining and redefining Christian faith.[32] Although he correctly warns against the twin dangers of Christians using the righteous as an alibi, on the one hand, and Jews rushing to embrace them, as atoning on the other, it is clear that the actions of these people were neither normative then nor atoning now. Rather, such actions indict Christian complicity while demonstrating what could be accomplished by a group of people determined to answer God's question to Cain in the affirmative. In Le Chambon, during the Holocaust, Hanukkah and other Jewish festivals were celebrated with the help and support of devout Christians. It is entirely appropriate that the Jewish people whose lives were saved by the villagers erected a plaque in the center of Le Chambon memorializing the righteous .

Far beyond the European continent, *Weapons of the Spirit* has touched lives and won awards. For example, in Japan, where there are no significant numbers of either Jews or Christians, the film received several prizes. Sauvage reports speaking to Japanese high-school students about their reactions. The students were fascinated by three basic questions: What makes us human beings? What is human solidarity? and What are we responsible for? The Japanese, he reports, were "fascinated by *good* people."[33] What can be learned from this experience? For one thing, models of goodness transcend national and religious boundaries even while simultaneously remaining elusive. Modeling acts of *tikkun* themselves serve as an incentive for such actions. Human solidarity in the face of oppression is reminiscent of Wiesel's emphasis on solidarity as a dimension of the additional covenant. One irony here is that at the time of this writing the film has yet to be screened on French television, probably because of its unsparing look at French collaboration.[34] Nevertheless, Sauvage, who founded the Friends of Le Chambon to educate people about goodness, and his film are making important progress in this vital pedagogical task.

## SO MANY MIRACLES

The Canadian actor Saul Rubinek's *So Many Miracles* explores a different dimension of altruism in telling the story of his parents' Holocaust experience while simultaneously attesting to his own understanding of second-generation Jewish identity. Made in Canada and directed by Katherine Smalley and Vic Sarin, the film is narrated by Saul Rubinek. Rubinek accompanies his parents on their return to Poland to visit Zophia Banya, the Christian woman who hid them for over two years and wants to see them again before she dies. Zophia had been a customer in the Rubineks' small grocery store before the war, and they had extended credit to her and shown other kindnesses. Unlike either the religious factor that played such a dominant role in the case of the Chambonnais rescue or the anti-Nazism of the Belgian rescuers, the action of Zofia Banya appears motivated to a large extent by prewar friendship, and thus illustrates what Hilberg terms a "selective helper."

On the eve of their departure, Saul articulates his understanding of the relationship between experiencing the Holocaust and being a second-generation witness. He realizes that the only way for him to comprehend the European catastrophe is to "deal with what happened to my parents as individual people and their own experiences and to identify with what happened." This is not out of a desire to "reach what happened historically through them." Rather, this quest is far more personal. Rubinek undertakes it, he attests, "Just because it is important for me to understand my parents." This desire to know and understand the parents is the linchpin of second-generation cinematic discourse.

In terms of structure, *So Many Miracles* portrays the prewar, Holocaust, and post-*Shoah* lives of the Rubineks. Differing from the films of Abramowicz and Sauvage, Rubinek utilizes actors to recreate crucial events in the lives of his parents during the *Shoah*, therefore enabling him to portray these events in color, which emphasizes their continuing contemporary impact. Interestingly, Insdorf reports that the actors were not professionals, "but Polish townspeople who offered to participate" in the film.[35] Additionally, each of the Rubineks serves—at one point or another—as narrator of the film, thus underscoring several significant themes: the difference between survivor memory and second-generation inherited memory, the familial cohesiveness and mutual support characteristic of many survivor families, the continuing impact of the *Shoah*, and Saul Rubinek's determination to explore his relationship to the *Shoah* and to model the *tikkun* of bearing witness to that relationship.

In relating their experiences, Frania and Israel Rubinek tell of the murder of Pinczow's Jews, including Israel's grandfather. Witnessing this from his hiding place leaves Israel literally speechless. The parents detail their own desperate journey to Zofia's cottage, where they were hidden for twenty-eight months. Of the four films under discussion, *So Many Miracles* provides the most detailed account of survivors' inner thoughts and emotions while in hiding. For example, peering through a slit in the

Banya's front door—on which the camera focuses—Israel remembers envying a fly and the family's chickens, who, he attests, "have more rights than a human being." Frania, for her part, recalls Zofia's warm embrace when they arrived at the farmhouse and remembers thinking that "a mother does not greet her own child the way she greeted me." The Rubinek's reflections assume even greater intensity as this scene is dramatized by the actors.

Israel Rubinek also reveals a little-known dimension of the relationship between Jews in hiding and their Christian rescuers: the Jewish victim as teacher of gentiles. During the two-and-one-half years of hiding, he serves as Zofia's son Maniek's surrogate father, teaching the youth how to read and write. Consequently, if Zofia is Frania's "foster mother," then Israel is Maniek's "adoptive father." "Parenting" Maniek, Israel attests, helped take his own mind off the Gestapo and the situation he was in. Constantly in fear of being discovered by the Nazis, the Rubineks also feared being betrayed by Ludwig, Zofia's husband. Physically abusive to his wife, Ludwig is a sullen man who ignores his own son and has grave doubts about hiding Jews, going as far as threatening to turn them over to the Gestapo. Israel states that the man did not betray them to the Gestapo because he—Israel—spoke to him humanely and made him "believe that he was a good, good man." As these words are spoken, the camera cuts to a black-and-white shot of Ludwig dressed in his peasant cap and jacket.

Fogelman provides additional detail about the relationship between Israel Rubinek and Ludwig.[36] Rubinek took two measures to protect himself and Frania. First, he slept with a knife in case Ludwig tried to attack them. Secondly, he determined to make a friend of the man. Consequently, he began reading newspapers to Sophia's husband and explaining politics to him. When farmers visited on Sunday, Ludwig repeated what he had heard. "In no time at all," writes Fogelman, "Ludwig became known as the most politically savvy man in the village."[37] Thus, Rubinek teaches both the son and the father. Paradoxically, when the Rubineks were no longer able to pay their helpers, Ludwig became more protective, sharing his wife's emotional attachment to Israel and Frania.

This film, like the others in this chapter, raises the complex issue of rescuer motivation. Such motivation runs the gamut from sheer altruism, with no money involved, to hiding Jews only for payment.[38] However, even when Jews literally paid *for* their lives, they were not infrequently betrayed by their alleged helpers and paid *with* their lives.[39] As the camera profiles Zofia's wrinkled face, she attests that during the war she "felt so much pity for [the Rubineks]. It was impossible to betray them." Yet rescue was an awesome and ominous task. When Frania asks if she and Israel could hide in Zofia's home, Zofia responds by saying she wanted to think about it. In fact, the Banyas were paid by Frania's sister, who, owing to her "Aryan" appearance, passed as a Christian. Nevertheless, even when her husband initially wanted to throw out the Rubineks, Zofia resisted. "It would," she says, " be on my conscience for all of my life." At this point the camera switches to a black-and-white wartime photo of Zofia's face. Her actions emphasize the accuracy of Pierre Sauvage's observation that frequently it was the women who made the initial decision concerning whether or not to help Jews.

The perspective of the child rescuer is far less complex. For example, actors dramatize the time that two German soldiers slept in the Banyas' kitchen while Frania and Israel hid in the secret potato cellar under the stove. Maniek slept next to the stove and throughout the night, every ten to fifteen minutes, intentionally cried and coughed in order to mask the sounds of Israel's own coughing. After the Germans left, the Rubineks asked him why he coughed all night. Frania recalls that Maniek said to her husband, "You don't understand anything. I did it so you could cough." While Frania terms this episode "a miracle of miracles," the camera cuts to the door in the side of the stove that led to the Rubinek's hiding place. The now adult Maniek reflects that even though he was very young then, he "felt an obligation, a human duty." It is appropriate at this point to note that Fogelman observes of child rescuers that they "ignore danger either through a deliberate if unconscious misjudgment of the seriousness of the situation or by making light of danger altogether.[40] Maniek's adult reflection may mask what he felt when, as a child, he coughed to protect the Rubineks.

Like Abramowicz and Savauge, Rubinek articulates the dimensions of his own second-generation witness while revealing fundamentally different ways that survivor children discover their Jewish identity. Unlike Sauvage, the young Rubinek was raised Jewishly and frequently heard his parents' Holocaust stories. Traveling to Poland and meeting Zofia and Maniek, Saul contends that all the courage and love that he has seen enable him "to remember without the weight of any bitterness." The camera shows an emotional reunion between the rescuers and the rescued. Shortly after the film was completed, the eighty-four-year-old Zofia died as the result of an accidental fall. The camera cuts to Saul Rubinek's face as he expresses his thankfulness at having had the chance to meet Zofia, whom he compares to a "grandmother I never knew." Exploring his own relationship to the Holocaust and his Jewish identity, this second-generation witness becomes a "Rider towards the Dawn."

So Many Miracles emphasizes the crucial distinction between the official indifference of the Catholic Church and Zofia's life-saving action. The camera frequently shows interior scenes of the church in which Zofia prays, inviting the viewer to contrast the behavior of the institution with that of the person. Unlike Zofia, however, the elder Rubineks express their anger at God. Each of them reveals an aspect of the Jewish quarrel with the deity. Frania questions God's existence, while Israel's protest from within leads him to contend—with Wiesel—that, "Yes I believe in God, but I'll take him to court." But the film's theology has less to do with God than it does with miracles. Survival itself is a miracle made possible by an entire range of other miraculous events. For example, Frania's sister happened to rent a room in a house owned by Ludwig's sister. This enabled her to learn her family's hiding place and to send money for the Banyas. Moreover, in showing the resoluteness of an unsophisticated woman determined to save Jewish lives, the film challenges its viewers to question their own moral and ethical precepts. Unlike the rescuers in Belgium, the Banyas had no network or organization. Quite to the contrary: they told no one of their deed because they feared betrayal. The film's universal message is that even in the midst of radical evil, resistance can save lives.

## VOICES FROM THE ATTIC

Debbie Goodstein is a daughter of Job whose parents are Polish Jews. She directed and narrates *Voices from the Attic* (1988), a one-hour film that expresses the quest of a second-generation witness to gain mastery of her Holocaust legacy. In this case, Goodstein and five of her cousins travel to Poland in order to meet Maria Gorocholski, the peasant woman who saved Mrs. Goodstein's life by permitting her and fourteen other members of her extended family to hide in the Gorocholskis' attic. The film combines interviews and archival footage in telling the tale of a "selective helper." In addition, Goodstein acknowledges the scholarly guidance provided by Annette Insdorf. Several important second-generation themes emerge in *Voices from the Attic*. For example, Goodstein speaks of the "conspiracy of silence" among certain survivors, the role of the Holocaust in shaping second-generation perceptions, the crucial importance of listening to survivor testimony, and the need to make a pilgrimage to Europe.

Goodstein poetically voices the continuing impact of the *presence of the absence* in the lives of the second generation. She states, "For as long as I could remember I've had nightmares and relived things that happened before I was born in a place I've never seen. I was haunted by stories that I'd never heard." This unarticulated legacy is expressed in the way Holocaust imagery informs the lives of the second generation. For example, one of the cousins was afraid to ride subways for a time because she was reminded of death trains. This recalls the observations of Helen Epstein and Art Spiegelman on the role played by Holocaust imagery in the lives of survivors' offspring. Further, Goodstein attests that she and her cousins "were brought into the world more suspicious than [their] European-born parents had been, knowing what could happen." This distrust of the social world leads to being fearful for one's own safety.

Goodstein also articulates the power of Holocaust secrets kept by survivors. For example, like Ariel in Wiesel's *The Fifth Son*, Jason Kole in Friedmann's *Damaged Goods*, and Abraham Ravett's *Half-Sister*, Goodstein only learns much later about the Holocaust death of a relative. She is eighteen before discovering that her mother and aunts had a younger sister whose existence was never discussed. The filmmaker also discovers previously unknown information about the deaths of two other people hidden in the attic: her grandmother and a little boy. Furthermore, buttressing the contention of Fogelman's *Breaking the Silence*. Goodstein observes that despite her parents conspiracy of silence, "or as a result of it, [the Holocaust] even managed to make its way into the next generation."

In order to come to grips with her Holocaust legacy, Goodstein undertakes her journey. But this odyssey is not without pain. For example, the filmmaker' s mother and aunt decline—on camera—to accompany her to Poland. Her mother states, "I don't need to do things that will cause me unhappiness." For Goodstein, however, it is crucial to travel to Poland for three reasons: in order to put the "pieces of stories" she had heard into context, to understand the impact of the Holocaust on her own life, and—like Abramowicz, Sauvage, and Rubinek—to make a pilgrimage to meet a rescuer. Aunt Sally Frishberg, "the living Anne Frank," is Goodstein's guide, transmitting the family's Holocaust story to Debbie and her five cousins who accompany her and her husband to Cracow, Warsaw, Auschwitz, and their hometown of Urzejowice.

Post-Holocaust Poland remains a land of contradictions. During the *Shoah* some three million Polish Jews were murdered. Auschwitz was located on Polish soil. The Polish home army frequently murdered Jews and, in 1946 in Kielce, a pogrom took the lives of forty-two Jewish survivors. Yet, among the rescuers honored by Yad VaShem, "By far the vast majority . . . are Polish and Dutch."[41] *Voices from the Attic* powerfully captures the current expression of Polish ambiguity concerning the Jews. On the one hand, Aunt Sally is warmly embraced by former neighbors and friends. She also thanks her neighbors for their help when she returned from the attic. However, on the other hand, there are disquieting signs. A Polish child says "Heil Hitler" to one of the cousins. Moreover, the camera shows a freshly painted swastika on the wall of the home Debbie's parents were forced to leave over forty years earlier. Debbie responds by observing that "some of these children inherited a hatred of us the way we inherited a fear of them." Sally tells the cousins that three months after the war, some Polish men came to their house and told them that Poland was for Poles. Jews should go to Palestine, or be killed.

But Poland proves the crucible in which Debbie Goodstein forges a fuller discovery of the past that her parents and her cousins' parents had tried to suppress. In fact the film underscores the diversity of rescuer motivation. For example, initially the Goodsteins survived by literally living underground for three months. As in the case of Zoltan Klein in Brand's *Kaddish*, the Goodsteins had dug holes in the earth, and some farmers shared food with them. Stanislav Gorocholski, one of the farmers, had been a childhood friend of Sally's mother. Sally herself believes that she knows why the farmers did not betray them. Her explanation is a variant of Pierre Sauvage's "conspiracy of goodness" theory. For instance, she contends that the sight of little children among their group "softened the hearts" of the farmers.[42]

Debbie's parents' lives had been saved by the Gorocholski family, whose original motivation was economic. Mr. Gorocholski kept refusing to hide the family because his wife was too fearful. Sally's mother, however, finally bribed them. Aunt Sally recalls that he told the group that his wife was willing to chance hiding them providing they turn over their jewelry and furs. Like the Banyas in *So Many Miracles*, the Gorocholskis display what Fogelman terms "economically based Judeophilism." This was, notes Fogelman, "a factor in many rescues."[43] Yet, because the Gorocholskis saved thirteen lives during the Holocaust, sixty people are alive today.

With the other second-generation witnesses who have made films honoring the rescuers, the main purpose of Goodstein's trip to Poland is to meet her parents' helper. Aunt Sally, speaking in Polish, introduces her family to the now-widowed Maria Gorocholski. The cousins look raptly at the eighty-year-old woman. The entire entourage then go to the attic, where Sally describes the conditions under which they lived for two torturous years. She recalls the summer's unbearable heat and being covered by snow in the winter. The family "scrounged for crumbs in the straw." Sally reflects on her own "survivor mission." Each time that she tells her story, she feels that she is doing what her murdered uncle Naphtali was supposed to do. In a highly charged emotional scene she also weeps bitterly when recalling the deaths of her little sister, a young boy, and her grandmother, and the unspoken yet omnipresent pain of her parents.

Sally articulates a universal understanding of Jewish chosenness. Moreover, she contends that Jews cannot cease being Jewish. For example, she asks why don't the Jewish people "un-Jew" themselves? Responding to her own query, Sally views Jewish suffering in the Holocaust in terms of what today would be termed *human rights*. Asking herself for what reason the Jews suffered, Sally responds, "This is the Jewish way of defining the human right to be what one is." Consequently, for Aunt Sally, Jewish and human destiny are inextricably linked in a type of political theology that appears to be a secular variant of Israel as Isaiah's suffering servant.

The film concludes with a party in the Gorocholski home. At this point Goodstein asks the family two questions; why did you rescue, and did the children suspect that anyone was in their attic. In response, the Gorocholski spokesperson contends that in terms of the first question it was really a "simple matter." We did not understand the consequences of our actions. "Those who had a good heart," he continues, "took in a family to prevent their death." This, of course, is a postwar reflection on the situation. The children did suspect that some people were in their attic. Yet, even after forty years, Maria Gorocholski does not like to talk to her neighbors about what she did because something terrible might happen. On behalf of the second generation, Goodstein toasts the Gorocholski family and Sally's daughter thanks Maria.

Goodstein articulates her second-generation witness legacy in terms of both a *tikkun olam* and a *tikkun atzmi*. Despite her ambivalence about the Polish people and the knowledge that the Gorocholski's motives "were not entirely selfless," she is grateful that they were willing to risk their lives in order to save her family. Consequently, her film leaves open for further exploration both the issue of altruistic behavior and the complexity of Jewish-Christian relations. Moreover, she compares the generational legacy of the Holocaust for both murderers and victims. Noting, correctly, that antisemitism had not disappeared with the Jews of Poland, she contends that it is a "hand-me-down" from previous generations. Antisemitism haunts Polish children, she contends, the way her own parents' survivor guilt continues to haunt the second generation. This observation highlights the fact that children of the perpetrators have their own peculiar Holocaust inheritance. The work of the Israeli psychologist Dan Bar-On in his book *The Legacy of Silence* is especially pertinent in this area.[44]

Goodstein also derives a particularist lesson from her journey. Although the Holocaust remains an unmasterable trauma, her trip to Poland does result in a feeling that she has more understanding of events. In her own words, "I don't have to live in an imaginary attic. I have been in the real one and left it." This observation emphasizes both the cathartic nature of Goodstein's experience and the difference between survivors and the second generation. Elsewhere, Goodstein observes that "the crux of [her film is] that the survivors never let themselves mourn." Consequently, the burden of guilt and grief got passed on to the next generation."[45] Concerning the third generation, the filmmaker expresses her wish to tell the family story to any children she might have. Her hope is that the third generation will not feel the survivors' tragedy, but instead be "inspired by their strength and courage."

## CONCLUSION

Second-generation witness tributes to the righteous engage the dialectic between a *tikkun olam* and a *tikkun atzmi*. These films underscore the notion of a personal mending in several ways. First, the survivors, with the exception of the Sauvage family, who had abandoned Judaism prior to the war, raised their children Jewishly. Secondly, each of the righteous believed that Jews deserved respect. As Nazism singled out Jews for destruction, the rescuers were committed to saving Jews as Jews. This commitment stemmed from several sources, including religious concerns, political opposition to Nazism and all forms of fascism, ties of prewar friendship, morality, and Judeophilism. Meeting their parents' helpers, the second-generation witnesses have the opportunity to personally see those whose intervention during the *Shoah* made their own lives possible. More pieces of their own biography begin to come together.

The universalist dimension of these films is attested by the altruistic behavior of the rescuers. None of these people view their actions as heroic. Indeed, some wish to keep such activities secret even now. Several emphasize the continuity between Judaism and Christianity, stressing the Jewish origins of their faith. The acts of the righteous may yet prove exemplary both in redefining Christianity and in modeling exemplary conduct, thereby demonstrating that such behavior is both possible and salvific. Many rescuers attest that if it were not the Jews, it would have been others that they would have helped. In short, what makes people help those in distress? Despite their differing interpretations of altruism, Abramowicz, Sauvage, Rubinek, and Goodstein agree that the prosocial actions of the few stand as witness to the best in humanity and indictment of the worst.

The commitment of the second-generation witnesses to commemorate the acts of the rescuers insures that these acts become part of the Jewish story of the Holocaust. Important lessons are learned. For example, each of the films stresses the vital role played by women in rescuing Jews.[46] Further, the second-generation witnesses come to know the offspring of the helpers. The postwar fate of the helpers, while not discussed in the films, is itself a fact with which the second-generation becomes familiar. That so many of these people were reviled by their own countrymen and found themselves in extreme economic distress prompted Eva Fogelman to become the founder of the Jewish Foundation for Christian Rescuers.[47] The example of the few who helped stands as an indictment of the many who failed. By making the stories of the rescuers public, the second generation undertakes a pedagogical effort whose scope is universal. Implicit in all the films about the rescuers is the assumption that goodness can be taught and that the memory of the righteous will be for a blessing.

We now turn to the book's conclusion, asking what we have learned about the contribution of the contemporary children of Job towards helping shape Holocaust memory. Further, the last chapter inquires what these "Riders towards the Dawn" might possibly contribute to the emergence of a new form of Jewish expression in America.

# CHAPTER 7

# *Whither the Future?*

> Those many survivors who had lost their faith in the war did not
> know what to pass on to their children. The Holocaust had become
> the touchstone of their identities as Jews and it became a touch-
> stone for their children as well. The trouble was that while it con-
> ferred an identity, it provided no structure, no clue to a way of life.
> —Helen Epstein[1]

An Australian friend, himself the son of Holocaust survivors, writes of
accompanying his parents to a *Yom HaShoah* service held at the Martyrs'
Monument at Melbourne's Carlton Cemetery. The service, which
occurred when he was a youngster, took place on a dark and overcast
day. A driving rain began falling during the ceremony, thereby heightening the ensuing drama. In a haunting tone, the rabbi, head of Melbourne's
*Beth Din* (Rabbinical Council), began retelling the tale of Moses leading
the Israelites from Egyptian bondage. The speaker emphasized the fact
that Moses himself carried the bones of Joseph and his brothers on his
shoulders during the generation of Jewish endurance in the desert. The
presence of these bones enabled Moses to persevere, build an army, and
prepare the people to enter the Promised Land. The rabbi then exclaimed
that the bones on his back prompted Moses to cry, "*Kadimah*! Forward!
Only Forward!" for behind him, if ever they were to turn back, were the
bones of the dead. Making a midrash, the rabbi draws a lesson for post-
Auschwitz generations. While the Jewish community must go forward, he
observes, it must simultaneously carry the bones of those who perished in
the Holocaust.[2]

Although this means that the dead may never rest in peace, the
rabbi reminds his audience of a twofold particularist truth: memory
links the generations and, unless the Jewish people themselves bear witness, the world will soon forget the *Shoah*.[3] My friend, the young writer-
to-be, learned an important lesson about inheriting the legacy of the
Holocaust and the role played by the *Shoah* as a source for contemporary Jewish identity. Fifty years after the event, second-generation witnesses, many of whom are parents, are attempting to move
forward Jewishly while symbolically carrying the "memory bones" of
the victims.

## WORKING THROUGH THE HOLOCAUST

This memory, as we have seen in the preceding chapters, assumes the form of the *presence of an absence*, over which the second generation keeps guard. Further, this memory expresses itself behaviorally in both a particularist and universalist manner, seeking to achieve a *tikkun* of the self and a mending of the world. Like their counterparts in France and Israel about whom Hartman observes, "This generation creates its own, often exotic world coiled round that absence, and offers the glimpse of a transformative art,"[4] the American second-generation witnesses seek to confront the *Shoah*, in the process shaping its memory in ways that continue to underscore their own relationship to Jewish history. The contemporary children of Job, by focusing on the "sequelae of a catastrophic memory," remind us of a twofold truth; the Holocaust continues to wound, and the *Shoah* forms the identity of children of survivors in a profoundly important manner.

Contemporary children of Job "work through" the Holocaust in a variety of ways, although certain common themes emerge among both particularist and universalist authors. For example, the second generation is especially sensitive to the continuing impact of the Holocaust on Jewish identity and world history. Consequently, their creative works are marked by a personal encounter with the issue of theodicy in the form of an accidental or untimely death (Finkelstein's *Summer Long-a-Coming*, Salamon's *White Lies*, Rosenbaum's "Lost, in a Sense" in *Elijah Visible*), disappearance (Friedmann's *Damaged Goods*), or suicide (Spiegelman's *Maus*). This loss of innocence connects the second-generation witnesses and their parents to the issue of Jewish fate. Further, the works of this generation stress the fact that after Auschwitz only an applied theology that strives to enhance human dignity and to uphold justice in an unjust world is worthy of the name theology. Implicitly, all share Wiesel's belief that God must not be justified at the expense of humanity. Moreover, these works each attest to the fact that listening to and sharing tales of the Holocaust themselves constitute secular liturgical acts much in the manner suggested by Greenberg.

Second-generation witnesses have a complex relationship to their Holocaust legacy. Hartman articulates this complexity in terms of trauma and memory. He observes that the eyewitness generation expressed a return of memory despite trauma; this "second-generation expresses the trauma of memory turning in the void."[5] Further, this void or absence makes the second generation especially sensitive to trivialization or distortion of the *Shoah*. This phenomenon is especially clear in the works of Spiegelman, Salamon, and Steinfeld. Spiegelman is besieged by those wishing to commercialize the Holocaust, while Salamon's heroine is angered by offspring of nonwitnessing Jews who either do not know or do not care about the destruction of European Jewry. Steinfeld, for his part, portrays indifference to the *Shoah* among both psychiatrists and the non-Jewish Canadian community. Further the theme of second-generation guilt and mourning is found among the particularist and universalist works in both novels/short stories and films.

Many second-generation witnesses conduct their own *din Torah*, in which the deity is indicted for the sin of indifference, if not commission, concerning Auschwitz. Among the examples that come to mind here are Barbara Finkelstein, Lev Raphael, and Art Spiegelman. Covenantal Judaism is, however, far from over. Rather, its scope and shape have become transformed. Contemporary children of Job elect to live as Jews, if not by observing traditional rituals, then by means of behavior and self-identification, thus modeling Greenberg's understanding of voluntary covenant. Further, the notion of an additional covenant that arises from the works of Wiesel permits these witnesses to attest their post-Holocaust Jewish identity in spite of a hermeneutics of suspicion concerning the biblical covenant. Additionally, their attempts to achieve a *tikkun* of the self and the world reflect Fackenheim's understanding of both the possibility and necessity of this repair after Auschwitz, even though it be fragmentary.

Collectively, the creative works of second-generation witnesses model an understanding of the post-Holocaust covenant that insists that the burden of maintaining the covenant now stands on the shoulders of humanity. Albert Friedlander notes this shift in his poetic retelling of an Elijah parable for an age that has witnessed Auschwitz. "For the Messiah's pathway," he writes,

> once seen by the patriarch Jacob as a golden ladder—was seared and torn by the passing of the chariots [was there one chariot, or were there six million that the disciple Elisha saw?]. Once the ladder was built from heaven to earth; now it must reach from earth to heaven, and must be constructed by man.[6]

Second-generation witnesses, in all their diversity, are among the primary architects of this post-Auschwitz covenant that acknowledges both the fact of divine absence and the need for Jewish identity.

On the psychosocial level, the works of the second-generation witnesses announce an important perceptual shift. From being viewed collectively, in the decade of the seventies, as psychologically damaged people, the contemporary children of Job have, in the decade of the eighties, been perceived—certainly by themselves—as guardians of their parents' Holocaust legacy. Common themes in second-generation texts include a focus on images of survivors and the flawed dynamics of intergenerational communication among numb or victim families. Survivor parents in these families are seen both as heroic and as insensitive or intrusive. For example, lack of parental boundaries is an almost uniformly reported perception in the second-generation texts with which this book deals. The other side of this psychosocial coin is the apparent indifference of survivor parents as seen in Salamon's *White Lies* and Mrs. Gelfman in Danny Fisher's film *A Generation Apart*.

An intense emotional life is a further shared second-generation phenomenon. This intensity eventuates in the knowledge that the *Shoah* continues to shape the identity of the second generation. Further, members of the second-generation frequently report hiding from the *Shoah* as children, and feeling that their Holocaust legacy was comprised of terrible secrets that threatened to overwhelm them. Thus, witnesses who seem at first to have little in common, such as Fogelman, Goodstein, Spiegelman, Fischer, Bukiet, Steinfeld, and Rosenbaum, are united by their identity as contemporary children of Job. Moreover, they discover that this identity is marked both by the *Shoah* and distinctive traits of North American culture, such as comic books and Vietnam War protests; homosexuality and racism; antisemitism and indifference. As the "first and the last," this generation is in effect a bridge between a world that was exterminated and one that seeks a way of shaping its own response to the Holocaust.

The contemporary children of Job work through the Holocaust in a manner that empowers them to interpret the meaning of their parents' experience. Second-generation working-through involves finding their own voice and developing their own rituals of Holocaust memory. The films of Fogelman, Fischer, and Brand, and the Australian film *Angst*, reveal that this encounter only occurs as the offspring become young adults, a time when they themselves begin to develop an appreciation of parenting and can speak to their own parents more directly about the Holocaust, and when the parents themselves may be ready to speak about the *Shoah* in a more systematic way.

Further, offspring of survivors frequently "parent" their parents. This "parenting" occurs, at least in "survivor" or "numb" families, on the levels of culture and language. On the level of language, because English is their native tongue, American children of Job are able to make themselves understood in a way unavailable to most of their parents. This means that the second generation feels that it has a mission to bear witness for its parents. Yet the relationship between culture and identity for contemporary children of Job is complex. In one sense, the second generation is at home in the American cultural ethos, sharing its quest for ethnic identity and a search for meaning in existence. In another sense, however, children of survivors are apart from American culture in their having been raised in homes where the presence of the Holocaust cast an indelible shadow over their lives.

## RIDERS TOWARDS THE DAWN

In the first chapter I referred to Friedlander's study of "those who come out of the darkness and have not forgotten it, but who also know that dawn lies ahead, and that they must journey towards it."[7] Friedlander focuses on the generation contemporaneous with the *Shoah*, Jewish and Christian thinkers and writers in various countries, and reports their responses to the multifaceted crises engendered by the murder of the Jewish people. Although beginning in the past and not abandoning it, Friedlander notes that they "have moved forward into new life."[8] While restricting himself to the witnessing generation, Friedlander's designation sheds light on much of the second-generation witness work.

As "riders towards the dawn," the contemporary children of Job are determined to embrace their Holocaust legacy and to transmit it to their own children and to the world at large. In order to accomplish this task, as adults they have consciously sought to open lines of communication with their parents, no matter how difficult their earlier relations. This metamorphosis is seen clearly in Wiesel's *The Forgotten* when the adolescent Malkiel exclaims to his father: "You have no right! You have no right to saddle me with a burden like that! Let me live my adolescent life. Don't force me to grow up so fast" (103). Yet, as an adult, Malkiel tells Elhanan that the survivor is at the center of his existence. Survivors and their offspring have begun speaking to each other about the *Shoah*. Learning more, by what Fogelman terms "breaking the silence," children of Job begin their task of more fully understanding themselves and their own relationship to their parents, to the Holocaust, and to Jewish history. Additionally, as the second generation creates written and visual texts, these documents themselves become ways of commemorating and shaping Holocaust memory. Furthermore, this process has served to help members of the second generation more fully embrace their Holocaust inheritance.

## CHILDREN OF JOB AND COVENANTAL JUDAISM

Writing in *The Jewish Bible after the Holocaust: A Re-reading*, Fackenheim places Judaism's covenantal response to catastrophe in historical perspective. He argues that the nature of such responses cannot be known in advance and that one must be attentive to various clues, some of which may at present not even be apparent. I cite his comment in full:

> That Judaism could survive the destruction of the Second Temple, a catastrophe culminating in the loss of the Bar Kochba war—that it could survive in an exile with no end in sight—was not known until a response

was found, in what might be called exile-Judaism. Whether Judaism can survive the vastly greater catastrophe of the Holocaust, too, cannot be known prior to a post-Holocaust Judaism that will have to pass tests, some of which we have as yet no inkling of.[9]

As noted in chapter 1, Fackenheim argues that all post-Auschwitz generations are Job's children, that is, the second set of daughters and sons. The first set are the *k'doshim* (holy ones) who perished in the *Shoah*. Consequently, the second children of the Job of the gas chambers can no longer read the *TaNaK* (Hebrew Bible) or any part of Jewish history as if Auschwitz never happened. At least one dimension of this rereading in light of the Holocaust is the embrace—even if un-self-consciously—of post-Auschwitz covenantal modes that permit expression of Jewish commitment on both the particular and universal planes, albeit in distinctively post-Enlightenment ways.

This study has suggested that creative responses by second-generation witnesses comprise a link in the chain of post-Auschwitz Jewish identity that is currently being forged. For instance, responding to Martin Buber's questions concerning the possibility of Jewish life after Auschwitz, Fackenheim writes: "there must be a possibility, for there is a reality."[10] The living children can, observes Fackenheim, never replace those who were murdered, yet they have "written a new page in Jewish history" by founding a new Jewish state.[11] The creative works of second-generation witnesses mark a transitional stage in memorialization of the *Shoah*.[12] Consequently, memory is being preserved by those who were not there for those who come after. Furthermore, the rituals of second-generation witnesses help define both the shape of Holocaust memory and the nature of Judaism for those living in the aftermath. The protagonists in the novels and films reject nihilism and seek instead a *tikkun*. Furthermore, each of the novels embraces the Wieselian belief that post-Auschwitz literature must play a moral role: it seeks enlightenment rather than entertainment. Further, literature can change lives. Hence, the attempt to achieve this *tikkun* has implications on both the personal and transpersonal level.

A sharper cleavage distinguishes the particularist and universalist films. For example, particularist films focus on the results of difficult intergenerational communication, distrust of the social world, which for understandable reasons is viewed as anomic and highly dangerous, and dislike of Christianity both for its historical role in sowing the seedbed for the Holocaust and for the murderous acts of individual Christians during the *Shoah*. *Angst*, for its part, focuses a new look at the relationship between humor and horror in speaking about how certain second-generation members confront their Holocaust inheritance. These films seek a *tikkun* of the self and of family relations. In so doing, they also address the issue of parent-child relations both within and outside the Jewish world. *A Generation Apart* emphasizes this dimension of the film when Danny Fischer notes, "Everyone has parents, and everyone has problems with them."

The universalist films, for their part, highlight the moral example of non-Jewish rescuers and helpers who during the time of severe testing revealed the *tikkun* of ordinary decency. Varied in their motivation, the rescuers are united in their twofold belief that what they did was not heroic and, given the choice between saving lives and acquiescing to death, they chose life. Further, the universalist films pay homage to the fact that humans are capable of acting courageously in the face of terrible evil. Bearing witness to acts of goodness (*Hakarat HaTov*), the second-generation witnesses who made these films are aware of the fact that they would not have been born if the helpers had not saved their parents' lives. Consequently, these films are both highly personal yet have universal implications in terms of raising fundamental moral and ethical issues by inviting viewers to respond to the implicit question, "How would I behave in those circumstances?" Acts of goodness were exceptionally rare during the *Shoah*. Yet, the acts of the "moral minority" comprise a vital chapter in the study of the Holocaust.[13] Moreover, the universalist films underscore the crucial role played by women in rescuing Jews and invite their viewers to ask, as does Pierre Sauvage, whether this role has until recently not been appreciated owing to the norms of a patriarchal culture. Further, the special circumstances of child survivors, portrayed with intensity and compassion in *As If It Were Yesterday*, focus attention on a hitherto neglected group of Holocaust victims.

Their differences notwithstanding, these films do share some important similarities as well. First and foremost, they raise theological issues. Why did the Jewish people suffer during the Holocaust? Where was God? Why did the "moral minority" help? Why were the majority of European Christians either murderers or bystanders? In addition, the particularist and universalist films—like their literary counterparts—highlight the rituals that have emerged with special force after the *Shoah* (e.g., lighting yarhrzeit candles), the *tikkun* of family, and the voluntary nature of the post-Auschwitz covenant. Further, both particularist and universalist second-generation filmmakers acknowledge the impossibility of complete reenacting of *Shoah* rituals as well as the fragmentary nature of the tales that they themselves tell.

In covenantal terms, these novels and films embody Greenberg's voluntary covenant, with its stress on a twofold insight: the increasing hiddeness of the divine in history, and the corresponding necessity of viewing apparently secular acts as masking holiness. In this view, the writing of second-generation novels and the making of films dealing with the maturation of the second generation constitute "secular liturgical acts," which comprise part of the ritual of post-Auschwitz Jewish life. Further, the contemporary children of Job adhere to Wiesel's additional covenant as an anchor for their Jewish affirmation, one that enables them to bear witness even if they no longer feel that the biblical covenant makes any coercive claim on them.

Theologically, the creative works of the second-generation witnesses shift the focus from an interventionist deity to an emphasis on the role played by the human covenantal partner in maintaining Jewish identity. While some of these witnesses feel that the Sinaitic covenant makes no credible post-Auschwitz claim, and others are either ambivalent about, or view with suspicion, the biblical warrant for Jewish identity after Auschwitz, all are committed to this identity. Collectively, the contemporary children of Job are demonstrating through various means their attempt to construct a post-Auschwitz covenant that impels them to learn more about Jewish history and themselves. This covenant reconstruction reminds one of the truth of Greenberg's observation about the "low priority" of theology among Jewish people.

Nevertheless, the creative works of the daughters and sons of Job attest to the distinctive nature of the second-generation witness in America. On the one hand, these witnesses are an integral part of American culture in terms of aesthetics, multiculturalism, ethnic identity, language, and dress. On the other hand, by virtue of inheriting the Holocaust, the second-generation witnesses remain apart from American culture in several crucial ways—for example, their determination to achieve a *tikkun* of bearing witness to an event that, for most Americans, ended in the dim past fifty years ago. Further, while fully participating in the postmodern ethos that celebrates the autonomy of the self and the irrelevance of traditional forms of Jewish identity, these witnesses voluntarily seek to express their own sense of covenant and Jewish commitment. Their post-*Shoah* midrash on Jewish identity continues to shape both contemporary memory of the Holocaust and late-twentieth-century Jewish ritual. Finally, the contemporary children of Job are preparing their own testament as a legacy for the third, and subsequent, generation(s). This legacy will, in turn, become part of the chain of tradition that helps shape future memory of the *Shoah*.

# NOTES

## CHAPTER 1. INTRODUCTION

1. Wiesel is cited in Hillel Goldberg, "Holocaust Theology: The Survivor's Statement," *Tradition* 20.2 (1982), 150.

2. Elie Wiesel, *The Forgotten*, trans. Stephen Becker (New York: Summit Books, 1992), 196.

3. Figure cited by Lucy Steinitz and David Szony, eds., *Living After the Holocaust: Reflections by Children of Survivors Living in America* (New York: Bloch, 1979), vi.

4. Geoffrey H. Hartman, "Introduction: Darkness Visible," in G. H. Hartman, ed., *Holocaust Remembrance: The Shapes of Memory* (Cambridge: Blackwell, 1994), 7. Hereafter, this text will be cited as "Introduction."

5. Hartman, "Introduction," 7.

6. Cheryl Pearl Sucher, "History Is the Province of Memory," *Midstream* 35.3 (1989), 56.

7. Hartman, "Introduction," 7.

8. Ellen Fine, "The Absent Memory: The Act of Writing in Post-Holocaust French Literature," in *Writing and the Holocaust*, ed. Berel Lang (New York: Holmes and Meier, 1988), 41.

9. Nadine Fresco, "Remembering the Unknown," *International Review of Psycho-Analysis* 11.4 (1984), 419.

10. Alain Finkielkraut, *The Imaginary Jew*, trans. Kevin O'Neill and David Suchoff (Lincoln: University of Nebraska Press, 1994), 113.

11. In addition to the work of Finkielkraut, see also the novels of Henri Raczymow, which evoke what Fine terms the "*absence* of memory" (see above, note 8). Further, Juliette Dickstein has intelligently analyzed this phenomenon in the works of still a third French second-generation witness writer; see her "Inventing French-Jewish Memory: The Legacy of the Occupation in the Works of Patrick Modiano 1968–1988," Paper presented at the Association for Jewish Studies Annual Meeting, December 1994.

12. Robert J. Lifton, "Witnessing Survival," in *Genocide and Human Rights: A Global Anthology*, ed. Jack Nusan Porter (Lanham, MD: University Press of America, 1982), 264.

13. Dina Wardi, *Memorial Candles: Children of the Holocaust*, trans. Naomi Goldblum (London: Tavistock/Routledge, 1992). Wardi explains the burden of being designated a memorial candle. She writes:

> in most of the survivors' families one of the children is designated as a "memorial candle" for all of the relatives who perished in the Holo-

caust, and he is given the burden of participating in his parents' emotional world to a much greater extent than any of his brothers or sisters. He is also given the special mission of serving as the link which on the one hand preserves the past and on the other hand joins it to the present and the future. (6)

14. Robert M. Prince, "Knowing the Holocaust," *Psychoanalytic Inquiry* 5.1 (1985), 51.

15. Robert M. Prince, "Second-Generation Effects of Historical Trauma," *Psychoanalytic Review* 72.1 (1985), 23.

16. For a significant collection of essays dealing with the impact of the Holocaust on second-generation witnesses, see Efraim Sicher, ed., *Breaking Crystal: Writing and Memory after Auschwitz: Essays on the Post-Holocaust Generation* (Urbana: The University of Illinois Press, 1997).

17. Aaron Hass, *In the Shadow of the Holocaust: The Second Generation* (Ithaca: Cornell University Press, 1990), 48.

18. This dialectical tension is also seen in approaches to the Holocaust itself where the debate concerns the relationship between Jewish and non-Jewish victims of Nazism. Perhaps the two best-known survivors who have joined the issue are Elie Wiesel, for whom the *Shoah*'s universal implications derive from its Jewish specificity, and Simon Wiesenthal's universalist view.

19. Elie Wiesel, *Survivors' Children Relive the Holocaust, New York Times,* 16 November 1975.

20. This view is especially prominent in the writings of Elie Wiesel, Irving Greenberg, and Shlomo Riskin. Wiesel observes that "for a survivor to get married in 1945 and have children is a covenant equal to that between Abraham and God" (*Against Silence: The Voice and Vision of Elie Wiesel,* ed. Irving Abrahamson [New York: Holocaust Library, 1985]. Greenberg, for his part, observes that "the perspective of Auschwitz sheds new light on the nature of childrearing and faith. It takes enormous faith in ultimate redemption and meaningfulness to choose to create or even enhance life again. In fact, faith is revealed by this not to be a belief or even an emotion, but an ontological life-force that reaffirms creation and life in the teeth of overwhelming death. One must silently assume redemption in order to have the child—and having the child makes the statement of redemption" ("Cloud of Smoke, Pillar of Fire: Judaism, Christianity, and Modernity after the Holocaust," in *Auschwitz: Beginning of a New Era?: Reflections on the Holocaust,* ed. Eva Fleischner [New York: KTAV, Cathedral Church of St. John the Divine, Anti-Defamation League of B'nai B'rith, 1977], 42). Rabbi Riskin contends that "what makes Jews remarkable is not that they believe in God after Auschwitz, but that they have children after Auschwitz. That they affirm life and the future" (cited by William B. Helmreich, *Against All Odds: Holocaust Survivors and the Successful Lives They Made in America* [New York: Simon and Schuster, 1992], 120).

21. Wiesel, "Some Words for Children of Survivors: A Message to the Second Generation," in *The Holocaust: Forty Years After,* ed. Marcia Sachs Littell, Richard Libowitz, and Evelyn Bodek Rosen (Lewiston: Edwin Mellen Press, 1989), 7.

22. *The Testament of Job*, ed. Robert A. Kraft (Missoula: Society of Biblical Literature and Scholars' Press, 1974).

23. William Helmreich writes of a "curtain of silence" that descended on survivors discussing the Holocaust with their offspring. This "curtain" dropped in the mid-1950s (Helmreich, *Against All Odds*, 133).

24. On this matter see Metzudat David and Metzudat Zion in *Mikra'ot Gedalot* on Job 42:14 (New York: Abraham Friedham, n.d.), 53b. I am grateful to Rabbi Neal G. Turk who brought these sources to my attention.

25. Eliezer Berkovits, *Faith After the Holocaust* (New York: KTAV, 1973), 5.

26. Deborah E. Lipstadt, "We Are Not Job's Children," *Shoah* 1.4 (1979), 16.

27. Emil Fackenheim, *The Jewish Bible after the Holocaust: A Re-reading* (Bloomington: Indiana University Press, 1990), 26.

28. Fackenheim, *Jewish Bible*, 26.

29. Terrence Des Pres, "The Dreaming Back," *Centerpoint* 4.13 (1980), 14.

30. Eliezer Ben Yehuda, *Dictionary and Thesaurus of the Hebrew Language* (New York: Thomas Yoseloff, 1959), 7870.

31. Menachem Z. Rosensaft, cited in Judith Miller, *One by One, by One: Facing the Holocaust* (New York: Simon and Schuster, 1990), 226.

32. Deborah E. Lipstadt, "Children of Jewish Survivors of the Holocaust: The Evolution of a New-Found Consciousness," in *Encyclopaedia Judaica Year Book 1988/89* (Jerusalem: Keter, 1989), 148.

33. Eva Fogelman, "Intergenerational Group Therapy: Child Survivors of the Holocaust and Offspring of Survivors," *Psychoanalytic Review* 75.4 (1988), 619.

34. For an interesting second-generation suggestion about what constitutes a usable theological past after Auschwitz, see Stephen L. Jacobs, *Rethinking Jewish Faith: The Child of a Survivor Responds* (Albany: SUNY Press, 1994).

35. Eugene Borowitz, *Renewing the Covenant: A Theology for the Postmodern Jew* (Philadelphia: Jewish Publication Society, 1992).

36. Elie Wiesel, *A Jew Today*, trans. Marion Wiesel (New York: Vintage Books, 1979), 241–42.

37. Helmreich, *Against All Odds*, 139.

38. Elie Wiesel, *The Oath* (New York: Avon Books, 1974), 67.

39. Hass, *In the Shadow of the Holocaust*, 69.

40. Albert Friedlander, *Riders Toward the Dawn: From Ultimate Despair to Temperate Hope* (London: Constable, 1992).

## CHAPTER 2. FROM PATHOLOGY TO THEOLOGY: THE EMERGENCE OF THE SECOND-GENERATION WITNESS

1. Rosensaft is cited in Judith Miller, *One by One, by One: Facing the Holocaust* (New York: Simon and Schuster, 1990), 225.

2. Much has been written on this point. Helpful studies include Helen Epstein, *Children of the Holocaust: Conversations with Sons and Daughters of*

*Survivors* (New York: G. P. Putnam Sons, 1979), especially chapter 12 (hereafter, this work will be cited as *Conversations*); Deborah E. Lipstadt, "Children of Jewish Survivors of the Holocaust: The Evolution of a New-Found Consciousness," in *Encyclopaedia Judaica Year Book 1988/89* (Jerusalem: Keter, 1988/89), subsequently cited as "New-Found Consciousness"; Aaron Hass, *In the Shadow of the Holocaust: The Second Generation* (Ithaca: Cornell University Press, 1990), especially the introduction and chapter 2; Hass, *The Aftermath: Living with the Holocaust* (Cambridge: Cambridge University Press, 1995), chapter 8; and William B. Helmreich, *Against All Odds: Holocaust Survivors and the Successful Lives They Made in America* (New York: Simon and Schuster, 1992), particularly chapter 4.

3. Epstein, *Conversations*, 98.

4. Yael Danieli, "Differing Adaptational Styles in Families of Survivors of the Nazi Holocaust," in *Children Today*, September–October 1981, 7.

5. Danieli, 34.

6. Danieli, 35.

7. Danieli, 10.

8. Helmreich, *Against All Odds*, 144.

9. Lipstadt, "New-Found Consciousness," 147.

10. Lipstadt, "New-Found Consciousness," 148.

11. Hass, *In the Shadow of the Holocaust*, 89.

12. Hass, 89.

13. Hass, 89.

14. Jack Nusan Porter, "Is There a Survivor's Syndrome? Psychological and Socio-Political Implications," in Jack Nusan Porter, ed., *Confronting History and Holocaust: Collected Essays* (Lanham, MD: University Press of America, 1983), 100.

15. Lipstadt, "New-Found Consciousness," 148.

16. Bela Savran and Eva Fogelman, "Psychological Issues in the Lives of Children of Holocaust Survivors: The Children as Adults," in Lucy Y. Steinitz and David M. Szony, eds., *Living after the Holocaust: Reflections by Children of Survivors in America* (New York: Bloch Publishing Company, 1979), 152. Hereafter, this will be cited as *Living after the Holocaust*.

17. See note 16, above.

18. See note 2, above.

19. Steinitz, *Living after the Holocaust*, iii.

20. Steinitz, *Living after the Holocaust*, iii.

21. Steinitz, *Living after the Holocaust*, v.

22. Epstein, *Conversations*, 338.

23. Lipstadt, "New-Found Consciousness," 141.

24. Epstein, *Conversations*, 13.

25. Epstein, *Conversations*, 11.

26. Epstein, *Conversations*, 10.

27. Epstein, *Conversations*, 9.

28. Irving Abrahamson, ed., *Against Silence: The Voice and Vision of Elie Wiesel* (New York: Holocaust Library, 1985), 3:321.

29. Abrahamson, 3:320.

30. Abrahamson, 3:320.

31. Abrahamson, 3:323.

32. Wiesel, *The Forgotten*, trans. Stephen Becker (New York: Summit, 1992), 147.

33. Alvin H. Rosenfeld, *A Double Dying: Reflections on Holocaust Literature* (Bloomington: Indiana University Press, 1980), 19.

34. Ted Solotaroff and Nessa Rapoport, eds., *Writing Our Way Home: Contemporary Stories By American Jewish Authors* (New York: Schocken Books, 1992), xxiii. In addition to the novels and films discussed in this study, there exist second-generation poetry and art. For the former see Stewart J. Florsheim, ed., *Ghosts of the Holocaust: An Anthology of Poetry by the Second Generation* (Detroit: Wayne State University Press, 1989), and Charles Fishman, ed., *Blood To Remember: American Poets on the Holocaust* (Lubbock: Texas Tech University Press, 1991). Important studies of second-generation art include the following works by Stephen C. Feinstein: Feinstein, ed., *Witness and Legacy: Contemporary Art about the Holocaust* (Minneapolis: Lerner Publications Company, 1995), catalogue of the Witness and Legacy exhibition held by the Minnesota Museum of American Art, St. Paul, Minnesota, 29 January–14 May 1995; and "Mediums of Memory: Artistic Responses of the Second Generation," in Efraim Sicher, ed., *Breaking Crystal: Writing and Memory after Auschwitz: Essays on the Post-Holocaust Generation* (Urbana: University of Illinois Press, 1997). See also Vivian Alpert Thompson, ed., *A Mission in Art: Recent Holocaust Work in America* (Macon, GA: Mercer University Press, 1988). An intriguing second-generation portrait is drawn by Pat Conroy in his *Beach Music* (New York: Doubleday, 1996). Conroy's work reveals the penetration of second-generation awareness in the writings of non-Jewish professional novelists. Shyla Fox, a daughter of Job, is overwhelmed by her legacy—her father was forced to be a member of the Judenrat [Nazi-appointed Jewish Council]—and commits suicide. Her very name, which can be translated as "question" [She'alah], is emblematic of the popular perception that these second-generation witnesses are damaged. Conroy's otherwise insightful novel is flawed in that it relegates the second-generation to the category of pathology.

35. Eva Fogelman, "Mourning Without Graves," unpublished paper. Cited in Lipstadt, "New-Found Consciousness," 148.

36. Lawrence L. Langer, *Holocaust Testimonies: The Ruins of Memory* (New Haven: Yale University Press, 1991), 39.

37. Langer, 39.

38. Geoffrey H. Hartman, ed., *Holocaust Remembrance: The Shape of Memory* (Cambridge: Basil Blackwell, 1994), 6.

39. Hass, *In the Shadow of the Holocaust*, 150.

40. Epstein, *Conversations*, 23.

41. Harry James Cargas, ed., *Harry James Cargas: Conversations with Elie Wiesel* (South Bend: Justice Books, 1992), 56–57.

42. Cargas, 57.

43. Alan L. Berger, "Elie Wiesel's Second-Generation Witness: Passing the Torch of Remembrance," in Harry James Cargas, ed., *Telling the Tale: A Tribute to Elie Wiesel on the Occasion of His 65th Birthday: Essays, Reflections, and Poems* (St. Louis: Time Being Books, 1993), 119–36.

44. Michael Berenbaum, *Elie Wiesel: God, the Holocaust, and the Children of Israel* (New York: Behrman House, 1994), 127. This work will subsequently be cited as *Elie Wiesel*.

45. Berenbaum, *Elie Wiesel*, 127.

46. Berenbaum, *Elie Wiesel*, 127.

47. Berenbaum, *Elie Wiesel*, 140–41.

48. Berenbaum, *Elie Wiesel*, 141.

49. Berenbaum, *Elie Wiesel*, 141.

50. Berenbaum, *Elie Wiesel*, 143.

51. Berenbaum, *Elie Wiesel*, 144.

52. For an important literary study of the Holocaust as a reversal of the Exodus in Wiesel's *Night*, see Lawrence S. Cunningham, "Elie Wiesel's Anti-Exodus," in Harry James Cargas, ed., *Responses to Elie Wiesel: Critical Essays by Major Jewish and Christian Scholars* (New York: Persea Books, 1978), 23–28. For comprehensive studies of this theme, in addition to Berenbaum, see Ellen S. Fine, *Legacy of Night: The Literary Universe of Elie Wiesel* (Albany: SUNY Press, 1982); Robert McAfee Brown, *Elie Wiesel: Messenger To All Humanity*, rev. ed. (Notre Dame: University of Notre Dame Press, 1989); and Colin Davis, *Elie Wiesel's Secretive Texts* (Gainesville: University Press of Florida, 1994).

53. Berenbaum, *Elie Wiesel*, 146.

54. Berenbaum, *Elie Wiesel*, 146.

55. Berenbaum, *Elie Wiesel*, 128.

56. Berenbaum, *Elie Wiesel*, 128.

57. On this point see Alan L. Berger, "The Holocaust, Second-Generation Witness, and the Voluntary Covenant in American Judaism," *Religion and American Culture* 5.1 (1995), 23–47.

58. Irving Greenberg, *The Jewish Way: Living the Holidays* (New York: Summit Books, 1988), 325. Hereafter, this book will be cited as *The Jewish Way*.

59. Greenberg, *The Jewish Way*, 325.

60. Greenberg, *The Jewish Way*, 320.

61. Greenberg, *The Jewish Way*, 321.

62. Greenberg, *The Jewish Way*, 321.

63. Greenberg, *The Jewish Way*, 321.

64. Greenberg, *The Jewish Way*, 228.

65. Greenberg, *The Jewish Way*, 224.

66. Greenberg, "The Third Great Cycle of Jewish History," in Irving Greenberg, *Perspectives: A CLAL Thesis* (New York: The National Center for Learning and Leadership, no date), 12. Hereafter, this will be cited as *Perspectives*.

67. Greenberg, *The Jewish Way*, 320.

68. Greenberg, *The Jewish Way*, 320.

69. Greenberg, "Voluntary Covenant," in *Perspectives*, 34.

70. Greenberg, *The Jewish Way*, 321.

71. Greenberg, "Religious Values After the Holocaust: A Jewish View," in Abraham J. Peck, ed., *Jews and Christians after the Holocaust* (Philadelphia: Fortress Press, 1982), 84. Greenberg opines that "survivor accounts or ghetto diaries will likely be among the new Scriptures" (85).

72. Greenberg, "Religious Values," 84.

73. Greenberg, "Voluntary Covenant," 38.

74. Greenberg, "Voluntary Covenant," 36.

75. Emil Fackenheim, *God's Presence in History: Jewish Affirmations and Philosophical Reflections* (New York: New York University Press, 1970), 84.

76. Bella Savran and Eva Fogelman, "Psychological Issues in the Lives of Children of Holocaust Survivors: The Children As Adults," in *Living after The Holocaust*, 154.

77. Savran and Fogelman, "Psychological Issues," 155.

78. Richard L. Rubenstein and John K. Roth, eds., *Approaches to Auschwitz: The Holocaust and Its Legacy* (Atlanta: John Knox Press, 1987), 319.

79. Rubenstein and Roth, 321.

80. Rubenstein and Roth, 321.

81. Emil L. Fackenheim, *To Mend the World: Foundations of Future Jewish Thought* (New York: Schocken Books, 1982), 256. This work will henceforth be cited as *To Mend*.

82. Fackenheim, *To Mend*, 256.

83. This is the subtitle of Fackenheim's book, and it has a direct bearing on the works of the second generation.

84. Fackenheim, *To Mend*, 262.

85. Fackenheim, *To Mend*, 262.

86. Fackenheim, *To Mend*, 262.

87. Fackenheim, *To Mend*, 254.

88. Fackenheim, *To Mend*, 218.

89. Fackenheim, *To Mend*, 222.

90. Fackenheim, *To Mend*, 217.

91. Fackenheim, *To Mend*, 276.

92. Fackenheim, *To Mend*, 268.

93. Fackenheim, *To Mend*, 292–93.

94. For an example of this post-Auschwitz *tikkun* in Australian second-generation literature, see Alan L. Berger, "From Theology to Morality: Post-Auschwitz *Tikkun Olam* in the Works of Serge Liberman," *Australian Journal of Jewish Studies*, 91–92 (1995), 104–23.

95. Richard L. Rubenstein, *Power Struggle: An Autobiographical Confession* (Lanham, MD: University Press of America, 1986), 14.

96. See Rubenstein's essay "The Unmastered Trauma: Interpreting the Holocaust," in his *After Auschwitz: History, Theology, and Contemporary Judaism*, Second Edition (Baltimore: Johns Hopkins University Press, 1992), 81–122.

97. Rubenstein, "Covenant and Holocaust," in *Remembering for the Future*, Papers presented at International Scholars' Conference (Oxford: Pergamon Press, 1988), Theme 1, 665.

98. Rubenstein, "God after the Death of God," in *After Auschwitz*, 296–306.

99. Rubenstein, "God after the Death of God," 301.

100. Rubenstein, "Covenant and Holocaust," 668.

101. Rubenstein, "Covenant and Holocaust," 668.

## CHAPTER 3. SECOND GENERATION
## NOVELS AND SHORT STORIES:
## JEWISH PARTICULARISM

1. Helen Epstein, "Guardians of the Legacy," *Jerusalem Post Supplement—Holocaust Survivors Gathering*, 14 June 1981, 7.

2. Eugene Borowitz, *Renewing the Covenant: A Theology for the Postmodern Jew* (Philadelphia: Jewish Publication Society, 1991), 5.

3. Thomas Friedmann, *Damaged Goods* (Sag Harbor, NY: Permanent Press, 1984). All citations are from this edition.

4. See, for example, Barbara Finkelstein's *Summer Long-a-Coming* (discussed in this chapter) and Julie Salamon, *White Lies*, which is treated in chapter 4.

5. William Helmreich, "Entering and Leaving Judaism and the Problematics of Orthodox Judaism in Contemporary America: A Review Essay," *American Jewish History*, 79.3 (1990), 398–405.

6. Robert J. Lifton, "Witnessing Survival," in Jack Nusan Porter, ed., *Genocide and Human Rights: A Global Anthology* (Lanham, MD: University Press of America, 1982), 265.

7. Aaron Hass, *In the Shadow of the Holocaust* (Ithaca: Cornell University Press, 1990), 52–53. Lev Raphael specifically comments on this issue. See chapter 4.

8. Eva Fogelman, "Intergenerational Group Therapy: Child Survivors of the Holocaust and Offspring of Survivors," *Psychoanalytic Review* 75.4 (1988), 635.

9. Fogelman, "Intergenerational Group Therapy," 635.

10. Maurice Blanchot, *The Writing of the Disaster*, trans. Ann Smock (Lincoln: University of Nebraska Press, 1986), 1.

11. Friedmann, *Hero Azriel: A Collection of Tales* (Marblehead, MA: Micah Publications, 1979), 54. The title of Friedmann's book is a veiled reference to the *Shema* prayer, which begins, "Hear, O Israel . . ."

12. See Rabbi Joseph Soloveitchik, *Halakhic Man* (*Ish HaHalakha, galui venistar*), trans. Lawrence Kaplan (Philadelphia: Jewish Publication Society, 1983).

13. Irving Greenberg, *The Jewish Way: Living the Holidays* (New York: Summit, 1988), 336.

14. Greenberg, *The Jewish Way*, 343.

15. Greenberg, *The Jewish Way*, 343.

16. Greenberg, *The Jewish Way*, 341.

17. Barbara Finkelstein, Lecture at Syracuse University, October 5, 1987.

18. Finkelstein, Lecture.

19. Finkelstein interviewed by Douglas Collins, "Shadows Cast on the Wall of a Cave," *Syracuse Jewish Observer* 26 October 1987, 9.

20. Finkelstein interview, 13.

21. Finkelstein, Lecture.

22. Finkelstein, Lecture.

23. For an authoritative study of these testimonies see Lawrence L. Langer, *Holocaust Testimonies: The Ruins of Memory* (New Haven: Yale University Press, 1991). Hereafter, this text will be cited as *Holocaust Testimonies*.

24. Barbara Finkelstein, *Summer Long-a-Coming* (New York: Harper and Row, 1987). Page numbers are from this edition. The discussion of Barbara Finkel-

stein and Art Spiegelman in this chapter is an expanded version of what appears in Efraim Sicher's, ed. important collection of essays, *Breaking Crystal: Writing and Memory After Auschwitz: Essays on the Post-Holocaust Generation*, Urbana: The University of Illinois Press, 1997.

25. Greenberg, "Cloud of Smoke, Pillar of Fire: Judaism, Christianity, and Modernity after the Holocaust," in Eva Fleischner, ed., *Auschwitz: Beginning of a New Era? Reflections on the Holocaust* (New York: KTAV, Cathedral Church of St. John the Divine, Anti-Defamation League of B'nai B'rith, 1977), 54.

26. Isaac Bashevis Singer, *Enemies, A Love Story* (New York: Fawcett Crest Books, 1972), 33.

27. Finkelstein's novel is one of the few second-generation works that portrays a child of survivors who is apparently indifferent to the catastrophe. Steve excuses his reaction by comparing himself to German tourists sunbathing on the beach near his New Jersey shore home. The Germans were murderers, yet they are enjoying themselves. What happened to Perel, on the other hand, was an accident. Steve's denial of his Holocaust inheritance appears to conform more to that of adolescence rather than a mature assumption of identity. On this distinction see chapter 5.

28. On this theme see Anson Laytner, *Arguing With God: A Jewish Tradition* (Northvale, NJ: Jason Aronson, 1990).

29. Elie Wiesel, *A Jew Today*, trans. Marion Wiesel (New York: Vintage Books, 1979).

30. For an insightful and nuanced discussion of Berkovits's position see Steven T. Katz, "Eliezer Berkovits's Post-Holocaust Jewish Theodicy," in Steven T. Katz's *Post-Holocaust Dialogues: Critical Studies in Modern Jewish Thought* (New York: New York University Press, 1983). Michael Wyschogrod speaks pointedly of the "destructive potential" of the *Shoah* in his essay "Some Theological Reflection on the Holocaust," in Lucy Y. Steinitz and David Szony, eds., *Living after the Holocaust: Reflections by Children of Survivors in America*, 2nd rev. ed. (New York: Bloch, 1979), 65–68.

31. Frederick P. W. MacDowell, "Ellen Glasgow," *Dictionary of Literary Biography 9* (Detroit: Gale Research Co., 1981), 45–46.

32. This sense of mission is also forcefully articulated by Jamaica Just in Julie Salamon's *White Lies*; see chapter 4.

33. Art Spiegelman, *Maus I: A Survivor's Tale: My Father Bleeds History* (New York: Pantheon Books, 1986), and *Maus II: A Survivor's Tale: And Here My Troubles Began* (New York: Pantheon Books, 1991).

34. Spiegelman, *The Complete Maus* (New York: The Voyager Company, 1994). The CD-ROM contains sketches, family photographs, and two-and-one-half hours of audio.

35. Spiegelman interviewed by Aron Hirt-Manheimer, "The Art of Art Spiegelman," *Reform Judaism* (Spring, 1987), 23.

36. Spiegelman, Hirt-Manheimer interview, 23.

37. Spiegelman, Hirt-Manheimer interview, 32.

38. Spiegelman, Hirt-Manheimer interview, 32.

39. Spiegelman interviewed by Lawrence Wechsler, "Mighty Maus," *Rolling Stone* 20 November 1986, 148.

40. Langer, *Holocaust Testimonies*, 67.

41. Langer, *Holocaust Testimonies*, 67.

42. Spiegelman interviewed by Jonathan Rosen, "Spiegelman: The Man Behind *Maus*," *The Forward* 17 January, 1992, 1.

43. Hugh Nissenson, *My Own Ground* (New York: Farrar, Straus and Giroux, 1976).

44. Spiegelman interviewed by Ester B. Fein, "Holocaust As a Cartoonist's Way of Getting to Know His Father," *The New York Times* 10 December 1991, C1.

45. Richard D. Olson, "'Say! Dis Is Grate Stuff': The Yellow Kid and the Birth of the American Comics," *Library Associates Courier Syracuse University*, 28.1 (1993), 19 and 23.

46. Spiegelman, Hirt-Manheimer interview, 23.

47. Kominsky-Crumb, presently editor of *Weirdo* magazine, reflects the heightened feminist and Jewish concerns voiced during the late 1980s. For a helpful review on this issue see Roberta Smith, "The Unruly Parallel World of Women's Comics," *The New York Times* 20 November 1994.

48. Spiegelman, Hirt-Manheimer interview, 22.

49. Spiegelman, Rosen interview, 11.

50. Terrence Des Pres, "Holocaust Laughter," in Berel Lang, ed., *Writing and the Holocaust* (New York: Holmes and Meier, 1988), 231–32.

51. Des Pres, "Holocaust Laughter," 229.

52. Lawrence L. Langer, "A Fable of the Holocaust," *The New York Times Book Review* 3 November 1991, 1.

53. Langer, "Fable," 35.

54. Langer, "Fable," 36.

55. Geoffrey H. Hartman, "Introduction: Darkness Visible," in Geoffrey H. Hartman, Editor, *Holocaust Remembrance: The Shapes of Memory* (Cambridge: Blackwell, 1994), 21. Albert Friedlander goes further in attesting that Spiegelman's work "is something entirely different . . . and totally American."

> With all its harsh presentation of the victims and their imperfections, *Maus* is in the end a celebration of the human spirit, and does as much for the American Jewish scene as it achieves for the Holocaust. The public and personal response to the victims, the attempts of the next generation to come to terms with the *tremendum*, and the fundamental decency which exists between the generations are captured here; and the comic book has come into its own. (Albert H. Friedlander, *Riders towards the Dawn: From Holocaust to Hope* [New York: Continuum, 1994], 164).

56. Hillel Halkin, "Inhuman Comedy," rev. of *Maus II*, *Commentary* February 1992, 56.

57. Langer, *Holocaust Testimonies*, 6.

58. For a perceptive analysis of language in Spiegelman's work see Alan Rosen, "The Language of Survival: English as Metaphor in Spiegelman's *Maus*," *Prooftexts* 15:3 (1995), 249–62.

59. Ellen Fine, "The Absent Memory," in Berel Lang, ed., *Writing and the Holocaust* (New York: Holmes and Meier, 1988), 55.

60. Helen Epstein, *Children of the Holocaust: Conversations with Sons and Daughters of Survivors* (New York: G.P. Putnam's Sons, 1979), 231.

61. Spiegelman, Hirt-Manheimer interview, 23.

62. Primo Levi, *The Drowned and the Saved*, trans. Raymond Rosenthal (New York: Summit Books, 1986), 201.

63. Elie Wiesel, *One Generation After*, trans. Lily Edelman and Elie Wiesel (New York: Random House, 1970), 35.

64. Wiesel, *One Generation After*, 35.

65. Greenberg, *The Jewish Way*, 320.

66. Spiegelman, Rosen interview, 11.

67. Spiegelman, Rosen interview, 11.

68. Spiegelman, Rosen interview, 11.

69. Spiegelman, Rosen interview, 11.

70. Author's telephone discussion with Rosenbaum, 7 August, 1996. This reference will hereafter be cited as Rosenbaum discussion.

71. Alan L. Berger, rev. of *Stories of an Imaginary Childhood*, in *Shofar* 12.1 (1993), 114.

72. Melvin J. Bukiet, *Stories of an Imaginary Childhood* (Evanston: Northwestern University Press, 1992).

73. Bukiet, "Memory Macht Frei," unpublished essay.

74. Bukiet, "Memory Macht Frei."

75. Bukiet, *While the Messiah Tarries* (New York: Harcourt Brace, 1995). Bukiet's Holocaust novel *After* (New York: St. Martin's Press, 1996) appeared too late for inclusion in this study.

76. Bukiet, *While the Messiah Tarries*.

77. Bukiet's story is an implicit critique of the Fortunoff Video Archives for Holocaust Testimonies at Yale University. He raises important questions about the routinization of survivor testimony. The point of view contained in "The Library of Moloch" stands in sharp contrast to the near reverence accorded to the oral historian at Yad VaShem who interviews Rukhl and Yankl Szuster in Barbara Finkelstein's *Summer Long-a-Coming*. The name *Moloch* is itself significant. A semitic deity of great antiquity, *Moloch* was worshiped in ancient Israel by burning children as sacrificial offerings. Bukiet's tale suggests that survivors' testimony, like the burning children of old, is being offered as a sacrifice to the appetite of the "culture industry" in the guise of video archives.

78. Personal correspondence from Steinfeld to the author, 3 August 1994.

79. J. J. Steinfeld, *Dancing at the Club Holocaust: Stories New and Selected* (Charlottetown, P.E.I., Canada: Ragweed Press, 1993). Steinfeld's other collections include *Forms of Captivity and Escape* (Saskatoon: Thistledown Press, 1988); *Unmapped Dreams: The Charlottetown Stories* (Montague, P.E.I., Canada: Crossed Keys, 1989); and *The Miraculous Hand and Other Stories* (Charlottetown, P.E.I., Canada: Ragweed Press, 1991).

80. Primo Levi, *The Drowned and the Saved*, 198–203.

81. The phenomenon of attempting to hide from evil is presented in still another way by Finkelstein. Years ago, Charlie, the Szuster's black handyman, had been falsely accused of raping a white girl in Alabama. Discovering faded newsclippings, Brenda is sickened to read the Klan's antisemitic and racist

response to the not-guilty verdict. The fact that the trial occurred two days before the Nazis murdered Brenda's maternal grandfather and two aunts links the evil of American racism and the scourge of European antisemitism; this type of linkage is also made by Carol Ascher in *The Flood* (see chapter 4).

82. Thane Rosenbaum, *Elijah Visible: Stories* (New York: St. Martin's Press, 1996), 200. All citations are from this edition and appear in parenthesis in the text.

83. Rosenbaum discussion.

84. Rosenbaum discussion.

85. Rosenbaum discussion. Here Rosenbaum echoes Spiegelman's position when the latter contends that *Maus* enabled him to continue his relationship to his father.

86. Rosenbaum discussion. Rosenbaum shares Steinfeld's view that Holocaust memories may be genetically transmitted.

87. This same reversal of classical norms to indicate the shattering nature of the Holocaust is reflected in *Dancing on Tisha B'Av*, the title of Lev Raphael's collection of short stories. Raphael's work is discussed in chapter 4 of this book. See my review of *Elijah Visible* in *Tikkun*, 11.5 (September/October, 1996), 85–86. Rosenbaum extends the theme of reversal even to the point of distorting history. For example, an Auschwitz tattoo appears on the right arm of a survivor in "The Rabbi Double-Faults." See discussion of the story in this chapter.

88. Irving Greenberg, "Lessons to be Learned from the Holocaust," unpublished paper.

89. Elie Wiesel, *Night*, trans. Stella Rodway (New York: Bantam Books, 1986), 65.

## CHAPTER 4. SECOND-GENERATION NOVELS
## AND SHORT STORIES: JEWISH UNIVERSALISM

1. Menachem Z. Rosensaft, "Reflections of a Child of Holocaust Survivors," *Midstream* 27.9 (1981), 33.

2. Jack Nusan Porter, "Is There a Survivor's Syndrome? Psychological and Socio-Political Implications," in Jack Nusan Porter, *Confronting History and Holocaust: Collected Essays* (Lanham, MD: University Press of America, 1983), 100.

3. Carol Ascher, *The Flood* (Freedom, CA: Crossing Press, 1987). Citations are from this edition.

4. Ascher, "Fragments of a German-Jewish Heritage in Four 'Americans,'" *American Jewish Archives*, special issue, "The German-Jewish Legacy in America, 1938–1988 A Symposium," 40.2 (1988), 381. Hereafter, this reference will be cited as "Fragments."

5. Ascher, "Fragments," 382.

6. Ascher, "Fragments," 383.

7. Lore Grozsmann Segal, *Other People's Houses* (New York: Harcourt, Brace, and World, 1964). Helpful discussions of this book include Alan L. Berger, "Jewish Identity and Jewish Destiny, the Holocaust in Refugee Writing: Lore Segal and Karen Gershon," *Studies in American Jewish Literature* 11.1 (1992); and Cynthia Ozick, "A Contraband Life," *Commentary* 39 (March 1965).

8. Michael A. Meyer, *Jewish Identity in the Modern World* (Seattle: University of Washington Press, 1990), 33.

9. Meyer, *Jewish Identity*, 50.

10. Irving Greenberg, *The Jewish Way: Living The Holidays* (New York: Summit, 1988), 321.

11. Greenberg, "Cloud of Smoke, Pillar of Fire: Judaism, Christianity, and Modernity after the Holocaust," in Eva Fleischner, ed., *Auschwitz: Beginning Of A New Era?* (New York: KTAV, The Cathedral Church of St. John the Divine, Anti-Defamation League of B'nai B'rith, 1977), 42.

12. Ascher, "Fragments," 371.

13. Ascher, "Fragments," 371.

14. Ascher, "Fragments," 371.

15. For an exposition and critique of Berkovits's position see Alan L. Berger, "Holocaust and History: A Theological Reflection," *Journal of Ecumenical Studies* 25.2 (1988); and Steven T. Katz, "Eliezer Berkovits's Post-Holocaust Jewish Theodicy," in Steven T. Katz, *Post-Holocaust Dialogues: Critical Studies in Modern Jewish Thought* (New York: New York University Press, 1983).

16. Richard L. Rubenstein, *After Auschwitz: History, Theology, and Contemporary Judaism*, Second Edition (Baltimore: The Johns Hopkins University Press, 1992), 3–13, 157–200; and *Power Struggle: An Autobiographical Confession* (Lanham, MD: University Press of America, 1986), 1–21. Rubenstein's critique is of biblical and rabbinic notions of an intervening deity. As we saw in chapter 2, his own view of deity has undergone transformation.

17. Rubenstein, *The Cunning of History: The Holocaust and the American Future* (New York: Harper and Row, 1978), 91.

18. Of the vast literature on Jewish self-hate, the best contemporary work is Sander L. Gilman, *Jewish Self-Hatred: Anti-Semitism and the Hidden Language of the Jews* (Baltimore: Johns Hopkins University Press, 1986).

19. Meyer, *Jewish Identity*, 50.

20. Meyer, *Jewish Identity*, 50.

21. Salamon interviewed by Alexander Wohl, "Interview With Julie Salamon," *Baltimore Jewish Times* 19 February 1988, 60.

22. Julie Salamon, *White Lies* (Boston: Hill and Company, 1987). All citations in the text are from this edition.

23. Salamon, Wohl interview.

24. Aaron Hass notes the commonality of this phenomenon. He writes that "emotional explosions and irrational reactions were common in many survivor homes" (*In the Shadow of the Holocaust: The Second Generation* [Ithaca: Cornell University Press, 1990], 64).

25. Lucy Y. Steinitz and David Szony, eds., *Living after the Holocaust: Reflections by Children of Survivors in America* (New York: Bloch Publishing Company, 1979), 43. Julie Salamon's *The Net of Dreams* (New York: Random House, 1996) is a poignant memoir in which the author shares her search for a *tikkun atzmi*. Her book details the 1993 journey she took to Poland and Hungary with her mother and stepfather. At Steven Spielberg's invitation, they visit the set of *Schindler's List*. Salamon's account actually tells of two journeys: one to eastern Europe, and the other to the depths of her own soul. In the process she discovers much about her parents, their Holocaust past, and its impact on her own identity as a second-generation witness. *White Lies* is a fictional account of her experiences as a daughter of Job.

26. William Helmreich, *Against All Odds: Holocaust Survivors and the Successful Lives They Made in America* (New York: Simon and Schuster, 1992), 142.

27. Eva Fogelman and Bela Savran, "Psychological Issues in the Lives of Children of Holocaust Survivors: The Children As Adults," in Steinitz and Szony, eds., *Living after the Holocaust*, 149.

28. Hass, *In the Shadow of the Holocaust*, 37. Also on this matter, see Anna Kolodner, "The Socialization of Concentration Camp Survivors," Ph.D. dissertation, Boston University, 1987. Clearly, as the writings discussed in this chapter show, the issue is what one does with this perception.

29. Helen Epstein, *Children of the Holocaust: Conversations with Sons and Daughters of Survivors* (New York: G. P. Putnam's Sons, 1979), 11.

30. Epstein, *Children of the Holocaust*, 127–38.

31. This survivor sense of gratitude is chronicled by Dorothy Rabinowitz in her book *New Lives: Survivors of the Holocaust Living in America* (New York: Knopf, 1976).

32. Robert M. Prince, "Knowing the Holocaust," *Psychoanalytic Inquiry* 5.1 (1985), 51.

33. Prince, "Knowing the Holocaust." Prince articulates three main themes that emerge from the "conscious rationales" given by members of the second generation for wanting to tell their children about the Holocaust. The first is a "desire to preserve the past." Some second-generation witnesses contend that this "would insure that the Holocaust is never forgotten." Others claim they want their children to "have a Jewish identity," and the "Holocaust is part of the history of the Jewish people." Secondly, the Holocaust is a paradigm for educating their children about "the nature of the world" and the danger of "succumbing to a false sense of security." This is clearly the case with Spiegelman. Prince identifies the third theme as a "desire for their own children (the third generation) to know and understand them." Thus, "passing on knowledge of their parents' history is a means of revealing themselves to their own children" (52).

34. Robert J. Lifton, *History and Human Survival* (New York: Random House, 1970), 198.

35. Primo Levi, *Survival in Auschwitz: The Nazi Assault on Humanity*, trans. Stuart Woolf (New York: Collier Books, 1961), 82.

36. Lifton, *History and Human Survival*, 201.

37. The phrase is used by Emil Fackenheim.

38. For an important study that focuses exclusively on female response during the *Shoah*, see Carol Rittner and John K. Roth, eds., *Different Voices: Women and the Holocaust* (New York: Paragon House, 1993).

39. The role of helpers also forms a thread in the tapestry of survival woven in the stories of Vladek Spiegelman in *Maus* and by the Szusters in *Summer Long-a-Coming*. For a more detailed discussion of this phenomenon see chapter 6 of this work.

40. Elie Wiesel, *One Generation After*, trans. Lily Edelman and Elie Wiesel (New York: Schocken Books, 1982), 72.

41. A best-case study of postmodernism is the work of Robert P. Scharlemann, ed., *Theology at the End of the Century: A Dialogue on the Postmodern*

(Charlottesville: University Press of Virginia, 1990). See Scharelmann's introduction, especially pp. 2–7. I am grateful to Professor Charles E. Winquist for bringing this work to my attention.

42. Hass, *In the Shadow of the Holocaust*, 116.

43. This phenomenon is also seen in Brenda Szuster's reaction to the racism that indicted Charly for a crime he did not commit, although in Finkelstein's novel, it is not personal empathy but the phenomenon of injustice (e.g., anti-semitism and racism) that is stressed.

44. Cynthia Ozick, "Rosa," *The New Yorker* 21 March 1983, 38–71.

45. This approach calls to mind Brenda Szuster's observation that her family is hiding from the world.

46. Lev Raphael, *Dancing at Tisha B'Av* (New York: St. Martin's Press, 1990); *Winter Eyes* (New York: St. Martin's Press, 1992).

47. Raphael interviewed by Paul Han, "Author Speaks on Holocaust Day," *Yale Daily News* 12 April 1991, 6.

48. Raphael interviewed by Ronald Gans, "An Interview With Lev Raphael," *Christopher Street* 13.5 (1990), 31–32.

49. Hass, *In the Shadow of the Holocaust*, 48.

50. Hass, *In the Shadow of the Holocaust*, 44.

51. Recall the positions of Wiesel, Greenberg, and Riskin on this issue; see chapter 1, note 20.

52. Hass, *In the Shadow of the Holocaust*, 65.

53. "Inheritance," in *Dancing On Tisha B'Av*, 171–88.

54. Benjamin Ferencz, *Less than Slaves* (Cambridge: Harvard University Press, 1979), 66.

55. Ferencz, *Less than Slaves*, 67.

56. Raphael, Han interview, 6.

57. "Caravans," in *Dancing on Tisha B'Av*, 69–82.

58. "Abominations," in *Dancing on Tisha B'Av*, 215–31.

59. "An Interview With Lev Raphael," *Frontiers* 1 March 1991, 42. Cynthia Ozick, writing in the context of excluding women from Jewish ritual obligation, makes a similar claim. See, for example, "The Jewish Half-Genius," *Jerusalem Post*, International Edition, 8 August 1978, 10, 11.

60. As of this writing, the issue of Orthodoxy's stance towards homosexuality has been intensified by the debate over so-called gay clubs at Yeshiva University. Right-wing faculty, students, and supporters of the university want such clubs banned and threaten to withhold financial support. The left wing supports the presence of these clubs, as does the New York City human rights law banning discrimination based on sexual orientation. Dr. Norman Lamm, the President of Yeshiva University, has taken a public stand on the issue. His position is that it is against the (secular) law to discriminate against the gay clubs. Consequently, he has lost some fiscal support among the right wing. Prior to Dr. Lamm's public stance, the dilemma was well described by Gary Rosenblatt, editor of *The New York Jewish Week*. Rosenblatt wrote that Dr. Lamm is "caught between his personal beliefs and his public role" (cited in *Jewish Observer*, Syracuse, New York, 20 July 1995, 2.

61. Rabbi Gordon Tucker, of the Conservative movement, sensitively distinguishes between halakhic and metahalakhic views of homosexuality. Rabbi

Tucker's is a sensitive and insightful point of view, one that acknowledges the crucial distinction between the law as it is written and life as it is lived. This position is, however, neither normative nor universally accepted.

62. Michael Berenbaum, *After Tragedy and Triumph: Modern Jewish Thought and the Jewish Experience* (Cambridge: Cambridge University Press, 1990), especially the following essays: "The Nativization of the Holocaust," "The Uniqueness and Universality of the Holocaust," and "Public Commemoration of the Holocaust." Edward T. Linenthal, *Preserving Memory: The Struggle to Create America's Holocaust Museum* (New York: Viking, 1995).

63. Harold Flender writes that Nazi Germany never imposed the Nuremberg decrees on Denmark. Therefore, wearing the Yellow Star was not required of Danish Jews (*Rescue in Denmark* [New York: MacFadden-Bartell, 1968], 215–16). This observation detracts not one bit from the support given Danish Jews by King Christian X. As the Holocaust recedes further in time, however, and also becomes increasingly the focus of popular culture, historical accuracy becomes even more imperative.

64. For an insightful discussion of the historical reasons underlying persecution of gays see Steven T. Katz's magisterial study *The Holocaust in Historical Context: The Holocaust and Mass Death before the Modern Age* (New York: Oxford University Press, 1994). Katz argues that in the medieval worldview the homosexual was "merely a sinner" whereas the Jew was "a subversive cosmic being whose dark and promiscuous power was demonic" (526). During the *Shoah* Nazism expanded this theme by designating Jews as primal enemies of the proposed thousand-year Reich proclaimed by Hitler. Therefore, Jews were murdered in the name of metaphysics: Hitler wanted nothing less than to create a new-*Judenrein* (Jew-free) world. Elsewhere, Katz observes that: "In Nazi Germany, . . . Jews were singled out for "metaphysical," i.e., racial and manichaean, reasons." Katz, "Auschwitz and the Gulag: Discontinuities and Dissimilarities," in *Bearing Witness to the Holocaust 1939–1989*, ed. Alan L. Berger (Lewiston, NY: The Edwin Mellen Press, 1991), 73.

65. For an intelligent discussion of Spielberg's film and its cultural implications see Geoffrey Hartman, "The Cinema Animal: On Spielberg's *Schindler's List*," *Salmagundi* (Spring-Summer, 1995), 127–45. On the denial phenomenon, see Deborah E. Lipstadt, *Denying the Holocaust: The Growing Assault on Truth and Memory* (New York: Free Press, 1993).

66. Raphael, "To Be A Jew," in Lev Raphael, *Journeys and Arrivals* (Boston: Faber and Faber, 1996), 5.

67. "An Interview With Lev Raphael," *Frontiers* 1 March 1992, 43.

68. Irena Klepfisz writes passionately about antisemitism in the lesbian community. See her essay "Anti-Semitism in the Lesbian/Feminist Movement," in Evelyn Torten Beck, ed., *Nice Jewish Girls: A Lesbian Anthology* (Boston: Beacon, 1982), 51–60. Klepfisz argues that lesbians should realize that they face the same peril as Jews did in Nazi Germany. Further, contemporary lesbians assume the same attitude as the Jews did: they believe that they are protected under the law.

69. Raphael, "On a Narrow Bridge: A Jewish Writer's Journey," *Reconstructionist* (1992), 23.

70. For an interesting discussion of dissimilation and Jewish Feminists, see Susannah Heschel, "The Feminist Confrontation with Judaism," in Alan L. Berger, ed., *Judaism in the Modern World* (New York: New York University Press, 1994), 268–80.

71. On the concept of Jewish self-loathing see Gilman, *Jewish Self-Hatred*, as well as his essay "The Visibility of the Jew in the Diaspora: Body Imagery and Its Cultural Context," in Alan L. Berger, ed., *Judaism in the Modern World*. See also Michael A. Meyer's chapter on "Antisemitism," in his book *Jewish Identity in the Modern World*.

72. Greenberg, "Voluntary Covenant," in *Perspectives: A CLAL Thesis* (New York: The National Jewish Center for Learning and Leadership, n.d.), 38.

73. Greenberg, "Voluntary Covenant," 38.

74. Greenberg, "Voluntary Covenant," 37.

75. Epstein, *Children of the Holocaust*, 133–35.

## CHAPTER 5. SECOND-GENERATION DOCUMENTARIES AND DOCUDRAMAS: JEWISH PARTICULARISM

1. Aaron Hass, *In The Shadow of the Holocaust: The Second Generation* (Ithaca: Cornell University Press, 1990), 164.

2. Saul Friedlander, "Trauma, Transference, and 'Working Through' in Writing the History of the *Shoah*," *History and Memory* 4.1 (1992), 53.

3. Cited by William B. Helmreich, *Against All Odds: Holocaust Survivors and the Successful Lives They Made in America* (New York: Simon and Schuster, 1992), 146.

4. Annette Insdorf, *Indelible Shadows: Film and the Holocaust*, 2nd ed. (Cambridge: Cambridge University Press, 1989), chapter 12, "The Personal Documentary."

5. Insdorf, *Indelible Shadows*, 212.

6. Yossi's embrace of the traditional Jewish mourning custom stands in sharp contrast to Spiegelman's recitation from the *Tibetan Book of the Dead* at his mother's funeral.

7. Insdorf, *Indelible Shadows*, 224. Insdorf's comment was accurate at the time. It should, however, be noted that Yossi Klein is now Yossi Klein Halevi. His book, *Memoirs of a Jewish Extremist: An American Story* (Boston: Little, Brown and Company, 1995) is the memoir of a disillusioned ex-member of the Jewish Defense League. Klein Halevi's renunciation of extremism is further evidenced by his position as a senior writer for *The Jerusalem Report*.

8. Elie Wiesel, in Irving Abrahamson, ed., *Against Silence: The Voice and Vision of Elie Wiesel* (New York: Holocaust Library, 1985), 3:112.

9. Aaron Hass observes that, "for most survivors, their devotion and fidelity to the State of Israel has become their religious duty," Hass, *The Aftermath: Living with the Holocaust* (Cambridge: Cambridge University Press, 1995). This devotion is expressed in several ways: visits to Israel, political support, and financial commitment. Concerning the latter, William B. Helmreich cites an

astounding statistic. Quoting Benjamin Meed, president of the American Gathering and Federation of Jewish Survivors, Helmreich reports that survivors buy approximately 10 percent of the total number of Israel Bonds sold in the United States Helmreich, *Against All Odds*, 185–86.

10. Lawrence L. Langer, *Holocaust Testimonies: The Ruins of Memory* (New Haven: Yale University Press, 1991), chapter 3, "Humiliated Memory: The Besieged Self."

11. Langer, *Holocaust Testimonies*, 83–84.

12. Hass, *In the Shadow of the Holocaust*, 27–28.

13. David Mittleberg, "Impact of the Holocaust on Second Generation of Survivors: The Differential Socialization of Affirmative Commitment to the Collective," in *Remembering for the Future*, Theme 1, "Jews and Christians During and After the Holocaust" (Oxford: Pergamon Press, 1988), 1142. On the impact of the *Shoah* for second generation identity, see Pier Marton's *Say I'm a Jew*. This 1985 documentary film stresses the mourning phase of children of survivors.

14. On this point see Alan L. Berger, *Crisis and Covenant: The Holocaust in American Jewish Fiction* (Albany: SUNY Press, 1985), 68–79; and "Elie Wiesel's Second-Generation Witness: Passing the Torch of Remembrance," in Harry James Cargas, ed., *Telling the Tale: A Tribute to Elie Wiesel on the Occasion of His 65th Birthday: Essays, Reflections, and Poems* (Saint Louis: Time Being Books, 1993).

15. Eva Fogelman, "Intergenerational Group Therapy: Child Survivors of the Holocaust and Offspring of Survivors," *Psychoanalytic Review* 75.4 (1988), 625–26.

16. Primo Levi, *The Drowned and the Saved*, trans. Raymond Rosenthal (New York: Summit Books, 1988), 25.

17. Hass, *In The Shadow of the Holocaust*, 156.

18. On the theme of survivor mistrust of the social world see Hass, *The Aftermath: Living with the Holocaust*; and Anna Kolodner, "The Socialization of Children of Concentration Camp Survivors." Ph.D. Dissertation, Boston University, 1987.

19. Fogelman, "Intergenerational Group Therapy," 626.

20. Abraham Ravett, interviewed by this author, Boston, December 1994.

21. Ravett, interviewed by this author.

22. Ravett, Association for Jewish Studies Meeting, Boston, December 1994.

23. Ravett, interviewed by this author.

24. In this sense, Ravett's work recalls the relationships between Wiesel's Reuven and Ariel in *The Fifth Son*, Friedmann's Mordechai Kole and his son Jason, Finkelstein's Rukhl and Yankl Szuster and their daughter Brenda, and Raphael's various fathers and sons.

25. Ravett, interviewed by this author.

26. Seymour Fisher and Rhoda L. Fisher, *The Psychology of Adaptation to Absurdity: Tactics of Make-Believe* (Tuxedo Park, NY: Earlbaum Assoc., 1993). On the theme of humor and the Holocaust, see the following: Leslie Epstein, *King of the Jews: A Novel of the Holocaust* (New York: Coward, McCann and Geoghegan, 1979); Terrence Des Pres, "Holocaust *Laughter*?" in Berel Lang, ed., *Writing and the Holocaust* (New York: Holmes and Meier, 1988), 216–33; and the more

problematic study by Steve Lipman, *Laughter in Hell: The Use of Humor during the Holocaust* (Northvale, NJ: Jason Aranson, 1991).

27. Abraham Cykiert, "The Ghost of Betrayal," *Generation* 2.2 (April 1990/91), 33.

28. Study guides for these films were written by this author.

29. For a study of this phenomenon in American novels of the *Shoah*, see Alan L. Berger, "The Holocaust Survivor: Shifting Images in American Literature," in Marcia Sachs Littel, Richard Libowitz, Evelyn Bodek Rosen, eds., *The Holocaust Forty Years After* (Lewiston, NY: The Edwin Mellen Press, 1989), 61–71; and "La Shoa dans la littérature américaine: témoins, non-témoins et faux-témoins," *Pardes* 9–10 (1989), Numero special.

30. On the issue of intermarriage in the second generation, see Vera R. Obermeyer, "Patterns of Outmarriage and Inmarriage among the Children of Jewish Holocaust Survivors," *Journal of Reform Judaism*, Winter 1987. In certain cases, evidence indicates that intermarriage is seen as "a surrogate of Hitler's work" (Hass, *In the Shadow of the Holocaust*, 113). Yet, there are those who believe exactly the opposite: marrying out is a reaction to the Holocaust (Richard L. Rubenstein, "The Silence of God," chapter 6 in Richard L. Rubenstein and John K. Roth, eds., *Approaches to Auschwitz: The Holocaust and Its Legacy* (Atlanta: John Knox Press, 1987), 316.

## CHAPTER 6. SECOND-GENERATION DOCUMENTARIES AND DOCUDRAMAS: JEWISH UNIVERSALISM

1. Pierre Sauvage, interviewed by Richard Bernstein, "A Movie Maker Preserves Those Who Preserved Him," *New York Times* 27 August 1989.

2. Raul Hilberg, *Perpetrators, Victims, Bystanders: The Jewish Catastrophe 1933–1945* (New York: HarperCollins, 1992), 213.

3. On this phenomenon see the following studies: Eva Fogelman, *Conscience and Courage: Rescuers of Jews during the Holocaust* (New York: Anchor Books, 1994); David P. Gushee, *The Righteous Gentiles of the Holocaust: A Christian Interpretation* (Minneapolis: Fortress Press, 1994); Kristen R. Monroe, Michael C. Barton, and Ute Klingermann, "Altruism and the Theory of Rational Action: Rescuers of Jews in Nazi Europe," *Ethics* 10.1 (1990), 103–22; and Samuel P. and Pearl M. Oliner, *The Altruistic Personality: Rescuers of Jews in Nazi Europe* (New York: Free Press, 1988).

4. Nechama Tec, *When Light Pierced the Darkness: Christian Rescue of Jews in Nazi-Occupied Poland* (New York: Oxford University Press, 1986).

5. Important studies of the helpers include Hillel Levine, *In Search of Sugihara: The Elusive Japanese Diplomat Who Risked His Life to Rescue 10,000 Jews* (New York: The Free Press, 1996); Mordecai Paldiel, *The Path of the Righteous: Gentile Rescuers of Jews during the Holocaust* (Hoboken, NJ: KTAV, 1993); Eric Silver, *The Book of the Just: The Unsung Heroes Who Rescued Jews from Hitler* (New York: Grove Press, 1992); André Stein, *Quiet Heroes: True Stories of the Rescue of Jews by Christians in Nazi-Occupied Holland* (New York: New

York University Press, 1988); and Carol Rittner and Sondra Myers, eds., *The Courage to Care: Rescuers of Jews during the Holocaust* (New York: New York University Press, 1986). In addition, see footnote 3 above. Geoffrey Hartman, "The Cinema Animal: On Spielberg's *Schindler's List*," *Salmagundi*, 106–107 (Spring–Summer, 1995), 127–45, argues that Spielberg is not content struggling with an absent memory and instead aims for "visuality" that "leads to moments approaching Holocaust kitsch" (128 and 129).

6. Emil L. Fackenheim, *The Jewish Bible after the Holocaust: A Re-reading* (Bloomington: Indiana University Press, 1990), vi.

7. Emil L. Fackenheim, *To Mend the World: Foundations of Future Jewish Thought* (New York: Schocken Books, 1982), 307.

8. Eva Fogelman, *Conscience and Courage*, 305.

9. Pierre Sauvage, "Ten Things I Would Like to Know About righteous Conduct in Le Chambon and Elsewhere during the Holocaust," *Humboldt Journal of Social Relations* 13.1–2 (1985/86), 239. Hereafter, this source will be cited as "Ten Things."

10. Annette Insdorf, *Indelible Shadows: Film and the Holocaust* (Cambridge: Cambridge University Press, 1989), 229.

11. Insdorf, *Indelible Shadows*, 229.

12. The hidden children received widespread public attention with the convening of the First International Gathering of Children Hidden During World War II held in New York City on 26 and 27 May 1991. Among those who spoke were Myriam Abramowicz, Yaffa Eliach, Eva Fogelman, Abraham and Golda Foxman, and Nehama Tec. For a journalistic account of how the conference came about and profiles of some of the participants, see Jane Marks, "The Hidden Children," in *New York* 25 February 1991. Professor Yaffa Eliach, herself a hidden child and creator of the Tower of Faces at the United States Holocaust Memorial Museum, notes the pain of the hidden children when she observes that "their Christian identity is better formed and stronger than their Jewish identity" (conversation with author, February 1996). Important studies of the hidden children include Deborah Dwork, *Children With a Star: Jewish Youth in Nazi Europe* (New Haven: Yale University Press, 1991); Jane Marks, *The Hidden Children: The Secret Survivors of the Holocaust* (New York: Ballantine Books, 1993); and André Stein, *Hidden Children: Forgotten Survivors of the Holocaust* (New York: Penguin Books, 1994). Stein tells Yaffa Eliach's story in chapter 3, entitled "Child of Shadow, Child of Light." Eliach herself has written sensitively about hidden children, whom she terms "both insiders and outsiders at the Kingdom of Death." See her article "From Hiding Place to Center Stage: A Child of the Holocaust," presented at the Second International Gathering of the Hidden Child, Jerusalem, 12–15 July 1993.

13. Author's telephone discussion with Myriam Abramowicz, 7 February 1992. Hereafter this will be cited as Abramowicz discussion.

14. The AJB, Association of Jews in Belgium, was established by the Nazis.

15. See the following works: Yehuda Bauer, *American Jewry and the Holocaust: The American Joint Distribution Committee, 1939–1945* (Detroit: Wayne State University Press, 1981); Bauer, *Flight and Rescue: Brichah—The Organized Escape of the Jewish Survivors of Eastern Europe, 1944–1948* (New York: random House, 1970); Ernst and Linn E. Papanek, *Out of the Fire* (New York:

William Morrow, 1975); Nechama Tec, *Defiance: The Bielski Partisans* (New York: Oxford University Press, 1993); and Tec, *In The Lions Den: The Life of Oswald Rufeisen* (New York: Oxford University Press, 1990).

16. Shuttling between foster homes, Betty's experience of anomie and stress is like that of Lore Grozman Segal. See chapter 4, note 7.

17. Ella Mahler, "About Jewish Children Who Survived WW II on the Aryan Side," *Yad Vashem Bulletin* 12 (December 1962), 49.

18. Abramowicz discussion.

19. Abramowicz discussion.

20. Abramowicz discussion.

21. Abramowicz discussion.

22. Pierre Sauvage, interviewed by Mary Johnson, "A Filmmaker's Odyssey," *Facing History and Ourselves News*, Winter 1989–90, 18.

23. Pastor Donadile's respect for Judaism is similar to that of Father Capart in Abramowicz's *As If It Were Yesterday*. This attitude is in striking contrast to the countless millions of allegedly professing Christians who oriented themselves by the "Teaching of Contempt" when it came to Jews and Judaism.

24. Sauvage, Bernstein interview.

25. Richard L. Rubenstein and John K. Roth, *Approaches to Auschwitz: The Holocaust and Its Legacy* (Atlanta: John Knox Press, 1987), 200–201.

26. Pierre Sauvage, "Ten Things," 254.

27. Author's telephone discussion with Sauvage, 1 February 1992. Further reference to this source will be cited as Sauvage discussion.

28. Sauvage discussion.

29. Sauvage, Bernstein interview.

30. Sauvage, Bernstein interview.

31. It is interesting to note that Fogelman's *Breaking the Silence* also utilizes the Partisan song.

32. Sauvage discussion.

33. Sauvage discussion.

34. This situation may well change now that President Jacques Chirac has publicly acknowledged French complicity with Nazism and the deportation of Jews during World War II. See the article "Chirac Affirms France's Guilt in Fate of Jews," *New York Times* 17 July 1995, 1 and 3.

35. Insdorf, *Indelible Shadows*, 232. For the complete text of the film see Saul Rubinek, *So Many Miracles* (Markham, Ontario: Viking, 1988).

36. Fogelman, *Conscience and Courage*.

37. Fogelman, *Conscience and Courage*, 138.

38. Fogelman, *Conscience and Courage*, and Tec, *When Light Pierced the Darkness*.

39. J. Presser, *The Destruction of the Dutch Jews* (New York: E. P. Dutton, 1969), and Tec, *When Light Pierced the Darkness*.

40. Fogelman, *Conscience and Courage*, 223.

41. Fogelman, *Conscience and Courage*, 352n.12.

42. This same sight, however, did not soften the heart of the German nurse in Abramowicz's *As If It Were Yesterday*, or so many other Nazi hearts. If we are looking for a theory of goodness, it will have to be more inclusive than the asser-

tion of softening the heart. If anything, it is more to the point to assert that, like the Pharaoh of old, Nazism was a case of hardening the heart.

43. Fogelman, *Conscience and Courage*, 184.

44. Dan Bar-On, *The Legacy of Silence* (Cambridge: Harvard University Press, 1989); see also Peter Sichrofsky, *Born Guilty*, trans. Jean Steinberg (New York: Basic Books, 1988).

45. Debbie Goodstein, interviewed by Katherine Dieckmann, "Documenting Distant Voices," *Elle* April 1989, 68.

46. For an insightful discussion of women rescuers see "Men and Women Rescuers," chapter 13 in Fogelman, *Conscience and Courage*, 237–51. Fogelman argues-against the sex-based theory of Carol Gilligan's "different voice"— that rescue activity depends more on skill level than on gender.

47. It is also important in this context to note the establishment of two other foundations to aid the helpers. For example, in 1986 Rabbi Harold Schulweiss and Eva Fogelman co-founded the Jewish Foundation for Christian Rescuers, now under the auspices of the Anti-Defamation League. More recently, Steven Spielberg has established the Righteous Persons Foundation. This organization is, however, concerned primarily with strengthening Jewish communal life, although part of its mission statement is to "promote tolerance and understanding and building alliances between Jews and non-Jews," as well as "encouraging Jews to participate in the critical work of *tikkun olam*."

## CHAPTER 7. WHITHER THE FUTURE?

1. Helen Epstein, *Children of the Holocaust: Conversations with Sons and Daughters of Survivors* (New York: G. P. Putnam's Sons, 1979), 260.

2. Serge Liberman, "The Storyteller," in Serge Liberman, *The Battered and the Redeemed* (Balaclava, Australia: Fine-Lit, 1990), 14.

3. The rabbi, reports Liberman, "told of Jeremiah who said that a catastrophe was as a disaster that had befallen at sea. For a short time, the signs remained, and were seen, and remembered. But then the waters swelled, the tides rose over, and all became as if nothing had happened" ("The Storyteller," 15).

4. Geoffrey Hartman, *The Shapes of Holocaust Memory* (Cambridge: Basil Blackwell, 1994), 18.

5. Hartman, *Shapes*, 18.

6. Albert Friedlander, *Out of the Whirlwind: A Reader of Holocaust Literature* (New York: Schocken Books, 1976), 536.

7. Albert Friedlander, *Riders towards the Dawn: From Holocaust to Hope* (New York: Continuum, 1994), 12.

8. Friedlander, *Riders towards the Dawn*, 13.

9. Emil L. Fackenheim, *The Jewish Bible after the Holocaust: A Re-reading* (Bloomington: Indiana University Press, 1990), xi.

10. Fackenheim, *The Jewish Bible*, 94.

11. Fackenheim, *The Jewish Bible*, 94.

12. That the Holocaust has entered a new phase of memorialization is indicated by the role and function of Holocaust memorials in various countries. On

this issue, see the following works: Edward T. Linenthal, *Preserving Memory: The Struggle to Create America's Holocaust Museum* (New York: Viking, 1995); Judith Miller, *One, by One, by One: Facing the Holocaust* (New York: Simon and Schuster, 1990); and James E. Young, *The Texture of Memory: Holocaust Memorials and Meaning* (New Haven: Yale University Press, 1993). On the phenomenon of shaping Holocaust memory by nonwitnesses, see Geoffrey Hartman's introductory essay, "Darkness Visible," in Hartman, ed., *Holocaust Remembrance: The Shapes of Memory* (New York: Bloch, 1979).

13. The phrase "moral minority" was coined by Professor Lawrence Baron. See his study "The Moral Minority: Psycho-Social Research on the Righteous Gentiles," in Franklin H. Littel, Alan L. Berger, and Hubert Locke, eds., *What Have We Learned: Telling the Story and Teaching the Lessons of the Holocaust* (Lewiston, NY: Edwin Mellen Press, 1993).

# INDEX

"*Abominations.*" *See* Raphael, Lev.

Abramowicz, Myriam: African-Americans and Jews, 167; and comparison with Sauvage, 168, 170, 172; antisemitic restrictions in Belgian, 162; *As If It Were Yesterday*, 4, 20, 161, 162–167, 189; collaboration in Belgium, 163, 164; and comparison with Rubinek, 174, 176; deportation of rescuers with hidden children, 162; description of rescuers, 162, 164; discussions between helpers and the helped, 163; emotions of rescuers, 163; hidden children and identity confusion, 167; and Hidden Child Meeting, 167; hidden children, terror, and uncertainty, 165, 166; hidden children and post-Auschwitz life, 166; hidden children and psychological scars, 165–166, 167; hidden children and their mothers, 163, 164; Holocaust experience and Belgium's Jews, 162; humanizing plight of the Jewish people, 165; impact upon non-Jewish audiences, 167; implications of *tikkun* of ordinary decency, 161; Jewish self-help during the *Shoah*, 164; and post-Auschwitz universal role, 167; and prosocial actions of rescuers, 181; reaction of Jewish audiences, 167; and reference to Hillberg, 162; rescuer attitudes towards Jews and Judaism, 163; rescuer motivation, 164, 166–167; revisionists and non-Jewish righteous, 167; role of women rescuers, 165; second-generation mission, 161; the *Shoah* and identity of hidden children, 162, 165, 166, 167; the *Shoah*'s universal impact, goodness and moral behavior, 161; and *tikkun* of ordinary decency, 31; use of humor, 164

"*Academic Freedom.*" *See* Steinfeld, J. J.

*After Auschwitz*. *See* Rubenstein, Richard L.

"*An Act of Defiance.*" *See* Rosenbaum, Thane.

*Ahavat Yisrael*: in Brand's *Kaddish*, 135

*Aleinu* (Aleynu): and the perfection (*tikkun*) of the world, 4; expression of the messianic hope, 28

*Alinsky's Children*. *See* Shapiro, Own J.

*aliyah*: in Fischers' *A Generation Apart*, 137

*Am Yisrael Hai*, 140

*Angst*: Australian documentary, 131, 150–152; comedic dissonance and Holocaust legacy, 150, 151; dynamics within survivor household, 150; effect of Holocaust on Jewish identity, 150, 151; humor as mask for angst, 150; memories of lonely/unhappy childhood, 150; and reference to Epstein, 150; and reference to Fishers, 151; and reference to Zable, 150; relationship of humor

215

*Angst (continued)*
and horror, 188; second
generation and bearing witness to
the Holocaust, 152; second-
generation behaviors, 151; second-
generation coping with Holocaust
legacy, 151, 152; second-
generation gestalt, 150; second-
generation guilt, 150; second
generation and Holocaust imagery,
151; second-generation lesson,
152; second-generation pain and
anger, 150, 151; second generation
and relationship of humor and
rage, 151; second generation and
relationship to parents' experience
and Jewish tradition, 151, 186;
second generation as "Riders
towards the Dawn," 152; second-
generation lesson, 152; second-
generation understanding of
Holocaust, 150 separation of
second-generation children from
peers, 151; tragic dimension of
humor, 151. *See* Deb Filler. *See*
Sandy Gutman. *See* Moshe
Waldoks.

antisemitism: in *Breaking the Silence*,
143; in *The Flood*, 89, 90, 91, 92,
93, 94, 95; and homophobia and
racism, 87, 88, 92, 95, 117; and
Jewish identity, 90–91, 94–95; in
*Open Secrets*, 155, 156, 157; and
Poland, 124; and second-
generation particularist writers,
87; and second-generation
universalist writers, 88, 90, 92, 95,
107, 126; in *Voices from the Attic*,
180; in *Weapons of the Spirit*,
169; in *White Lies*, 107; in *Winter
Eyes*, 124, 125

Armenian genocide, 9

*As If It Were Yesterday. See*
Abramowicz, Myriam.

Ascher, Carol: American culture and
Jewish identity, 90–91; and
American racism, 88, 89, 90, 92,

93, 95, 126; and antisemitism and
Jewish psyche, 90, 94–95; and
comparison with Bukiet, 90, 92;
and comparison with Finkelstein,
90, 93; and comparison with
Fogelman, 143; and comparison
with Freidmann, 90; and
comparison with Raphael,
110–111, 116, 119, 122, 123,
125; and comparison with
Salamon, 90, 94, 96, 101, 102,
104, 109; and comparison with
Spiegelman, 90; and effect of
Holocaust legacy, 90; *The Flood*,
4, 88–95, 109, 155; and innocent
suffering, 92; and Jewish self-hate,
93; and meaning of "flood," 95;
and late-nineteenth-century
German antisemitism, 94; and
particularist themes, 89–90; and
post-Auschwitz Jewish identity,
89, 90–91, 93; and post-Auschwitz
theodicy and Jewish identity, 94;
and post-Auschwitz theology,
91–93; and reference to
Greenberg, 91–92; and reference
to Meyer, 90–91, 94; and
reference to Rosensaft, 95; and
reference to Roethke, 95; and
reference to Wiesel, 91; and
refugees, 89, 90, 91, 92, 93, 95;
Rubenstein and death-of-God
theology, 93; and second-
generation identity and quest for
*tikkun olam*, 126; and survivors'
Post-Holocaust lives, 89, 90; and
theodicy, 93; and *tikkun olam*, 92,
94, 95; uniqueness of the
Holocaust, 93, 94; and universalist
motifs, 90, 126; writing as act of
*tikkun*, 126–127

Auerbach, Erich: mimesis, 14

Auschwitz, 22, 27, 30; in
Abramowicz and Hoffenberg's
*As If It Were Yesterday*, 166;
and Bukiet, 71, 73, 74; in
Fischers' *A Generation Apart*,

136, 137, 138, 140; in
Friedmann's *Damaged Goods*,
37, 41; in Goodstein's *Voices
from the Attic*, 178; and issue of
*Wiedergutmachung*, 114; and
Ravett's *"Everything's For You,"*
147; in Rosenbaum's *"Elijah
Visible,"* 81–84 *passim*; in
Salamon's *White Lies*, 96, 100,
104–106; and trial of God, 133
Avuyah, Elisha Ben, 93


Bar Kohkba, 44
bar mitzvah: in Bukiet's *Stories of an
Imaginary Childhood*, 73, 77–78;
in Raphael, 110, 116; in
Rosenbaum's *"The Rabbi
Double-Faults,"* 83, 84; in
Sauvage's *Weapons of the Spirit*,
172; in Spiegelman's *Maus*, 69,
70
Baron, Salo W.: and "lachrymose
conception" of Judaism, 146
Bar-On, Dan: *The Legacy of Silence*,
180
Bauman, Zygmunt: modernity,
morality, and rationality, 145
*"Because of the War."* See Steinfeld,
J. J.
Beit Lochamei Hagetaot, 149
Ben-Yehuda, Eliezer: definition of
*Tikkun Olam*, 8, 88
Berenbaum, Michael: and additional
covenant, 36; analysis of Wiesel's
literary corpus, 23–25; and
universalizing the Holocaust and
its legacy, 118
Bergen-Belsen, 27; in Bukiet's
*"Himmler's Chickens,"*, 74; in
Fischers' *A Generation Apart*, 137;
in Friedmann's *Damaged Goods*,
37, 41, 44, 46; and Rosenbaum,
72
Berkovits, Eliezer: Holocaust,
modernity, and Christianity, 54;
and Jewish peoplehood, 135; and

Post-Auschwitz theology, 93;
survivors as *k'doshim* (holy ones)
and nonwitnesses, 6–7
*Beth Din*, 183
Bible: and Fackenheim's two-
dimensional abyss, 160; Hebrew,
102; and law, 105; in Raphael,
123
*"Bingo by the Bungalow."* See
Rosenbaum, Thane.
Blanchot, Maurice, 42
Blumenthal, Gina: *In Dark Places*,
130, 131; and Susan Sontag, 131,
134
*The Book of Job*, 2; and meaning of
innocent suffering, 5; and mystery
of man and God, 5; theodicy in
light of Auschwitz, 5; significance
of daughters' names, 6
Borowitz, Eugene: Jewish modernity
and postmodern Judaism, 35; and
Jewish particularism, 35;
*Renewing the Covenant: A
Theology for the Postmodern Jew*,
9, 35; covenant and "common
self's concentration on
immediacy," 9; second-generation
link with prior Jewish generations,
22
Braham, Randolph: and Brand's
*Kaddish*, 134
Brand, Steven, 131–132; and *Ahavat
Yisrael*, 135; and comparison with
Berkovits, 135; and comparison
with Fischers, 137, 138, 139, 140;
and comparison with Fogelman,
153; and comparison with
Goodstein, 179; and comparison
with Greenberg, 134, 140; and
comparison with Raphael, 132,
134; and comparison with Riskin,
140; and comparison with
Rubenstein, 133; and comparison
with Salamon, 132; and
comparison with Singer, 132; and
comparison with Sontag, 134; and
comparison with Wiesel, 133, 135,

Brand, Steven *(continued)*
140; death of survivor-father, 134;
difference between survivors and
nonwitnesses, 132; effects of
Holocaust and Jewish identity,
132–136; effects of Holocaust
legacy, 133, 134, 135; effects of
intergenerational tension, 132;
family ritual enactment, 132;
father-son relationship, 132, 133,
134, 135; fear of Nazis, 132;
Holocaust and American culture,
134; importance of Israel to
survivors, 133; and interpretation
of parents' experience, 186; issues
of loss and mourning, 134; Jewish
continuity, 134, 135; Jewish
peoplehood, 135; *Kaddish*, 4,
130–136, 154; materialism and
apocalyptic violence, 134; meaning
of survival for the Jewish people,
135; mimesis of parents, 134; need
for post-Holocaust Judaism, 133;
post-Auschwitz Jewish identity,
134, 135; post-Auschwitz Jewish
theological dynamic, 136; and
*presence of an absence*, 132;
prophetic view of Jewish identity,
135; reference to Prince, 132;
rejection of orthodoxy but not
Judaism, 133; and second-
generation anxiety and Jewish
identity, 132; and second-
generation connection to
Holocaust, 133, 134, 135, 136;
and second-generation Holocaust
imagery, 132; second-generation
identity, parent-child relationship,
and politics, 133; second-
generation identity, *Shoah*, and
Israel, 135–136; stages of Jewish
identity, 131, 132, 135–136;
survivors not viewed as victims,
135; trial of God, 133; and Yael
Danieli, 131; and Yaffa Eliach, 131
*Breaking the Silence. See* Fogelman,
Eva.

Buber, Martin: "eclipse of God," 83;
and Jewish life after Auschwitz,
188; "Job's of the gas chambers," 5
Buchenwald, 30; in Friedmann's
*Damaged Goods*, 44
Bukiet, Melvin J., 20; America and
assimilation, 73; Christianity,
Jewish persecution, and Jewish
self-hatred, 73; and comparison
with Ascher, 90; and comparison
with Steinfeld, 75; and comparison
with Finkielkraut, 73; and
comparison with Ravett, 146, and
comparison with Singer, 72; and
comparison with Spiegelman, 73;
and comparison with Wiesel, 73,
75; "*Himmler's Chickens*," 74;
and Holocaust and Jewish identity,
71, 73, 74; and Jewish history and
Jewish heritage, 73; "*The Library
of Moloch*," 74–75; and loss of
innocence after Auschwitz, 73; and
messianic credo, 74; and oral
history archives, 74–75; and pre-
Holocaust Jewish consciousness,
73; and pre-*Shoah* and European
Jewry, 72–73; and reference to
Fackenheim, 75; and reference to
Greenberg, 75; and sacrality of
survivor testimony, 75; and
second-generation Jewish identity,
73; and second-generation
pilgrimage to Auschwitz, 73; and
second-generation remembrance,
73; and second-generation witness,
73, 74, 75; and survivor memory
and second-generation
imagination, 72; *Stories of an
Imaginary Childhood*, 4, 37, 71,
72; and *tikkun atzmi*, 73; and
unity of the second-generation,
186; *While the Messiah Tarries*, 4,
37, 71, 73–74, 92

Camus, Albert: *The Plague*, 168
"*Caravans*." *See* Raphael, Lev.

*"Cattle Car Complex." See* Rosenbaum, Thane.

*cheyder* (religious school), 116

*Children of the Holocaust: Conversations with Sons and Daughters of Survivors. See* Epstein, Helen.

Chmielnicki: massacre in Poland, 44

*"The Coinciding of Sosnowiec, Upper Silesia, Poland, 1942, and Banff, Alberta, Canada, 1990." See* Steinfeld, J. J.

*"Connections." See* Raphael, Lev.

*Conscience and Courage: Rescuers of Jews During the Holocaust. See* Fogelman, Eva.

counting of Omer, 38, 44

covenant: at Sinai, 5, 21, 25, 26, 140, 190; post-*Shoah*, 8, post-Auschwitz, 9, 21, 22, 22–33 *passim*, 153, 190

Covenant Theology: of Wiesel, 8, 10, 22–25; of Fackenheim, 22–23, 28–31; of Greenberg, 8, 10, 22–23, 25–28; and Spiegelman's *Maus*, 69–70; of Rubenstein, 8, 10, 22–23, 31–33; post-Auschwitz, 9, 21–22; and second-generation witness, 21–33 *passim*, 69–70

Cykiert, Abraham, 151; and comparison with Wiesel, 152; desanctification of the *Shoah*, 152; tragic dimension of humor, 151–152

Dachau, 31

*Damaged Goods. See* Friedmann, Thomas.

*Dancing at the Club Holocaust. See* Steinfeld, J.J.

*Dancing on Tisha B'Av. See* Raphael, Lev.

Danieli, Yael: and Brand's *Kaddish*, 134; intergenerational processes,

13–14; survivor family types and second-generation identity, 14; survivors and offspring as heterogeneous population, 14; *victim families*, 47

*davening*, 49; in Ascher's *The Flood*, 90

Des Pres, Terrance: and Finkelstein's *Summer Long-A-Coming*, 57; and Spiegelman's *Maus*, 63; universal impact of the *Shoah*, 7

Displaced Persons Camps: marriage and birth rate among Jewish survivors, 5; as birth place of second-generation, 20, 71

*Docu-dramas. See The Dr. John Haney Sessions. See Open Secrets. See also* Owen J. Shapiro. *See also* Thomas Friedmann.

*The Dr. John Haney Sessions. See* Shapiro, Owen J.

East European death camps: in *Angst*, 151

Eliach, Yaffa, 131; and Hidden Children, 210 n. 12

*Elijah Visible. See* Rosenbaum, Thane. *See also "Elijah Visible."*

Enlightenment: and Jewish self-hatred, 125

Epstein, Helen, 20, 35, 183; and American culture and the second generation, 17; and *Angst*, 150; *Children of the Holocaust: Conversations with Sons and Daughters of Survivors*, 16, 17, 102; and Friedmann's *Damaged Goods*, 44–45; and genealogy and Holocaust, 101; "Heirs of the Holocaust," 17; interview of Eli Rubenstein, 21; and kinship among second generation, 115, 137; and second-generation discussion group, 141; second-generation issues and Jewish history, 146; second-generation

Epstein, Helen *(continued)*
legacy of icons and images, 17–18, 52, 67, 177–178; second generation, invisibility, and visibility, 144; survivors as heterogeneous population, 13
*'erev Shabbat*, 116; in Brand's *Kaddish*, 133; in Fischers' *A Generation Apart*, 136
European Jewry: in Ascher's *The Flood*, 92, 93; and Bukiet, 72; connection of tragedy to American Jews and American culture, 9; and post-Auschwitz ritual tradition of Hanukkah, 140; prewar Jewish life, 153; and Holocaust, 57; in Raphael's *"Abominations,"* 119; in Ravett's *"Everything's For You,"* 148; in Salamon's *White Lies*, 184–185; in Spiegelman's *Maus*, 64
*"Everything's For You." See* Ravett, Abraham
Exodus: from Egypt, 120, 137; as foundational tale for Jewish identity, 154

Fackenheim, Emil: call for mending the world, 22; and Christian acts of *tikkun*, 30–31; "Commanding Voice" of Auschwitz, 28–29, 31, 139; covenantal theology of, 28–31, 187–188; nature of *Shoah*, 7; *The Jewish Bible after the Holocaust: A Re-reading*, 187; notion of *tikkun*, 10; and partial *tikkun* of rupture, 8, 29; post-Auschwitz generations as "replacement children," 7, 187; post-Holocaust *tikkun*, 29–30, 185; second generation and post-Auschwitz *tikkun*, 31, 47; shift in thought, 23; "614th Commandment," 29, 53, 76, 81; and survivor testimony, 75; task of post-Holocaust generations, 7;

*tikkun* of "ordinary decency," 31; and *tikkun* of the world, 107; two-dimensional abyss, 160; use of *kl'al Yisrael*, 7
Ferencz, Benjamin: and issue of *Wiedergutmachung*, 114
Filler, Deb: giving voice to father's experience, 152; performer in *Angst*, 150; *Punch Me in the Stomach*, 152; second-generation pain and anger, 150; separation of second generation from peers, 151. *See Angst.*
Final Solution, 159
Fine, Ellen: and difference between survivors and second generation, 96; and second-generation guilt, 67; and task facing second-generation witnesses, 2
Finkelstein, Barbara, 20, 84; and comparison with Ascher, 90, 93; and comparison with Fischers, 137; and comparison with Fogelman, 142; and comparison with Friedmann, 50, 52, 54, 56, 57, 59, 71; and comparison with Raphael, 111, 112; and comparison with Ravett, 150; and comparison with Rosenbaum, 80; and comparison with Salamon, 98, 99, 100, 103, 104, 105, 106; and comparison with Sauvage, 168; and comparison with Spiegelman, 60, 61, 62, 66, 67, 70, 71; and comparison with Steinfeld, 78; and *din Torah*, 185; effect of Holocaust legacy, 48, 50–58 *passim*; and writer Ellen Glascow, 56; and Fackenheim's 614th Commandment, 53; Holocaust, modernity, and Christianity, 54; images of survivor parents, 10, 48–58 *passim*; issue of indirect communication, 50–51, 56; mimesis of parents' Holocaust experience, 14, 22, 55, 57, 67;

new post-Holocaust rituals in Jewish practice, 49, 51, 56; and reference to Fogelman, 100; and reference to Greenberg, 55, 59; and reference to Singer, 59; and reference to Wiesel, 53–55, 58, 59; rejection of orthodoxy but not Judaism, 36, 55–56, 59; sanctification of life, 59; and second-generation guilt, 67; second-generation Jewish identity in America, 52, 56, 58, 59; second-generation mission, 58; second-generation *din Torah*, 52–53; second generation and religious response to Auschwitz, 49, 52–54; second-generation witness ritual, 56; *Summer Long-A-Coming*, 4, 22, 36–37, 48–59, 90, 96, 97, 155, 184; and task as writer, 48; theodicy, 22, 49–50, 52–55, 57, 58, 184; *tikkun atzmi*, 56, 59; *tikkun* of bearing witness, 55, 59; *tikkun* of family, 31; *tikkun* of ordinary decency, 58 *tikkun* of story-telling, 52; traditional rituals and Holocaust remembrance, 52, 56; transformation of image of God, 55; transmission to third generation, 58, 59 ; validity of Orthodoxy after Auschwitz, 52–54

Finkielkraut, Alain: comparison with Bukiet, 73; image of protagonist, 42; second generation social type, 2

First International Conference of Children of Holocaust Survivors (1984), 18

First-generation witnesses: as a new first generation in America, 19; American culture and wartime experiences, 15; attitude toward traditional Judaism, 36; and "conspiracy of silence," 6; and death of eyewitnesses, 1; experiences of during the Holocaust, 2; and indirect communication, 39; parenting after the Holocaust, 2–3, 10, 35–36; post-Auschwitz survival, 60–61, 68; post-war family types, 14

Fisher, Seymour and Rhoda Drs.: humor as means of managing terror, 151

Fischer, Jack and Danny: and comparison with Brand, 137, 138, 139, 140; and comparison with Fackenheim, 139; and comparison with Finkelstein, 137; and comparison with Friedmann, 140; and comparison with Ravett, 147; and comparison with Salamon, 136, 137; and comparison with Spiegelman, 137, 140; and comparison with Wiesel, 139; difference between survivors and second-generation, 136, 138, 139; and distinction between experience and imagination, 136, 139; dynamics of contemporary Jewish identity, 140; effect of Holocaust legacy, 136, 137, 138–140; family ritual enactment, 136, 140; *A Generation Apart*, 4, 131, 136–140, 144, 154, 186, 189; intergenerational communication, 136, 137, 138–139; and interpretation of parents' experience, 186; memory and survivor families, 139; *presence of an absence*, 139; Jewish reproduction after the *Shoah*, 140; and parent-child relations, 189; and reference to Hass, 137–138; and reference to Langer, 136; second-generation denial, 137; second-generation identity and parental expectations, 136, 137–138; second-generation guilt, 137–138; and second-generation kinship, 137, 139, 186; second-

Fischer, Jack and Danny *(continued)* generation perceptions of Holocaust legacy, 139; second generation as "witnesses to memory," 139; second-generation "replacement" children, 138; the *Shoah* and second-generation identity, 136, 137, 138, 139, 140; survival of the Jewish people, 140; survivor child-rearing practices, 138, 186; survivor memories, 136–137, 138–139; survivors and depersonalization, 138; survivors and post-Auschwitz faith, 140; and *tikkun* of family, 31; *tikkun* of human relations, 137; traditional ritual and Holocaust remembrance, 140; transmission to third generation, 137

*The Flood. See* Ascher, Carol.

Fogelman, Eva, 140–141: adolescent attitude toward Jewish legacy, 143; art as second-generation testimony, 143; *Breaking the Silence*, 4, 10, 16, 130, 131, 140–146, 154; and child rescuers, 176; and comparison with Ascher, 143; and comparison with Friedmann, 142; and comparison with Finkelstein, 142; and comparison with Fischers, 144; and comparison with Klein, 143; and comparison with Raphael, 143; and comparison with Ravett, 147; and comparison with Salamon, 142, 145; and comparison with Spiegelman, 142, 143; and complexity of moral decisions, 161; *Conscience and Courage: Rescuers of Jews During the Holocaust*, 141; and "conspiracy of silence," 141, 142, 178; difference between first- and second-generation witness, 143; and "economically based Judeophilism," 179; effects of *Shoah's* legacy, 143; Holocaust's lessons and non-Jews, 145; immigrant and survivor experience, 143; indirect communication, 142; initiation of children-of-survivor awareness groups, 15–16, 140–141; intergenerational communication, 142, 143, 144, 145, 187; issues of loss and mourning, 142; and Jewish Foundation for Christian Rescuers, 181; and Jewish identity after the Holocaust, 130; memory and Jewish historical experience, 144; psychological aspects of Holocaust legacy, 141, 143; and reference to Epstein, 144, 146; and reference to Gruenbaum, 141, 144, 145; and reference to Hass, 143; and reference to Levi, 142; and reference to Lifton, 131, 144–145; and reference to Mason, 131; and reference to Rosensaft, 141, 145; and reference to Waldoks, 144, 145; relationship of second-generation identity, Jewish history, and parents' experience, 141, 142, 143, 144, 145–146, 186; and Rubinek's *So Many Miracles*, 175; second-generation anger, 143; and second-generation denial, 41–42; and second-generation discussion group, 141, 145–146; second-generation expression of Jewishness, 29, 143; second generation and moral improvement of society, 145; second generation and particularist lesson, 146; second generation and memory of the *Shoah*, 145; second generation and *tikkun* of family relations, 144; second generation and *tikkun* of self, 144; second generation as "replacement" children, 144; and second-generation sense of mission, 15, 145; second-generation witness and memory, 142, 143; societal impact of *tikkun* of bearing witness, 145; societal indifference during the *Shoah*, 145; survivor parents as overprotective, 10; survivors and "death imprint,"141, 142; survivors' distrust of outside world, 144; survivors' flawed parenting skills, 142; survivors, second-generation witnesses, and American ethnic groups, 9, 19; survivors' separation anxiety, 144; *tikkun* of ordinary decency, 145; transmission to third generation, 142, 143; and unity of the second-generation, 100, 186; universal dimension of second-generation, 144

*Forms of Captivity and Escape. See* Steinfeld, J.J.

Fresco, Nadine, 95–96; and second generation in France, 2

*"Fresh Air." See* Raphael, Lev.

Friedlander, Albert: and post-Holocaust covenant, 185; second generation as "Riders Towards the Dawn," 11; *Riders toward the Dawn: From Ultimate Despair to Temperate Hope*, 11; American version of subtitle, *From Holocaust to Hope*, 11; and witness generation, 187

Friedlander, Saul: "working through" the Holocaust, 129

Friedmann, Thomas, 20; biblical and Holocaust literature, 46; *Damaged Goods*, 4, 5, 36–47, 90, 97, 106, 140, 178, 184; and central issues raised, 38, 47; and comparison with Ascher, 90; and comparison with Fogelman, 142; and comparison with Raphael, 111, 114, 119, 122; and comparison with Ravett, 146; and comparison with Rosenbaum, 79; and comparison with Salamon, 96, 104, 106–107; and comparison

with Spiegelman, 42, 46, 60, 61, 62, 67, 69, 70, 71; and comparison with Steinfeld, 78; validity of Orthodoxy after Auschwitz, 45–47; and distinctive element of writing, 38; and Finkelstein's *Summer Long-A-Coming*, 53, 56, 57; image of protagonist, 42, 46, 67; image of survivor parents, 10, 37–47 *passim*; issue of indirect communication, 39–41; meaning of absent grandparents, 40–41; orthodox world and rituals, 38–47 *passim*; parents' "conspiracy of silence," 41, 178; parents' survival lessons, 41, 47; post-Auschwitz second-generation identity, 45–47; rejection of orthodoxy but not Judaism, 36, 47; second-generation denial, 41–42; second-generation images of survivors, 42; second-generation shaping memory of the *Shoah*, 43; second-generation witness and study of *Shoah*, 44–47; and Shapiro docudramas, 152; *Shoah* treated in American context, 38, 42; and similarity to Fackenheim, 47; and similarity to Greenberg, 43–44, 46, 47; and similarity to Wiesel, 39, 42, 47; theodicy, 39, 184; *tikkun atzmi*, 41, 45; traditional ritual and Holocaust remembrance, 43–44; transmission to third generation, 45; treatment of survivor community, 42–43

*"The Funeral." See* Steinfeld, J.J.

Gelfman, Shelley: artist and second-generation adult-child, 137

*Gemara*, 54

*gematria*, 69

*A Generation Apart. See* Fischer, Jack and Danny.

Genocide Treaty, 15

Glascow, Ellen, 56
Goodstein, Debbie: and Polish antisemitism, 180; and comparison with Abramowicz, 178; and comparison with Brand, 179; and comparison with Epstein, 177; and comparison with Fogelman, 178, 179; and comparison with Friedmann, 178; and comparison with Ravett, 178; and comparison with Rubinek, 178, 179; and comparison with Sauvage, 178, 179; and comparison with Spiegelman, 177; and comparison with Wiesel, 178; and complexity of Jewish-Christian relations, 180; and "conspiracy of goodness," 179; difference between survivors and second generation, 180; distrust of social world and fear for safety, 178; and "economically based Judeophilism," 179; and generational legacy for murderers and victims, 180; importance of survivor testimony, 177; and issue of altruistic suffering, 180; and issue of mourning, 180; Jewish suffering and the Holocaust, 179–180; and meeting parents' rescuer, 178, 179; and particularist lesson, 180; pilgrimage to Europe, 177, 178, 179, 180; and political theology, 180; Post-Holocaust Poland, 178–179; and prosocial actions of rescuers, 181; and reference to Bar-On, 180; and reference to Insdorf, 177; second generation and Holocaust imagery, 177; and rescuer motivation, 179, 180; second-generation mission, 161; second generation and parent's survivor guilt, 180; second-generation perception and the Holocaust, 177; second generation and *presence of the absence*, 177; second-generation witness and Holocaust legacy, 177, 178; second-generation witness and *tikkun atzmi*, 180; second-generation witness and *tikkun olam*, 180; *Shoah's* universal impact, goodness and moral behavior, 161; survivor "conspiracy of silence," 177; survivor Holocaust secrets, 178; "survivor mission," 179; and *tikkun* of family, 31; transmission to third generation, 180; and unity of the second-generation, 186 universal understanding of Jewish chosenness, 179; *Voices from the Attic*, 4, 20, 161, 177–180

Greenberg, Irving: and American Jews and second-generation witness, 25, 81; and applied theology, 8, 88; covenant transformation, 25; covenantal theology of (Voluntary Covenant), 8, 10, 22, 25–28, 47, 55, 69–70, 84, 88, 110, 125–126, 130, 168, 185, 189; dialectic of *tikkun atzmi* and *tikkun olam*, 27; divine hiddenness, 26–27, 189; Holocaust memory and ritual observance, 43–44, 49; and Jewish peoplehood, 135; and Jewish reproduction after the *Shoah*, 140; the masking of holiness, 25, 189; and post-Auschwitz problem of theodicy, 49, 83; and Purim as *the* holiday of the diaspora, 27; reference to Rabbi Soloveitchik, 43; religious testimony after Auschwitz, 164–165; sanctification of life, 59; second generation, theology, and identity for, 27, 33, 36; secularization and Jewish affirmation, 25–27, 36, 46, 69, 158, 184; shift in thought, 23; and survivor testimony, 75, 82; theology and Post-Auschwitz Judaism, 83–84, 91–92, 190

Gruenbaum, Henry Dr.: and second-generation children as "compensation," 144; and second-generation discussion group, 141; survivor parents and second generation reconnection, 145

Gutman, Sandy (a.k.a. Austen Tayshus): impact of Holocaust on second generation, 152; as newlywed, 152; performer in *Angst*, 150; second generation and survivor relationship, 152; second-generation pain and anger, 150–151; transmission to third generation, 152; tragic dimension of humor, 151–152. *See Angst*.

*haham*: in Shapiro, 153

*Hakarat Hatov*: and second-generation witness and non-Jewish rescuers, 160, 189

*halakha/halakhic*, 43, 70

*Half-Sister. See* Ravett, Abraham.

Halkin, Hillel: and Spiegelman's *Maus*, 64

Hanukkah: and Fischers' *A Generation Apart*, 140; and *Hallel*, 140; and post-Auschwitz context, 140; and Sauvage's *Weapons of the Spirit*, 172

Hanukkiah: in Sauvage's *Weapons of the Spirit*, 171

Hansen, Marcus, 19

*Happuch*, 6

Hartmann, Geoffrey H.: and age of testimony, 21; eyewitness generation and return of memory, 184; role of second-generation witnesses, 1–2, 184; second-generation Holocaust legacy, trauma, and memory, 184; and "sequelae of a catastrophic memory," 3; and Spiegelman's *Maus*, 63–64; universal impact of the *Shoah*, 7

*Hasidei Umot Ha-Olam*, 31; and essence of religious behavior, 160; frameworks of non-Jewish helpers and rescuers, 159–160; and meaning of religion, 160; and mending of the world, 160; motivations of non-Jewish helpers and rescuers, 159, 160; and second-generation filmmakers, 130, 158–182 *passim*; and Spiegelman's *Maus*, 69; and universalist implications of films about, 160

Hasidic dance: in Rosenbaum's *"The Rabbi Double-Faults,"* 83, 84

Hasidism, 93–94; in Raphael's *Winter Eyes*, 125

Hass, Aaron, 3, 129; and absence of grandparents, 40; and distrust of non-Jewish social world, 101; and early awareness of children of survivors, 11; difference between first- and second-generation transmission, 143; and Holocaust-induced flawed parenting, 112, 113; and post-Auschwitz covenant theology, 21; and post-Auschwitz Jewish African-American relations, 108, 109; and empathy for survivor parent's experiences, 15; and second-generation guilt, 137–138; and second-generation identity and fear, 111; and second-generation and family's European history, 15

Helmreich, William: *Against All Odds: Holocaust Survivors and the Successful Lives They Made in America*, 10; "curtain of silence," 82; *A Generation After*, 99; second generation trends and tendencies, 14; survivor-parent images and second-generation witness, 10–11, 51, 81, 99;

Hidden Child Meeting (1991): and Myriam Abramowicz, 167, 210 n. 12

Hidden Children, meeting, experiences of, identity. *See* Abramowicz, Myriam.

Hillberg, Raul: types of non-Jewish helpers and rescuers, 159, 162, 168, 173

*"Himmler's Chickens." See* Bukiet, Melvin.

Hiroshima, 8

*"History." See* Steinfeld, J. J.

Hoffenberg, Esther: antisemitic restrictions in Belgian, 162; *As If It Were Yesterday*, 4, 161, 162–167; collaboration in Belgium, 163, 164; deportation of rescuers with hidden children, 162; description of rescuers, 162, 164; discussions between helpers and the helped, 163; emotions of rescuers, 163; hidden children and identity confusion, 167; hidden children memories, terror, and uncertainty, 165; hidden children and post-Auschwitz life, 166; hidden children and psychological scars, 165–166, 167; hidden children and their mothers, 163, 164; Holocaust experience and Belgium's Jews, 162; humanizing plight of the Jewish people, 165; implications of *tikkun* of ordinary decency, 161; Jewish self-help during the *Shoah*, 164; reaction of Jewish audiences, 167; and reference to Greenberg, 164–165; and reference to Hillberg, 162; rescuer attitudes towards Jews and Judaism, 163; rescuer motivation, 164, 166–167; role of women rescuers, 165; second-generation mission, 161; the *Shoah* and identity of hidden children, 162, 165, 166. 167; the *Shoah's* universal impact, goodness and moral behavior, 161; use of humor, 164

Holocaust: contemporary source of identity for second-generation witnesses, 1, 3, 4; continuing aftermath of, 2, 3; and issue of comparative suffering, 120; as *novum* in history, 120; second-generation images of and bearing witness to, 3, 19–20; transmission from generation to generation, 1–2; watershed event in Jewish and human history, 22. *See also Shoah*

Holocaust denial: phenomenon of, 120

Holocaust Memory: in contemporary Jewish and American culture, 11; and historical, interpretative, and phenomenological questions, 120; and linking generations, 183; and mending of the world, 184; and paradigm shift, 20; and particularist truth, 183; particularist and universalist expressions, 184; and *presence of an absence*, 184; shaped by second-generation writings and films, 9, 19–22, 129; and Spiegelman's *Maus*, 66; and *tikkun* of self, 184

Homosexuality: and Conservative Judaism, 118; and modernity's challenge to classical Judaism, 188; and Orthodox Judaism, 118; and Reconstructionist and Reform Judaism, 118

Huber, Kurt: Munich philosopher, 30

*"Ida Solomon's Play." See* Steinfeld, J. J.

*In Memory. See* Ravett, Abraham.

*"Inheritance." See* Raphael, Lev.

Insdorf, Annette: and Brand, 132; and Goodstein's *Voices from the Attic*, 177; and Rubinek, 174; and second-generation "cinematic return," 161; documentary and personal voice, 130

Jerusalem Temple: destruction of First, 44, 121; destruction of Second, 26, 44, 121; and Kamtza and Bar-Kamtza talmudic tale, 156; sacrifice at, 46

Jew-hatred: and Spiegelman's *Maus*, 71

Jewish history: as paradigm for type of covenant, 26; transmission of early transformative events, 1; transmission of the Holocaust story, 1, 57

Jewish identity: and dialectical tension between universalism and particularism, 4; particularist expression of, 4, 35; and relationship to *Shoah*, 1, 10, 19–22, 28; and second-generation witnesses, 2–3, 16, 19–22, 28, 29 *passim*; universalist expression of, 4, 6

kabbalistic tradition: and sexual intercourse as a *tikkun* of the world, 116–117

*kaddish*, 65; in Brand, 132, 134

*Kaddish. See* Brand, Steven.

Kafka, Franz: *"Josephine the Singer,"* 62; *"The Mouse Folk,"* 62

Kamtza and Bar-Kamtza: talmudic tale of, 153, 156, 157

*k'doshim*: and Fackenheim's covenantal theology, 187

*k'lal Yisrael*: in Fischers' *A Generation Apart*, 140

Klepfisz, Irena, 124; Jewish feminism, traditional teachings and orthopraxy, 125

Kominsky-Crumb, Aline: *Wimmen's Comix*, 62

Korda, Gabriela, 126

Kuperstein, Ilana: second-generation identity as American and Jews, 153; second-generation Jewish identity and Holocaust , 130

*Kristallnacht*, 31

*lager*, 43

"lamed-vovnicks," 45

Langer, Lawrence: "deep memories," 43; and "humiliated memory," 136; interviews with Holocaust survivors, 61; and Spiegelman's *Maus*, 63, 66; "witnesses to memory," 20

Le Chambon-sur-Lignon: and deeds of the righteous, 161; and rescuer network, 159–160

*"Lessons." See* Raphael, Lev.

Levi, Primo: *The Drowned and the Saved*, 68; and memory, 142; and *Muselmänner*, 105; and Steinfeld, 76

Lewinska, Peglia: Polish prisoner at Auschwitz concentration camp, 30

Liberman, Serge, 183, 212 n. 2, 212 n. 3

*"The Library of Moloch." See* Bukiet, Melvin.

Lichtenberg, Bernhard, 30–31

*"The Life You Have." See* Raphael, Lev.

Lifton, Robert J.: and death imprint, 112; and first-generation witnesses post-Holocaust life, 2; phenomenon of *psychic numbing*, 39, 104; and the *Muselmänner*, 105; and second-generation discussion group, 141; and second generation as social movement, 144–145

Linenthal, Edward T.: and universalizing the Holocaust and its legacy, 118

Lipstadt, Deborah: "complex web of issues" and children of survivors, 14; nonwitnesses and survivor experiences, 7; children of survivors and other catastrophic events, 9

*"The Little Blue Snowman of Washington Heights." See* Rosenbaum, Thane.

Lodz Ghetto, 149
"*Lost in a Sense.*" *See* Rosenbaum, Thane.

*Magen David*, 80; in Fischers' *A Generation Apart*, 138; in Shapiro's *Open Secrets*, 157
Maidanek: and Rosenbaum, 72; and Sauvage's *Weapons of the Spirit*, 169
Maimonides: twelfth principle of faith, 73
Marrano Jews, 109
Mason, Edward: director of Fogelman's *Breaking the Silence*, 141
*Mattan Torah*: and trial of God in Auschwitz, 133
*Maus. See* Spiegelman, Art.
Meyer, Michael A.: antisemitism and Jewish identity, 90–91, 94; and "Judaism of defiance," 102
*mezzuzoth*, 38–39, 157
Mittelberg, David: and second-generation socialization, 138
*Moviegoer:* and Solomon, 96
Munch, Eduard: *The Scream*, 68
*Muselmänner*, 105

Nachman of Bratslav, Reb, 143
Nagasaki, 8
Nathan, Ruth: and Australasian Holocaust Descendants Gathering, 150; and transmission of "holocaust of the mind," 150
Neige: and *As If It Were Yesterday*, 162
Neusner, Jacob: survivors and earlier second-generation American Jews, 19
*New Yorker:* and Spiegelman, 59
*New York Times:* and Solomon, 96; and Spiegelman, 63
*New York Times Book Review*, 63

Nissenson, Hugh: *My Own Ground*, 62
Norich, Samuel: and second-generation discussion group, 141

*Open Secrets. See* Shapiro, Own J.
*Ostjuden*, 94, 102
Ozick, Cynthia: *Rosa* and attitudes towards survivors, 109

"*The Pants in the Family.*" *See* Rosenbaum, Thane.
*parsha Truma*, 69
Passover: in Fischers' *A Generation Apart*, 137; in Rosenbaum's "*Elijah Visible*," 82; in Raphael's "*Abominations*," 121; in Shapiro, 153
Porter, Jack Nusan: "sociopolitical syndrome" and Holocaust inheritance, 15–16, 87, 101
Post-Auschwitz Jewish Thought: figure of Job, the Holocaust, and contemporary Jewish identity, 6
Post-Auschwitz Jewish Identity: and second-generation artistic works, 15; significance of inheriting the Holocaust, 7
Post-Holocaust Theology: as applied theology, 8, *passim*; and Greenberg, 8, 88, *passim*; and Pierre Sauvage, 168, 170, *passim*; and second-generation witnesses, 22, 27, 88, 184, *passim*; and Wiesel, 8, *passim*
*Punch Me in the Stomach. See* Filler, Deb.
Prince, Robert M.: second generation and Holocaust imagery, 67, 101, 132; second-generation themes, 104, 204 n.33
Purim: in Brand's *Kaddish*, 134; and Spiegelman's *Maus*, 70; as rabbinic

covenantal paradigm, 26–27; and role of Esther and Mordecai, 26

"*The Rabbi Double-Faults.*" *See* Rosenbaum, Thane.

Raphael, Lev: "*Abominations,*" 117–120; absent grandparents, 111, 122; and antisemitism and the gay movement, 124; and antisemitism and homophobia, 88, 111, 112, 115, 117–119, 120, 123, 125, 126; "*Caravans,*" 115, 123, 125; and Christian rescuers, 119–120; and comparison with Ascher, 110–111, 116, 119, 121, 123, 125; and comparison with Brand, 132, 134; and comparison with Friedmann, 111, 114, 119, 122; and comparison with Finkelstein, 111, 112; and comparison with Fogelman, 143; and comparison with Greenberg, 110, 125–126; and comparison with Klepfisz, 124, 125; and comparison with Salamon, 110–111, 112, 115, 116, 119, 122, 123; and comparison with Sauvage, 172; and comparison with second-generation filmmakers, 130; and comparison with Spiegelman, 110, 111, 114, 116, 119, 120, 123; and comparison with Steinfeld, 112, 122; and comparison with Wiesel, 110, 113, 114, 117, 119, 121; and compulsion to bear witness to the Holocaust, 111; and concern with gay and bisexual issues, 21, 110–126 *passim*; "*Connections,*" 122; and "conspiracy of silence," 113, 114, 122, 123; *Dancing on Tisha B'Av,* 4, 88, 110, 113, 121, 122; and "death imprint" among survivors, 111, 112; and *din Torah,* 185; and "dissimilation,"

125; distant parental relationships, 111, 112, 113, 115, 122, 126; and effect of Holocaust legacy, 111, 113, 115, 116, 117, 119, 122, 123, 124, 125; and estrangement, Jewish heritage, and American culture, 111, 115–116, 123, 124; "*Fresh Air,*" 112, 113; and gay triumphalism, 121, 126; and "God is dead" approach, 32; and gulf between survivors and offspring, 111, 112, 113, 114, 115–116, 120, 122–123, 126; the Holocaust and abortion, 112; the Holocaust and universal tolerance, 110, 115, 119; and homophobia within the Jewish community, 118; "*Inheritance,*" 113–114; issue of loss and mourning, 111, 122; and issue of *Wiedergutmachung,* 113–114, 115; and Jewish identity and sexual orientation, 110, 113, 115, 117–119, 121–126; and Jewish self-hatred, 110, 120, 122, 125, 126; as a Jewish writer 110; and kinship among second-generation, 115; and Lambda Literary Award, 110, 111; "*Lessons,*" 122; "*The Life You Have,*" 112; and the presence of an absence, 111, 122; and psychological effect of Holocaust, 88, 116, 123, 125; and reference to Epstein, 115; and reference to Hass, 111, 112, 113; and reference to Lifton, 112; relationship of Holocaust to contemporary Jewish identity, 110, 115, 116, 122, 123, 125; and repair of the social order, 110–111, 121–122; and reproduction after the Holocaust, 112; and second-generation and emotional burden, 113, 116, 122–123, 124, 125; and second-

Raphael, Lev *(continued)*
    generation identity and fear, 111;
    and second-generation identity,
    psychosocial terms, and
    theological issues, 111, 112, 116,
    121, 123; and second-generation
    identity and *tikkun olam*, 126;
    second-generation isolation and
    friendship, 116; and second-
    generation Jewish identity and
    ethnicity, 124–126; and second-
    generation mission and straight
    and gay communities, 110,
    118–119; and second-generation
    as replacement children, 114; and
    second-generation witness and
    authenticity, 119; and second-
    generation identity as Jewish and
    gay, 110, 111, 118–126; second-
    generation witness and survivor
    suffering, 112, 114–115, 116; and
    second-generation witness and
    unwarranted suffering, 124;
    "*Separate Lives*," 122; and
    siblings of nonwitnessing parents,
    117; and singularity of survivor
    families, 122; survivors' flawed
    parenting skills, 112, 114, 115,
    122, 123, 126; survivor images,
    10, 111, 112, 115, 116, 123;
    survivor rage, 116, 122; and
    survivor revenge, 112; and *tikkun*
    of family, 31, 119; and *tikkun* of
    the self, 119, 126; "War Stories,"
    113; *Winter Eyes*, 4, 88, 110, 122,
    126, 172; and writing as act of
    *tikkun*, 121–122, 126–127
*rasha*: in Shapiro, 154
Ravett, Abraham, 146; and
    comparison with Bukiet, 146–147;
    and comparison with Finkelstein,
    150; and comparison with
    Friedmann, 146; and comparison
    with Klein, 147; and comparison
    with Rosenbaum, 150; and
    comparison with Salamon, 150;
    and comparison with Spiegelman,
    147, 150; and comparison with
    Wiesel, 147; divine compassion
    during the Holocaust, 149;
    *Everything's For You*, 4, 131, 147;
    father-son relationship, 147, 149;
    *Half-Sister*, 4, 131; Holocaust
    history and understanding of
    Holocaust, 147; Holocaust past
    and American present/future, 148;
    *In Memory*, 4, 131, 149;
    interaction of Jews and Christians
    after Holocaust, 148; issues of loss
    and mourning, 148; "memory,"
    reconstruction, and mourning,
    146; and parental "conspiracy of
    silence," 146, 178; presence of an
    absence, 146; relationship to God,
    149; relationship of self and
    history, 149; and role of silence,
    146–147, 150; second-generation
    anger, 148; second generation and
    elusive presence of Holocaust,
    147; second-generation Holocaust
    icons, 147; second-generation
    identity and bearing witness, 146,
    149, 150; second generation and
    murdered prewar family, 146,
    147, 148, 149; second generation
    and nature of post-Auschwitz
    memory, 146, 150; second
    generation and *tikkun atzmi*, 150;
    second-generation and survivor
    secrets, 149; survivor bitterness,
    148; survivors' experience and
    second-generation identity, 148;
    survivors' post-Auschwitz lives,
    148; survivor testimony as new
    post-Auschwitz ritual, 150; third
    generation witness, 147, 149;
    *tikkun* of bearing witness and
    Holocaust legacy, 149; traditional
    rituals and Holocaust
    remembrance, 149; witnessing
    generation and offspring, 149
*Raw* magazine: and Spiegelman, 59
Riskin, Shlomo: and Jewish
    reproduction after the *Shoah*, 140

Roethke, Theodore, 95
*"Romancing the Yohrzeit Light." See*
    Rosenbaum, Thane.
Rosenbaum, Thane, 72; *"An Act of
    Defiance,"* 79, 80; *"Bingo by the
    Bungalow,"* 80; *"Cattle Car
    Complex,"* 80; *Elijah Visible*, 4, 37,
    80, 97; *"Elijah Visible,"* 81; and
    comparison with Buber, 83; and
    comparison with Finkelstein, 80;
    and comparison with Friedmann,
    79; and comparison with
    Greenberg, 81, 82, 83, 84; and
    comparison with Ravett, 150; and
    comparison with Rubenstein, 83;
    and comparison with Salamon, 80;
    and comparison with Spiegelman,
    80; and comparison with Steinfeld,
    79; and comparison with Wiesel,
    81, 82, 83, 84; and "conspiracy of
    silence," 82; difference between
    survivors and second-generation,
    81; death imprint, 80; dynamics in
    survivor families, 81; and effect of
    Holocaust legacy, 79–81; and
    Fackenheim's 614th
    Commandment, 81; images of
    survivors, 80, 81; and implicit
    theological position, 81; issues of
    loss and mourning, 79, 80; *"The
    Little Blue Snowman of
    Washington Heights,"* 79; *"Lost, in
    a sense,"* 80, 184; mimesis of
    parents' Holocaust experience,
    79–80; modernity, America, and
    Post-Holocaust Judaism, 81, 82;
    *"The Pants in the Family,"* 80, 81;
    and psychological legacy of *Shoah*,
    79, 80, 81; *"The Rabbi Double-
    Faults,"* 82; reference to Helmreich,
    81, 82; *"Romancing the Yohrzeit
    Light,"* 81; second-generation guilt,
    79; second-generation sense of loss,
    80; second-generation mission, 80,
    81; second-generation witness and
    Holocaust inheritance, 71–72, 79,
    81, 84; and survivor *din Torah*, 81;

survivors' flawed parenting skills,
    79, 80; survivor testimony and
    prophet Elijah, 81, 82; and
    theodicy, 80, 184; theology and
    Post-Auschwitz Judaism, 82–84;
    and *tikkun atzmi*, 80; transmission
    of Holocaust legacy, 80, 82, 84;
    and unity of the second-generation,
    186; untimely death, 80;
    unwarranted suffering, 80; as
    witness to the *presence of an
    absence*, 79
Rosenbush, Miriam Strilky: *The
    Legacy: Children of Holocaust
    Survivors*, 130
Rosenfeld, Alvin: *A Double Dying:
    Reflections on Holocaust
    Literature*, 19; "phenomenology of
    reading Holocaust Literature," 19,
    22
Rosensaft, Menchem Z., 13, 87; and
    second-generation discussion
    group, 141; second-generation
    movement and human rights
    issues, 145; second generation and
    mission, 8, 95
Rubenstein, Eli: covenant and second-
    generation post-Holocaust
    lifestyle, 21–22
Rubenstein, Richard L.: *After
    Auschwitz*, 32; covenantal
    theology of, 10, 22–23, 31–33, 60,
    70; earlier theological writings, 32,
    133; encounter with Dean
    Heinrich Grüber, 31–32; and
    Fackenheim's "614th
    Commandment," 29; and "God
    After the Death of God," 32; and
    "God is Dead" theology, 22–23,
    31, 83, 93; notion of covenant 8;
    shift in thought, 23
Rubinek, Saul: and altruism, 172; and
    child rescuer, 176; and comparison
    with Abramowicz, 174, 176; and
    comparison with Goodstein, 179;
    and comparison with Sauvage,
    174, 175, 176; and comparison

Rubinek, Saul *(continued)*
with Wiesel, 177; continuing
impact of the *Shoah*, 174;
dynamics of survivor families, 174;
film's theology, 177; film's
universal message, 177; first- and
second-generation memory, 174;
indifference of institutional
Catholic Church, 176; Jewish
victims and fear, 175; Jewish
victims teaching gentiles, 175; and
moral and ethical precepts, 177;
and prewar, Holocaust, and post-
*Shoah* lives, 174; and prosocial
actions of rescuers, 181; and
reference to Fogelman, 175, 176;
and reference to Hillberg, 173; and
reference to Insdorf, 174;
relationship between first- and
second-generation witness, 174;
rescuer motivation, 174, 175–176;
and "Rider Towards the Dawn,"
176; role of women rescuers, 176;
second-generation desire to
understand parents, 174; second-
generation identity and parents'
Holocaust experience, 173–174;
second-generation mission, 161;
second generation, the *Shoah*, and
*tikkun* of bearing witness, 174,
176; second-generation witness,
176; *Shoah's* universal impact,
goodness, and moral behavior,
161; *So Many Miracles*, 4, 20,
161, 172–177; structure of film,
174; survivor anger at God, 177;
survivor children and Jewish
identity, 176; survivors' experience
while hiding, 174–175; *tikkun* of
ordinary decency, 161;


Sachsenhausen, 22
Salamon, Julie, 20, 95; antisemitism,
racism, and American culture,
107, 109, 126; attitudes towards
survivors, 109; and children of
survivors and of nonwitnesses,
100, 101, 109–110; and
comparison with Ascher, 90, 96,
101, 104, 109; and comparison
with Brand, 132; and comparison
with Finkelstein, 96, 97, 99, 100,
103, 104, 105, 106; and
comparison with Fischers, 136,
137; and comparison with
Fogelman, 142, 145; and
comparison with Friedmann, 96,
97, 104, 106–107; and
comparison with Raphael,
110–111, 112, 115, 116, 119,
122, 123; and comparison with
Ravett, 147, 150; and comparison
with Rosenbaum, 80, 97; and
comparison with Spiegelman, 97,
99, 100, 101, 102, 107, 109; and
comparison with Wiesel, 97, 107;
critique of postmodernism, 108;
dynamics in survivor families,
106, 110; and focus on
multiculturalism, 21; and
Holocaust, Jewish identity, and
American culture, 96, 102–103,
106, 109; and Holocaust legacy,
memory, and imagery, 96, 97,
100, 101, 103; and indifference of
survivor parents, 186; indirect
communication, 97–98, 101, 102;
issues of loss and mourning, 96,
101, 104–106; and mimesis of
parents' Holocaust experience, 99,
104; and morally corrupt political
system, 88; murdered siblings and
survivor households, 106; and *Net
of Dreams, The*, 203 n. 25; and
particularist and universalist
themes, 96, 103–104, 106, 107,
108, 126; and post-Auschwitz
theodical issues, 104–106, 184;
and quest for social justice, 96;
and reference to Epstein, 101,
102; and reference to Fackenheim,
107; and reference to Fine, 96;
and reference to Hass, 101, 108,

109; and reference to Levi, 105; and reference to Lifton, 104–105; and reference to Mengele, 106; and reference to Meyer, 102; and reference to Ozick, 109; and reference to Porter, 101; and reference to Prince, 101, 103; and reference to Steinitz, 98; second-generation and action of helpers, 107; and second-generation ambivalence, 96, 109; and second-generation feelings of unworthiness, 97; and second-generation guilt, 97–98; and second-generation identity and America, 96, 102–103; and second-generation identity and *tikkun olam*, 126; and second-generation identity and witness, 96, 97, 102, 103, 107; and second-generation jealousy, 99; and second-generation sense of isolation, 99–101; and second-generation, social justice, and social responsibility, 107–109; second-generation and suffering, 104–106; second-generation and survivor tales, 107, 110; second-generation welfare mothers, 108; seeking a *tikkun olam*, 96, 103; survivor families as *other*, 101; survivor silence, 101, 103; and theology of protest, 96; and *tikkun* of bearing witness, 96, 107; and *tikkun* of the helpers, 31; and a *tikkun* of the social order, 96; and *tikkun* of the world, 107; traditional ritual and Holocaust remembrance, 102; transmission to third generation, 104; and trivialization/distortion of the *Shoah*, 184–185; and view of the *Shoah*, 96; *White Lies*, 4, 5, 88, 90, 95–110, 122, 184, 186; presence of an absence, 96, 106–107; writing as act of *tikkun*, 126–127

Sanctification of life (*kedushat haHayim*): third element of Wiesel's Additional Covenant, 24–25

Sauvage, Pierre, 159; and acts of resistance, 170; and antisemitism, 169; and applied theology, 168, 170; Biblical ethic and authentic religious response, 169, 170; and Catholic minority, 169; Christianity, complicity, apostasy, and altruism, 171, 172; and comparison with Abramowicz, 168, 170, 172; and comparison with Finkelstein, 168; and comparison with Greenberg, 168; and comparison with Raphael, 172; and comparison with Rubinek, 174, 176; and comparison with Spiegelman, 172; and comparison with Wiesel, 172; complex emotions of rescued Jews, 170–171; and "conspiracy of goodness," 171, 172, 179; and deportation of French Jews, 169; and description of rescuers, 169, 170; and ecumenism, 170; and French collaboration, 169, 172; and Friends of LeChambon, 172; and fundamentalist Christians, 169; and issue of memory, 172; and Jewish identity, 171, 172; and Jewish responses to Nazi persecution, 172; and Jewish self-discovery, 172; and Jewish self-help, 172–173; Le Chambon and deeds of the righteous, 161, 172; notion of choice, 171; and reaction in Japan, 172; and reference to Camus, 168; and reference to Hillberg, 168; religious belief and Nazi resistance, 168, 169; and rescuer prosocial behavior, 168, 169, 170, 171, 181; rescuer motivation, 168, 169, 170; second-generation mission, 161; *Shoah's* universal impact, goodness, and

Sauvage, Pierre *(continued)*
  moral behavior, 161, 172; and
  *tikkun atzmi*, 172; and *tikkun*
  *olam*, 172; and *tikkun* of ordinary
  decency, 31, 161; and universal
  implications, 172; and universe of
  human obligation, 168; *Weapons*
  *of the Spirit*, 4, 20, 161, 168–177;
  and role of women rescuers, 189
Savran, Bella: and children-of-
  survivor awareness groups, 15–16,
  140–141; second-generation
  expression of Jewishness, 29;
  second generation and mission, 15
Schindler, Oskar: and moral
  motivation during the *Shoah*, 160
Second-generation witnesses (writers):
  and antisemitism, 87, 88; and
  applied theology, 10, 22, 27, 88,
  184; artistic work and theological
  context, 12, 21–22, 131; attitude
  toward orthodoxy, 36;
  autobiographical nature of artistic
  work, 19, 33; connection to other
  catastrophic events, 9, 15, 25, 90;
  constantly present and continually
  elusive legacy of, 3, 18, 184; and
  contemporary Jewish identity, 2,
  19–20, 23, 28, 35, 36, 84, 87,
  131, 182, 184, 185, 188, 190; and
  dialectic between *tikkun olam* and
  *tikkun atzmi*, 181, 188; and *din*
  *Torah*, 185; and distinctive Jewish
  path of particularism, 4, 7–8, 25,
  33, 35–85 *passim*, 87, 88, 188;
  and distinctive Jewish path of
  universalism, 4, 6, 8, 25, 84, 85,
  87–127 *passim*, 131, 181, 188;
  distinctive images and witness and
  memories of Holocaust, 3, 8, 11,
  19, 20; and distinctive post-
  Auschwitz covenant theology,
  21–22, 23, 24, 185, 190; and
  distinctive traits of American
  culture, 186, 190; distrust of social
  world, 188; and divine hiddenness,
  189; and features shared by

particularists and universalists,
  4–5, 6, 11–12, 87, 88, 184, 185,
  188; focus of testimony, 2, 188;
  "guardians of an absent meaning,"
  2; and feelings of guilt,
  ambivalence, loss, mourning, and
  denial, 16, 35, 87, 185; as
  heterogenous population, 13–14,
  157; images of survivors, 10, 36,
  185–186; impact of family type
  upon, 14; implicit second-
  generation theology, 88, 131;
  inform and sensitize about the
  Holocaust, 11, 16–17, 20, 84,
  184, 187, 190; and innocent
  suffering, 8; and intense emotional
  life, 186; intergenerational
  communication, 35, 131, 185,
  187; and interpretation of parents'
  experience, 186; and issue of
  theodicy, 184; and Jewish fate,
  184; and lack of parental
  boundaries, 186; lives shaped by
  Holocaust, 1, 3, 22, 24, 36, 84,
  87, 88, 186; mimesis of parents'
  Holocaust experience, 14–15, 35;
  moral role of post-Auschwitz
  literature, 188; number living in
  the United States, 1; as offspring of
  Jewish Holocaust survivors, 1, 10,
  19–20, 88, 131; and offspring of
  helpers, 181; and parent-child
  relations, 188; and partial *tikkun*
  of rupture, 8, 11, 29, 31;
  pathologized by studies, 13, 16,
  185; personal relationship to
  *Shoah*, 1, 15, 18, 20, 87, 131, 186,
  187; and post-Auschwitz
  covenant, 190; and post-
  Auschwitz Jewish life in America,
  10; postmodern and post-
  Holocaust worldviews, 9, 22, 28;
  and postwar fate of helpers, 181;
  reaction to Nazism, 36; reference
  to Fogelman, 181; reference to
  Porter, 87; relationship between
  sacred and secular, 88, 184; as

"replacement" children, 5; relationship to other American ethnic groups, 9, 16, 20, 186; responsibility for "parenting parents," 3, 186; as "Riders Towards the Dawn," 182, 187; and secular acts masking holiness, 189; secular midrash on post-Auschwitz Jewish identity, 9; and separation anxiety, 10, 131; and "sequelae of a catastrophic memory," 184; shape and ritualize Holocaust memory, 2–3, 11, 20–21, 33, 36, 85, 87, 182, 184, 186, 187, 188; *Shoah* and contemporary Jewish identity, 10, 21, 33, 37, 84, 87, 88, 184, 187, 188; specific identity rather than syndrome, 13; and Spielberg's "Survivors of the *Shoah* visual history project," 9; and Steinfeld's work, 87; and survivors' experiences and non-witnessing world, 118; and theological resonance, 88; and theology of protest, 36; and *tikkun* of bearing witness, 31, 88, 131, 190; and *tikkun* of family, 31; and *tikkun olam*, 84, 87, 185; and *tikkun* of ordinary decency, 88; and *tikkun* of the self, 31, 33, 36, 84, 87, 185; traditional imagery and Jewish legacy, 9, 28; transmission to third generation, 7, 187, 190; as transitional stage in Holocaust memorialization, 188; and tributes to the righteous, 181; and trivialization/distortion of the *Shoah*, 184; as voice of survivor parents, 3, 131, 185, 186; as witness to the *presence of an absence*, 2, 20; and women rescuers, 181

Second-generation witnesses (filmmakers): and abbreviated or lost childhoods, 129; and altruistic behavior of rescuers, 181; autobiographical nature of, 19; and child survivors, 189; and comparison with Greenberg, 130, 158; and comparison with Raphael, 130; and comparison with Wiesel, 158; deeds of the righteous and moral behavior, 160; and dislike of Christianity, 188; and divine hiddenness, 189; and documentaries, 130; and docudramas, 130, 158; and effects of the *Shoah*, 127, 129, 130; focus on psycho-social issues, 129–130, 158; and *Hasidei Umot HaOlam*, 158, 181; Holocaust and philosophical, psychohistorical, and theological contexts, 131, 189; and individual voice of survivors, 129; and intergenerational communication, 188; and issues of loss and mourning, 129, 157; and Jewish identity after the Holocaust, 130, 158; and lack of extended family, 129; and moral example of non-Jewish rescuers, 189; and murdered grandparents, 129; and mystery of goodness and evil, 161; and non-Jewish rescuer motivation, 161, 189; and parent-child relationships, 157; particularist in nature, 4, 160, 188–189; and post-Auschwitz covenant, 189, 190; and post-Auschwitz Jewish life in America, 10, 190; and post-Auschwitz ritual tradition, 189; psychological and theological dimensions of, 127, 157, 158; reaction to deeds of the righteous, 161, 189; reference to Fackenheim, 160; reference to Fogelman, 161; reference to Insdorf, 161; relationship between particularism and universalism, 160, 189; rescuers and notion of choice, 189; the righteous and personal mending, 181; rituals and second-generation Jewish identity, 158,

Second-generation witnesses
(filmmakers) *(continued)*
189; role of women rescuers, 189;
second-generation bearing witness,
158, 161, 189; and second-
generation feelings of unworthiness,
129; second generation and Jewish
commitment, 158, 190; second
generation and Jewish history, 158;
second generation and Holocaust
legacy, 158, 161, 189, 190; second-
generation identity and the
Holocaust, 158, 161; second-
generation identity, survivor
parents' experience, and non-Jewish
rescuers, 161, 189; second
generation and sanctification of life,
158; second-generation witness and
non-Jewish rescuers, 159–182
*passim*, 189; and secular acts
masking holiness, 189; secular
midrash on post-Auschwitz Jewish
identity, 9; and shaping Holocaust
memory, 129; and survivors'
"conspiracy of silence," 129; and
survivors' flawed parenting skills,
129, 158; and *tikkun* of bearing
witness, 190; and *tikkun* of family,
31, 129, 188, 189; and *tikkun* of
self, 129, 158, 181, 188; and
*tikkun* of ordinary decency,
160–161, 189; and *tikkun* of
society, 129; and transmission to
third generation, 129, 190;
universal legacy of the Holocaust,
130, 158, 160; universalist in
nature, 4, 160, 181, 189
Segal, Lore Grozsmann: *Other
People's Houses*, 89
"*Separate Lives.*" *See* Raphael, Lev.
Shabbat: in Friedmann's *Damaged
Goods*, 38, 44; in Finkelstein's
*Summer Long-a-Coming*, 49, 50,
52, 58; in Brand's *Kaddish*, 132
Shapiro, Owen J: *Alinsky's Children*,
4, 152; American culture, Jews,
and the Holocaust, 153;
antisemitism, 155, 156, 157;
classical texts and post-Auschwitz
Jewish life, 155, 156, 157; and
comparison with *Breaking Silence*,
154; and comparison with *The
Flood*, 155; and comparison with
*A Generation Apart*, 154; and
comparison with *Kaddish*, 154;
and comparison with *Summer
Long-a-Coming*, 155; and
comparison with Spiegelman, 157;
and comparison with Wiesel, 157;
difference between documentaries
and docudramas, 152–153;
distinction between survivors and
offspring, 153, 157; *The Dr. John
Haney Sessions*, 152, 153, 154;
dynamics in survivor household,
155; family and transmission of
Jewish identity, 155, 157;
Holocaust, personal identity, and
second-generation therapy group,
153; Jewish particularist concerns,
154, 155; memory and Judaism,
155, 157; *Open Secrets*, 152,
154–157; post-Auschwitz
covenant, 153; *presence of an
absence*, 153, 155; and reference
to Friedmann, 152; reference to
Kuperstein, 153; relationship
between pre- and post-Auschwitz
Jewish identity, 156–157; religious
survivors and Holocaust legacy,
154; second-generation alienation
and separation, 153; second-
generation anger and confusion,
155; second generation and
forgiveness, 156; second
generation and Holocaust legacy,
154, 155, 157; second-generation
identity as American and Jews,
153; second-generation identity as
evolving process, 154; second-
generation issues, 156; second-
generation memory of the
Holocaust, 157; second generation
and post-Auschwitz rabbinic

teachings, 156, 157; second-generation quest, 153; second generation reaction types, 153–154; second generation and survivor parents' suffering, 153; second generation and survivor testimony, 157; second-generation and vengeance, 156; *Shoah* and contemporary Jewish identity, 153, 157; survivor distrust of social world, 155; survivor silence, 157; traditional rituals, Talmudic tales, and post-Holocaust Judaism, 153–154, 156, 157; universalist concerns, 154

Shavuot, 43, 44

*shekhinah*, 55, 116

*shiva*, 65

*Shoah*: and connection to second-generation, 3, 5, 16, 19–22, 24, 26; and contemporary Jewish identity, 1, 6, 10, 20, 22, 183; continuing and multidimensional sequelae, 19; increasing focus of American culture, 64; and murdered European-Jewish culture, 2, 11, 20. *See also* Holocaust

*Shul*, 42, 46, 81; in Brand, 132

*sinat hinam*: in Kamtza and Bar-Kamtza talmudic tale, 156

Singer, Isaac Bashevis: and comparison with Brand, 132; *Enemies, a Love Story*, 49, 132; and Finkelstein's *Summer Long-A-Coming*, 59; and treatment of evil, 49

Singerman, Al: and second-generation guilt, 99

Six Day War: in Raphael, 124

*So Many Miracles. See* Rubinek, Saul.

solidarity: and Jewish existence, 24; treatment within Wiesel's Additional Covenant, 24, 46, 88, 110, 172

Soloveitchik, Rabbi Joseph, 43; and murder of Jews of Europe, 57; and State of Israel, 133

Soltaroff, Ted, 19

Sontag, Susan: in Brand, 134; and Blumenthal's *In Dark Places*, 131, 134

Spiegelman, Art, 20, 25; affinities between postmodern and post-Holocaust worldviews, 63; and antisemitism, 71; as biographical and autobiographical writer, 60; and aesthetics of comic books, 21, 62, 63–64, 68; and comparison with Ascher, 90; and comparison with Finkelstein, 60, 61, 62, 66, 67, 70, 71; and comparison with Fischers, 137; and comparison with Fogelman, 142, 143; and comparison with Friedmann, 42, 46, 60, 61, 62, 66, 67, 69, 70, 71; and comparison with Goodstein, 177–178; and comparison with Kafka, 62; and comparison with Levi, 68; and comparison with Raphael, 110, 111, 114, 116, 119, 120, 123; and comparison with Ravett, 147, 150; and comparison with Rosenbaum, 80; and comparison with Salamon, 98, 99, 100, 101, 102; and comparison with Sauvage, 172; and comparison with Steinfeld, 78; and comparison with Wiesel, 61, 70; and *din Torah*, 70, 185; dynamics in survivor households, 61, 66; and effect of Holocaust legacy, 60, 61, 64, 66–68, 71; and "God is dead," 32; and Holocaust memory, 66–67, 68; images of survivor parents, 60–61, 64, 65, 66–68, 109; implicit covenantal view, 33, 69–70; and Jewish history and identity, 60, 62, 65, 69, 71; and Jewish self-understanding, 60, 62, 69, 70, 84; *Maus I: A Survivor's Tale*, 3, 4–5, 37, 59–71 *passim*, 90, 97, 109, 140, 157; *Maus II: And Here My Troubles Began*, 59–71 *passim*, 90,

Spiegelman, Art *(continued)*
97, 109, 140, 157; and mimesis of
parents' Holocaust experience, 14,
67; and mother's suicide, 65–66;
murdered siblings and survivor
households, 61, 107; and
nonwitnessing Americans, 66; and
parents' Holocaust experience,
60–61; parents' survival lessons,
66; and Nazi antisemitism and
mouse image, 63; and reference to
Des Pres, 63; and reference to
Greenberg, 69; and reference to
Hartman, 63–64; and reference to
Langer, 63, 66; and reference to
Rubenstein, 60, 70; "righteous
helper," 69; second-generation
guilt, 63, 65–68; second-
generation Jewish identity in
America, 62, 64, 66, 69, 70–71;
and second generation and
parents' victimization, 60, 65; and
second-generation research into
the Holocaust, 63; second-
generation witness, 60, 66, 71;
survivor guilt, 68; survivor
separation anxiety, 66; survivors'
flawed parenting skills, 61, 66;
survivor mourning, 68; survivors'
post-Auschwitz survival, 60–61,
68, 70; and survivor-psychiatrist,
Pavel, 68, 151; and theodicy, 184;
*tikkun* of bearing witness, 66;
*tikkun* of the helpers, 31; and
rejection of traditional Judaism
and its mythic structure, 36, 69,
70–71; and trivialization/distortion
of the *Shoah*, 184; transmission to
third generation, 71; and unity of
the second-generation, 186; as
witness to the *presence of an
absence*, 61, 64, 68
Spielberg, Steven: *Schindler's List*,
120
"The Star of David." *See* Steinfeld, J. J.
"Starring at Auschwitz." *See*
Steinfeld, J. J.

State of Israel, 26, 27, 45, 55, 82, 83,
124; in Brand's *Kaddish*, 133, 134,
135–136; and Ravett, 146
Steinfeld, J. J.: "Academic Freedom,
76; "Because of the War," 77–78,
122; biblical and Holocaust
legacy, 79; and comparison with
Bukiet, 75; and comparison with
Finkelstein, 78; and comparison
with Freidmann, 78; and
comparison with Raphael, 112,
122; and comparison with
Rosenbaum, 79; and comparison
with Spiegelman, 78; and
comparison with Wiesel, 77; "The
Coinciding of Sosnowiec...," 76;
*Dancing at the Club Holocaust*, 4,
37, 76–77; and death of the
innocent, 76; and effect of
Holocaust legacy, 77, 78; and
Fackenheim's 614th
Commandment, 76, 78; *Forms of
Captivity and Escape*, 37, 77;
"The Funeral," 76; and "God is
dead," 32; "History," 77; history
and second-generation, 77; and
Holocaust and second-generation
identity , 71, 75–76; "Ida
Solomon's Play," 76; and implicit
covenantal view, 33; and issue of
indirect communication, 76, 77;
and mimesis of parents' Holocaust
experience, 76; reference to Levi,
76; and second-generation guilt,
76; and second-generation
revenge, 76–77; and *Shoah's*
psychic legacy, 75, 77–78; "The
Star of David," 76; "Starring at
Auschwitz," 75; and survivor
identity, 78; and *tikkun atzmi*, 78,
87; traditional ritual and
Holocaust remembrance, 77, 79;
transmission to third generation,
77, 78–79; and
trivialization/distortion of the
*Shoah*, 184, 185; and unity of the
second-generation, 186

Steinitz, Lucy Y.: and impact of Holocaust legacy, 97; *Living After the Holocaust: Reflections by Children of Survivors in America*, 16, 102

Stonewall riots, 117

*Stories of an Imaginary Childhood.* See Bukiet, Melvin.

Sucher, Cheryl Pearl: first- and second-generation memory, 2–3

*Summer Long-A-Coming. See* Finkelstein, Barbara.

Survivor families: complexity of survivor parent-child relationships, 10; images of survivor parents, 10–11, 35–36; nature of relationship, 2–3, 61; second generation understanding of survivor parents, 11; and post-Auschwitz rituals, 36; second generation and role in family, 11; postwar family types, 14

Szony, David M.: *Living After the Holocaust: Reflections by Children of Survivors in America*, 16

*Tallit*, 52, 69

Talmud: and sanctity of human life, 159; and silence of *Mattan Torah*, 133

*Tam*: and Fischer's *A Generation Apart*, 137; in Shapiro, 154

TaNaK: and Fackenheim's covenantal theology, 188

*Tashlich*, 38

*The Testament of Job*, 7; reinterpretation of the biblical tale, 6; connection to second-generation artistic works, 6; points concerning second generation, 6; and second-generation "replacement" children, 137

*Tefillin*, 52, 69; in Brand's *Kaddish*, 132

Theological sequelae: covenantal affirmations of, 8; and second-generation artistic works, 10, 33; types of, 8

Third Generation Witnesses, 7

*Tibetan Book of the Dead*, 65

*Tikkun*: in the *Aleinu* prayer, 4; of bearing witness, 149, 174; and dialectic between *tikkun olam* and *tikkun atzmi*, 181, 184; and kabbalistic tradition, 116–117; of ordinary decency, 88, 160–161; not a resolution of the *Shoah*, 11; as witness of *Shoah's* sequelae, 19

*Tikkun*, 71

*Tikkun atzmi* (repair or mending of the self), 184; in Bukiet's *Stories of an Imaginary Childhood*, 73; as expression of particularist path, 4; as expression of universalist path, 87, 126; in Finkelstein's *Summer Long-A-Coming*, 56, 59; in Fogelman's *Breaking Silence*, 145; in Friedmann's *Damaged Goods*, 41, 45, 47; in Goodstein's *Voices from the Attic*, 180; and Greenberg's Voluntary Covenant, 27; in Raphael's *"Abominations,"* 119; and Ravett, 150; and Rosenbaum's *Elijah Visible*, 80; and second-generation filmmakers, 129, and second-generation identity quest, 84, 87; in Steinfeld's *"Because of the War,"* 78; in Sauvage's *Weapons of the Spirit*, 172

*Tikkun olam* (moral improvement or repair of the world), 184; and act of writing, 121; as expression of universalist path, 4, 8, 87, 92; definition of, 8, 88; and Fackenheim's Covenantal Theology, 29–30, 47; in Goodstein's *Voices from the Attic*, 180; and Greenberg's Voluntary Covenant, 27; and non-Jewish helpers and rescuers, 160; in Sauvage's *Weapons of the Spirit*, 172

Tisha B'Av, 44; in Raphael's *Dancing on Tisha B'Av*, 121
to'evah: in Raphael's "Abominations," 117–118
Trial of God in Auschwitz, 133
Tshuvah: in Raphael, 120

*Voices from the Attic*. See Goodstein, Debbie

Waldoks, Moshe, 152; performer in *Angst*, 150; and response of altruism, 145; and second-generation children as "compensation," 144; second-generation pain and anger, 151; second-generation sensitivity to civilization's failure, 145. See *Angst*.
*Wall Street Journal*: and Solomon, 96
Walt Disney: *Bugs Bunny*, 62; *Mickey Mouse*, 62, 63; *Porky Pig*, 62
Wardi, Dina, 3; image of second generation as symbolic "memorial candles," 44
"We are Here" (*mir szeinen doh*): Partisan song in Fogelman's *Breaking the Silence*, 146; in Sauvage's *Weapons of the Spirit*, 172
*Weapons of the Spirit*. See Sauvage, Pierre.
*While the Messiah Tarries*. See Bukiet, Melvin.
*White Lies*. See Salamon, Julie.
"White Rose": Munich student resistance group, 30
Wiesel, Elie, vii–viii, 1, 53; as applied theology, 8; and comparison with Bukiet, 73, 75; and comparison with Friedmann, 39, 42, 47; and comparison with Goodstein, 178; and comparison with Raphael, 119, 121; and comparison with Spiegelman, 61, 70; and comparison with Steinfeld, 77;
covenantal theology of (Additional Covenant), 8, 10, 22–25, 45, 47, 55, 58, 59, 84, 88, 110, 158, 172, 185, 190; desanctification of the *Shoah*, 152; difference between the first- and second-generation witnesses, vii–viii *passim*, 18, 139; distinction between memory and imagination, viii, 113, 139; *The Fifth Son*, 2, 5, 23, 39, 107, 114, 139, 157, 178; first-generation "children of Job," vii; and First International Conference of Children of Holocaust Survivors (1984), 18; *The Forgotten*, 1, 18, 23, 157, 187; *The Gates of The Forest*, 54; and guilt of bystanders, 117; identity of "children of Job," vii; and indifference of the world, 107; *A Jew Today*, 53–54; and Jewish reproduction after the *Shoah*, 140; moral role of post-Auschwitz literature, 188; murdered siblings and survivor households, 107, and "mystical madness," 107; need for sequel to the *Book of Job*, 5–6; and Nobel Peace Prize, 25; *The Oath*, 5, 11, 23, 114; position concerning second-generation witness, vii, 18, 81, 113; relationship between the *Shoah* and Israel, 135; sanctification of life, 59, 88; second-generation "children of Job," vii–viii *passim*; second generation, Holocaust, and Jewish identity, 10, 73, 97; second-generation act of remembering, vii; second-generation guilt, vii; second generation and parental expectations, viii; second generation and parents' experience, vii, viii; second-generation question, vii; and second generation as replacement

children, 114; second generation and survivor silence, vii; second generation, survivors, and faith in God, viii; shift in thought, 23; and survivor testimony, 75, 82, 113; *The Testament*, 23; theology and Post-Auschwitz Judaism, 83, 84, 91; *The Town Beyond the Wall*, 117; and trial of God, 133, 177, 184; use of dialogue, 147

*Wiedergutmachung*, 113–114, 115

*Winter Eyes. See* Raphael, Lev.

witnesses: meaning historically, 24; as element of Wiesel's Additional Covenant, 24, 46

World Gathering of Holocaust Survivors (Jerusalem 1981), 7; in Brand's *Kaddish*, 135

Wyschogrod, Michael: Holocaust, modernity, and Christianity, 54


Yad VaShem: in Brand's *Kaddish*, 135; in Finkelstein's *Summer Long-A-Coming*, 53, 56; and honor of rescuers, 178; Israel's Holocaust memorial museum and archive, 48

Yahrzeit, 44; in Ascher's *The Flood*, 90; and *El Male Rahamim*, 149; in Finkelstein's *Summer Long-A-Coming*, 49, 50–51; and second-generation filmmakers, 189; and Shapiro docudramas, 153, 155, 157

*yarmukah*/yammie, 38; in Brand's *Kaddish*, 132, 133, 134; in Steinfeld's *"Because of the War,"* 77; in Friedmann's *Damaged Goods*, 40

Yiddish: in Finkelstein's *Summer Long-A-Coming*, 56; as language of an annihilated culture, 38; in Raphael's *"Inheritance,"* 115; and Ravett, 146, 147, 148; in Shapiro's *Open Secret*, 156

*Yom HaShoah*, 183

Yom Kippur: in Raphael's *"Abominations,"* 120; *Yizkor* (memorial) service on, 149


Zable, Arnold: and *Angst*, 150; and memoir *Jewels and Ashes*, 150

*zaddik ve-ra lo*: in Ascher's *The Flood*, 92